Youths in Challenging Situati

This book investigates and explores the complex dynamics of youth in contemporary society, especially in troubled and crisis-ridden contexts. On the one hand, teenagers and young adults experience social suffering, marginalisation, gender and ethnic bias, and an increased risk to be radicalised and involved in extremism and related violence. On the other hand, it is shown that young people are resilient, and they have a remarkable ability to adapt and cope with extremely difficult situations.

This interesting ambivalence is vividly illustrated by a number of studies in countries as varied as Ethiopia, Zambia, South Africa, Botswana, Brazil, Hong Kong, Kuwait, India, Israel, Britain, Italy, Malta, Spain, Portugal and Cyprus. Each of the 16 chapters throws a different light on the impact of destabilising circumstances and how youths cope with them in order to gain positive self-esteem and sense of a meaningful life. Overall, the experiences of young people are a distillation of the particular traumas and challenges that their society faces. Understanding those experiences and how they are coped with helps to make sense of all societies.

This book was originally published as a special issue of *Contemporary Social Science*.

Charalambos Tsekeris is a sociologist working as a Researcher at the National Centre for Social Research, Athens, Greece; and Professor Extraordinary in the School of Public Leadership at Stellenbosch University, South Africa. He is also a Research Associate at the Research Centre for Greek Society, Academy of Athens, and at the Anti-Corruption Centre for Education and Research, Stellenbosch University.

Lily Stylianoudi is a social and legal anthropologist working as a Research Professor and Director of the Research Centre for Greek Society, Academy of Athens, Greece. She has done extensive fieldwork in Ethiopia and Greece. Her research interests include juvenile deviant behaviour, clinical anthropology, social problems and research methods in social science.

Contemporary Issues in Social Science

Series editor: David Canter, University of Huddersfield, UK

Contemporary Social Science, the journal of the **Academy of Social Sciences**, is an inter-disciplinary, cross-national journal which provides a forum for disseminating and enhancing theoretical, empirical and/or pragmatic research across the social sciences and related disciplines. Reflecting the objectives of the Academy of Social Sciences, it emphasises the publication of work that engages with issues of major public interest and concern across the world, and highlights the implications of that work for policy and professional practice.

The *Contemporary Issues in Social Science* book series contains the journal's most cutting-edge special issues. Leading scholars compile thematic collections of articles that are linked to the broad intellectual concerns of *Contemporary Social Science*, and as such these special issues are an important contribution to the work of the journal. The series editor works closely with the guest editor(s) of each special issue to ensure they meet the journal's high standards. The main aim of publishing these special issues as a series of books is to allow a wider audience of both scholars and students from across multiple disciplines to engage with the work of *Contemporary Social Science* and the Academy of Social Sciences.

Most recent titles in the series:

Exploring Social Inequality in the 21st Century
New Approaches, New Tools, and Policy Opportunities
Edited by Jennifer Jarman and Paul Lambert

Political Activism across the Life Course
Edited by Sevasti-Melissa Nolas, Christos Varvantakis and Vinnarasan Aruldoss

Crime and Society
Edited by Donna Youngs

Youths in Challenging Situations
International and Interdisciplinary Perspectives
Edited by Charalambos Tsekeris and Lily Stylianoudi

For a full list of titles in this series, please visit www.routledge.com/Contemporary-Issues-in-Social-Science/book-series/SOCIALSCI.

Youths in Challenging Situations

International and Interdisciplinary Perspectives

Edited by
Charalambos Tsekeris and Lily Stylianoudi

Routledge
Taylor & Francis Group

LONDON AND NEW YORK

ACADEMY
of SOCIAL SCIENCES

First published 2019
by Routledge
2 Park Square, Milton Park, Abingdon, Oxon, OX14 4RN, UK

and by Routledge
52 Vanderbilt Avenue, New York, NY 10017

First issued in paperback 2020

Routledge is an imprint of the Taylor & Francis Group, an informa business

British Library Cataloguing-in-Publication Data
A catalogue record for this book is available from the British Library

ISBN 13: 978-0-367-58749-9 (pbk)
ISBN 13: 978-1-138-61655-4 (hbk)

Typeset in Myriad Pro
by codeMantra

Publisher's Note
The publisher accepts responsibility for any inconsistencies that may have arisen
during the conversion of this book from journal articles to book chapters, namely
the possible inclusion of journal terminology.

Disclaimer
Every effort has been made to contact copyright holders for their permission to
reprint material in this book. The publishers would be grateful to hear from any
copyright holder who is not here acknowledged and will undertake to rectify any
errors or omissions in future editions of this book.

Contents

CONTENTS

Citation Information

The chapters in this book were originally published in *Contemporary Social Science*, volume 12, issues 3–4 (September–December 2017). When citing this material, please use the original page numbering for each article, as follows:

Introduction
Youngsters and adolescents in troubled contexts: worldwide perspectives
Charalambos Tsekeris and Lily Stylianoudi
Contemporary Social Science, volume 12, issues 3–4 (September–December 2017)
pp. 165–174

Chapter 1
The contribution of guardian care and peer support for psychological resilience among orphaned adolescents in Ethiopia
Daniel Sewasew, Orna Braun-Lewensohn and Ebabush Kassa
Contemporary Social Science, volume 12, issues 3–4 (September–December 2017)
pp. 175–188

Chapter 2
Ethnicity, politics and Zambian youth
Derek Roberts and Simusa Silwamba
Contemporary Social Science, volume 12, issues 3–4 (September–December 2017)
pp. 189–201

Chapter 3
Youth identity in desegregated schools of Johannesburg
Marie Jacobs
Contemporary Social Science, volume 12, issues 3–4 (September–December 2017)
pp. 202–214

Chapter 4
Violence and youth voter turnout in sub-saharan Africa
Dabesaki Mac-Ikemenjima
Contemporary Social Science, volume 12, issues 3–4 (September–December 2017)
pp. 215–226

Chapter 13

Imagining the future in a difficult present: storylines from Spanish youth
María Luz Morán and Laura Fernández de Mosteyrín
Contemporary Social Science, volume 12, issues 3–4 (September–December 2017)
pp. 347–360

Chapter 14

Young individuals as microcosms of the Portuguese crisis
Magda Nico
Contemporary Social Science, volume 12, issues 3–4 (September–December 2017)
pp. 361–375

Chapter 15

Investigating the roots of political disengagement of young Greek Cypriots
Ioanna Christodoulou, Charis Pashias, Sotiris Theocharides and Bettina Davou
Contemporary Social Science, volume 12, issues 3–4 (September–December 2017)
pp. 376–392

For any permission-related enquiries please visit:
http://www.tandfonline.com/page/help/permissions

Foreword
Youth in Challenging Contexts

It is generally accepted that it is difficult to be a young person in these less than certain times. But the challenges that face teenagers and young adults are even more demanding in those many contexts around the world that are especially troubled and crisis-ridden. They are even more likely, than the adult, established population, to experience marginalisation, gender and ethnic bias and to be politically radicalised. As a consequence, there is an increased risk of their involvement in extremism and related violence.

In an exploration of these complex dynamics of youths in especially challenging situations around the world, Charalambos Tsekeris and Lily Stylianoudi from the Academy of Athens, Greece have brought together, for this volume, 15 contributions. They come from academics in countries as varied as Israel and India, Hong Kong and Kuwait, Botswana and Brazil. Each of these papers throws a different light on the impact of destabilising circumstances, and how youths cope with them.

The surprising findings of how young people cope with extremely difficult situations is often how resilient they are. They typically have a remarkable ability to adapt and cope with adversity. This is illustrated in the work of Daniel Sewasew and his colleagues from the University of Bamberg in Germany in their chapter. They managed to get 300 orphaned adolescents in Dessie, Ethiopia to complete self-report questionnaires. The results indicated that the key to their resilience was the support of their peers, especially for girls, and to a lesser extent their guardians. Despite the recurrent catastrophes of war, draught and HIV/AIDS, the social support systems helped these teenagers to have positive self-esteem and sense of a meaningful life.

The positive impact of social support contrasts with the potential for damage that can be caused by institutional processes. This is illustrated by Roxana Cavalcanti, from London's University of Westminster, UK, in her study in Recife – Northeast Brazil – where the inappropriate introduction of policing methods had far more negative consequences than the authorities appreciated. She reports that the effects of attempts to reduce endemic violence by much more interventionist law enforcement were limited and short-term. The process converted young people living in the area from being victims to being suspects and perpetrators. Youths were consequently criminalised and exposed to much more violence.

Another illustration of the challenge of coping with debilitating circumstances is illustrated in the study carried out in Turin, Italy by Lara Monticelli and Simone Baglioni from Pisa, Italy and Glasgow, UK, respectively, at the height of the recent recession. Their interviewees were mainly in their 20s, unemployed or in a precarious situation moving between part-time and/or intermittent occupations. The lack of regular employment not only excluded them from the ability to own the consumerist symbols so significant in modern society but also reduced their ability for social engagement. Their precarious situation therefore put them in a vicious cycle that increased the social exclusion from one generation to the next.

The authors of the Turin study offer the optimistic note that whilst their interviewees felt powerless they were striving to maintain their agency. Whilst this is not currently manifested in any form of public, or political, stance it does seem possible that a collective voice may emerge that will have influence. This has been the case in other settings.

The political activism that disaffected youths express is reported in the chapter by Tin-yurt Ting from Hong Kong, where he interviewed those who took part in recent protests over democratic crises. He shows that such political activity is not a passive reaction to current repression. Rather, those he spoke to expressed a desire for an imagined future that related to their own identities and their own role in transforming society.

In Kuwait the turn away by young people from conventional political activity is rather different from that in Hong Kong. This is revealed by Emanuela Buscemi from the University of Aberdeen, UK in her chapter describing how Kuwaiti youths deal with the conflicting demands of a liberal modernity an unprecedented economic crisis and a repressive autocratic regime. She argues that access to social media helps to avoid state censorship and provides a forum for mobilising protests as well as channelling extremist propaganda. This provides a basis for different forms of activism. Some of this was expressed in political campaigns, but other aspects draw on Islamic extremism with associated violence. However, a further, more productive, route is through civic engagement, such as urban projects, art collectives and itinerant markets.

Two aspects to the 15 studies in this volume are particularly noteworthy; one is the outreach to many different places around the world by researchers based in Western universities. Social scientists in Britain, Germany and other developed European countries have their sights far beyond the day-to-day concerns of their host nations. Their researchers show young people as similar to the historical canaries in the coal mines that were more sensitive to danger than the miners who worked there. The experiences of people in their late teens and early 20s is a distillation of the traumas and challenges that their society faces. Understanding those experiences and how they are coped with helps us to make sense of all aspects of society. This volume is therefore a salutary and hopeful account of important research around the world.

Professor David Canter
Series Editor

INTRODUCTION

Youngsters and adolescents in troubled contexts: worldwide perspectives

Charalambos Tsekeris ⓘ and Lily Stylianoudi

ABSTRACT
A brief overview is presented of perspectives on current thinking on youth to contextualise the themed issue of *Contemporary Social Science* entitled 'Investigating Youth in Challenging and Troubled Contexts'. This provides an overview of up-to-date interdisciplinary, international research that investigates the complex dynamics of youth in contemporary society, especially in troubled and crisis-ridden contexts. The studies are brought together from many countries and cultures, including Ethiopia, Zambia, South Africa, Botswana, Brazil, Hong Kong, Kuwait, India, Israel, Britain, Italy, Malta, Spain, Portugal and Cyprus. Taken together the 15 papers show that current youth research contributes significantly to understanding emergent dynamic transformations which are reshaping the social structure (including politics and democracy), taking place at both local and global levels.

Introduction

There is a special value in considering youth and adolescents in troubled contexts. This throws light on their particular experiences at a formative stage in their lives. Such research, recent years, has considered such matters as social exclusion, marginalisation, unemployment, poverty, disempowerment and disenchantment, as well as promoting effective frameworks, interventions, strategies and innovations through a variety of policies. The latter have often taken account of interdependent issues of gender, race, ethnicity, sexuality, disability, inequality, migration, faith, activism, violence, extremism and political radicalisation. As Standing (2011) has pointed out, this has led to the recognition of the growth of a *precariat*, especially among youths in difficult or threatening environments.

As a contribution to this emerging field of research empirical studies that investigate the complex dynamics of youth in troubled or crisis-ridden contexts are brought together in this current issue of *Contemporary Social Science*, drawing on a wide range of countries and cultures, including, Botswana, Brazil, Britain, Cyprus, Ethiopia, Hong Kong, India, Israel, Italy, Kuwait, Malta, Portugal, South Africa, Spain and Zambia. Taken together the 15 papers show that current youth research contributes significantly to understanding emergent dynamic transformations which are reshaping the social structure (including politics

1

and democracy), taking place at both local and global levels. What these studies demonstrate is the need to tackle youth-relevant issues from many different social science perspectives that mutually and substantially complement each other.

Ambivalences in youth research

The concept of crisis includes the nonlinear dynamics of conflict, change and transition. When a community goes through a transitory period, as ongoing fieldwork since 2008 (Stylianoudi, 2010, 2017)[1] in a remote mountainous area of central Greece shows, the community often suffers from a disintegration of its social structure, resulting into the gradual emergence of a *disintegrating self*, especially for the young (and most vulnerable) individuals. Young individuals in transitory contexts thus see an uncertain future and environment, not knowing how to invest in their community or what to aspire to. They feel 'lost', with few hopes regarding their career paths. Under precarious working conditions, young adults in crisis-ridden countries, such as Greece, are now obliged to cope with various limitations which affect them at multiple levels, indicating different aspects of social and psychological complexities. They feel helpless and express feelings of disappointment, uncertainty, pessimism, fear, anger, negativism, anxiety and depression (Chalari, 2014; Tsekeris, Kaberis, & Pinguli, 2015).

In addition, crisis disrupts youngsters' life trajectories and their existential need for self-development and re-orientation, as expressed within subjective living-with-parent's experiences (Tsekeris, Ntali, Koutrias, & Chatzoulis, 2017). Nevertheless, contemporary youth is characterised by strong ambivalences. For instance, many young people seem to make genuine efforts to defend collective values and civil society, to explore new alternative paths, strategies, solutions and ideas, and to create new small enterprises, start-ups and co-working habitats (Tsekeris, Pinguli, & Georga, 2015). In some cases, this is strongly reinforced by the huge opportunities provided by the internet and its facilities. Therefore, the unemployed and unemployable young people in today's reality are not necessarily a 'lost generation' (Asmussen, 2014; Santos, 2017); they are reflexive, knowledgeable and critical citizens, who energetically embrace risk and exploit chaos.

Of course, the degenerating – and almost pessimistic – situation for the youth began many years ago, through the (neoliberal) individualising processes associated with the logic of reflexive modernisation (Beck & Beck-Gernsheim, 2002; Beck, Giddens, & Lash, 1994). It reached its peak with the current (global) financial crisis – or at least it has made itself apparent within (and because of) the crisis. As a result, the proportion of younger citizens who trust established political parties (or representative institutions) and believe 'it is essential to live in a democracy' is surprisingly, falling to a minority at the international level (Foa & Mounk, 2017, p. 6) – that is, a disengagement process which potentially gives rise to negative narratives and authoritarian or populist interpretations of democracy.

To a large extent, this current themed issue deals with the fundamental concept of the youngsters' self, subjectivity and identity, as well as with various facets of their deep precariousness, insecurity and anxiety, relating to everyday social and subjective experiences. Although significant differences can be discerned due to cultural particularities, quite astonishingly, many things are similar for youngsters and adolescents from different countries. This arguably signifies the dynamic relational possibility that young people nowadays have to interact, communicate, exchange ideas and collaborate with their peers around the rapidly digitalised, networked and interconnected globe (see e.g. Tsekeris & Katerelos, 2014). That is, the constant and ubiquitous use of new information and communication technologies effectively undoes the borders that previously tightly isolated young adults and children (de Almeida, Delicado, de Almeida Alves, & Carvalho, 2014). Today's well-educated young generations obtain the tools and the capacity to freely express themselves and to access power outside of the old participatory structures and mechanisms (e.g. using the internet to gather information, express opinions, spread views or even influence decision-making processes).

Other new forms of participation to social life, political processes and democratic structures include peer-to-peer networks, discussion fora, signing petitions, participation in so-called new social movements, support groups, boycotting of products, demonstrations and international meetings (Goździk-Ormel, 2008, p. 26). These new meaningful forms move beyond the 'old' or 'received' youth paradigm depicting young people as apathetic, unengaged and uninterested in political processes.[2] It is now widely acknowledged that the youngsters can be highly political and civic minded, albeit in alternative ways, often being more active and innovative than a majority of adults. Political parties and elections alone do not amount to the 'political'. All forms of participation are political and young people's civic engagement is finding new forms of participation,

> as traditional politics feels unrepresentative and unable to address the concerns associated with contemporary youth culture ... [But] how much influence do young people really have through these new modes of participation? Are they truly at the decision-making table on issues that interest and affect them? Recognising something until recently overlooked, does not necessarily entail its augmentation. In other words, does decision-makers' admitting that young people do have a voice, also make it stronger? (Nica, 2014)

Lessons from Africa

No doubt, contemporary youth confronts challenging and troubled contexts in different ways across the world. In the beginning, the themed issue attracts original contributions from countries (and deprived areas) that are usually under-represented in most academic media. Four interesting and informative accounts come from Africa. First, Sewasew, Braun-Lewensohn, and Kassa (2017) investigate the contributions of guardian care and peer support to psychological resilience among orphaned young adolescents in Ethiopia (Dessie town). There the unique sociocultural context in which children grow up places many pressing responsibilities on them, thus moving them forward to become adults at a very early age. The painful experience of orphanhood is an additional contributor to life experience, which also acts as a strong resilience factor for the older group of children.

Secondly, Roberts and Silwamba (2017) demonstrate the complex, meaningful links between ethnicity, youth and political participation, particularly voting behaviour and tribal identity, in the Zambia context. Within conditions of fragile democracy and economic turbulence, they find that Zambian youth consider ethnicity to be an important part of personal identities (albeit not a political factor) and overwhelmingly perceive politicians to be engaging in political tribalism, which they broadly reject. Lower voter turn-outs, especially among Zambia's largest tribe, and the risk of democratic disengagement are the results of youth's widespread dissatisfaction with the perceived ethnic politics.

Thirdly, Jacobs (2017) did original ethnographic research in two desegregated schools in Johannesburg to explicate social processes of adolescent identity construction in post-apartheid South Africa, under conditions of de-racialisation of the school system. The research shows that the adolescents construct complex identity bricolages which represent not least answers to still existing discourses and practices of racialisation. Race and ethnic relations, as well as class and economic divisions, still structure social relations inside school. Nonetheless, South African teenagers seem to appropriate for themselves specific features from global popular culture in order to express or claim their particular symbolic identity, or to re-draw racial differentiations between social groups.

Fourthly, Mac-Ikemenjima (2017) offers an analytic starting point for bridging the theoretical gap in understanding the role of violence in low youth turnout during elections in sub-Saharan Africa. There recent waves of heightened political awareness have seen increasing numbers of youth engaging in protests and some actively mobilising their peers to vote. Using a large set of data from 20 countries in Africa, it is particularly interesting to find a negative correlation between violence and voting for youth. This correlation, albeit statistically weak, implies that violence could deter voting in elections (thus seriously undermining youngsters' capacity to determine the political futures of their respective countries), regardless the role of socioeconomic and political variables, such as level of education, employment status and association with a political party.

Activism and violence

Turning attention to Latin America, where diverse forms of routine violence are enduring problems, predominantly in the communities most affected by social inequalities, Cavalcanti (2017) examines youth perceptions of a managerial homicide reduction programme in Recife, the capital city of the state of Pernambuco in the northeast of Brazil. Original ethnographic data show a clear dissonance between what high-ranking officials, police and academics involved with public security interventions claimed (as a 'success') and what young people in poor and marginalised communities actually experienced. That is, increasing feelings of being trapped, isolated and criminalised as a result of increased policing. This intriguingly opens up the critique of the deficiencies and inadequacies of 'Global North' security strategies when applied to the South.

Furthermore, Ting (2017), in his original qualitative study, brings valuable lessons from the Far East about the complex links between youth, future orientations and embodied resistance. In particular, the author draws out the irreducible importance of future orientations, as they play out in youth activist strategies in Hong Kong. He argues that these orientations go beyond meta-narratives and social movement frames, and are embodied at the dynamic site of grassroots struggle. Hence, aspirations about the future both shape and are shaped by young people's political activism.

In a different geographical and cultural setting (Middle East), Buscemi (2017) presents a substantial account of the role of young people in contemporary Kuwait and their diverse – seemingly interdependent and possibly overlapping – resistant practices in the areas of political mobilisation (protests staged in Kuwait mainly in 2012), political radicalisation (political violence, Islamic extremism and terrorist episodes) and civic engagement (examples from an invigorated civil society) in the period 2009–2016. Such practices arguably tend to challenge (or transgress) dominant cultural and political paradigms, affecting symbolic identity construction and social patterns. They also signify the distance between the government and youth, as well as between conflicting local social requests and wider aspirations, instilled by modernity and its declinations.

Topical issues of political radicalisation are also critically discussed by Uboldi (2017) in his qualitative analysis of European jihadist terrorism 'from a subcultural perspective'. The author introduces a visual method as an alternative sociological tool not widely exposed to significant empirical scrutiny in the youth literature, imaginatively focusing on how youth groups construct their jihadist identity. The Western foreign fighters or native-born terrorists, who are all young people, like other members of criminal or noncriminal subcultures, express this identity through visual forms, namely through (emotionally loaded) images of the self, which circulate the web platforms and social network sites.

Revisiting complex processes of youth identity and violence, Armstrong and Rosbrook-Thompson (2017) elaborate their findings from two years' ethnographic fieldwork. They carefully investigate how gang activity in Newham (East London, UK) is combatted by a faith-based organisation, namely, Teaching Against Gangs. This organisation aims to radically reform the symbolic identities of young male gang members, advancing a new kind of masculinity that pertains to an awareness of the racial and racist (power) dynamics of criminal and wider society. It provides a focus on individuals thriving within fraternal networks, and the meaningful desire to canalise creative energies into legitimate entrepreneurial activities. Although this strategy poses only an indirect challenge to the racist societal structures it identified, it was effective in reducing levels of gang violence in East London. It thus shows that finding God could really work in gang intervention and the rehabilitation of gang members, 'but only if the search had a certain worldly resonance' (Armstrong & Rosbrook-Thompson, 2017).

Insights from south Europe

Moreover, this special issue offers a number of empirical contributions from Southern Europe. Uboldi (2017) explores the educational experiences of young pupils (aged between 16 and 21) from a disadvantaged social background, focusing on public and private secondary art schools (practical lyceums) in Milan, Italy. The author uses in-depth interviews with time line and focus groups to show how these pupils (perceived as incomplete neoliberal subjectivities), their choices and their educational representations, attitudes, and ambitions can possibly be interpreted in terms of Pierre Bourdieu's concept of 'outcasts on the inside' (Bourdieu & Accardo, 1993, p. 602). Her original sociological analysis arguably opens up a significant question about what can/should be done in the future, in order to deepen and continue to develop such a critical youth research paradigm.

A town near to Milan, and former economic and industrial centre, Turin, is the locus of Monticelli and Baglioni's (2017) research on the subjective feelings and perceptions on social exclusion, joblessness and powerlessness among a group of young unemployed and precarious people. Due to Turin's post-industrialisation dynamics, youngsters from blue-collars families have now a low sense of belonging to communities, limited income and scarce opportunities to plan for the future and foresee a passage into an adult, independent life. Yet, an analytic focus on deprived experiences of consumption (in particular, consumption of leisure goods) reveals that while work has not lost its conventional material and symbolic meaning, young people attribute great importance and value to experiences of consumption as a way for them to gain social status, as well as to socialise with peers, friends and acquaintances.

Visanich (2017) draws qualitative data (through the use of in-depth interviews) from another Southern European country, the small island state of Malta, a location that is still relatively traditional due to the strong influence of Catholic morality and kinship ties. The author focuses on tertiary education students (aged between 21 and 26) and examines the sociological implications and the contextual framework of structural conditions of their personal anxiety – that is, a framework characterised by the ambivalence (or cultural dualism) between modernity and tradition.[3] On the one hand, the degree of youth's anxiety is increased by changes in the educational system, employment prospects and personal debts. On the other hand, the familial support network, which offers both financial and emotional support, seems to reduce anxiety, as well as the uncertainty which is created by youth's reflexive deliberations and 'institutional individualisation'.

Using a similar sample (tertiary education students aged between 20 and 25), Morán and Fernández de Mosteyrín (2017) explore how Spanish young people imagine and represent their future through autobiographical narratives (collected in the form of 'letters'), in a context characterised by high uncertainty and a far-reaching economic, social and political crisis. This multidimensional crisis disrupts and dysfunctionalises hitherto youth strategies, disarticulates students' imagined futures and has adverse consequences on their transitions to adult life. In their narrative analysis, nevertheless, the authors show how, in the process of imagining their future, Spanish youth manage to reconsider their expectations and generate new solutions, linking individual experiences to the collective, generational dimension.

This individual-collective link is also discussed in Nico's (2017) qualitative contribution, pertaining to a relational understanding of how the current financial crisis has been experienced by young people in Europe, particularly in Portugal. Here, an original methodological approach to life-histories, with the application of some co-constructed instruments, casts light on how Portuguese youth's educational, residential, occupational and romantic lives were particularly pervaded and affected by the crisis. It also elucidates how a popular generational (neoliberal) discourse neglects the relational context in an individual's own biography, thus bypassing its historical location and interpretation:

> the appropriation of individualisation discourses by political agents may not be a one-way street, but part of a circular movement in which the dissemination of this individualised neo-liberal discourse is able to re-contaminate the individual's discourses and ways of thinking. (Nico, 2017)

Finally, Christodoulou, Passias, Theocharides, and Davou (2017) use focus groups to study the dynamic processes that underlie the dramatic drop recorded in political interest of young Greek Cypriots, who, as most young people in Europe, feel extremely insecure and uncertain for their future, are quite pessimistic and cynical, and highly disillusioned with traditional politics. Interestingly, Cypriot youngsters' increased abstention from political participation and collective action is linked to Euroscepticism and a high degree of emotional distance from important changes to come with the possible reunification of

Cyprus. In the last instance, such findings signify an urgent need to get inspired and 'rediscover passion for ideas' (Christodoulou et al., 2017), which seemingly youth all over Europe and the world cannot find any more in traditional politics.

Conclusions

This current themed issue offers an international coverage of original empirical studies from many different countries, such as Ethiopia, Zambia, South Africa, Botswana, Brazil, Hong Kong, Kuwait India, Israel, Britain, Italy, Malta, Spain, Portugal and Cyprus. The extent of this coverage depicts a growing cross-cultural sensitivity and understanding of the huge complexity of youth identities and behaviours, including their emergent relational consequences on global transformation, politics and democracy. In addition, it demonstrates the value of combining various disciplinary perspectives, methods and tools within the wide and diverse field of social science, thus maximising the impact and significance of social research.

Interestingly, contemporary youth research shows the urgent and pressing need to build citizen dialogue mechanisms to debate, discover and solve the massive challenges of engagement and inclusion. This will arguably bring democratic institutions closer to younger citizens (especially those in ethnic minorities or in migration contexts), who desire to be heard, recognised and respected (Montgomery, 2015) and are often dangerously trapped in a *vicious circle* between socioeconomic barriers and political disengagement (Dezelan & Lisney, 2015).

In general, youth is nowadays more educated, networked and informed than ever before. It is thus an immense source for new ideas, perspectives and initiatives. Yet, they are more disadvantaged and marginalised than in the past, growing up poorer than their parents (Dobbs et al., 2016), with whom they are often inextricably bound up. Indisputably, further empirical social research is needed to inform youth policy domains against variegated and diffuse phenomena of social marginalisation, exclusion, injustice, inequality, subordination and suffering. But before elaborating on the appropriateness of any youth policy, one should reflect on the significant dissonance between policy and the actual realities of youth's lives (Pechtelidis & Giannaki, 2014), as well as on the critical relational observation that

> youth and policy are themselves mutually constitutive and that how either is understood at any time and in any location is conditional upon political circumstances ... austerity (like policy) should be understood as discourse and, as such, is a social product. This means that austerity policy is, itself, socially shaped and its provisions and exclusions sanctioned in culturally and historically specific ways and through differing local and global practices. (Bradford & Cullen, 2014, p. 4)

Notes

1. This fieldwork study, titled as 'Rural Crisis and Social Pathology', is directed by Professor Lily Stylianoudi and funded by the Research Centre for Greek Society of the Academy of Athens (Athens, Greece).
2. Yet, in the diverse field of youth (policy) paradigms, a rough distinction is often made whether young people are seen as a problem or as a resource. In countries where young people are seen as a *problem*, there is a particular focus on issues such as homelessness, unemployment,

marginalisation, social exclusion and so on. In countries where young people are seen as a *resource*, the central emphasis is on policies that help youngsters to develop themselves, mainly by focusing on education, training and political participation. The best example for the 'resource approach' is Denmark and Sweden; a good example of a mixture of resource and problem could include Germany, Greece and the Netherlands (Wallace & Bendit, 2009).

3. For an extensive study of this cultural dualism in the context of Greek society, see Diamandouros (1994).

Acknowledgments

We are grateful to Professor David Canter and the staff from the Academy of Social Sciences for their valuable help during the whole course of doing this themed issue. We would also like to heartily acknowledge all CSS's external reviewers for their valuable help in reviewing the submissions and bringing the manuscripts to their current form.

Disclosure statement

No potential conflict of interest was reported by the authors.

Notes on contributors

Charalambos Tsekeris is currently a Research Associate at the Research Centre for Greek Society of the Academy of Athens, Adjunct Lecturer at the University of Athens, Senior Researcher at the Laboratory of Virtual Reality, Internet Research & E-Learning (Panteion University), Professor Extraordinary at Stellenbosch University, and Research Professor at Aegean College, Athens, Greece. His current academic interests involve relational approaches in youth research and the social science in general, reflexivity and the self, human complex systems and psychosocial networks. He is the coeditor of *The Social Dynamics of Web 2.0* (Routledge 2014) and editor of *Revisiting the Self: Social Science Perspectives* (Routledge 2015).

Lily Stylianoudi is a social and legal anthropologist, Research Professor and Director of the Research Centre for Greek Society (RCGS) of the Academy of Athens, Athens, Greece. She has participated in many research projects and done extensive fieldwork in Ethiopia (Amhara), as well as in different regions in Greece. Professor Stylianoudi is the editor of *Greek Society / Elliniki Koinonia*, RCGS's Year Book and of RCGS's Publication Series. Her main research and academic interests include juvenile deviant behaviour, clinical anthropology, social problems, migration studies, epistemology, research methods and interpretative tools in the social sciences.

ORCID

Charalambos Tsekeris ⓘ http://orcid.org/0000-0002-3304-5331

References

Armstrong, G., & Rosbrook-Thompson, J. (2017). 'Squashing the beef': Combatting gang violence and reforming masculinity in East London. *Contemporary Social Science, 12*(3–4), 285–296.

Asmussen, J. (2014, June). Let's stop talking about Europe's 'Lost Generation' of young jobless. *Friends of Europe*. Retrieved September 1, 2017, from http://www.friendsofeurope.org/smarter-europe/lets-stop-talking-about-europes-lost-generation-of-young-jobless

Beck, U., & Beck-Gernsheim, E. (2002). *Individualization: Institutionalized individualism and its social and political consequences*. Thousand Oaks, CA: Sage.

Beck, U., Giddens, A., & Lash, S. (1994). *Reflexive modernization: Politics, tradition and aesthetics in the modern social order*. Cambridge: Polity Press.

Bourdieu, P., & Accardo, A. (1993). *La Misère du Monde*. Paris: Éditions de Seuil.

Bradford, S., & Cullen, F. (2014). Youth policy in austerity Europe. *International Journal of Adolescence and Youth, 19*(1), 1–4.

Buscemi, E. (2017). Resistant identities: Culture and politics among Kuwaiti youth. *Contemporary Social Science, 12*(3–4), 258–271.

Cavalcanti, R. P. (2017). Marginalised youth, violence and policing: A qualitative study in Recife, Brazil. *Contemporary Social Science, 12*(3–4), 227–241.

Chalari, A. (2014). The subjective experiences of three generations during the Greek economic crisis. *World Journal of Social Science Research, 1*(1), 89–109.

Christodoulou, I., Passias, C., Theocharides, S., & Davou, B. (2017). Investigating the roots of political disengagement of young Greek Cypriots. *Contemporary Social Science, 12*(3–4), 376–392.

Conti, U. (2017). Between Rap and Jihad. Spectacular subcultures, terrorism and visuality. *Contemporary Social Science, 12*(3–4), 272–284.

de Almeida, A. N., Delicado, A., de Almeida Alves, N., & Carvalho, T. (2015). Internet, children and space: Revisiting generational attributes and boundaries. *New Media & Society, 17*(9), 1436–1453.

Dezelan, T., & Lisney, J. (2015). *Young people and democratic life in Europe*. Brussels: European Youth Forum.

Diamandouros, N. (1994). *Cultural dualism and political change in post-authoritarian Greece, Estudio/working 1994/50*. Madrid: Centro de Estudios Avanzados en Ciencias Sociales, Instituto Juan March de Estudios e Investigaciones.

Dobbs, R., Madgavkar, A., Manyika, J., Woetzel, J., Bughin, J., Labaye, E., & Kashyap, P. (2016). *Poorer than their parents: Flat or falling incomes in advanced economies*. San Francisco, CA: McKinsey Global Institute.

Foa, R. S., & Mounk, Y. (2017). The signs of deconsolidation. *Journal of Democracy, 28*(1), 5–15.

Goździk-Ormel, Ż. (2008). *Have your say! Manual on the revised European charter on the participation of young people in local and regional life*. Paris: Council of Europe.

Jacobs, M. (2017). Youth identity in desegregated schools of Johannesburg. *Contemporary Social Science, 12*(3–4), 202–214.

Mac-Ikemenjima, D. (2017). Violence and youth voter turnout in Sub-Saharan Africa. *Contemporary Social Science, 12*(3–4), 215–226. https://doi.org/10.1080/21582041.2017.1369558

Montgomery, V. (2015). Participation and integration: The contextual factors influencing minority and migrant participation. In M. Barrett & B. Zani (Eds.), *Political and civic engagement: Multidisciplinary perspectives* (pp. 71–84). London: Routledge.

Monticelli, L., & Baglioni, S. (2017). Young and unemployed: Aspiring workers or consumers? Youth social exclusion in the Era of consumer capitalism. *Contemporary Social Science, 12*(3–4), 316–332.

Morán, M. L., & Fernández de Mosteyrín, L. (2017). Imagining the future in a difficult present: Storylines from Spanish youth. *Contemporary Social Science, 12*(3–4), 347–360. https://doi.org/10.1080/21582041.2017.1372620

Nica, M. (2014, March). What of youth's new forms of political participation? *European Students' Forum*. Retrieved September 2, 2017, from http://www.aegee.org/what-of-youths-new-forms-of-political-participation/

Nico, M. (2017). Young individuals as microcosms of the Portuguese crisis. *Contemporary Social Science, 12*(3–4), 361–375.

Pechtelidis, Y., & Giannaki, D. (2014). Youth policy in Greece and the current economic and political crisis. *Autonomie locali e servizi sociali, 37*(3), 461–478.

Roberts, D., & Silwamba, S. (2017). Ethnicity, politics and Zambian youth. *Contemporary Social Science, 12*(3–4), 189–201.

Santos, B. (2017). A New vision of Europe: Learning from the south. In G. K. Bhambra & J. Narayan (Eds.), *European cosmopolitanism. Colonial histories and postcolonial societies* (pp. 172–184). London: Routledge.

Sewasew, D., Braun-Lewensohn, O., & Kassa, E. (2017). The contribution of guardian care and peer support for psychological resilience among orphaned adolescents in Ethiopia. *Contemporary Social Science, 12*(3–4), 175–188.

Standing, G. (2011). *The precariat: The New dangerous class.* London: Bloomsbury Academic.

Stylianoudi, L. (2010, April). *Transformations of the social fabric and cohesion at a mountainous area of central Greece.* Paper presented at the Conference on Ideologies and Social Realities of Migration in Contemporary Greece, Athens.

Stylianoudi, L. (Ed.) (2017). *Elliniki Koinonia: Yearbook of the research centre for Greek society, Vols. 10–11.* Athens: Academy of Athens.

Ting, T. (2017). Struggling for tomorrow: The future orientations of youth activism in a democratic crisis. *Contemporary Social Science, 12*(3–4), 242–257.

Tsekeris, C., Kaberis, N., & Pinguli, M. (2015). The self in crisis: The experience of personal and social suffering in contemporary Greece, *Hellenic observatory papers on Greece and Southeast Europe,* GreeSE Paper No. 92, 1–40.

Tsekeris, C., & Katerelos, I. (2014). *The social dynamics of Web 2.0: Interdisciplinary perspectives.* London: Routledge.

Tsekeris, C., Ntali, E., Koutrias, A., & Chatzoulis, A. (2017). Boomerang kids in contemporary Greece: Young people's experience of coming home again, *Hellenic observatory papers on Greece and Southeast Europe,* GreeSE Paper No. 108, 1–49.

Tsekeris, C., Pinguli, M., & Georga, E. (2015). Young people's perception of economic crisis in contemporary Greece: A social psychological pilot study. *Crisis observatory research papers,* Paper No.19/2015, 1–26.

Uboldi, A. (2017). Disadvantaged students and Art school: The outcasts on the inside between acquiescence and contestation. *Contemporary Social Science, 12*(3–4), 297–315.

Visanich, V. (2017). Youth in the Age of anxiety: The case of a Southern European location. *Contemporary Social Science, 12*(3–4), 333–346.

Wallace, C., & Bendit, R. (2009). Youth policies in Europe: Towards a classification of different tendencies in youth policies in the European Union. *Perspectives on European Politics and Society, 10*(3), 441–458.

The contribution of guardian care and peer support for psychological resilience among orphaned adolescents in Ethiopia

Daniel Sewasew, Orna Braun-Lewensohn and Ebabush Kassa

ABSTRACT

The main purpose of this study was to investigate the contributions of guardians' care, and peer support to psychological resilience. Three-hundred orphan adolescents (OAs) living in Dessie, Ethiopia, aged 12–20 ($M = 15.5 \pm 1.23$), of which 165 (55%) were boys, filled out self-reported questionnaires, which included resilience, guardian care and peer support scales. Results show that the majority of the OA living in Dessie town are resilient. Older adolescents are more resilient than younger ones, and girls obtain more support from their peers compared to the boys. Age, guardian care and peer support were significantly positively related to resilience; together, they accounted for 35.6% of the explained variance. More specifically, peer support accounted for the highest proportion, followed by guardian care and age. The results of this study are discussed based on the cultural competence theory. The unique cultural context in which Ethiopian children grow up places many responsibilities on them, and thus moves them forward to become adults at a very early age. The experience of orphanhood could be an additional contributor to life experience which also serves as a strong resilience factor for the older group children. Practical implications will be offered to foster resilience among orphan and vulnerable adolescents in deprived areas.

Introduction

Resilience is the ability to adapt and successfully cope with adversity, life stressors and potentially traumatic events. It is a cumulative matrix of capacities, resources, strengths, knowledge and adaptive skills that continue to grow over time, which equips individuals with a variety of coping and adjustment skills despite personal vulnerabilities and adversities (Henderson & Thompson, 2010; Shulman, 2009; Tefera, 2005).

Resilience can lead to good outcomes despite a high-risk status (such as resilience in overcoming the odds) and may provide sustained competence under threat (resilience as stress resistance) and recovery from trauma. Fabes and Martin (2001) noted that although teenagers face increasing risks associated with violence, sexual abuse, parental loss and emotional abuse, only a few of them exhibit extreme or long-term behavioural or psychological problems. This means that even though adolescents face various difficulties and adversities, they rely on personal and social resources to overcome them (Braun-Lewensohn, Sagy, & Roth, 2011). Therefore, it is important to look at children, adolescents and their families not through a deficit lens which obscures recognition of their capacities and assets, but through their individual and unique strengths (Benard, 1997).

Different researchers have identified naturally occurring resources and protective factors associated with resilience, i.e. factors that appear to contribute to resilience in the face of adversities. These include confident relationships with other persons, sociability, capacities for appropriate expression of emotion, positive peer relationships, guidance and monitoring from adults, willingness to engage in styles of coping that are prosocial and helping others (Sun & Stewart, 2007; Tefera, 2007). Efficacy of adolescents' resilience strategies indicates that both individual characteristics and environmental factors positively or negatively affect childrens' and (Torsheim, Aaroe, & Wold, 2001; Tusaie, Puskar, & Sereika, 2007). These associations indicate that self-esteem, peer support, parental support and social participation are important to children's resilience (Sun & Stewart, 2007). Another study (Broderick & Korteland, 2002) suggests that the efficacy of resilience schemes is considerably influenced by the individual's perceived autonomy in managing risk factors. Consequently, more positive adjustment has been shown when efficacy and autonomy have been employed to deal with risk factors which are perceived to be controlled. Furthermore, pursuing support in relation to uncontrollable risks is associated with fewer mental health problems.

Scholars (e.g. Botcheva & Feldman, 2004) have maintained that the way children and young people respond to adversities (parental loss, emotional trauma, deprivation of parental guidance and others) depends on the ecological cycles which surround them. Therefore, it seems important to note the culture of relations and values in the studied population. Moreover, in Ethiopia, the concept of resilience (adaptation) may be perceived as resulting from the collectivist way of life. In this collectivist-oriented mode of life, group interests, standards and activities are prominent. Resilience, in this case, is a group rather than an individual characteristic because social beliefs, practices and provisions play a much more important role in building resilience (Tefera, 2005).

Examining the Ethiopian ecology in relation to cooperation and altruism, some local investigations have indicated that dominant Ethiopian cultural values include sharing resources, helping one another and altruism (Tefera, 2007). Many Ethiopians believe that God ordered men to unite and cooperate with neighbours, relatives and others (Sumner, 1990). Scholars have also reported the prevalence of the values of Christianity, the dominant Ethiopian religious belief, exemplified by principles, such as 'love your fellow man as you love yourself', 'do unto others as you would have them do unto you' and the opposite (1990, p. 175). This emphasises the value of altruism and the importance of human relationships in Ethiopian culture.

There are also other socio-cultural factors that help enhance resiliency, such as division of labour, which is age graded. Household tasks are apportioned and everyone is expected to contribute to the household for healthy home functioning (Tefera, 2007). Even though child labour is considered a form of abuse, home labour divisions and expectations may help children exercise responsibility. However, Tefera and Mulatie (2014) noted that *orphan and vulnerable children* (OVC) failed to use protective factors to buffer different risks. Consequently, most were found to be less resilient to adversities.

Peer relationship and resilience

Peers are an important ecological circle for adolescents. Different scholars believe that peers greatly influence adolescent behaviour. According to Prevatt (2003), having a peer group from which to select friends, experiencing a more challenging learning environment in school and taking on new responsibilities in the family and community are beneficial to most adolescents.

Fabes and Martin (2001) have further explained that adolescents' capacities to confront challenges and adversities are greatly influenced by their relationships with others. Being liked and accepted by one's peers serves a protective function. Having someone to talk to, confide in and share helps adolescents to deal with stressors of everyday life (Haggerty, Sherrod, Garmezy, & Rutter, 1997). In addition, Ladd and Kochenderfer (2001) contend that peers, especially friends, provide various skills to children; peers can be used as sources of attraction, interaction and emotional support. Similarly, Brien (cited in Tefera, 2005) stated that peers are the most likely sources of overall support for adolescents, followed by mothers. Furthermore, in his research, Daniel (2006) pointed out that most OVC have close friends and their friends are sympathetic, encourage them to do good things and help them overcome their problems. The present study will try to overcome a gap in the literature and will investigate the way peer support facilitates resiliency in orphaned children in Ethiopia. We hypothesise that the more peer support the orphaned child has, the higher resiliency he/she will report.

Guardian care and resilience

Guardian care refers to the care and support provided by grandparents, older siblings, neighbours and other responsible individuals that care for the orphans. In the present study, guardian care and support are directly related to cultural practices in caring for and supporting the orphans (Hagos & Tefera, 2005).

Glenn and Wilson's (2008) cultural competence theory explains that cultural factors shape the type and content of competencies which individuals manifest. One such competency is a mutual exchange which is based on the well-documented norms of reciprocity that exist in poor neighbourhoods. Such competencies are necessary for survival in neighbourhoods whose economy embraces a conventional way of life. A child's successful development under conditions of poverty in collectivist societies is facilitated by strong family support and social networks of peers and respected elders. Similarly, the Amhara National Regional State Bureau of Labor and Social Affairs (ANRS BoLSA, 2008) pointed out that having someone who could provide a caring relationship would help foster protective factors in OVC by making them feel important and helping them develop a sense that others are concerned about them.

Regarding the cultural caring and supporting practices of Ethiopia, Tefera (2007) explained that family life has great value, and that family households are composed of the extended family system, which is greatly valued in Ethiopia. Furthermore, Tefera (2007) stated that donation of one's children by dying persons to others, especially to grandparents, siblings, relatives, neighbours and other trusted individuals, is common in Ethiopia. Donation facilitates the care and support of orphaned and vulnerable children. Furthermore, the Ethiopian collectivist-oriented lifestyle calls for relatives, neighbours and other community members to care for the disadvantaged (Tsegaye, 2001).

In addition, Abebaw (2007) maintained that Ethiopian culture is characterised by the high value given to religion, which promotes respect for elders and parents, and multiple attachments with siblings, aunts, uncles, godfathers, and other extended family members and even neighbours. Moreover, Befikadu (2005) reported that single orphans who are not taken care of by their surviving parent, and double orphans, are usually integrated into their extended families. In many settings, grandparents appear to be the most common caregivers.

In sum, it may be said that a supportive social environment like the Ethiopian collecti-vist-oriented lifestyle may help develop personal qualities that enable orphans and vulner-able adolescents to cope with life challenges which result from parental loss. Altogether, a supportive social environment (i.e. extended family, relatives and others) has the potential to contribute much to enhancing orphaned and vulnerable adolescents' resiliency. The present study will try to address this hypothesis and to investigate it empirically.

Socio-demographic factors and their relationships with the study variables

Age effects
Many authors (e.g. Beka, Daga, Doboro, & Dominiko, 2014; Cobb, 2001; Kassa, 2006; Tefera, 2007) have found significant relations between age and resilience. Older children, especially late adolescents, are happier, more dependable and more resilient than younger children. Nevertheless, a few studies of 9–14-year-old children and adolescents have found decreases in individual resilience (e.g. self-esteem) with increasing age, suggesting that the relevant individual characteristics are acquired in middle childhood. In contrast, results in terms of developmental changes related to environmental factors are less consistent (Bolognini, Plancherel, Bettschart, & Halfon, 1996; Frost & McKelvie, 2004; Watkins, Dong, & Xia, 1997). Hormonal and physiological changes of early adoles-cence increase the risk of stress and lessen resilience. The response of children to stress and adversity will obviously be modified by their age and thus their capacity to under-stand the experience. This shows that age is an important mediating factor in reducing stress and enhancing resilience.

Gender effects
Regarding peer relations and resilience, Sun and Stewart (2007) reported that adolescent girls are better at seeking social support and coping through the utilisation of social resources than adolescent boys. This research result also corroborates other research find-ings such as those of Brown and Gilligan (1993), who asserts that females are more caring, more responsible and more sociable than males. Similarly, one local study in Ethiopia (Mulugeta, 2008) also maintains that women under difficult circumstances were able to look for support from family members, friends and other kin. In other words, females discuss their problems and share experiences on how to alleviate problems, all of which give them relief from stress in adverse circumstances. In contrast, boys from all age groups tend to make more use of adaptive coping strategies that focus on immediate

problems. Strategies are externalised and commonly include direct action, distraction, positive self-instruction (Hampel & Petermann, 2006) and physical recreation, such as sports, to cope with adversity (Frydenberg & Lewis, 1993).

The study population – orphans in Ethiopia

Due to HIV/AIDS and other catastrophes, such as prolonged war, recurrent drought and scarcity of land, Ethiopia is a country with high numbers of OVC and adolescents. The situation in the Amhara region, particularly in Dessie town, is more severe than national conditions. For instance, ANRS BoLSA (2008, p. 22) reported that in the region there are about 62,820 orphans and vulnerable children, and in Dessie town, there are about 8379 OVCs. Consequently, orphans and vulnerable children and adolescents have faced various problems, for example, deprivation of parental guidance and monitoring, emotional distress as a result of the loss of parents, living outside family settings, with unmet needs and violated rights (Hagos & Tefera, 2005). Additionally, OVCs face family, school and community-related problems including negative discrimination, rejection and social isolation (Tefera & Mulatie, 2014). In the present study, we define an orphaned adolescent as an individual between the ages of 12 and 20, who has lost one or both of their parents.

Several studies in Ethiopia have focused on OVCs and their risk factors such as child abuse and neglect (e.g. Sewasew & Mengiste, 2014), or their personal resilience (e.g. Beka et al., 2014; Tefera & Mulatie, 2014). However, little attention and interest have been devoted to identifying good practices of childcare (guardian care) or peer relationships, which can promote successful adaptation among OVCs. In addition, these previous study samples were taken from non-risk participants (e.g. regular secondary school students). To the best of our knowledge, no study has examined the complex relations of guardian care in the Ethiopian cultural context.

The present study

In conclusion, there is a scarcity of information regarding the contribution of social factors (e.g. guardian care and peer support) that have the potential to enhance orphaned adolescents' adaptation in complicated and stressful situations. Additionally, resilience has not been adequately examined within a wider cultural context, especially with regard to collectivist and interdependence-oriented cultures. The present study will try to address the contributions of guardian care and peer support for psychological resilience among orphaned children. In accordance with the literature review, four hypotheses are proposed:

1. Older adolescents are more resilient than young and middle school-aged adolescents (Beka et al., 2014; Cobb, 2001; Kassa, 2006; Tefera, 2007).
2. Females obtain more support from their peers than male adolescents (Mulugeta, 2008; Sun & Stewart, 2007).
3. Significant relationships will be exhibited between the different study's variables. Thus, peer support, guardian support, and resiliency will be linked to each other positively (ANRS BoLSA, 2008; Ladd & Kochenderfer, 2001; Tsegaye, 2001; Tefera, 2005).

4. Finally, a model which will include age group, guardian care and support, as well as peer support will indicate that all make a significant contribution to orphaned adolescent resilience (Fabes & Martin, 2001; Tefera, 2007).

Methods

Procedure

After obtaining the approval of the research review committee for the questionnaire, 10 assistant data collectors were selected and trained on data collection procedures, research ethics, commitment and appropriate recording of data. On the first day of data collection, the researchers visited care-providing organisations for orphaned children. All of the directors of the organisations were cooperative and they gave the complete list of registered orphaned children. On another day, all orphaned children were told the objective of the study. After securing consent, each data collector administered the back and forth translated Amharic (local language) version of the questionnaire to each respondent at their homes. Seventeen participants did not complete the questionnaire properly. These respondents were excluded from the analysis. Therefore, the analysis was based on data obtained from 283 orphaned adolescent respondents.

Participants

Three-hundred adolescents (165 boys (55%) and 135 girls (45%)) were selected for this study using systematic random sampling. The participants, aged 12–20, with $M = 15.5$ and $SD = 1.23$ were divided into three main groups: early adolescents (12–14-years-old): 103 (36.4%); middle adolescents (15–17-years-old): 137 (48.4%) and older adolescents (18–20-years-old): 43 (15.2%). Regarding guardianship, 39.92% of the respondents were living with their single parents (36.39% with their mothers and 3.53% with their fathers). Most of the respondents (60.08%) were living with relatives such as grandparents (19.8%), aunts/uncles (16.25%), siblings (17.67%) and other relatives (2.83%). As for gender, 61% of the boys and 58.9% of the girls were living with members of the extended family.

Measures

Demographic characteristics: All respondents provided information regarding their gender, age, type of orphancy and living conditions (with whom do they live).

A *measure of resilience (CD-RISC)* (Connor & Davidson, 2003): The Connor–Davidson Resiliency Scale (CD-RISC) – which has 25 items, each rated on a 5-point scale (0 = not true at all to 4 = true all the time) – was used to measure general resilience ability of the respondents. Higher scores indicate higher resilience. Examples of items are: 'I am able to adapt to changes', 'I have close and secure relationships' and 'Under pressure, I can focus and think clearly'. The major advantage of the CD-RISC is its simplicity, which enables a precise and reliable translation from English to Amharic (local language) and vice versa, thereby minimising the potential for misunderstandings emanating from cultural differences. Secondly, the CD-RISC was developed in 2003 to remedy limitations of earlier resilience scales and has been tested across cultures in various studies of non-psychiatric populations of 12 years of age and above. CD-RISC has been reported to have sound psychometric properties with greater reliability and validity than previous scales (Connor & Davidson, 2003). The present research has adopted this questionnaire and added three items to address the Ethiopian context: 'I can handle unpleasant feelings', 'I like challenges' and 'I work to attain my goals'. The adapted questionnaire (resilience measure) consisted of 28 items with a minimum score of 28, a maximum score of 112 and an average score of 70. Cronbach alpha reliability equalled 0.66.

Measure of guardian care (Tefera, 2005): The present research added four items to the original scale, which included 15 items. The minimum score is 15 and the maximum score is 40. High scores indicate high support. The answers range from 'rarely true = 1' to 'true all the time = 4'. Examples of items include 'My guardians helped me to recover from my grief', 'Living with the guardians makes me happy' and 'In times of problems I can communicate with my guardians freely'. The Cronbach alpha for the present study was 0.71.

Measure of peer support/relations (Cutrona & Russel, 1987): This is a 27-item, 4-point Likert-type scale (rarely true = 1 to 'true all the time = 4). The minimum score is 25 and the maximum score is 100. High scores indicated high support. Sample items were 'I have friends to share my problems', 'I get much satisfaction from the groups I am part of' and 'Because of peer support I am involved in income generating activities'. In the present study, the Cronbach alpha for the present study was 0.90.

Data analyses

In this study, descriptive statistics, one-way ANOVA, *t*-tests, Pearson correlations and hierarchical regression analysis were used to analyse the obtained data.

Results

In accord with the study's first hypothesis, significant differences among the three groups of adolescents were shown. The results indicated that late adolescents are the most resilient group in comparison to the other groups. Furthermore, middle adolescents are more resilient than early adolescents. Large effect size (Cohen's *d*) was observed between the early or middle adolescent groups, and the late adolescent group (see Table 1).

In accord with the second hypothesis, a significant difference between genders was shown in peer support. Females reported more support than their male counterparts; however, the effect size was small (see Table 2).

Table 1. Differences among the age groups on resiliency.

Variable	Early adolescence (a) (12–14), N = 103		Middle adolescence (b) (15–17), N = 137		Late adolescence (c) (18–20), N = 43		F	Cohen's d
	M	SD	M	SD	M	SD		
Resilience	78.31	14.33	79.91	13.41	86.21	8.06	$5.62^{ac, bc, ab,*}$	0.12^{ab}
								0.57^{bc}
								0.68^{ac}

Note: $N = 283$. The age classification is based on Jaffe (1998) categorisation.
*$p < .05$.

Table 2. Differences among genders on peer support.

| | Female | | Male | | | |
| | N = 129 | | N = 154 | | | |
Variable	M	SD	M	SD	t	Cohen's d
Peer relation (support)	70.88	14.91	69.81	13.02	4.19*	0.08

Note: N = 283.
*p < .05.

Table 3. Correlations between the study's variables.

	M	SD	Guardian care	Peer support	Resilience
Guardian care	48.05	9.42	1		
Peer support	70.34	13.96	0.55**	1	
Resilience	80.35	13.36	0.49**	0.56**	1

Note: N = 283.
*p < .05
**p < .0.

Table 4. Hierarchical regression of resilience on the independent variable treated.

Variables	R^2	R^2	B	β	SE	t
Peer support	0.22	0.22	0.39	0.40	0.06	6.89***
Guardian care	0.35	0.12	0.31	0.26	0.08	4.42***
Age group	0.36	0.01	1.40	0.08	0.95	1.47

Note: N = 283.
***p < .00.

In accord with the study's third hypothesis, the relationships between the three main variables were strong, positive and significant (see Table 3).

Finally, in order to examine the last hypothesis, a hierarchical regression was run. In each step, one variable was entered and results are presented in Table 4.

The fourth hypothesis was partially supported; peer support as well as guardian care, but not age, made a significant contribution to orphans' resiliency.

Discussions

The main purpose of this study was to investigate the contributions of age, guardian care and peer support to orphans' resiliency. First, we wanted to find out if there were differences between our age groups on resilience. We also examined differences among genders on peer support, and lastly, we evaluated our entire model. We now discuss each of our hypotheses and results accordingly.

Age and resiliency

Our first hypothesis was supported with each of the older age groups being more resilient than their younger counterparts. These results are consistent with other similar research outcomes. For instance, Cobb (2001) reported that generic stress has an effect on early adolescents as a result of rapid hormonal and physiological changes and this was found to be an additional risk factor that lessens early adolescent resiliency. In addition, Tefera

(2007) reported that older children who are encouraged to express their feelings through participating in mourning rituals with the help of an adult recover from grief more quickly than younger children. Similarly, Kassa's (2006) research found that older children, especially late adolescents are happy, dependable and more resilient than younger children. These explanations also corroborate the results of the present study.

The Ethiopian cultural context pushes young children and adolescents to become adults at a very early age as the situations which they encounter place many responsibilities on their shoulders. The experience of orphanhood could be an additional contributor to life experience, which also serves as a strong resiliency factor for the older group children. Therefore, consistent with scholars' research findings, the present study findings showed that children in late adolescence are found to be more resilient than children in early and middle adolescence. Hence, age is an important mediating factor in reducing stress and enhancing resiliency.

Gender and peer relation

Our results also indicated that female adolescents use more peer support than their male counterparts. These findings are consistent with previous research findings. For example, Sun and Stewart (2007) reported that adolescent girls are better at coping by using social resources than adolescent boys. This result also corroborates other research findings, such as those of Gilligan (2016), who explains that females are more caring, more responsible and sociable than males. Similarly, Mulugeta (2008) reported that in relation to non-kin support, friends rather than family members are the primary sources of support for low-income women, especially for women who are living under difficult circumstances. Moreover, Mulugeta (2008) also explained that women under difficult circumstances were able to seek support from family members, friends and other kin. In other words, females discuss their problems and share experiences on how to alleviate problems, all of which give them relief from stress in adverse circumstances. Furthermore, due to strict norms and taboos, Ethiopian girls are afraid of openly requesting any help from their family unless they are facing a problem beyond their control; consequently, they prefer to consult and seek advice from their peers.

Guardian care to orphaned adolescents' resiliency

The findings of the research show that guardian care and support made a significantly positive contribution to adolescents' resilience, with peer support as the most salient contributor. This result is consistent with former local and foreign research. For instance, Tsegaye (2001), Tefera (2005) and ANRS BoLSA (2008) reported that a supportive social environment and the presence of others such as grandparents, siblings and other relatives could provide protective factors for children under adverse circumstances. Other scholars such as Tefera (2005) and Kassa (2006) also indicated that such caring relationships in a family environment would contribute to the resilience of orphaned and vulnerable children by boosting their self-esteem and their sense of the meaningfulness of life. In addition, Befikadu (2005) reported that double orphans and single orphans who were not taken care of by their surviving parents are usually integrated into their extended families. In many settings, grandparents appear to be the most common caregivers.

Above all, the theory of cultural competence (Glenn & Wilson, 2008) explains the significant contribution of guardian care to orphan resiliency. Guardians take this role upon themselves because the Ethiopian collectivist-oriented lifestyle calls for relatives, neighbours and other community members to care for the disadvantaged children (Tsegaye, 2001). At the same time, religious guardians feel satisfaction that their nurtured orphans have survived. So there is a mutual exchange which is based on the well-documented norms of reciprocity that exist in poor neighbourhoods (Glenn & Wilson, 2008).

Similarly, the present research found that the presence of guardians (such as single parents, grandparents, siblings, relatives and others) helped orphaned and vulnerable adolescents to develop high resiliency. This shows the contribution of the collectivist culture in promoting orphan adolescent (OA) resilience. This is especially true of Dessie dwellers, who are known for their prosocial or altruistic behaviours for the disadvantaged. For instance, despite the increasing number of orphaned and vulnerable children, most of them lead independent lives, helping themselves, their siblings and the elderly with the support of their grandparents, other relatives, neighbours and foster parents (ANRS BoLSA, 2008).

Peer relations to orphaned adolescent resiliency

The present research also showed that peer support makes a significant contribution to adolescent resilience. The Pearson correlation test showed that there is a significant and positive correlation between peer support and adolescent resilience. Furthermore, the regression analysis revealed that peer relations make the highest contribution, followed by guardian care and support.

The present research findings are in line with other research findings. For example, Fabes and Martin (2001) explained that adolescent capacities to confront challenges and adversities are influenced greatly by their relationships with others, especially peers and friends. Being liked and accepted by one's peers serves a protective function; having someone to talk to, confide in and share helps adolescents to deal with stressors of everyday life. In addition, Ladd and Kochenderfer (2001) reported that peers, especially friends, teach different skills to children; peers can provide sources of attraction, interaction and emotional support. In general, peers can be helpful in people's reactions to stressful and aversive situations which can be mitigated by the presence of a companion.

Similarly, Haslam, O'Brien, Jetten, Vormedal, and Penna (2005) pointed out that peers were the most likely sources of overall support for adolescents, followed by mothers. In addition, Daniel (2006) pointed out that a large percentage of OVCs have close friends and their friends are sympathetic, encourage them to do good things and assist them at difficult times. The heavy reliance on peers could be due to the open relations and communication that exist among peers at this age around the world. This openness is usually more restrained and conditional with family. Moreover, when children are orphaned, they preferred to get support from equivalent peers instead of guardians and elders who are perceived by these adolescents as less understanding of their situation and problems.

To sum up, the present research findings show that peers make a great and significant contribution to OA resilience. The findings of the study also revealed that the contribution of peer support is even greater than the contribution of guardian care and support. This implies that, in our context, peers can be considered as important sources in promoting OA resilience. Additionally, existing cultural values, such as sharing resources, helping one another, good practices of childcare and religious beliefs of the society, also serve as other sources of OA resiliency.

Study limitation

The study has several limitations. First, this is a cross-sectional study, which considers only the time when the adolescents filled out the questionnaires. Second, information about their experiences was provided only by the adolescents themselves, and therefore, the collected data are subjective and retrospective. In addition, because we lack base rate information about the rates of resilience in the adolescents prior to the study period, we cannot with certainty ascribe the mental health outcomes solely to the impact of the examined situation. In the future, it is important to use multi-informant and longitudinal methods with a qualitative component.

Conclusion and future research

This study sought to investigate the contributions of guardian care and peer support to psychological resilience. Data were collected from 300 orphaned adolescents in Dessie town. The study has added to the limited study documentation in Ethiopia. Based on the findings, it is safe to conclude that the majority of the orphaned adolescents living in Dessie town are resilient. Guardians and peer support have significant and positive effects on orphaned adolescents' resilience. Female adolescents are more likely to obtain support from their peers and older adolescents are more resilient than younger ones. The unique cultural context within which Ethiopian children grow up places many responsibilities on their shoulders and thus moves them forward towards adulthood at a very early age. Given that our study has shown the crucial role of guardian and peer support for psychological resilience among OVC under guardian supervision in a developing country like Ethiopia, we should be aware that the impact of adversity on children and adolescents psychological health and well-being is apparent whatever its type (e.g. divorce, separation) and regardless of the country where children are living. This study is a survey; however, the issue under investigation (resilience) is not well examined through a questionnaire. Hence, further studies should consider investigating the topic using a qualitative approach within the same cultural context. Moreover, this survey investigation has not recorded the age at which the respondent became an orphan, whether they are singly or doubly orphaned and, if the latter, the period between the bereavements. Also unrecorded is the time lapse between the respondent's becoming an orphan and the completion of the survey; hence, we suggest that further investigations should fill these gaps.

In helping orphaned and vulnerable children and adolescents, governmental and nongovernmental organisations, professionals such as psychologists, social workers, and others should exploit the social capital available for these children and adolescents, including extended families, friends and peers. Parents and/or guardians of non-resilient adolescents should allow their children to share experiences and learn from resilient orphaned and vulnerable adolescents.

Disclosure statement

No potential conflict of interest was reported by the authors.

Notes on contributors

Daniel Sewasew is an Assistant Professor and Doctoral fellow at University of Bamberg (Germany). He received his assistant professorship at University of Gondar (Ethiopia) in 2014. His major research interests include children with adversities, interplay of motivational and cognitive abilities in childhood, gender differences in scholastic achievement and latent variable modelling (SEM, IRT).

Orna Braun-Lewensohn is an Associate Professor and the head of the 'Conflict Resolution and Conflict Management' Program at the Ben-Gurion University of the Negev (Israel). Her major research interests include mental health outcomes and coping during or following stressful events. The focus of her research is personal as well as communal coping resources in different cultural groups.

Ebabush Kassa is lecturer and PhD candidate at the University of Andhra (India). He received his Master's Degree in Developmental Psychology from Addis Ababa University (Ethiopia) in 2009. His major research interests include psychological well-being of children and youth as a function of their micro and mesosystems and community at large.

References

Abebaw, M. (2007). Child rights in Ethiopia: Discussion of Ethiopian realities and implications. In B. Tefera & A. Minaye (Eds.), *Child rights, childhood education and the use of mother's tongue in schools: A voyage to reconstruct the Ethiopian child. The proceeding of 7th Ethiopian Psychologists Association National Conference* (pp. 23–29). Addis Ababa: Addis Ababa University Press.

ANRS BoLSA. (2008). *Situation analysis on orphan and vulnerable children in Amhara region: With special reference to urban towns in Amhara region. A study commissioned by Amhara National Regional State Bureau of Labor and Social Affairs and save the children* (Unpublished research report). Norway.

Befikadu, E. (2005). *A comparative study of the psychological and social adjustments of non-institutionalized and institutionalized HIV/AIDS orphans in Addis Ababa* (Unpublished MA Thesis). Addis Ababa University.

Beka, M. B., Daga, E. G., Doboro, E. D., & Dominiko, T. (2014). Risk factors and resilience: The case of second cycle primary school children in Wolaita zone, Ethiopia. *Journal of Social Science Studies, 1*(2), 249. doi:10.5296/jsss.v1i2.5920

Benard, B. (1997). *Turning it around for all youth: From risk to resilience.* ERIC/CUE Digest, Number 126. Retrieved from http://www.ericdigests.org/1998-1/risk.htm

Bolognini, M., Plancherel, B., Bettschart, W., & Halfon, O. (1996). Self-esteem and mental health in early adolescence: Development and gender differences. *Journal of Adolescence, 19*(3), 233–245.

Botcheva, L. B., & Feldman, S. S. (2004). Grandparents as family stabilizers during economic hardship in Bulgaria. *International Journal of Psychology, 39*(3), 157–168. doi:10.1080/00207590344000321

Braun-Lewensohn, O., Sagy, S., & Roth, G. (2011). Coping strategies as mediators of the relationship between sense of coherence and stress reactions: Israeli adolescents under missile attacks. *Anxiety, Stress, and Coping, 24*(3), 327–341. doi:10.1080/10615806.2010.494329

Broderick, P. C., & Korteland, C. (2002). Coping style and depression in early adolescence: Relationships to gender, gender role, and implicit beliefs. *Sex Roles, 46*(7–8), 201–213. doi:10.1023/A:1019946714220

Brown, L. M., & Gilligan, C. (1993). Meeting at the crossroads: Women's psychology and girls' development. *Feminism & Psychology, 3*(1), 11–35.

Cobb, N. (2001). *The child: Infants, children, and adolescents.* London: Mayfield.

Connor, K. M., & Davidson, J. R. T. (2003). Development of a new resilience scale: The Connor–Davidson resilience scale (CD-RISC). *Depression and Anxiety, 18*(2), 76–82. doi:10.1002/da.10113

Cutrona, C., & Russel, D. W. (1987). *Social Provision Scale.* Retrieved May 23, 2017, from https://public.psych.iastate.edu/ccutrona/socprov.htm

Daniel, M. (2006). *The psychosocial behavior of AIDS orphans: The case of AIDS orphans in five organizations in Awassa* (Unpublished MA Thesis). Addis Ababa University.

Fabes, B. R., & Martin, C. (2001). *Exploring development through childhood.* Boston, MA: Allyn and Bacon.

Frost, J., & McKelvie, S. (2004). Self-esteem and body satisfaction in male and female elementary school, high school, and university students. *Sex Roles, 51*(1–2), 45–54. doi:10.1023/B:SERS.0000032308.90104.c6

Frydenberg, E., & Lewis, R. (1993). Boys play sport and girls turn to others: Age, gender, and ethnicity as determinants of coping. *Journal of Adolescence, 16*(3), 253–266. doi:10.1006/jado.1993.1024

Gilligan, C. (2016). *In a different voice – Carol Gilligan*. Harvard University Press. Retrieved from http://www.hup.harvard.edu/catalog.php?isbn=9780674970960

Glenn, B. L., & Wilson, K. P. (2008). African American adolescent perceptions of vulnerability and resilience to HIV. *Journal of Transcultural Nursing, 19*(3), 259–265. doi:10.1177/1043659608317447

Haggerty, J. R., Sherrod, R. L., Garmezy, N., & Rutter, M. (1997). *Stress risk and resilience children and adolescents processes mechanisms and interventions*. New York: Cambridge University Press.

Hagos, B., & Tefera, B. (2005). *Psychosocial survey of OVC their families and communities: The case of OVC in Addis Ababa and Chilga* (Unpublished research report). Addis Ababa University.

Hampel, P., & Petermann, F. (2006). Perceived stress, coping, and adjustment in adolescents. *Journal of Adolescent Health, 38*(4), 409–415. doi:10.1016/j.jadohealth.2005.02.014

Haslam, S. A., O'Brien, A., Jetten, J., Vormedal, K., & Penna, S. (2005). Taking the strain: Social identity, social support, and the experience of stress. *British Journal of Social Psychology, 44*(3), 355–370.

Henderson, D. A., & Thompson, C. L. (2010). *Counseling children* (8th ed.). Belmont: Cengage Learning.

Jaffe, M. L. (1998). *Adolescence*. New York: Wiley.

Kassa, N. (2006). *Problems coping, resilience and support of AIDS orphans in Arada sub-city* (Unpublished MA Thesis). Addis Ababa University.

Ladd, G., & Kochenderfer, B. (2001). Friendship quality as a predictor of young children's early school adjustment. *ResearchGate*. Retrieved from https://www.researchgate.net/publication/14494863

Mulugeta, E. (2008). Negotiating poverty: Problems and coping strategies of women in five cities of Ethiopia. In E. Mulugeta (Ed.), *Urban poverty in Ethiopia: The economic and social adaptations of women* (pp. 47–55). Addis Ababa: Addis Ababa University Press.

Prevatt, F. F. (2003). The contribution of parenting practices in a risk and resiliency model of children's adjustment. *British Journal of Developmental Psychology, 21*(4), 469–480. doi:10.1348/026151003322535174

Sewasew, D. T., & Mengiste, M. M. (2014). Prevalence of physical and psychological forms of child abuse: Implication for intervention, Gondor, northwest Ethiopia. *Innovare Journal of Social Sciences, 2*(2), 17–22.

Shulman, L. (2009). *The skills of helping individuals, families, groups and communities* (6th ed). Belmont, CA: Brooks/Cole Cengage Learning. Retrieved from http://trove.nla.gov.au/work/20047697

Sumner, C. (1990). The Ethiopian understanding of human beings. In R. Pankhurst, A. Zekaria, & T. Beyene (Eds.), *Proceedings of the first national conference of Ethiopian studies* (pp. 335–343). Addis Ababa: Addis Ababa University Press.

Sun, J., & Stewart, D. (2007). Age and gender effects on resilience in children and adolescents. *International Journal of Mental Health Promotion, 9*(4), 16–25.

Tefera, B. (2005). Resilience and coping among war-affected children and implications for caring HIV/AIDS-affected children: Analysis of children's experiences in selected Eastern and central African countries. Unpublished Research Report. Submitted to Benard Van Leer foundation, The Netherlands.

Tefera, B. (2007). Raising AIDS orphan children in Ethiopia: Practices of care and support, challenges and future directions. In B. Tefera, & A. Minaye (Eds.), *Caring for orphaned and vulnerable children in Ethiopia.* (pp. 60–107). Addis Ababa: Addis Ababa University Press. Proceeding of the 6th Ethiopian Psychologists Association National Conference.

Tefera, B., & Mulatie, M. (2014). Risks, protection factors and resilience among orphan and vulnerable children (OVC) in Ethiopia: Implications for intervention. *International Journal of Psychology and Counseling, 6*(3), 27–31.

Torsheim, T., Aaroe, L. E., & Wold, B. (2001). The sense of coherence and school-related stress as predictors of subjective health complaints in early adolescence: Interactive, indirect or direct relationships? *Social Science & Medicine (1982), 53*(5), 603–614.

Tsegaye, C. (2001). Overview of services for orphans and vulnerable children in Ethiopia: A report paper presented at a workshop in Kigali, Ministry of Local Government and Social Affairs of the Republic of Rwanda (pp. 1–22).

Tusaie, K., Puskar, K., & Sereika, S. M. (2007). A predictive and moderating model of psychosocial resilience in adolescents. *Journal of Nursing Scholarship: An Official Publication of Sigma Theta Tau International Honor Society of Nursing, 39*(1), 54–60.

Watkins, D., Dong, Q., & Xia, Y. (1997). Age and gender differences in the self-esteem of Chinese children. *Journal of Social Psychology; Worcester, MA, 137*(3), 374–379.

Ethnicity, politics and Zambian youth

Derek Roberts and Simusa Silwamba

ABSTRACT

Zambia is a very young nation in the midst of economic and political turbulence. The current trials are exacerbated by a youth bulge. Zambian youth have been exposed to a globalising world, and their expectations often exceed the current realities of the country. The country's economy has been decimated by daily power outages and falling copper prices. The fragile democracy has seen ethnic politics expand in the face of two presidential elections in less than two years. There have been concerns about the potential for increased political and ethnic violence as a result of these financial and political challenges. In this article, we draw upon a survey of 419 public university students in order to uncover how ethnic identities contribute to the democratic landscape for the nation's youth. We find that Zambian youth consider ethnicity to be an important part of personal identities, but they do not believe ethnicity should be a political factor. Contrary to this desire, the youth overwhelmingly perceive politicians to be engaging in political tribalism. The data suggest that the youth's widespread dissatisfaction with the perceived ethnic politics has contributed to lower voter turnouts, especially among Zambia's largest tribe.

Introduction

Zambia is a nation that has been facing significant financial and political upheaval for the past two years. The death of President Michael Sata in 2014 left a power gap that resulted in two highly contentious presidential elections within a period of two years. Though Vice President Guy Scott became the first white African head of state in decades, the constitution only allowed him to fill the position on an acting basis. The two main candidates from January 2015, Edgar Lungu and Hakainde Hichilema, ran against one another again in August 2016. Not only were the elections close in regard to time, they were also close in results. Neither candidate won a majority of the registered voters in 2015, which became a requirement in 2016. Moreover, there were widespread concerns of increasing political violence, including along tribal lines. The undesirable prospect of a run-off election – the third election within two years – increased the political tension leading to the 2016 election.

The urgency of the latest general election was heightened by an energy and economic crisis. Daily power outages (i.e. load shedding) lasting several hours became the norm in

June 2015. The effect on the economy has been dramatic. Inflation has negatively affected the purchasing power of most Zambians. The value of the Zambian kwacha against the US dollar went from k7.4/$1 in June 2015 to a current rate of k10.1/$1, with a low of k13.9/$1 in November 2015 (XE, 2017). Compounded by the global decline in copper prices, the energy crisis has resulted in an economic crisis for ordinary Zambians. In addition to small businesses, many of the nation's mines have closed or laid off thousands of workers. The decline of Zambia's main economic industry had many voters concerned about the nation's development as they headed to the polls.

The political and economic problems facing Zambia pose a particular challenge to the youth. Indeed, Zambia is a very young and rapidly growing country. Zambia's population has more than doubled since 1980. Between the census surveys of 1980 and 2010, the nation's total population increased from 5.7 to 13.1 million (Central Statistical Office [CSO], 2015). Recent estimates place the total population above 16 million (CSO, 2017). The growth in population is a result of a significant youth bulge in both urban and rural areas. Nationwide, people aged 24 or young made up two-thirds of the population at the 2010 census (CSO, 2012). Zambians under the age of 15 comprised 45.4% of the total population in the same census. In addition to one of the lowest (disability adjusted) life expectancies in the world (Kabir, 2008; Mathers, Sadana, Salomon, Murray, & Lopez, 2001), the country's youth bulge is influenced by high rates of adolescent fertility and marriage (United Nations Population Fund, 2015). The youth bulge in Zambia makes the local context even more challenging and troubling, as a large percentage of the population will soon need jobs and homes of their own. Indeed, youth bulges in developing nations have been associated with higher risks of violent conflict (Hilker & Fraser, 2009). How are the youths to provide for themselves and contribute to national development? Will they simply join the 9 in 10 working Zambians who are engaged in informal employment (CSO, 2011)? Will they become invested in politics as a way to shape a better future? With more than a quarter of youths unemployed (Muzira, Njelesani, & Zulu, 2013), these were important questions leading up to the 2016 election. Youthful frustration resulted in numerous riots and closures at the nation's public universities. Within this research project, we seek to show how Zambian youth assess the nation's political leaders and their impact on youth lives. Given the public concerns over tribalism in development and politics, we focus on the potential role of tribal identity in shaping youth perceptions.

Literature review

Ethnic identities and politics

Africa's pre-colonial societies were often built upon systems connected to family, clan and ethnicity (Isaacs, 1975). Such groups also played a pivotal role in the construction of political institutions. Like social beings from other parts of the globe, people in Africa also sought ways to organise themselves. According to Gluckman (2007), ethnically based societies allowed people to strengthen and form new social bonds that provided social security. For other scholars, identifying with a single ethnicity was not a socially beneficial process. Rather, it could be a way for social elites to play identity politics in multiethnic societies in order to enhance their own status (Horowitz, 1985). Moreover, it can impede democratic development (Juma, 2012). Nonetheless, for many Africans, ethnicity trumps nationality. In a geographical landscape shaped by colonial powers uninterested in pre-colonial ethnic borders, this has resulted in numerous violent conflicts (Badru, 2010; Berman, 1998; Mazrui, 1975; M'Poyo Kasa-Vubu, 1985; Wele, 2010).

The majority of political parties in southern Africa have engaged in ethnic politics (Vail, 1989). In addition to mono-ethnic political engagement, many countries have seen closely related groups form alliances in order to gain the power of more distant ethnic groups (Mwakikagile, 2001). However, some political leaders have intentionally sought to mobilise and include citizens from a variety of ethnic backgrounds in political positions in an effort to reduce ethnic tensions exacerbated by those exploiting ethnic politics. Nelson Mandela, for example, invited the Inkatha freedom fighters into his government in order to promote peace between the Xhosa and Zulu. At various times in Zambia's history, political leaders have both taken advantage of and tried to eradicate ethnic politics. In the following paragraphs, we focus on the position of ethnic politics in Zambia.

Ethnic politics in Zambia

Ethnic identities have long influenced the political landscape in Zambia, formerly known as Northern Rhodesia. There was less ethnic tension prior to gaining independence in 1964, as different ethnic groups had one common goal of attaining independence. Following independence, however, the country began to experience greater fragmentation along ethnic lines. The united fight against British colonialism helped people overlook ethnic divisions, but this quickly changed (Wele, 2010). Less than three years after gaining independence, the political party in power, the United National Independence Party (UNIP) divided itself into regions of preference (Wina, 1985). Two coalitions among the four major ethnic groups were born within the party. The Bemba and Tonga united, while the Lozi aligned themselves with the Ngoni. President Kaunda was later faced with growing tension between the two factions and the emergence of rival parties forming along ethnic lines (Bond, 1976), inspiring him to create the national motto of 'One Zambia, One Nation'.

Despite Kaunda's efforts, the post-independence political landscape was characterised by incidences of tribal and regional party politics by political players (Phiri, 2006). Ethnic politics failed to disappear, because political actors found it to be an easily deployed tool for mobilising constituents and discrediting competitors. Another reason ethnic politics were resistant to Kaunda's efforts is that they were already a well-established practice decades before independence. Despite the period of ethnic unity immediately preceding independence, Mwewa (2011) has argued that ethnic identity politics existed in Northern Rhodesia as far back as 1923, when welfare societies first formed. These predecessors to black political parties increased in prominence in the mid-1940s (Rotberg, 1965). By 1948, the first native political party (Northern Rhodesia African National Congress) emerged as a party for the Lozi and Tonga. As other political parties developed along ethnic lines and increased their political activities, growing ethnic tensions nearly caused an internal collapse of Northern Rhodesia (Mulford, 1967). Recent history has not seen a decline in ethnic identity politics in Zambia. Similar to other multiethnic states, ethnic identity has continually been utilised for political mileage (Macola, 2010). Later in his three-decade reign, Kaunda's own party was labelled as a Bemba party. In response, he transformed Zambia into a one-party state from 1972 until 1990. This superficial solution to ethnic politics did not, however, significantly alter the area's long history of ethnic politics. Political party formation, coalition building and voting patterns in Zambia have consistently followed ethnic lines, enhanced through linguistic and regional collaborations (Posner, 2005).

Youth and ethnic politics

Having discussed ethnic identity politics in Africa and Zambia, we now briefly turn our attention to the correlation between the perceived ethnic identity politics and youth political participation. While we have discussed some of the detrimental invocations of ethnicity above, it is important to note that ethnic identity is associated with positive self-evaluation and self-esteem (Phinney & Ong, 2007). Among other benefits, one's ethnic identity can help serve as a cushion between perceived societal discrimination and depression. Given the youthful demographic developments across Africa, the future of the continent will be shaped by the societal treatment of current youth as they try to find their position in multiethnic states and determine the extent to which they desire to be politically involved (Mandela Institute for Development Studies [MINDS], 2016). While youth are often among the most passionate activists for change and development, they are not always included in the implementation of reforms. Many of the youth who served as the driving force behind Tunisia's Jasmine Revolution, for example, have withdrawn from the voting process as a result of a lack of confidence in the electoral process. Similarly, Egyptian youth have become reluctant to participate in elections following the revolution that brought an end to the Mubarak regime (Karkara, 2011).

The general withdrawal of youth from politics in developing countries has been exacerbated by leaders engaged in ethnic politics. Across sub-Saharan Africa, the practitioners of ethnic politics from older cohorts have often sought to keep youth at bay in order to maintain power (Murunga & Nasong'o, 2007). Zambian youth have similarly been challenged by ethnic politics (Vail, 1989). Alternatively, the political elite have encouraged the youth to serve as enforcers in order to intimidate opponents. In Zambia, this tradition of violent youth cadres dates back decades (Bond, 1976). With a history of political leaders who take advantage of youth and ethnic identities in order to secure their own positions, we seek to understand how contemporary university students perceive and respond to ethnic politics.

Methods

Data for this article are drawn from a survey of undergraduate students at one of Zambia's public universities. A convenience sample of 419 undergraduate students was recruited from multiple schools across the university. With permission of the lecturers, surveys were passed out to students in the class. Those students who consented to participate in the study then completed the surveys face-to-face. While some of the preceding literature and other scholars (adamantly) insist on the conceptual superiority of ethnicity over tribe (Lentz, 1995; Paglia, 2007; Wiley, 1982), it is important to note that the survey used the language of the tribe. Scholars certainly should give thought to the use of tribe in a postcolonial context, and the lead author did not opt for its use in the survey without thoughtful consideration of the local linguistic customs. Not only is ethnicity a complex concept that poses challenges to even well-established scholars, it is also a largely unknown one in Zambia. From government leaders to street vendors, the Zambian habitus is permeated by the notion of the tribe. Accordingly, the decision to ask about tribal issues was a methodological one. Since many students are wholly unfamiliar with the meaning of ethnicity, asking them about it would pose a risk to the study's validity.

The surveys were distributed shortly after the highly contentious 2016 general election, in which the ruling party narrowly maintained the presidency. There were repeated concerns of tribalism throughout the build-up to the election, making this study a timely probe into the relationship between tribe and politics among the nation's youth. In addition to demographic questions, the survey contained questions about participants' preferred political party and their participation in the most recent general election. Participants then responded to a series of five-point Likert scale statements designed to assess their perceptions about tribal identities and relations (e.g. 'I trust people from other tribes', 'My tribe is important to me'), including the role of tribe in politics (e.g. 'Voters should consider a politician's tribe when voting', 'My tribe is well represented within government', 'Politicians use their tribal identity to secure votes'). Given the use of a convenience sample, we do not aim to generalise our findings to all university students or youth in Zambia. The following sections present descriptive statistics of the sample. We also provide results of a bivariate analysis to show how tribe and politics are related to the student participants.

Data and descriptive analysis

Convenience samples are not designed in order to have a participant make-up that is similar to the population in order to allow broad generalisations. Nonetheless, it is worth noting that this sampling technique resulted in a diverse sample of students across a variety of key demographic variables. Table 1 shows the demographic breakdown of respondents over several key variables.

The sample was closely balanced according to sex. A slight majority ($n = 217$) of the participants were male. The 202 female participants made up 48.2% of the sample, which is close to the university's female make-up of 46.5% (Ministry of General Education, 2016). The mean age of respondents was 22.42 years. All of the participants were legal adults who fell within the Zambian definition of youth (i.e. 16–35 years). The majority of Zambians still reside in rural areas, but the urban population is growing at twice the rate (4.2% vs. 2.1%) of the rural population (CSO, 2012). Unlike the general population make-up, the students sampled were primarily from urban areas. Approximately two-thirds of participants ($n = 269$) stated that they grew up in urban areas.

Participants were asked to self-identify their own tribe in an open-ended question. There are more than 70 recognised tribes in Zambia, 33 of which were represented by participants in this study. The nation's four largest tribes – Bemba, Ngoni, Tonga, Lozi – were all among the top five most common tribal identities provided by participants. As in the larger society, the largest tribal group consisted of those identifying as Bemba ($n = 114$).

Zambia's public universities were often portrayed as a site of political wrangling in the year leading up to the most recent general election, which was held in August 2016. However, students were as equally likely to vote as they were to not vote. Precisely half ($n = 205$) of the valid responses indicated that the participant had voted. A large

Table 1. Participant demographics.

Variable	Attribute	n	Valid%	Mean/median
Sex				
	Male	217	51.79	
	Female	202	48.21	
Age				
				22.42 years
Tribe				
	Bemba	114	27.21	
	Tonga	52	12.41	
	Chewa	32	7.64	
	Lozi	30	7.16	
	Ngoni	26	6.21	
	Other	165	39.38	
Place of Origin				
	Rural	144	34.87	
	Urban	269	65.13	
Political Affiliation				
	MMD	2	0.49	
	PF	109	26.78	
	UNIP	3	0.74	
	UPND	129	31.70	
	Other	21	5.16	
	None	143	35.14	
Voted in Election				
	Yes	205	50.00	
	No	186	45.37	
	Ineligible	19	4.63	

number of students surveyed ($n = 186$) chose not to vote. A small number ($n = 19$) of students indicated that they did not vote as a result of being ineligible. The breakdown of voter participation according to the tribe is shown in Figure 1. Notably, participants who self-identified as Bemba or Namwanga were the only respondents who were more likely to not vote than to vote.

The Zambian political system accommodates many different parties. There is a widespread turnover among the parties at the top of the political landscape, and parties that ruled in the past now receive negligible support. The nation's previous ruling parties received very little support from the students in this study. Only three students support theUNIP. The Movement for Multiparty Democracy, which last ruled in 2011, only received support from two participants. The majority of students support the two parties that received the vast majority of votes in the recent election. The Patriotic Front (PF) maintained the presidency in the election, but only one-quarter ($n = 109$) of participants sided with the incumbent party. The United Party for National Development (UPND) lost a highly contested election, but it received more support than the PF among participants ($n = 129$). Interestingly, more than one-third of all respondents ($n = 143$) indicated that they did not support any political party.

Discussion

In this section, we will extend the statistical analysis to include the results of the bivariate analysis. Given the sampling technique, we discuss results from the non-parametric analysis of variance, Kruskal–Wallis. Table 2 shows results from the Kruskal–Wallis tests. The first grouping variables of interest pertain to the respondents' tribe.

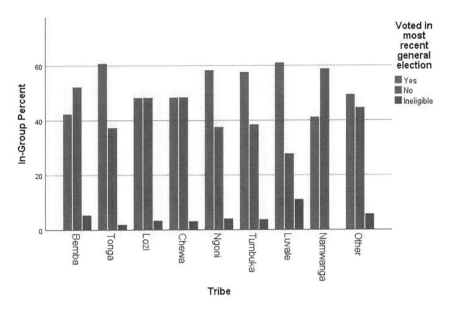

Figure 1. Voter participation according to the tribe.

For a clear majority of participants, tribe remains an important part of one's identity in contemporary Zambia. More than 7 out of 10 (71.3%) respondents agreed – somewhat or strongly – with the general statement that a person's tribe is an important part of their identity. There was no significant difference in the importance of tribal identity according to the tribe in the sample ($p = .070$). In addition to the generic statement about the importance of tribal identity, we asked participants to respond to the statement 'My tribe is important to me.' The students were more likely to agree with this specific statement about their own tribe's importance to them, as nearly three-quarters (74.6%) agreed with the statement. Like the generic question about tribal identity, there were no significant differences in the importance of one's own tribe according to the tribe ($p = .216$).

Participants were also asked to respond to numerous Likert scale statements designed to assess their perceptions of different tribes, as well as their own. Responses to statements like 'My tribe is better than other tribes', 'I trust people from other tribes' and 'There should be greater cooperation among all Zambian tribes' did not vary significantly according to the tribe. For each of these statements, respondents seemed to oppose tribalism (e.g. they disagreed that their tribe was better than others). This suggests that the national motto of One Zambia, One Nation has been internalised by participants. Intended to promote national unity across tribal lines, the motto is ubiquitous in Zambia. It is heard regularly at public meetings, spoken at the beginning of newscasts and located on the currency. When considered in combination with the statements in the preceding paragraph, this suggests that tribe can be an important part of one's identity without being a source of prejudice or discrimination. However, the responses to two statements contradict this trend among respondents. The views that 'People from my tribe work harder than people from other tribes' ($p = .006$) and 'People from my tribe are more honest than people from other tribes' ($p = .017$) differed significantly according to the tribe. The majority of participants disagreed with these biased statements. The greatest rejection

Table 2. Non-parametric statistical analysis (Kruskal–Wallis).

Test variables	Tribe	Grouping variables				
		Tribe is important for R's own identity	R says own tribe is better than others	R's tribe is well represented in govt	Govt concerned about R's tribe	Should consider politician's tribe
Tribe important for R's identity	.070	–	.000**	.773	.407	.010*
Tribe important identity – general	.216	.000**	.127	.037*	.793	.029*
Participates in tribal traditions	.485	.031*	.009**	.008**	.142	.000**
R's tribe works harder	.006**	.008**	.000**	.017*	.111	.000**
R's tribe more honest	.017*	.032*	.000**	.020*	.480	.000
R trusts own tribe	.055	.000*	.000**	.002**	.460	.014*
R trusts other tribes	.587	.006**	.070	.000**	.067	.524
R's tribe better than others	.618	.012*	–	.026*	.092	.068
Should be tribal cooperation	.174	.000**	.819	.169	.417	.000**
Tribe well represented in govt	.013*	.240	.823	–	.000**	.001**
Govt concerned about R's tribe	.363	.202	.694	.000**	–	.013*
Should consider politician tribe	.696	.110	.038*	.000**	.007**	–
Politicians use tribe for votes	.078	.505	.239	.062	.470	.464
Riots ok protest against govt	.904	.231	.099	.095	.071	.375

*Significant at $a = .05$.
**Significant at $a = .01$.

of the statements came from Bemba participants, as over half of them (55%) strongly disagreed. The majority of Luvale students (61.1%), however, did not disagree with the statements. It may come as little surprise to those familiar with the centuries-long conflict between the Lunda and Luvale that the Luvale responses to these biased statements were significantly different from other tribes. While the majority of Zambia has been free of violent tribal conflict, the tensions between the neighbouring tribes from North-Western Province have been a consistent concern for the nation's leaders.

Notwithstanding the significant differences pertaining to honesty and work ethic, participants largely showed themselves to be interested in a positive coexistence between tribes while still allowing one's own tribe to be an important aspect of one's identity. The students completing the survey appreciated the personal significance of tribal identity, but their opinions about tribal identity and government showed that they did not think tribe should be an omnipresent factor. A strong majority of participants (87.2%) strongly disagreed with the statement, 'Voters should consider a politician's tribe when voting.' There was no significant difference in response to this statement according to the tribe ($p = .696$), as the students across all tribes rejected the idea of taking a politician's tribe into consideration when voting.

The vast majority of students surveyed felt that tribe should not be a consideration in voting. There was, however, a significant ($p < .001$), positive association between participating in one's tribal traditions and whether a politician's tribe should be considered. The data show that the majority (61.7%) did not agree that they regularly participate in their tribal traditions, suggesting there was a difference between appreciating one's own tribe and having one's tribe play an active role in their identity construction. Those who participated least in tribal traditions disagreed most that a politician's tribe should be a consideration. Those who participated more regularly were more likely to say that tribe should be a political consideration. In other words, the more active participants were in their own tribal traditions, the more important the tribal identity of a politician was to them. Accordingly, since most participants did not regularly participate in their tribe's traditions, most participants did not think it appropriate to consider a politician's tribe. Nonetheless, there was a significant, moderate relationship between tribe and political affiliation (Cramer's $V < .001$; $p < .001$). For most tribal groups within the sample, no single party won the majority of student support. However, Figure 2 shows that the majority of students identifying as Tonga, Lozi and Luvale favoured the main opposition party, UPND. We discuss this further below.

Despite the youth's rejection of political tribalism, we find that what should be and what is are not always the same. Nearly two-thirds (65.4%) of the respondents agreed with the statement that politicians use their tribal identity to secure votes. For the university students surveyed, this means politicians are not behaving like the students would want them to. There were no significant differences in the perception that politicians use their tribal identity for votes according to the tribe ($p = .078$) or any other grouping variable of interest (see Table 2). This is noteworthy, as it shows that students from a variety of tribes consider politicians to be people who inappropriately take advantage of tribal identities. This perception that politicians take advantage of their own tribal

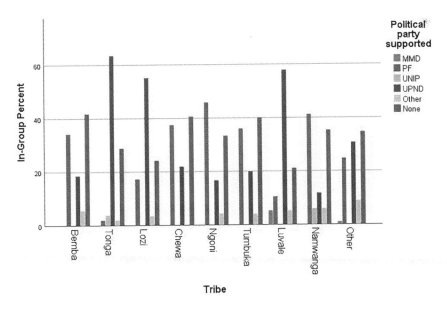

Figure 2. Political affiliation according to the tribe.

identities for political gain was so widespread that it did not even have a significant impact on voter participation ($p = .997$), suggesting it is just an undeniable part of Zambia's political landscape. We might expect that students from tribes that are not well represented in government would be more likely to agree that politicians from other tribes have been behaving inappropriately in this regard, but the data show this was not the case ($p = .062$).

We have shown that the majority of Zambian youth surveyed do not think one's tribal identity should be a political consideration, while simultaneously perceiving politicians to be abusing tribal identities for political gain. We now turn our attention to whether the existence of such political tribalism is seen as beneficial to participants' tribes. The data show that, while politicians may benefit from their tribal identity, the students did not think this had a positive trickle-down effect. Only 25.4% of participants agreed that government leaders are concerned about the welfare of their tribe. The negative view about government leaders did not differ significantly according to the tribe ($p = .363$). Similarly, only one-quarter (26.5%) of participants agreed with the statement, 'My tribe is well represented in government.' Responses to this statement did differ significantly according to the tribe ($p = .013$), and it was, once again, the Tonga, Lozi and Luvale who stood out. While responses for most tribes were fairly evenly split across the Likert scale, the majority of youth from these three tribes disagreed with the statement that their tribe is well represented in government. In light of this perception, we can appreciate why the majority of participants from these tribes favoured the main opposition party. Still, this seems to contradict participant responses pertaining to the appropriateness of tribal identity within politics. Like participants from other tribes, the Tonga, Lozi and Luvale youth strongly disagreed with the statement that voters should consider a politician's tribe. Yet, participants from these tribes seemed to be more focussed on tribal identities within politics, as they were significantly more likely to believe their own tribe had been left behind within government. As a result, they mirrored the larger voting population from their tribes in voting for UPND in an effort to secure a more desirable political outcome for their tribes.

Conclusion

Postmodernism has caused some to believe that racial and ethnic identities will lose significance. Certainly, if this were to be true, we would expect to see it among the youth. Our research suggests that this may not be the case for Zambian youth. Despite the national motto and prominent proclamations from leaders – including the current president – that their tribe is Zambian, the decades-long effort to minimise the importance of tribe for personal identities has not succeeded among our participants. Within a Zambian context, this study suggests that tribe does still matter a great deal to the youth. That these are the better educated among the nation's youth is noteworthy, as it contradicts the thought that tribe or ethnicity only matter to the uneducated.

In addition to showing that tribe still matters for personal identity construction, we have shown that the youth in our study broadly reject political tribalism. Among participants, there is a clear belief that political leaders misuse tribe to further their own agenda. Participants did not believe that this tribalistic aspect of politics was beneficial to their own tribe. The responses to statements about tribal representation within government and the government's concern with participants' tribes shed light on the political frustration experienced by the student participants. They do not think tribe should matter in politics, but they think the older politicians are using tribe anyway. Moreover, tribe is being used to help the power elite, but it is not viewed as something beneficial to the participants' own tribes, which is an important part of their self-identity. As the political world operates in ways youth deem inappropriate and unbeneficial for themselves, the youth are at risk of turning away from democratic engagement.

The most sizeable group within our study has already shown a willingness to turn its back on the democratic process. The majority of Bemba youth in the study did not vote in the most recent general election. Considering where the Bemba participants came from, it is clear they did not skip the election as a result of having to travel insurmountable distances from the university to their home provinces. On the contrary, they tended to live closer than participants from the tribes that had higher voter turnout. Could this be a temporary disinterest because of the lack of a Bemba candidate? Or perhaps a result of the common misperception that the Bemba is always in control of Zambian politics? It is not within the purview of our study to answer these questions, but this is not something to be ignored by future research. Zambia is a very young country, and if the youth of the largest tribal group do not participate in elections, it could lead to problems that challenge the nation's reputation as a bastion of peace. Together with youth from other tribal backgrounds, Bemba youth may benefit from greater outreach on behalf of the nation's political leaders.

Despite broad denunciation of tribalism in politics from various political entities, none of Zambia's political parties have been able to convince the youth in this study that they are better than the rest in this regard. Our findings point to the need for Zambian politics to become more issues based. Unlike political parties in more mature democracies (e.g. Germany, the United Kingdom and the United States), Zambia's parties have not established clear positions on the ideal role of government and the distinctive goals of their party. Indeed, political actors and would-be representatives seem indifferent to which party they belong, as party jumping has become quite common (MINDS, 2016). To the Zambian youth included in our study, as well as general observers, this may make politicians seem as though they are only out to gain power, joining whichever party can grant them such power. Among our participants, there was no significant association between party affiliation and view that politicians use their tribal identity for political gain ($p = .288$). Indeed, this shows that none of the parties have been able to establish themselves as an organisation that is perceived by participants to be above tribalism in politics. Having shed light on this issue with our convenience sample, we suggest that future research include a national study of Zambian youth (including non-students) that assesses both political perceptions and participation.

Disclosure statement

No potential conflict of interest was reported by the authors.

Funding

This work was supported by the Swiss Programme for Research on Global Issues for Development [grant number 400240_147210].

Notes on contributors

Derek Roberts is a Lecturer in the Dag Hammarskjöld Institute for Peace and Conflict Studies at the Copperbelt University in Zambia. In addition to issues of cultural identity, he is interested in the role of race and social class in shaping contemporary urbanisms in ordinary cities. His ongoing projects include a study of informal settlements in Zambia's second city. He holds a PhD in Sociology from Michigan State University.

Simusa Silwamba is a PhD student in the Dag Hammarskjöld Institute for Peace and Conflict Studies at the Copperbelt University in Zambia. His research interests include land tenure and ethnic politics.

References

Badru, P. (2010). Ethnic conflict and state formation in post-colonial Africa: A comparative study of ethnic genocide in the Congo, Liberia, Nigeria, and Rwanda-Burundi. *Journal of Third World Studies, 27*(2), 149–169.

Berman, B. (1998). Ethnicity, patronage and the African state: The politics of uncivil nationalism. *African Affairs, 97*(388), 305–341.

Bond, G. C. (1976). *The politics of change in a Zambian community*. Chicago, IL: University of Chicago Press.

Central Statistical Office. (2011). *Labourforce survey report 2008*. Lusaka.

Central Statistical Office. (2012). *2010 census of population and housing: Population summary report*. Lusaka.

Central Statistical Office. (2015). *Zambia demographic and health survey 2013–14*. Lusaka.

Central Statistical Office. (2017). *The monthly, volume 170*. Lusaka.

Gluckman, M. (2007). Social beliefs and individual thinking in tribal society. In R. Manners, & D. Kaplan (Eds.), *Anthropological theory* (pp. 453–465). Piscataway,NJ: Transaction Publishers.

Hilker, L. M., & Fraser, E. (2009). *Youth exclusion, violence, conflict and fragile states*. London: Social Development Direct.

Horowitz, D. L. (1985). *Ethnic groups in conflict*. Los Angeles: University of California Press.

Isaacs, H. R. (1975). *Idols of the tribe: Group identity and political change*. Cambridge, MA: Harvard University Press.

Juma, C. (2012). *How tribalism stunts African democracy*. . Cambridge, MA: Harvard University Press.

Kabir, M. (2008). Determinants of life expectancy in developing countries. *The Journal of Developing Areas, 41*(2), 185–204.

Karkara, R. (2011). *Essential reader on strengthening meaningful and ethnical participation of children and youth – social coherence and human rights. Draft 1 for UNICEF Turkey and Youth Habitat*. Ankara.

Lentz, C. (1995). 'Tribalism' and ethnicity in Africa: A review of four decades of Anglophone research. *Cahiers des Sciences Humaines, 31*, 303–328.

Macola, G. (2010). *Liberal nationalism in Central Africa: A biography of Harry Mwaanga Nkumbula*. New York, NY: Palgrave Macmillan.

Mandela Institute for Development Studies. (2016). *Youth participation in elections in Africa: An eight-country study*. Johannesburg.

Mathers, C. D., Sadana, R., Salomon, J. A., Murray, C. J. L., & Lopez, A. D. (2001). Healthy life expectancy in 191 countries, 1999. *The Lancet, 357*, 1685–1691.

Mazrui, A. A. A. (1975). *Soldiers and kinsmen in Uganda: The making of a military ethnocracy*. London: Sage.

Ministry of General Education. (2016). *2015 educational statistical bulletin*. Lusaka.

M'Poyo Kasa-Vubu, J. (1985). *Joseph Kasa Vubu, mon pere: De la naissance d'une conscience nationale a l'independence*. Brussels: Chabassol.

Mulford, D. C. (1967). *Zambia: The politics of independence, 1957-1964*. London: Oxford University Press.

Murunga, G. R., & Nasong'o, S. W. (2007). *Kenya: The struggle for democracy*. London: Zed Books.

Muzira, T., Njelesani, M. C., & Zulu, J. J. (2013). *The condition of young people: UN Zambia signature issues series – #2*. Lusaka: United Nations Country Team, Zambia.

Mwakikagile, G. (2001). *Ethnic politics in Kenya and Nigeria*. Huntington, NY: Nova Science Publishers.

Mwewa, C. (2011). *Zambia: Struggles of my people & Western contribution to corruption and underdevelopment in Africa*. Lusaka: Maiden Publishing House.

Paglia, P. (2007). *Ethnicity and tribalism: Are these the root causes of the Sudanese civil conflicts? African conflicts and the role of ethnicity: A case study of Sudan*. Retrieved from www.africaeconomicanalysis.org/articles/pdf/sudan0807.pdf

Phinney, J. S., & Ong, A. D. (2007). Conceptualization and measurement of ethnic identity: Current status and future directions. *Journal of Counseling Psychology, 54*(3), 271–281.

Phiri, B. J. (2006). *Political history of Zambia: From colonial rule to the third republic, 1890-2001*. Trenton, NJ: Africa World Press.

Posner, D. N. (2005). *Institutions and ethnic politics in Africa*. New York, NY: Cambridge University Press.

Rotberg, R. I. (1965). *The rise of nationalism in Central Africa: The making of Malawi and Zambia, 1873-1964*. Cambridge, MA: Harvard University Press.

United Nations Population Fund. (2015). *Zambia Annual report 2015*. Lusaka.

Vail, L. (1989). *The creation of tribalism in Southern Africa*. Los Angeles: University of California Press.

Wele, P. (2010). *Kaunda and Mushala rebellion*. Ndola: Mission Press.

Wiley, D. (1982). Using 'tribe' and 'tribalism' categories to misunderstand African societies. *New England Social Studies Bulletin, 39*(2), 15–17.

Wina, S. (1985). *The night without a president*. Lusaka: Multimedia Publications.

XE. (2017). *XE currency charts: USD to ZMW*. Retrieved from http://www.xe.com/currencycharts/?from=USD&to=ZMW&view=2Y

Youth identity in desegregated schools of Johannesburg

Marie Jacobs

ABSTRACT

Since the end of apartheid, South African schools went through deep changes with the deracialisation of the school system and a fairer allocation of educational resources (funding, equipment, facilities). School vision and mission had to promote values of the rainbow nation in order to enrol learners from different communities. Despite the recognition of diversity, race and ethnic relations still structure social relations inside school. This research shows how South African teenagers from desegregated school of Johannesburg construct their identity in relation to the diverse communities where they evolve. We expose their representation of a world affected by the apartheid legacy of racialised borders and socio-economical divisions but open to identity 'bricolages' and aspirations which allow overtaking them. Religion, popular and global culture, and democratic values are sources of identification to analyse to understand youth identity in contemporary South Africa.

Introduction

Known as the 'generation Y', youth who were born just before or after the first democratic elections in South Africa are generally referred to as the 'born free generation'. However, those young people were not completely free regarding the opportunities offered by a society still deeply structured by the old racial hierarchy of apartheid. Therefore, how does this 'post-apartheid generation' construct their identity today given the diverse social and cultural contexts where they evolve? For those who are given social opportunities through schooling, living in an urban environment like Johannesburg, they move between social structures inherited from the past but still strongly present, and emerging frames influenced by contemporary society changes.

> The official order of apartheid encompassed and embodied the everyday world in which the subjects of South Africa found themselves. This order continued to permeate the new South Africa and has a material existence in many schools today. It continues to confront young people as they seek to establish their identities. (Soudien, 2001, p. 315)

This article explores the deracialisation of identity of pupils at ex-Model C[1] schools in Johannesburg. It shows how the schooling experience influences their representations and offers various opportunities of identifications in order to transcend social and racial segregation processes influencing their path and their social environments or, on the contrary, reproduce racial and social barriers. During apartheid, racial identity assigned to their parents and grandparents was conceived in an essentialist perspective but today's youth define themselves in a more complex and reflexive way. The apartheid legacy and socio-economic divisions affect their representations but this study highlights ambivalent and reversible identity dynamics at work leading to a different kind of identity *bricolages* of past and present identifications.

Research methodology and context of study

This study relies on qualitative data collected in the framework of a doctoral research conducted in two ex-Model C schools of Johannesburg (Bafana High and Makeba High). These schools were chosen based on four criteria in order to enlarge research perspectives on differentiated school environments: position on the school quasi-market, school mission and vision, composition of the school population and the environmental context of the school (the type of urban district around and its impact on school life). Pupils at Bafana High are mainly (80%) from neighbouring districts such as Hillbrow, Berea, Yeoville (areas charecterised by high immigrant populations). A fifth of them come from townships such as Soweto or Alexandra. This gives an outline of social status and cultural characteristics of the school population. Bafana is located in a district of Johannesburg seen as very unsafe and precarious given its high rate of crime and poverty, a number of homeless people, and a large immigrant population.

At the second school, Makeba High, while a large proportion of the teaching staff remains white, the school hosts predominantly 'coloured' and 'black' pupils (according to the racial classification of apartheid). The school particularly draws families from Soweto since it is located close to the township. The school governing body[2] wants to preserve a balance in the composition of the school population by drawing children from white families living in the suburb in an attempt to reduce the number of students leaving for the more privileged schools in the north.

The ethnographic study (Glaser & Strauss, 1967; Woods, 1990, 2011) was conducted over one school year, observing students inside classrooms and during informal school periods such as break times and while entering and leaving the school. The study consisted of attending school on a regular basis (twice a week for each school) and following four grade 11 and 12 classes. We observed English, Life Orientation (similar to social studies), History and Geography classes in particular. The research fieldwork was planned in two stages. Firstly, the extensive stage consisted of collecting *in situ* observations to embrace the different dimensions of school life at Bafana High and Makeba High. It consisted of identifying significant observation points to study how the youth socialised. Secondly, the intensive stage focused on different peer groups by following them inside classrooms and during break time. We formed focus groups with these classrooms and did 40 comprehensive interviews with pupils. Students were chosen depending on their peer groups. We started by interviewing pupils who were more open and easier to establish contact with, then moved on to the peer groups who were more difficult to approach. In order to collect a representative sample of different types of identity constructions among the youthful sociability of every school, pupils were chosen according to variables such as gender, cultural membership claimed, optional subjects (Business, Accounting, Math, Math literacy, Afrikaans, isiZulu, French, History and Life Sciences) and school achievements.

Emergent fit theory was used as a method to select the relevant empirical data and to generate codes. It consists of continuously cross-checking the empirical data with the product of analysis and to adjust it gradually (Guillemette, 2006). At first, data were organised according to three descriptive axes: pupils/institution, pupils/peer groups, pupils/agents. Then, several codes linked to identifications/differentiation dynamics (identity repertoires mobilised by the pupils in their social relations at school) were highlighted for each of these three axes. Constant comparison between different incidents noticed in each school, and then between both schools, elicited the properties and dimensions of each code to theoretically saturate the core and related concepts (Glaser & Strauss, 1967). Comprehensive interviews allowed us to prove the pertinence of these concepts for the analysis of the whole empirical corpus.

Ethnic and race relations in South African schools

Since the end of apartheid, the South African society has faced the challenge of desegregation. As society was organised in a hierarchy according to racial groups, affecting every economic and social dimension of life, deracialisation is closely linked to the issue of social mobility. The affirmative action politics (Maré, 2001) of the democratic government of South Africa came into force to invert social divisions caused by apartheid so that individuals belonging to historically disadvantaged groups had the opportunity to cross borders that were previously impossible to penetrate.

In South Africa, social research studies on diversity and identity usually use the racial relations concept as a starting point to study dominant social relations (Soudien, 2004). But race as a category has an ideological meaning and poses several difficulties for empirical research. The main difficulty is linked to the use of this notion in the constructivist perspective. Several authors (Jenkins, 1986; Rex & Mason, 1986; Yetman, 1999) recognise that race relations and ethnic relations concepts are often used without clear distinction so that they appear as synonyms. Various attempts to conceptualise both these notions have followed but without convincing results. Rex (1986), for instance, explains: '[...] the element essential to the understanding of racism namely that ethnic groups sometimes had identities imposed on them to restrict their mobility and to facilitate their exploitation and oppression'.

Jenkins (1986), according to an American and cultural anthropology point of view, underlines several particularities to differentiate ethnicity from race relations. Firstly, ethnic relations relate to actors who define themselves according to their social situation. The main focus concerns the maintaining of boundaries between 'us' and 'them' as ethnic identity depends on mutual imputations exchanged between group members and outsiders. Then, it becomes interesting to study specific mobilisation of common racial categories even if the research study is anchored in the ethnic paradigm. 'A far wider set of situations are based upon cultural differentiation of groups than those which are commonly called racial [...] few of them have anything like the same conflictual consequences that racial situations do' (Rex in Jenkins, 1986, p. 176). This means that if we study ethnic boundaries and the constitution of ethnic groups, we must not neglect the categorisation question. Therefore, two dimensions of ethnicity can be highlighted: the process of identification within the group and the process of categorisation at work through ethnic boundaries and outside the group (Jenkins, 1986). The underlining of the categorisation process allows studying power relations amongst ethnic relations and the existence of domination strategies that could produce social and ethnic boundaries. These power relations will help us understand the meaning social actors give to the use of racial categorisations. For this research, we assume that racial categories are generally the legacy of past power relations even if some social groups continue using these racial markers to define themselves.

In this manuscript, identity is studied according to a relational and contextual perspective. 'The construction of an identity is made within social contexts that determine the position of the agents and, for this reason, orient their representations and choices' (Cuche, 1996, p. 182). This work relies on the thesis that identity in the late modernity is in constant crisis, permanently threatened and in transition (Dubar, 2002). As the importance of reflexive and narrative identity increases, the more community identities or social institutions come under pressure. This generates the complexity and duality (diachronic and synchronic) of the identity making (Dubar, 2002, p. 11). Identity is simultaneously always identity for oneself and identity for others. Therefore, youth identity in this research is studied by examining dynamics of identity differentiation and/or identity affiliation to reference groups. Two concepts, identity (role) repertoires (Hannerz, 1980) and categorisation are considered in this work to analyse how individuals mobilise different identity resources and get involved in diverse social situations according to opportunities or constraints.

The politics of identity making in privileged schools

Both schools under study belong to what we have called the 'intermediate segment' (Payet & Deneuvy, 2011) of the school quasi-market (situated between the township schools and northern Johannesburg upper class schools) with reference to their particular position on the local hierarchy according to the school's reputation and characteristics (matric pass rate, facilities, school population and location). Schools from the intermediate segment face major changes (deracialisation and desegregation processes) that concern the South African society itself. We consider them as 'experimental spaces of the Rainbow Nation'. For instance, previously known as Model C schools, these were generally the first to open their doors to 'non-white' pupils before the end of apartheid, and were actively involved during the transition to the new national model of education.

However, several researches (Dolby, 2001; Soudien, 2007; Vally & Dalamba, 1999) pointed out the persistence of symbolic power relations in ex-Model C schools where dominant discourses from apartheid still structure school life.

> The official order of apartheid encompassed and embodied the everyday world in which the subjects of South Africa found themselves. This order continued to permeate the new South Africa and has a material existence in many schools today. It continues to confront young people as they seek to establish their identities. (Soudien, 2001, p. 315)

Often, we observed that their vision is anchored in the Rainbow Nation discourse to promote cultural diversity and acknowledgment of differences, instead pupils collide with structures and ways of working still influenced by the apartheid regime since the teaching staff composition remains almost the same as the past. Behind a carefully inclusive school vision, their educational project remains in a precarious position between the re-assessment of conceptions and practices from the dominant white culture and inclusion strategies still confined into an assimilationist perspective (McKinney, 2010; Soudien, 2007). Therefore, these schools situated on the intermediate segments are structured by concomitant and rival integration discourses 'that construct, maintain, and change social identities in those communities and the wider society' (Chick, 2002, p. 463).

What this study has come to show is that peer relationships at school reflect the paradoxical and complex character of the deracialisation process at work. If the pupils willingly use the new South African political discourse (Rainbow Nation, unity and diversity ideal) to introduce their school as a place promoting cultural diversity, they admit that it is difficult to build friendship relations outside of old racial categories. While these teenagers claim their membership to a wide African community, it seems difficult for them to see beyond racial identities interiorised during apartheid.

> **Nkuli:** Some people find it better to interact with the same cultural group like you understand each other more. Some people find it difficult to interact with black in coloured or black in white, they rather be black to black or white to white or Indian and Indian. Since the racial thing, there are some people that do not like certain groups of people because of the way they look and the stuff we believe in.

Both the complex nature of inter-cultural relations amongst pupils inside school and the re-racialisation of identifications processes points out how much the subjacent political issue of racial classifications is problematic when it comes along with the Rainbow Nation vocabulary. The African National Congress partisans specifically carried a non-racialism philosophy during the struggle to defend the idea of a society liberated from racial constraints (Mistry, 2001). But when Black Economic Empowerment policy was established to transform institutional structures and counterbalance major inequalities between the different population layers, apartheid racial classifications were asserted as a selection grid to determine access to the work market according to affirmative action criteria while it would have been possible to benefit from this democratic opportunity to innovate a new non-racial vocabulary both in the political, economic and cultural field (Maré, 2001). As Ansell (2006, p. 340) points out, 'the abstract ideal of non-racialism that served so well during the period of transition has run up against the imperatives of transformation'. We can see the effects of those concomitant discourses, color-blind ideology and race-based policies of employment, on the identity making inside privileged schools. If racial identities remain salient in all sort of affective expression of cultural and political belonging and taste (Dolby, 2001), privileged schools are seen as a symbol of social mobility and pupils tend to claim their belonging to an upper social class unlike the racial categories remaining in the tacit school discourse.

> BEE doesn't work. You can't say in a company okay your company must employ blacks, in our country we have blacks, coloureds and Indians. The white people own all the major companies, but you can't say it's the white people, it's the black people. We're South African, like I said in my English speech, we mustn't say I'm black, he's white, she's Indian. We must think we are coloured ... [Pupils laugh at him and say along to correct him 'South African'!]. (notebook, Makeba High)

On the one hand, pupils continue using racial classification because the school context has not completely erased this social representation; on the other hand, pupils are willing to refer to other categories of identification that reflect their social aspiration and socioeconomic status. The following extract is very significant because it illustrates interferences in terms of individual identifications between the economic discourse on affirmative discrimination and the political discourse on the Rainbow Nation. What real possibilities of identification do these young people have? In this situation, what revolts the learner is the fact that *other*, the 'foreigner', uses the same racial categories of apartheid to define him while he actually demands the right, just like his interlocutor who calls himself Brazilian, to be identified as South African. This identity request is even stronger as we are in the context of the soccer World Cup in which patriotic fervour is very meaningful.

> During the World Cup I was at a game. I asked some guys where they were from. They won't say okay I'm a black Brazilian, I'm a white Brazilian, they all said I'm Brazilian. So the other guy said to me, are you coloured, are you black coloured, are you black South African? I was like, what's the difference! I'm asking the same question you answered. I'm South Africa it's like that! So ja, I think so because education is the key to success, it will open doors for our youth but we all have the same thing. (notebook, Makeba High)

Consequently, pupils attending privileged schools circulate between different social worlds where the possibilities of identification are various but also very unsteady.

> Their identities are incoherent and discontinuous. They are of their apartheid pasts, but simultaneously against it. Identity formation in school is a process in which young people bring resources, find new ones and constantly work to make sense of their identity positions relative to others. (Soudien, 2007, p. 96)

We are now going to explore these other possibilities of identification, in other words, values and referents that are meaningful in the identity making process. Our purpose is to show how these pupils take a stand on these values and referents and construct ambiguous affiliations between religious principles, traditional practices and beliefs, and global popular music tastes and styles.

Youth identity making beyond racial borders

To understand how the young people construct their identity inside these desegregated schools of Johannesburg, we must keep in mind the fact that these pupils are caught in the ambiguous position between the deracialisation discourse of the school, their family beliefs and tradition and their social aspirations. Different sources of identification are described, but two are particularly meaningful in the identity making of pupils we interviewed: religion and the global youth culture. Our purpose is to show how an ambivalent deracialisation/re-racialisation process that is linked to the school context where these pupils evolve structures these identification dynamics. In the informal spaces where these pupils find themselves, aside from the cultural project of the school, there is a counter culture that emerges. These young people know how much they need to adjust their identity to the school values but, conscious of how they are labelled and grouped, they need to express what really makes sense for them. Therefore, their identity making is strained between their will to cross the barriers of race and class and the problem they face when their home environment is not in alignment with the school (Soudien, 2007).

Religious beliefs and practices: a way to emancipate oneself?

We can analyse how young people use this religious repertoire to define themselves by describing two tendencies.

Firstly, youth tend to claim their religious membership to free themselves from pre-scripts and from traditional beliefs to emphasise the modern character of their individuality. Some pupils are in an awkward position with their family cultural inheritance and they want to emancipate themselves from customs and traditional rules. Since at school pupils have the opportunity to discuss democratic issues, they are encouraged to question their beliefs regarding rights guaranteed by the Constitution (for example, *lobola* (dowry or bride price), gender equality, sexual violence). Everything takes place as though this strong identification to religious referents, sometimes reacting against their parents, allows them to negotiate better their membership to modern values. It appears that democratic values taught at schools make them think about the consequences of some normative representations conveyed by their cultural inheritance. Defining themselves 'Christian' constitutes an emancipating identity repertoire where the question of individual choice is central. Religious beliefs would fulfil this role of re-reading their belonging to traditional and family culture, bringing about a responsible individual capable of making choices. Both extracts below illustrate this central question of individual freedom that conditions their self-development. Mahosazana and Jabulile both prefer Christian referents to traditional cultural practices as they openly chose this identity affiliation to introduce themselves.

> **Mahosazana**: I would say I'm a modernised cultural person and Christian coz I was born in a Christian family and my parents were fully converted to Christianity. When my dad converted to Christianity completely I did not get all that, like all that slaughtering of the cow. They take the skin of the cattle and they make a little ribbon for the boy and the girl and you wear it until you are in your twenties. My brother cut it off coz my dad converted completely to Christianity now.

For Jabulile, difference of beliefs between her parents and herself created a gap of incomprehension. She is completely aware of the consequences of being involved in the Christian community (against matrimonial expectations) and considers her choice as a mean to gain maturity. We can see how this Christian affiliation provides opportunities of self-development and social mobility.

> **Jabulile**: My parents aren't in the same church as I am. And you know they are still traditionalists. [...] They still live in the Old Testament time, they still believe in slaughtering and sacrifices and everything. But you know that Jesus Christ didn't just do all of that, right? [...] They want to impose ideas on me. And now I'm 17 years old. I've got a mind of my own now. I understand what life is. I understand implications that go with the choices that I make, that every choice that I make has to be consistent with what I want, or else I'm not gonna be happy.

The second tendency refers to the condition of life of some pupils. At school, they often discuss typical problems related to youth that can potentially lead to serious results. Many of them deplore peer pressure in relation to teenage temptations such as smoking, sexuality and more serious petty crimes such as drugs and theft. In very insecure social environments, a religious community represents a valve of protection against bad influences. It represents a way to protect them against all types of danger that comes along with adolescence and urban lifestyle.

Precious: When I was in Gr9 I was in a gang here at school. We were like six girls, and so those girls were smoking, drinking here at school. So I also began to know that attitude. But then I changed and then I realized this is wrong. So I went to Miss Purple and talked to her. Then I was in a process of like I can't drink anymore, I can't smoke. [...]

Marie: And what happened? How get involved in that gang?

Precious: I think it was peer pressure. I could not control myself. You know, you also want to be famous at school, so people could see. Because it's that stage of being a teenager. So I got to that point where I say let me just join because it is fun. I thought it was good but it is actually bad. [...] Maybe it's because I go to church. I am a Christian. I may be a Zulu though we've got things that we follow in our traditions. But then I prefer being a Christian. So I just went to church, I started praying, ja. And I love church, so much.

Religious values and norms offer a structuring frame and a socialisation space when these teenagers experience precarious family situations or do not find the adult figures supposed to serve as examples. In particular, they instil solid values that work as identity resources for young people exposed to difficult circumstances in life, affected by violence and the weakening of the nuclear family structure. Religion also provides resources to guide their action when they have to face different social troubles: according to these pupils, 'church' constituted a protective firebreak against temptations from outside, the street, the media, or even the consumer society. For instance, Christianity as a source of identification would work more in the service of a common morality by offering a moral frame for the reading of social relations. This frame, represented by the emblematic face of the pastor, would protect them from bad influence ('protect from the bad stuff') to be able to remain on the 'right track'. All in all, religious beliefs refer to the eminently moral dimension of acting for pupils who have to stay on the right path in a context where freedom as leitmotiv casts them on the fragile thread of adolescence and its experimentations. This extremely Manichean conception of reality seems to reflect the individual responsibility that weighs on these pupils of desegregated schools. We can see how the South African society is involved in a national process of democratic transition. All South Africans did not necessarily fight for freedom and the abrogation of the apartheid regime, but for the most oppressed and underprivileged groups, expectations were huge in comparison with goals set by the young South African democracy. Youth who did not live under apartheid (but who experienced it in a postponed way through stories and experiences narrated by their parents and grandparents) are considered by older generations to be the *well-off* in this democracy. Parents want to carry out their desires of emancipation by planning the professional careers of their children. Heavy expectations apply a huge pressure on pupils who have to make the right choices. But the context where they live also has its difficulties. Pupils explain that they suffer or that they find it difficult to satisfy requests from their parents.

Youth popular culture: a social marker?

Youth sociability inside school are particularly characterised by the popular global culture such as musical tastes and corresponding dress styles (Zola, Usher, Jay-Z, and various DJs and rappers). It also appears as a new source of identification away from ancient identity assignments. If pupils can hardly display their musical or dress preferences because of their school uniform, they show creativity and employ various strategies to differentiate themselves and express their musical tastes. Dress styles and appearance adopted by youth hold a central place since it reinforces and makes noticeable their identification to the global youth culture. These practices founded on aesthetic values and specific criteria of style translate a will to become a particular expressive subject, able to distance oneself from community, religious expectations or from ancient racial nomenclature (Nuttall, 2008).

The work of Nuttall (2008) and Nkuna (2006) on typical youthful codes noticeable at 'The Zone' (a shopping centre popular with youth in an upmarket area of Johannesburg) show how this multiracial symbolic repertoire, typical of the middle class, consists of a register of identification peculiar to the Model C kid who favours the English language, R&B music and famous brand clothes. If American globalised culture offers new sources of identification, we can observe typically South African variations, local re-appropriations that have more links with an enhanced black self-awareness. This symbolic syncretic repertoire (Nuttall speaks about remix of composition (2004)) would constitute an alternative, as a mean and style of self-expression, to the politics of resistance against apartheid crystallised in the black man figure. This means that young people who identify themselves to this repertoire, peculiar to the Model C kid or 'The Zone', do not passively use these globalised cultural types but act actively and consciously in the development of these types and work out together this new multi-ethnic and syncretic repertoire. They think the music they listen to and associate with must pass on a message.

> **Banele**: I'm also into a bit of reggae I listen to a lot of reggae coz I believe for a song to actually matter it has to carry a message, and I believe reggae is music with a message. Reggae kind of keeps me grounded with my life as well.

> **Sweetness**: I love hip-hop so much. It's, you know, like it's poetry. It's somebody that expresses itself. People say hey, hip-hop is all about swearing, all about clothes or girls or people being naked. But hip-hop is about expressing yourself or something that you went through, it's a message.

This brings us to the following analysis: youth do not characterise themselves by a blind affiliation to the westernised global culture but do question sexist and violent behaviours that are broadcasted through the media. They are critical of the bad influences of some popular faces of musical global stages. Pupils explain that they choose what makes sense for them according to their experiences. This identity making inspired by global youth culture would work as a living medium and as a mean to interact together. While these young people seem to be aware of belonging to a globalised generation culture, they relate according to what they experience in their daily lives.

> **Linha**: No, I think music builds my personality because the songs … you know people don't actually listen, pay attention to what they said. Especially when it comes to rap, they have this big issue with rap. I get the fact that they swear a lot but there are some rap songs that are actually really nice. Some people are actually experiencing that now so how they dealt with it, how they made it, how they became who they are now.

These reconstructed identities reworded via new ways of living for middle class black youth refers to what Nuttall calls the *politics of aspiration*. The will to stay in the township is received, according to Y culture, as an obvious failure, while carrying ostentatiously a flashy combination township popular culture points out that they want to live their life in another way, that they have no intention of slaving away as their parents (Nuttall, 2008). This phenomenon is extremely significant in pupils' discourses about their choices of study, their professional choices and their future display. Linguistic expressions used by pupils are indeed particularly eloquent when they say 'high up there', 'look up to these people', 'sky up there'. This also applies to the 'business men' figure and the social image associated ('I want to be successful', 'make money', 'I want to achieve'). This figure translates a desire of social emancipation that goes through mimetic behaviours and the display of successful signs broadcast in American pop videos, magazines, films, etc.

> **Trevor**: I would want to be a soccer player, an analyst, be successful, be a happy South African, maybe have a family of my own [...] and, I want a BMW, coz my father owns one ... people look at us. Because, once you can see you are in a BM, you are there.

Therefore, global popular culture provides a new source of identification allowing pupils to identify more apparently to modernity, to the global youth. It especially consti-tutes an identity repertoire that facilitates pupils' interactions by creating a youthful syn-cretic culture. Access to global youth culture comes true, for example, by visiting different urban areas in Johannesburg, such as malls, bars and nightclubs of Soweto, Rosebank, or Sandton. Mobility between social privileged and modest areas corresponds with these Model C kids, who manage to cross ancient borders of racial segregation and new borders of social segregation. Global youth culture offers new identification resources that work as markers of social differentiation (for instance the fact of having a brand new mobile phone or trendy clothes bought in an upmarket neighbourhood). Finally, for some young people, these global cultural referents represent a fundamental identity support in the process of their identity making. Facing jamming of referents and identity twinges between different community belongings, these referents make it possible to either break or conjugate multiple identity identifications. Therefore, their youth culture combines global popular culture referents, traditional referents, cultural community values, religious norms and political convictions. Global referents are therefore re-appro-priated according to local stakes that the youth face as social and ethnic segregation, poverty, intergeneration conflicts, etc.

If the global youth culture gives common identity referents to the youth creating a wide youth culture, this identity repertoire produces at the same time new differentiation pro-cesses. There are also opportunities for the youth to claim their ethnic identity. Beyond or despite inherited racial representations, new ethnic boundaries are being defined from this global youth culture. As Dolby (2001) exposed in her study, we can also observe the re-racialisation of taste in those school contexts, when social barriers structure social relations between students. Because access to global youth culture represents a way to socially differentiate themselves (the ability to cross social and racial barriers), some dress styles are also associated with different living areas more or less segregated. Inside school, it is common to hear pupils speaking about the 'southern suburbs' and the 'northern suburbs' of Johannesburg. The 'north' and 'south' categories translate these social distinction logics that are expressed through ethnic and global cultural referents.

The racial dimension of youthful sociability inside schools and the existence of silent rivalries between social backgrounds give rise to various ethnic labels used to characterised peer groups: *gangsters* from Eldorado, *township boys* from Soweto, etc. These ethnic labels are associated and reinforced by ethnic markers inspired by different dress styles and music types. For instance, Kerian (who considers himself as Scottish) differentiates himself from pupils coming from Soweto by referring to the music popular culture ('I am a typical white boy, can I survive this school? The so-called gangster mentality and stuff like that'). The gangster mentality of street culture is associated with hip-hop or rap that Kerian considers as degrading music styles ('There is a gangster mentality. It's a streetwise mentality [...] the way I see it, you know, MTV, this hip-hop mentality is what's really sort of deteriorating the youth, you know'). He associates himself to the rock and roll or heavy metal music types since he is part of a band ('Because I can tell you now, go back 20 years, rap was something small. It was all the rock and roll, heavy metal moves and that sort of stuff.'). On the contrary, some other pupils, praise township culture (*gang style*, *township style*) and willingly defend their own style that is not fancy, that does not come from the privileged areas of the town. Some girls explained that they would not shop at certain malls because they preferred the township stores. The glamorous representation of the 'ghetto' as a place of criminality is recuperated in order to present Soweto as *a cool pace to be* and not as a place of poverty to be ashamed of and run away from. This ghetto lifestyle or gangster style refers to hip-hop cultural referents, to the globalised street culture that youth use in their identification to the township or to Soweto.

Conclusion

If 'race thinking' (Maré, 2001) still manipulates representations of social life, the youth of South Africa seem to be looking for new sources of identification. First of all, the vocabulary of democracy and citizenship conduct them to make a stand against or with their community inheritance and traditional practices as *lobola* or ancestor worship. Youth differentiate themselves by what they call their 'modern' way of living that contributes to the building of a reflexive look, sometimes critical, on their traditions. Religious belonging also opens other ways of identity construction outside their cultural groups, allowing them to move away from customs and inherited traditional values and practices. Calling themselves Christian would both allow teenagers to escape from community expectations and protect themselves from threats and family injunctions. It has a very salient status in the self-presentation of youth and promotes the deracialisation of their social representations. We also need to underline the role of globalised cultural referents in the syncretic reconstruction of identifications. Access to consumer society makes sense for these young people (Hammett, 2009). This generation increasingly identifies and consumes different global music types, dress styles and fashion. Therefore, they express themselves through behaviours and particular aesthetic practices characterised by a strong visibility potential that goes beyond borders and localities (Nayak, 2003). These 'generation markers' have expanded largely carving out new globally defined spaces in which ideas of self and others are imagined, produced and lived (Dolby, 2001). Following a self-differentiation attempt, youth appropriate themselves specific features from the global popular culture in order to express or claim their particular identity or to re-draw racial differentiations between social groups. Our work shows, as Dubar's thesis (2002) fore-quoted, that these pupils try to distinguish themselves from former community or institutional identity repertoires (inherited from apartheid) through an individualisation of their identifications (narrative identities) which are now mostly reflexive.

Notes

1. In 1991, formerly white schools, called ex-model C schools, were allowed to enrol pupils from all « races » (black, indian, coloured) and up to 50% of their population. Model C schools are government institutions partially administered and funded by parents and a school governing body.
2. The school governing body is a decisional entity created by the State at the school level, and is composed of elected members (mainly parents, teachers and administrative personnel), as well as students and coopted members of the school community.

Disclosure statement

No potential conflict of interest was reported by the author.

Funding

This work was supported by the F.R.S. FNRS (National Fund for Scientific Research, Belgium) under Grant [FC 78292].

Notes on contributor

Marie Jacobs has a PhD in social and political sciences from the Université catholique de Louvain (UCL, Belgium) and a PhD in sciences of education from the University of Geneva (Switzerland). Her research interests, based on ethnographic qualitative studies, concerned ethnic and race relations inside schools, comparative analysis of school systems and early school access and socialisation. She now leads her researches at the Lausanne University of Teacher Education (HEP Vaud).

References

Ansell, E. A. (2006). Casting a blind eye: The ironic consequences of colour-blindness in South Africa and the United States. *Critical Sociology, 32*, 333–356. doi:10.1163/156916306777835349

Chick, K. (2002). Constructing a multicultural national identity: South African classrooms as sites of struggle between competing discourses. *Journal of Multilingual and Multicultural Development, 23*, 462–478. doi:10.1080/01434630208666480

Cuche, D. (1996). *La notion de culture dans les sciences sociales*. Paris: La Découverte.

Dolby, N. (2001). *Constructing race. Youth, identity and popular culture in South Africa*. New York, NY: Suny Press.

Dubar, C. (2002). *La socialisation, construction des identités sociales et professionnelles*. Paris: Armand Colin.

Glaser, B., & Strauss, A. (1967). *The discovery of grounded theory: Strategies for qualitative research*. New York, NY: Aldine.

Guillemette, F. (2006). L'approche de la grounded theory; pour innover. *Recherches Qualitatives, 26*, 32–50. Retrieved from http://www.lar.univ-paris-diderot.fr/sites/default/files/fguillemette_ch.pdf

Hammett, D. (2009). Local beats to global rhythms: Coloured student identity and negotiations of global cultural imports in Cape Town, South Africa. *Social & Cultural Geography, 10*, 403–419. doi:10.1080/14649360902853270

Hannerz, U. (1980). *Exploring the city: Inquiries toward an urban anthropology.* New York: Columbia University Press.

Jenkins, R. (1986). Social anthropological models of inter-ethnic relations. In J. Rex & D. Mason (Eds.), *Theories of race and ethnic relations* (pp. 170–185). Cambridge: Cambridge University.

Maré, G. (2001). Race counts in contemporary South Africa: 'An illusion of ordinariness'. *Transformation, 47,* 75–93.

McKinney, C. (2010). Schooling in black and white: Assimilationist discourses and subversive identity performances in a desegregated South African girls school. *Race Ethnicity and Education, 13,* 191–207. doi:10.1080/13613321003726876

Mistry, J. (2001). *Conditions for cultural production in post-apartheid South Africa.* IWM Junior Visiting Fellows Conferences, 11. Retrieved from http://www.iwm.at/publications/visiting-fellows-conferences/vol-11/

Nayak, A. (2003). *Race, place and globalization. Youth cultures in a changing world.* London: Berg.

Nkuna, L. (2006). "Fitting in" to a "classy place": The zone and youth identity. In P. Alexander, M. Dawson, & M. Ichharam (Eds.), *Globalisation & new identities. A view from the middle* (pp. 261–274). Johannesburg: Jacana.

Nuttall, S. (2004). City forms and writing the 'now' in South Africa. *Journal of Southern African Studies, 30,* 731–748. doi:10.1080/0305707042000313988

Nuttall, S. (2008). Youth cultures of consumption in Johannesburg. In N. Dolby & F. Rizvi (Eds.), *Youth moves. Identities and education in global perspective* (pp. 151–177). New York, NY: Routledge.

Payet, J.-P., & Deneuvy, M.-A. (2011). La segmentation du marché scolaire en Afrique du Sud: les paradoxes d'une politique de déségrégation raciale. *Education Comparée, 6,* 91–110.

Rex, J., & Mason, D. (1986). *Theories of race and ethnic relations.* Cambridge: Cambridge University Press.

Soudien, C. (2001). Certainty and ambiguity in youth identities in South Africa: Discourses in transition. *Discourse: Studies in the Cultural Politics of Education, 22,* 311–326. doi:10.1080/01596300120094352

Soudien, C. (2004). Constituting the class: An analysis of the process of integration in South African schools. In L. Chisholm (Ed.), *Changing class. Education and social change in post-apartheid South Africa* (pp. 89–114). Cape Town: Human Sciences Research Council.

Soudien, C. (2007). *Youth identity in contemporary South Africa. Race, culture and schooling.* Claremont: New Africa Books.

Vally, S., & Dalamba, Y. (1999). *Racism, racial integration and desegregation in South African public secondary schools.* A report on a study by the South African Human Rights Commission (SAHRC). Retrieved from https://www.sahrc.org.za/home/21/files/Reports/RACISMRACIAL%20INTEGRATION_pdf1999.pdf

Woods, P. (1990). *L'ethnographie de l'école.* Paris: Armand Colin.

Woods, P. (2011). *Sociology and the School.* Abingdon: Routledge.

Yetman, N. R. (1999). *Majority and minority. The dynamics of race and ethnicity in American life.* Boston, MA: Allyn and Bacon.

Violence and youth voter turnout in sub-saharan Africa

Dabesaki Mac-Ikemenjima

ABSTRACT

Despite the growing literature on political violence in sub-Saharan Africa, there is, surprisingly, a limited number of studies exploring its relationship with voter turnout, and specifically youth turnout, in the region. Africa is a relatively young continent, and the majority of its population is youth, positioning them as an important voting group. However, recent studies have suggested a shift in youth interest from voting to other forms of political participation such as protest. This paper explores the relationship between violence and youth voter turnout in sub-Saharan Africa. Using cross-sectional nationally representative data from the Afrobarometer public attitude survey from 20 countries, a correlation analysis is carried out to explore the relationship between fear of violence and turnout (voted in the last elections) among youth. The analysis shows a negative relationship between violence and voting among youth. Analyses controlling for employment, education and party affiliation also show that none of these had an effect on the strength and direction of the relationship. This suggests that violence could be a factor in explaining youth voter turnout in sub-Saharan Africa.

Introduction

In sub-Saharan Africa, recent waves of heightened political awareness have seen increasing numbers of youth engaging in protests and some actively mobilising their peers to vote and contest in elections (Chaturvedi, 2016; Lambert, 2016; Oyedemi & Mahlatji, 2016).[1] However, while they are active on the streets in protest, youth do not appear to sufficiently utilise their energies towards electoral political processes through voting. Honwana (2012) suggests that the inability on the part of youth to channel their energies into election processes often results in disillusionment and the outcome of their protests being appropriated by individuals who represent the 'establishment' they seek to upturn. Other analyses suggest that apathy among young voters in sub-Saharan Africa, like their counterparts elsewhere in the world, is a result of disengagement from the political process (Resnick & Casale, 2011; Resnick & Casale, 2014; Scott, Vawda, Swartz, & Bhana, 2012).

Analyses of the factors which explain apathy among young voters in European contexts examine factors such as class, socio-economic and political socialisation (Fieldhouse & Cutts, 2012). In sub-Saharan Africa, recent analyses suggest that young people's access to information, their perception of the electoral context as being free and fair or otherwise, and the existing party system are key determinants of turnout (Resnick & Casale, 2014).

There is also a growing literature which associates turnout with violence in elections (Bekoe, 2010; Collier & Vicente, 2012). The evidence emerging from this body of work suggests that electoral outcomes are, at least in part, affected by perceived violence, fear of violence and voter intimidation. Although the literature analysing electoral violence and youth political participation in the region is growing, discussions on the potential relationship between violence and youth voter apathy is limited.

The aim of this paper is to explore the relationship between youth voter turnout and violence using a large data set of data from several countries in Africa. By youth voter turnout, the paper implies the proportion of young people who cast their votes on election day. This is distinct from registering to vote in elections, enrolling as a candidate in election or being part of an political party – all of which are forms of political participation. The paper is organised into five sections. Following this introductory section, the second will briefly review the relevant literature on youth political participation, and in particular violence in elections in sub-Saharan Africa. The third section describes the data and methodology of the study. In the fourth section, the results of the analysis are presented. In the fifth section, the results are discussed and conclusions are drawn.

Youth and political participation

Youth, defined here as individuals aged 18–35 consistent with the African Youth Charter (African Union, 2006), constitute a significant portion of Africa's population. An age-based definition is used in this paper as opposed to others such as youth as a period of transition (Jones, 2009; Utas, 2012) or defining youth based on patterns of consumption that differentiate different demographic groups (Herrera, 2006), in order to enable consistence across countries and ensure that the analysis is comparable across countries, majority of which define the upper age limit of youth as 35 years. Individuals aged 15–24 and 15–34 constituted 20.5% and 34.5%, respectively, of Africa's one billion population in 2009 (African Union, 2011; UNECA, 2009). With such a large proportion of the population, youth have the potential to shift the electoral and political balance towards the issues that affect them using their votes. Chuck (2012: online) observes this by pointing out that 'the sheer size of African youth population provides them with voting clout', which makes them a respectable demographic to be targeted during electoral campaigns. Given the high youth population in sub-Saharan Africa, voting trends and patterns within this group are important as they could influence future electoral outcomes. It is therefore imperative to understand the factors that influence young people's turnout during elections, in particular those factors that have the potential to deter their turnout during elections and overall participation in politics.

Youth political participation is understood as a range of activities in which young people engage to project their voices on the issues that affect them within the political processes of their countries (Weitz-shapiro & Winters, 2008). Forms of political participation vary and include voting in elections, contacting a local official, taking part in protests and affiliation with a political party (Ekman & Amnå, 2012; Weitz-shapiro & Winters, 2008). While there is an array of activities that constitute political participation, some of them take pre-eminence. For example, although other aspects of youth political participation are also analysed in the literature, voting and protest appear to be the two areas which have gained the most attention in recent times (Sukarieh & Tannock, 2015).

Also, while other forms of political participation, such as protest, are crucial for demanding political accountability and social justice, voting plays a major role in installing the individuals and institutions from whom accountability are often demanded.

Voting is the most direct form of political participation because it informs those who become the decision makers and leaders in democracies through elections. Analyses of developed-country political trends emphasise the shift in youth political participation from voting to protests (Henn & Foard, 2013; Ødegard & Berglund, 2008; Quaranta, 2015). Thus, an important aspect of the debate includes strategies towards re-engaging young voters. One strategy in particular which has gained traction within the political debate in the United Kingdom is the call for the reduction of the voting age to 16.[2] This is suggested as a potential route to swell the ranks of young voters in order to facilitate their reengagement with political processes. Recent studies (Resnick & Casale, 2011, 2014) in Africa suggest that youth turnout is lower than those of adults and youth are disengaging from voting. This raises the question: why are young people not active in voting during elections?

Determinants of youth political participation

Resnick and Casale (2011) list a range of factors affecting youth turnout in sub-Saharan Africa. These include social and economic factors, highlighting education and income as positively affecting young people's likelihood of voting. Further, they highlight that access to information and knowledge on political issues, civic engagement and the performance of the government in power in terms of improving the country's economic performance in the areas that affect youth (such as job creation) are other determinants of youths' political participation. Overall, Resnick and Casale (2011) found that young people are less likely to vote than adults, and this is more so among young people in urban areas than rural areas. Further to this, they note that the duration of an incumbent's stay (the longer the stay) in power decreases young people's likelihood of voting (Resnick & Casale, 2011).

Writing about youth voter apathy in the United Kingdom, Phelps (2006) concluded that the level of young people's participation in political processes is determined by their class, social capital and education. Similar lines of argument have been made in recent studies which link political participation with wellbeing indicators. For example, a study in Switzerland suggests that life satisfaction increases the likelihood of voting among youth (Lorenzini, 2015). A similar conclusion was drawn from a study in Latin America in which it was found that life satisfaction increases voting in elections but not other forms of political participation such as protests (Weitz-shapiro & Winters, 2008). Flavin and Keane (2012) found that people who are more satisfied with their lives are more likely to vote in elections. The above do address some factors that affect youth turnout in Africa; however, the influence or contribution of violence is conspicuously missing.

Straus and Taylor (2009) found in an analysis of elections in Sub-Saharan Africa between 1990 and 2008 that 20% of them had some form of electoral violence. Given the trend in which some African countries have largely had authoritarian regimes and where elections have been largely violent, it would appear that a generation of young people have emerged who have not known the alternative to violent elections, and this has perhaps developed into a culture of violence which possibly deters these young people from voting. Take Nigeria and South Africa for example; in Nigeria the first generation of young people born within its return to democracy in 1999 will vote for the first time in the 2019 general elections aged 20, while in South Africa, the first such generation only voted for the first time in 2014 aged 20.

Electoral violence, defined as 'any acts or threats of coercion, intimidation, or physical harm perpetrated to affect an electoral process, or that arise in the context of electoral competition' (UNDP, 2011, p. 5), can be a major deterrent to voting (Gutiérrez-Romero & Lebas, 2016). Gutiérrez-Romero and Lebas (2016) find from an analysis in Kenya that rumours of violence can adversely affect turn out. Forms of electoral violence which may impede voting include assassinations, deaths, injuries, harassment, intimidation of political rivals and their supporters, and short-term arrests (Bekoe, 2011). Bekoe (2011) points out that these can occur before, during and after elections. Furthermore, despite that electoral violence has been a critical aspect of the process of democratisation in Africa, Bekoe (2011) posits that electoral violence as a separate area of scholarship has received limited attention. Examples of countries where electoral violence has been a major feature of the electoral cycles include Cote D'Ivoire, Kenya, Nigeria and Zimbabwe (Bekoe, 2011). The scales of such violence are often short term and limited to certain geographical areas within a country. Nevertheless, they can have large-scale and long-term impact. For example, as Bekoe (2011) points out, the post-election violence in Nigeria in 2011 resulted in 800 deaths and 65,000 persons were displaced. These outcomes have, as found in earlier iterations of elections in northern Nigeria (Bratton, 2008), far reaching negative effects on voter turnout. Bratton (p. 8) argues that 'political intimidation apparently has an intended effect: it makes citizens so fearful that they abandon their right to vote'.

Höglund (2009) offers a more comprehensive appraisal of the consequences of electoral violence by positing that it can result in low pre-election voter registration and, subsequently, on turnout, and could result in the legitimacy of the electoral outcomes being questioned. Adolfo, Kavacs, Nystrom, and Utas (2012), identified the consequences of electoral violence to include the risk of affecting the electoral process, outcome and perceptions of the electoral outcome. A series of experiments conducted in various countries suggest that violence discouraged individuals in African countries from voting (Collier & Vicente, 2012). Although Collier and Vicente's work is not specific to youth, it offers some insight and should generate interest in understanding the role of violence in youth voter turnout. The potential effect of election-related violence is captured in a meeting note prepared by the International Peace Institute (2012, p. 1), which highlights that 'election-related violence can ... undermine democracy by eroding people's faith in the democratic process ... ' Furthermore, Africa Research Institute (2011) in a briefing note on electoral violence in Sierra Leone highlights that economic challenges resulting from high unemployment increases youths' susceptibility to taking part in elections violence. This suggests that economic factors, such as unemployment, could be predisposing factors to youth involvement in electoral violence, and they contribute to increased violence during elections which ultimately affects the margin of youth who vote. This paper aims to contribute to the scholarship on the relationship between violence and voting in elections, with a view to extending the debate on youth voter apathy beyond the traditional disengagement, socialisation and economic factors.

Methods

The data analysed in this paper were derived from the fourth round of a data set of representative cross-sectional surveys conducted between 2008 and 2009 by

Afrobarometer, an African public attitude survey, in 20 countries. The countries are: Benin, Botswana, Burkina Faso, Cape Verde, Ghana, Kenya, Lesotho, Liberia, Madagascar, Malawi, Mali, Mozambique, Namibia, Nigeria, Senegal, South Africa, Tanzania, Uganda, Zambia and Zimbabwe. The demographic characteristics of these countries are outlined in Table 1. The countries analysed have varying population sizes, youth as a proportion of the population and economic conditions. Nigeria is the most populous with an estimated 179 million, with the least populated being Cape Verde at 500,000. Botswana has the highest per capita GNI among all 20 countries, at $US 7770 Dollars, while Liberia has the least with $US 410 Dollars. In terms of youth as a proportion of the population, Uganda and Zimbabwe have the highest proportions of youth aged 10–24, making-up 34% of the populations for each country. The data on youth aged 10–24 are used for convenience and does not reflect the age bracket used for the analysis in this study.

The Afrobarometer survey in each country was conducted using a combination of multistage, clustered and stratified probability sampling procedures. This combination of sampling approaches was used in order to ensure that the data are representative of the population in each country. Results of studies from nationally representative data could be deemed to reflect situation for the entire population under study (Field, 2009). In the case of this paper, it is assumed that the findings are representative of the 20 countries and could be applicable within the wider sub-Saharan African context. The total sample size for all 20 countries covered by the survey is 27,713 individuals aged 18–90 +. For the purpose of the analysis in this paper, the sample was recoded and further divided into age-groups of 18–24, 25–35 and 36 +. The number of participants

Table 1. Demographic characteristics of sample countries*.

No	Country	Population (Million)**	% youth (Million)*** 10–24yrs	Per capita GNI $US***	Overall Sample****	Youth sample**** 18–24	25–35
1	Benin	10.6	32 (3.4)	790	1200	249	447
2	Botswana	2.0	33 (0.7)	7770	1200	247	348
3	Burkina Faso	17.4	33 (5.7)	750	1200	259	404
4	Cape Verde	0.5	32 (0.2)	3620	1264	307	371
5	Ghana	26.4	31 (8.3)	1770	1200	259	339
6	Kenya	44.5	32 (14.4)	1160	1104	226	431
7	Lesotho	2.1	35 (0.7)	1500	1200	273	287
8	Liberia	4.4	32 (1.4)	410	1200	249	418
9	Madagascar	23.6	33 (7.8)	440	1350	183	424
10	Malawi	16.8	33 (5.6)	270	1200	289	404
11	Mali	15.8	32 (5.0)	670	1232	211	345
12	Mozambique	26.5	33 (8.7)	610	1200	456	383
13	Namibia	2.3	33 (0.8)	5870	1200	346	377
14	Nigeria	178.5	31 (55.5)	2710	2324	729	961
15	Senegal	14.5	32 (4.7)	1050	1200	229	321
16	South Africa	53.1	27 (14.6)	7410	2400	472	714
17	Tanzania	50.8	32 (16.1)	860	1208	216	399
18	Uganda	38.8	34 (13.1)	600	2431	593	982
19	Zambia	15.0	33 (4.9)	1810	1200	298	442
20	Zimbabwe	14.6	34 (5.0)	860	1200	291	409

*Nigeria, South Africa and Uganda make up higher proportions with 8–9% of the sample, while others make up 4–5%. This does not affect the distribution of the data since sampling strategy used ensures that the data are representative for each country.
**World Bank (retrieved from http://data.worldbank.org/region/SSA).
***Data for age 10–24 used for illustrative purposes and does not reflect the age group used for this analysis.
****Afrobarometer 2008 data.

aged 18–24 is 6382 (23%), 25–35 is 9206 (33%) and the remaining 12,119 (44%) participants are aged 36 +. The main focus of the analysis in this paper are the age groups of
18–24 and 25–35, and comparisons are made with those aged 36+ as appropriate
throughout the analysis.

The analysis in this paper uses fear of violence as a proxy for actual violence. The item
for fear questioned: 'During election campaigns in this country, how much do you personally fear becoming a victim of political intimidation or violence?' and the response scale
included: 0 = A lot, 1 = Somewhat, 2 = A little bit, 3 = Not at all, 9 = Don't know, 998 =
Refused to answer. The item is consistent with the definition of electoral violence outlined
in the previous section, which describes violence in a political context as acts or threats of
coercion, intimidation, or physical harm that arise in the context of electoral competition
(UNDP, 2011), and research by Collier and Vicente (2014), who model perceived violence
as a proxy for violence. On the other hand, voting is captured as self-reported voting in the
most recent national elections applicable to each country. The item question for voting
was: 'With regard to the most recent national elections, which statement is true for
you?' The response scale for this item was recoded from the original seven points (see
notes in Table 2) to a dichotomous one for the purpose of the analysis in this paper.
Along with these, data for level of education, employment status and political party affinity
were analysed as control variables.

The data were first analysed to explore whether statistically significant differences exist
between the means of voting scores across three age groups of 18–24, 25–35 and 36+
using one way between groups analysis of variance (ANOVA). This was followed by correlation analysis exploring the relationship between the variables voting in elections and violence across each of the above three age groups. Further to this, partial correlations were

Table 2. Voting in elections by country.

Country	Voting (%) (18–24)		Voting (%) (25–35)	
	Yes	No	Yes	No
Benin	84.3	15.7	93.1	6.9
Botswana	11.7	88.3	55.2	44.8
Burkina Faso	45.2	54.8	75.5	24.5
Cape Verde	42.3	57.7	83.8	16.2
Ghana	43.6	56.4	90.6	9.4
Kenya	55.8	44.2	81.6	18.4
Lesotho	30.8	69.2	56.4	43.6
Liberia	58.1	41.9	80.1	19.9
Madagascar	50.3	49.7	66.5	33.5
Malawi	41.5	58.5	83.2	16.8
Mali	56.4	43.6	77.7	22.3
Mozambique	23.7	76.3	80.1	19.9
Namibia	18.2	81.8	75.6	24.4
Nigeria	49.5	50.5	62.3	37.7
Senegal	56.3	43.7	77.6	22.4
South Africa	21.0	79.0	67.2	32.8
Tanzania	43.5	56.5	87.2	12.8
Uganda	42.5	57.5	76.3	23.7
Zambia	37.4	62.6	60.4	39.6
Zimbabwe	30.2	69.8	63.3	36.7
Total	42.1	57.9	74.7	25.3

Notes: Scale used for data collection: 0 = You were not registered or you were too young to vote, 1 = You voted in the
elections, 2 = You decided not to vote, 3 = You could not find the polling station, 4 = You were prevented from
voting, 5 = You did not have time to vote, to 6 = Did not vote for some other reason. This is recoded to a dichotomous
yes/no scale for the purpose of analysis in this paper.

used to explore the mediating effect of employment status, education and political party affiliation on the relationship between voting and violence. Descriptive statistics were used to analyse the responses to each of the variables across countries. The results of the analyses are described in the following section.

Results

Voting across countries

The results of the analysis show that the proportion of the respondents who indicated voting in the recent national elections varies across countries and age groups. As shown in Table 2. A higher proportion of those aged 18–24 reported not voting in recent elections. One possible explanation for this may be the proportion of those under the age of 18 during the previous elections. The results show that 36.6% of this age group were not registered or too young to vote during the previous elections. Furthermore, more than 50% youth aged 18–24 in 14 of the 20 countries did not vote in the previous elections. This is in contrast to those aged 25–35 where all countries had just over 50% of respondents voting in previous elections. Furthermore, while the relatively low turnout among youth aged 18–24 across countries could be explained by the likelihood of a large proportion being below the voting age during the previous elections, it is interesting to find that in Botswana a high proportion of the respondents aged 25–35 (44.8%) reported not voting in the previous election. This however appears to mirror a pattern of low voter turnout that has existed throughout the country's democratic history.

Violence by country

Table 3 shows reported fear of violence in the 20 countries. For both age groups of 18–24 and 25–35, young people in Zimbabwe reported the highest proportion of respondents indicating 'a lot' of fear at 72.2% and 68.9%, respectively. This is followed by Kenya with 35.8% and 39.9% for 18–24 and 25–35 year olds, respectively, reporting 'a lot' of fear. When the scale options 'a lot', 'sometimes' and 'a little' are combined to constitute affirmative response (indicating respondents had fear), Zimbabwe has the highest proportion of respondents (93.9%) indicating fear, followed by Kenya (82.3%), Uganda (73%), Nigeria (72.6%), Namibia (62.1), Zambia (59.7%), South Africa (56.5%), Mali (56%), Ghana (55.2%), Liberia (54.2%), Malawi (53.6%) and Tanzania (50.5%). Botswana has the lowest proportion of respondents indicating fear of violence at 18.6%, followed by Cape Verde at 30.3%.

Differences in voting across age groups

A one-way ANOVA was conducted to explore differences in voting across three groups (group 1: 18–24 years; group 2: 25–35 years; group 3: 36 + years). The analysis found a statistically significant difference at the $p < .05$ level in voting scores for the three age groups: $F(2, 27,704) = 7.9$, $p < .01$. *Post hoc* comparisons using the Tukey honest statistical difference test showed that the mean score for group 1 ($M = 1.60$, $SD = 4.39$) was significantly different from group 2 ($M = 1.81$, $SD = 4.70$). There was also a significant

Table 3. Violence by country.

Country	Violence (%) 18–24						Violence[a] (%) 25–35					
	−1[a]	0	1	2	3	9	−1	0	1	2	3	9
Benin	.4	6.4	10.4	18.9	63.5	.4	.2	6.5	10.5	19.0	63.5	.2
Botswana	0.0	4.5	4.0	10.1	81.4	0.0	0.0	2.6	5.2	10.3	81.3	.6
Burkina Faso	0.0	19.3	10.4	12.0	52.5	5.8	0.0	19.6	13.9	14.9	49.8	2.0
Cape Verde	.7	7.2	6.2	16.9	67.4	1.6	.5	8.6	7.3	14.3	68.5	.8
Ghana	0.0	15.4	11.6	28.2	42.5	2.3	0.0	13.3	11.8	23.9	48.4	2.7
Kenya	0.0	35.8	23.0	23.5	16.8	.9	.2	39.9	25.1	19.7	14.8	.2
Lesotho	0.0	19.4	15.0	15.0	46.9	3.7	0.0	17.1	14.6	13.6	52.6	2.1
Liberia	0.0	10.4	15.7	28.1	42.6	3.2	0.0	11.2	14.4	30.6	41.4	2.4
Madagascar	0.0	7.7	19.7	21.3	44.8	6.6	0.0	7.5	17.5	23.3	46.5	5.2
Malawi	0.0	24.2	15.6	13.8	44.3	2.1	0.0	24.0	10.1	11.6	53.0	1.2
Mali	0.0	18.5	11.4	26.1	41.2	2.8	0.0	16.5	12.8	21.2	47.5	2.0
Mozambique	.9	17.1	9.2	13.6	51.1	8.1	.5	16.2	12.3	18.8	49.6	2.6
Namibia	0.0	12.4	18.8	30.9	34.7	3.2	0.0	11.9	25.7	30.0	30.0	2.4
Nigeria	0.0	24.7	19.6	28.3	24.8	2.6	0.0	21.7	24.5	27.8	23.6	2.4
Senegal	0.0	16.2	16.2	8.3	57.6	1.7	.3	15.0	15.9	17.1	50.8	.9
South Africa	0.0	9.3	16.1	31.1	36.0	7.4	0.0	8.5	17.4	31.5	38.5	4.1
Tanzania	0.0	13.9	15.3	21.3	47.7	1.9	0.0	13.3	14.0	23.3	48.9	.5
Uganda	0.0	32.9	15.5	24.6	23.1	3.9	0.0	32.3	18.2	26.1	21.7	1.7
Zambia	0.0	20.1	12.8	26.8	36.2	4.0	.2	17.4	15.2	25.1	39.8	2.3
Zimbabwe	0.0	72.2	12.4	9.3	5.8	.3	0.0	68.9	12.2	9.0	9.3	.5

[a]0 = A lot, 1 = Somewhat, 2 = A little bit, 3 = Not at all, 9 = Don't know, − 1 = Missing.

difference between group 2 and group 3 ($M = 1.59$, $SD = 4.05$). There was no statistically significant difference between group 1 and group 3.

Voting and fear of violence

Results of Pearson's correlation found a weak negative, statistically significant relationship between voting and violence ($r = -.048$), $p < .05$, $n = 6382$ for youth aged 18–24. Similar results were found for respondents aged 25–35 ($r = -.027$, $p < .05$, $n = 9206$) and 36+ ($r = -.020$), $p < .05$, $n = 12,119$).

The effect of variables such as respondents' employment status, education and political party affiliation was explored using partial correlations where each of these variables was controlled for. Zero-order correlations using employment status ($r = -.48$ for ages 18–24, $r = -.27$ for ages 25–35), education ($r = -.48$ for ages 18–24, $r = -.27$ for ages 25–35) and political party affiliation ($r = -.48$ for ages 18–24, $r = -.27$ for ages 25–35) showed that these had no effect on the direction and size of the relationship between voting and fear of violence.

Discussion and conclusion

This paper analysed the relationship between violence and voting among youth in 20 sub-Saharan African countries. The results presented in the previous section suggest that there is a negative relationship between the two variables, implying that violence could deter voting in elections, albeit small. Although a negative relationship was expected *a priori*, the weak relationship between the variables may suggest that despite violence being related negatively to turnout, it is not strong enough to deter voting. This perhaps explains why in countries such as Uganda, despite a high proportion of respondents reporting of fear of violence, 42.5% and 76.3% of youth aged 18–24 and 25–35, respectively, reported voting in elections, a substantial proportion of the youth turned out to vote. Variations in the sample such as the fact that in some countries, like Botswana and Cape Verde, participants reported low levels of fear of violence at 18.6% and 30.3%, respectively, while in countries such as Zimbabwe, as high as 93.9% of participants reported fear of violence, and this might have affected the overall results. Furthermore, the weakness of the correlation may be explained by the high proportion of respondents that indicated voting in the most recent elections compared to the fewer numbers of individuals who did not vote and to whom the focus of this paper holds more relevance (what factors prevented them from voting).

The results discussed here are for the overall sample and differences may exist between countries. For example, 50.5% and 37.7% of the respondents aged 18–24 and 25–35, respectively, from Nigeria reported not voting and over 70% of the youth respondents aged 18–24 indicated fear of violence. In comparison, 69.8% and 32.7%, respectively from Zimbabwe reported not voting and 93.9% reported fear of violence. While the reason for low turnout could be a result of their ineligibility to vote at the time of the election preceding the survey, not being registered to vote, disinterest, distance from their homes to the polling unit or other factors, what is noted here is that in both countries where the reported fear of violence is high, fewer youth indicated voting during the elections.

The importance of country-level variations is highlighted by the difference between Botswana and other countries in the study. Although Botswana is considered a leading democracy in Africa (Mfundisi, 2006), 88.3% and 44.8% of youth aged 18–24 and 25–35, respectively, reported not voting despite only 18.6% reporting fear of violence. Ntsabane and Ntau (2006) attribute the high rate of apathy among youth in Botswana to cultural factors which inhibit young people's voice in the public sphere. According to them, cultural practices, particularly the expectation that young people accede to the views of elders, affects the extent of young people's involvement in decision making. Mfundisi (2006) however contends that in addition to cultural factors, other factors including economic and social issues affect young people's participation. The analysis in this paper however suggests the contrary on the effects of economic and social factors.

When social, economic and political variables such as level of education, employment status and association with a political party were controlled for, these did not affect the strength and direction of the relationship between violence and voting. This suggests that regardless of their socio-economic status and political leanings youth turnout generally has a weak negative relationship with violence. Previous research using the Afro Barometer data set also found that level of education did not predict youth turnout in elections (Resnick & Casale, 2011). This could also suggest that where violence exists, it constitutes a barrier to youth turnout, regardless of their level of education, economic status or political connections and it is likely to deter youth from voting. Bratton (2008, p. 8) aptly captures the effect of electoral violence on voting in Nigeria as follows:

> For an average Nigerian ... a threat of violence reduces the odds of intending to vote by 52 percent. Moreover, intimidation's effect seems to be long lasting, since the model works almost as well if exposure to violence is measured in 2003 rather than 2007. To all appearances, Nigerians who encounter a threat against voting freely often withdraw from the electoral process entirely, that is, they abstain from voting. So political intimidation apparently has an intended effect: it makes citizens so fearful that they abandon their right to vote.

Overall, the results discussed in this paper have some relevance in terms of their implications for wider analyses on the causes of low youth turnout, their consequences and solutions. For example, if the analysis of further data finds that violence is a cause of low youth voter turnout, this would imply that large-scale violence, intimidation or threat of violence could prevent youth from maximising their large numbers in influencing electoral outcomes since they will be less likely to vote as Bratton argues above. This could be detrimental to the causes in which youth are invested and which affect the quality of their lives. Given their large population in many countries, if youth were to organise, mobilise and vote based on the agendas that affect them, they could determine the political futures of their respective countries. However, violence could be a threat to their ability to vote, hence also being a threat to the opportunity that their large numbers represent.

This paper is concluded by returning to its initial question: does violence have a relationship with youth voter turnout in sub-Saharan Africa? The results suggest that such relationship, although statistically weak, does exist. This is corroborated by similar studies in sub-Saharan Africa (Collier & Vicente, 2014). Given this, it is argued that there exists a relationship between violence and youth turnout to vote. As shown earlier, countries with higher elections' violence such as Zimbabwe and Nigeria, had a higher proportion of respondents who reported not voting. It is however noted that there are also exceptions such as Botswana, where although reported fear of violence was low, corresponding youth turnout was also low. This suggests that where causality is established between violence and voting in elections, it could be one of several factors in some contexts. This paper does not suggest or attempt to suggest a casual relationship between violence and voting, rather, it provides a useful starting point for bridging the gap in understanding the role of violence in low youth turnout during elections in sub-Saharan Africa.

Notes

1. The Cable News Network chronicles here (http://goo.gl/7HB4Gv) various online platforms through which youth attempt to mobilise their peers to participate in an informed way in the elections process for Nigeria's 2015 National elections.
2. Cameron says he is happy to hold vote on lowering voting age to 16 (retrieved from http://goo.gl/BsY9mx).

Acknowledgements

The data set used in the analysis for this paper was produced by the AfroBarometer survey group. The author would like to thank Adebayo Samuel and Emmanuel Sanyi for their useful comments to earlier versions of this paper.

Disclosure statement

No potential conflict of interest was reported by the authors.

Notes on contributor

Dabesaki Mac-Ikemenjima is an external research associate of the University of East Anglia. He completed his PhD in International Development at the University of East Anglia, undertaking a mixed-methods study on the role of young people's goals in the development of youth quality of life measures. His research interests include analyses on youth political participation, aspirations and measurement of youth quality of life in sub-Saharan Africa.

References

Adolfo, E. V., Kavacs, M. S., Nystrom, D., & Utas, M. (2012). *Electoral violence in Africa* (Policy Notes No. 2012/3). Uppsala: The Nordic Africa Institute.

Africa Research Institute. (2011). *Old tricks, young guns elections and violence in Sierra Leone* (No. Briefing Note 1102). London: Author.

African Union. (2006). *African youth charter*. Addis Ababa: Author.

African Union. (2011). *State of the African youth report*. Addis Ababa: Author.

Bekoe, D. (2010). *Trends in electoral violence in Sub-Saharan Africa* (No. Policy Brief 13). Washington, DC: United States Institute of Peace.

Bekoe, D. (2011). Introduction: The scope, nature, and pattern of electoral violence in Sub-saharan Africa. In D. Bekoe (Ed.), *Voting in fear: Electoral violence in Sub-saharan Africa* (pp. 1–13). Washington, DC: United States Institute of Peace Press.

Bratton, M. (2008). *Vote buying and violence in Nigerian election campaigns* (Afrobarometer Working Papers No. 99). Cape Town: Afro Barometer.

Chaturvedi, R. (2016). Agentive capacities, democratic possibilities, and the urban poor: Rethinking recent popular protests in West Africa. *International Journal of Politics, Culture, and Society, 29*, 307–325.

Chuck, A. (2012). *The decisive African youth vote*. Retrieved May 26, 2015, from http://www.atlanticcouncil.org/blogs/newatlanticist/

Collier, P. & Vicente, P. C. (2012). Violence, bribery, and fraud: The political economy of elections in Sub-saharan Africa. *Public Choice, 153*(1–2), 117–147.

Collier, P. & Vicente, P. C. (2014). Votes and violence: Evidence from a field experiment in Nigeria. *Economic Journal, 124*(574), F327–F355.

Ekman, J. & Amnå, E. (2012). Political participation and civic engagement: Towards a new typology. *Human Affairs, 22*, 236–300.

Field, A. (2009). *Discovering statistics using SPSS (and sex and drugs and rock "n" roll)*. London: Sage.

Fieldhouse, E. & Cutts, D. (2012). The companion effect : Household and local context and the turnout of young people. *The Journal of Politics, 74*(3), 856–869.

Flavin, P. & Keane, M. J. (2012). Life satisfaction and political participation: Evidence from the United States. *Journal of Happiness Studies, 13*, 63–78.

Gutiérrez-Romero, R., & Lebas, A. (2016). *Does electoral violence affect voting choice and willingness to vote? Evidence from a vignette experiment* (No. WPS/2016–35). Oxford: Centre for the Study of African Economies.

Henn, M. & Foard, N. (2013). Social differentiation in young people's political participation: The impact of social and educational factors on youth political engagement in Britain. *Journal of Youth Studies, 17*(3), 1–21.

Herrera, L. (2006). What's New about youth? *Development and Change, 37*(6), 1425–1434.

Höglund, K. (2009). Electoral violence in conflict-ridden societies: Concepts, causes, and consequences. *Terrorism and Political Violence, 21*(3), 412–427.

Honwana, A. (2012). *The time of youth: Work, social change, and politics in Africa*. Virginia: Stylus Publishing.

International Peace Institute. (2012). *Elections and stability in West Africa: The Way forward*. New York: Author.

Jones, G. (2009). *Youth*. Cambridge: Polity Press.

Lambert, M. C. (2016). Changes: Reflections on Senegalese youth political engagement, 1988–2012. *Africa Today, 63*(2), 33–51.

Lorenzini, J. (2015). Subjective well-being and political participation: A comparison of unemployed and employed youth. *Journal of Happiness Studies, 16*, 381–404.

Mfundisi, A. (2006). Civic participation and voting patterns in Botswana. *Journal of African Elections, 5*(2), 81–98.

Ntsabane, T. & Ntau, C. (2006). Youth and politics in Botswana. *Journal of African Elections*, 5(2), 99–113.

Ødegard, G. & Berglund, F. (2008). Political *participation in late modernity among Norwegian youth: An individual choice or a statement of social class? Journal of Youth Studies*, 11(6), 593–610.

Oyedemi, T. & Mahlatji, D. (2016). The "born-free" Non-voting youth: A study of voter apathy Among a selected cohort of South African youth. *Politikon*, 43(3), 311–323.

Phelps, E. (2006). *Young adults and electoral turnout in Britain: Towards a general model of political participation* (No. SEI Working paper No 92). Brighton: Sussex European Institute.

Quaranta, M. (2015). An apathetic generation? Cohorts' patterns of political participation in Italy. *Social Indicators Research*, 125(3), 793–812.

Resnick, D., & Casale, D. (2011). *The political participation of Africa's youth turnout, partisanship, and protest* (No. Working Paper No. 2011/ 56). Helsinki: UNU World Institute for Development Economics Research.

Resnick, D. & Casale, D. (2014). Young populations in young democracies: Generational voting behaviour in sub-saharan Africa. *Democratization*, 21(6), 1172–1194.

Scott, D., Vawda, M., Swartz, S., & Bhana, A. (2012). Punching below their weight: Young South Africans' recent voting patterns. *HSRC Review*, 10(3), 19–21.

Straus, S., & Taylor, C. (2009). Democratization and electoral violence in Sub-saharan Africa, 1990–2007. In *Annual meeting of the American political science association* (pp. 1–40). Toronto: American Political Science Association.

Sukarieh, M., & Tannock, S. (2015). *Youth rising? The politics of youth in the global economy*. London: Routledge.

UNDP. (2011). *Understanding electoral violence in Asia*. Bangkok: Author.

UNECA. (2009). *African youth report 2009: Expanding opportunities for and with young people in Africa*. Addis Ababa: Author.

Utas, M. (2012). *Urban youth and post-conflict Africa: On policy priorities* (No. 4). Uppasala: Nordic Africa Institute.

Weitz-shapiro, R., & Winters, M. S. (2008). *Political participation and quality of life* (No. Working Paper 638). Washington, DC: InterAmerican Development Bank.

Marginalised youth, violence and policing: a qualitative study in Recife, Brazil

Roxana Pessoa Cavalcanti ⓘ

ABSTRACT

Few studies have examined the relations between urban marginalised youth and the public security system in the northeast of Brazil. This article addresses this gap in the literature through an examination of youth perceptions of a security programme aimed at reducing violence. It also analyses the effects of this security programme by interrogating the hegemonic discourses of state-actors in the region, namely, agents of the criminal justice system. The analysis draws on ethnographic data collected between 2012 and 2016 in Recife, the capital city of the state of Pernambuco in the northeast of Brazil. This approach permits an examination of the nature of new security interventions, and a comparison between two distinct narratives about this new securitisation agenda. One overarching narrative focuses on young people's vulnerabilities, the other on claims of successful securitisation. An analysis of these narratives widens understandings of the effects and risks of security interventions, contributing to a debate about their impact on young people's lives and society at large.

Introduction

A significant literature has begun to emerge identifying the issue of youth violence in poor urban communities around the world (Feltran, 2011; Hagedorn, Davis, & Ebrary, 2008). In Brazil, these communities are often referred to as favelas[1] (slums and informal settlements) and *periferias* (peripheral areas). Outsiders tend to perceive these communities as undesirable places in which to live. They are working-class neighbourhoods where workers such as labourers, service-sector employees and domestic workers live. They are communities in which family ties, hard work and social mobility are highly valued. They are also replete with community associations, organisers and leaders. However, they have come to the attention of the wider public as violent places, known for their high murder rates and for the cinematographic representations ingrained in public consciousness through films such as *City of God* (2002) and *Elite Squad* (2007). The social sciences and the ethnographic literature that examine the troubled context in which violence has become a central part of public life have tended to ignore youth experiences and perceptions of security and justice in Brazil.

Sometimes this violence is associated with 'gangs' (Fernandes, 2013; Jones & Rodgers, 2009), or with other forms of organised crime – especially drug dealing and trafficking (Arias, 2006; Bourgois, 2003; Denyer Willis, 2015). Sometimes it takes the form of political or community resistance (Davies, 2006; Scheper-Hughes, 2004). Young people are some-times the perpetrators of lethal violence, but more often they are victimised by police and death squads (Arias, 2006; Huggins, 1997; Zaluar, 2010). The causes and sources of violence and insecurity are multifarious. They relate to complex historical, socio-economic and geo-graphical factors (Pereira, 2008). Less is known about how young people relate, respond and perceive this challenging context.

Pinheiro (2006, p. xviii) suggests that our failure to listen to young people has led to a failure to understand and respond to their needs. This article examines the narratives of young people and security agents about a process of regional securitisation. The study focuses in Recife, the second largest city in the northeast of Brazil, where a public security programme known as *Pact for Life* has been deployed to reduce high rates of murder since 2007. This article asks how young people living in Recife respond to the nature of state interventions. What effects do new forms of formal control have on the communities they live in? Ultimately, what role does the State and its policies play in the fluctuation – continuation, expansion or reduction – of diverse forms of violence in the most socially excluded communities?

These issues are important because the securitisation of urban spaces can produce unequal social relations along spatial, ethnic and class lines (Becker & Müller, 2013; Davis, 2013). Securitisation is conceptualised here as a process in which concerns about security, law and order dominate approaches to resolve social problems. This process is associated with political profiteering, law and order politics and with hegemonic punitive discourses. It is also connected to the global export of 'zero tolerance policing' (ZTP) (Young, 2011). The export of this approach to securitising urban spaces is a classic example of the ways in which criminological theories travel from the global North and become uncritically applied to South. Attempts to cleanse the streets of groups and com-munities who are perceived as disorderly, socially undesirable (e.g. the poor and margin-alised) are attractive to local elites, businesses and profit-seeking real estate developers – all of which are influential sectors in the city of Recife.

The following sections of this article explore, in order: theories of state and violence; some of the existing challenges that young people face in the Brazilian context; the methodology of this study; the genesis of a new security programme; the dominant (albeit ambiguous) discourse of successful state intervention among public security actors and, finally, the chal-lenge to this hegemonic discourse, emerging from the narratives of young people.

Violence and the state in Latin America

State theorists and social scientists have debated the extent to which Brazil's violent context is linked to the issue of state absence. O'Donnell (1993) argued that human rights violations were linked to the absence of the rule of law and of effective state insti-tutions in poor communities. His thesis embodies a common fallacy that Brazilian cities are divided between accessible and no-go areas. In the former the State is perceived as present while in the latter, allegedly the territory of criminals, it is absent. A book by Zuenir Ventura (1994), *Cidade Partida* ('The Divided City'), focuses on this dualistic ideology. This emphasis on 'division' and on 'duality' ignores the connections that do exist between different areas of the city. It becomes tempting to perceive favelas as not only poor but also dysfunctional areas, which have failed to integrate with the rest of the city; areas in which traffickers impede the progress and development of civil society because they will not tolerate forms of social or political organisation that might challenge their power. This common misconception fails to acknowledge the ways in which the State is present in different territories and the ways in which poor areas are connected to the political system and to the rest of the city.

Elizabeth Leeds (1996) argued that rather than being absent, the State is entangled in violent relations through patron–client relations with favela residents. In a similar line of argument, Arias (2006) deployed 'social network' theories to argue that violence in poor urban areas was in fact not caused by the absence of the State, but rather by an intricate network involving a variety of social actors: civil society (e.g. non-governmental organis-ations, residents' associations), the police, corrupt politicians and favela residents. This suggests a need to look beyond the hypothesis of 'State abandonment' (Wacquant, 2003) often applied to the poorest communities in the region. The State is often part of existing problems (Arias, 2006; Gledhill, 2013).

Moreover, in some aspects the Brazilian state, specifically during the rule of the Worker's party (2002–2014), had not 'abandoned' the poor. The Worker's party increased spending on education, health, conditional cash transfers (CCTs) and increased the minimum wage (Hall, 2008; Molyneaux, 2008). Although most of the increase in public spending was directed at the often-criticised CCTs, in the 2000s Brazil experienced a reduction in labour informality (Comin, Barbosa, & Carvalhaes, 2012) and poverty (Barros, Carvalho, Franco, & Mendonça, 2010; Neri, 2009). This period of economic growth, growing employ-ment and improvements in the life chances of Brazil's poorest came to a halt when the country entered a recession and the political right reclaimed the highest ranks of govern-ment (Cavalcanti, 2017).

Instead of examining 'State abandonment' per se, this article suggests that it is impor-tant to examine the nature of state interventions. This demands an analysis of how state interventions take place and how they are interpreted, experienced – challenged and negotiated (Darke, 2013) – by those at the receiving end. It also requires an understanding of the complex context in which the State exists and relates to its citizens. The following section focuses on the complexities of this context with particular reference to issues faced by young people.

Youth in Brazil's context

Since the 1980s both the homicide rate and the use of firearms in homicides have been rising in most Latin American countries (Arias & Goldstein, 2010). Just in 2014, approxi-mately 60,000 people were killed in Brazil (Cerqueira et al., 2016). Brazil has the highest homicide rate among the 12 most populous countries in the world (Waiselfisz, 2013). There is also an unequal distribution of deaths in the country, with the North and North-east regions seeing much higher increases in levels of lethal violence in the 2000s. In the Northeast, the homicide rate per 100,000 inhabitants went from 19.4 in 2000 to 33.5 in 2009 (Souza, Ribeiro, & Valadares, 2012, p. 52). While there is a geographical aspect to this phenomenon, there are also gender, ethnic and class dimensions to it. According to a large-scale national survey (Waiselfisz, 2011, p. 60), the likelihood of death for a young man who is not white, and is aged between 15 and 25 in 2008 was 127.6% greater than for a white male in the same age bracket. Most victims of homicide are poor young black males (Waiselfisz, 2014).

In 2010, the rate of youth homicide (15–29 years old) with a firearm in Brazil reached 42.5/100,000 of the population, as compared with 9.1/100,000 in 1980 (Waiselfisz, 2013, 13): almost a fivefold increase in 30 years. Overall levels of lethal violence continue to grow, making Brazil one of the least safe countries for young people. However, at a policy and legal level, a number of promising and progressive changes took place in the country in the 1990s and 2000s. For example, spending in public health and education increased, the family income benefit programme (known as *Bolsa Familia*) was implemented and accredited with reductions in levels of extreme poverty and income inequality (Hall, 2008; Molyneaux, 2008; Neri, 2009).

In 1990 Brazil replaced the discriminatory, repressive and segregationist legislation known as 'Minors' Code' with the Children and Adolescent's Act (*Estatuto da Criança e do Adolescente* or ECA). The Minor's Code in operation from 1927 to 1990 had discrimi-nated between the definitions of 'child' and 'minor' (Rizzini, 1997). Children were con-structed as deserving innocent individuals in need of adult protection while minors were constructed as undeserving young wrongdoers from poor and morally deficient families (Drybread, 2014, p. 757). This code made it legally possible to institutionalise chil-dren indeterminately whether or not they had broken the law (Drybread, 2009). ECA rede-fined childhood by including all children and adolescents as rights-bearing citizens and forbidding the institutionalisation of young people, unless they commit a heinous offence of violence such as rape, murder or kidnapping with a maximum sentence of three years (Drybread, 2014, p. 758). Young people under the age of 12 are considered chil-dren incapable of committing crimes and those between 12 and 18 years old are con-sidered adolescents, who cannot be held criminally responsible.

ECA became a reference for Latin America because of its emphasis on human rights and the respect for the development of children and adolescents (UNICEF, 2015). This legal change developed a new discourse that constructs young people as bearing rights instead of as objects of intervention (Moore, 2015, 273). However, it is still unclear how much the law has changed discriminatory practices. Police practices remain embedded in misconstructions that portray young, poor, black males as criminals and young, poor, black females as morally dangerous. These discriminatory practices resonate with wider inequalities in Brazilian society, revealing its racist and classist discrimination that conflate crime with poverty.

Despite the legal and policy gains Brazil has made over the last 25 years, the current econ-omic recession and growing unemployment (Amorim, 2016), coupled with the impeach-ment of President Rousseff of the worker's party in 2016 and the following conservative interim government pose new threats to young people in the nation. The interim govern-ment and its supporting conservative parliamentary caucus have proposed freezing public spending (Alessi, 2016), support for the reduction of the age of criminal responsibility and for the increase of sentences for young offenders from 3 to 10 years (Douglas, 2015). This punitive approach is fuelled by misconceptions about crime control that emerge in societies where fear of crime and high-crime rates are widespread (Garland, 2001).

In the Brazilian context, the rise in punitive penalty, as illustrated by the extreme growth of the prison population, has been associated with the intensification of the war on drugs, the inclusion of drug trafficking in the list of heinous crimes in the 1990s and the practice of incarcerating drug users and small-scale dealers as if they were drug traffickers (Carvalho, 2013; Darke & Garces, 2017). Moreover, as Azevedo and Cifali (2015) note, many punitive laws have been proposed and rapidly created in contexts of high public demand with large disparities in the use of penal policies and criminal justice institutions in each federative state. The state of São Paulo and the state of Pernambuco, for example, while under the rule of the PSDB party have experienced conservative tendencies in the field of public security policies, with increasing use of the prison and law-and-order politics during a period of national leftist redistributive policies.

These recent changes are expected to generate devastating social costs. Young people, while being one of the most victimised groups in Brazil, are continuously constructed as criminals in need of tougher penal sanctions. The remainder of this article examines a state intervention aimed reducing violence and the ways in which young people respond this attempt to securitise the problematic context in which they live.

Methodology

This article draws on multiple sources of qualitative data collected and analysed between 2012 and 2016. Ethnographic data were collected through observations, open-ended and semi-structured interviews (Emerson, Fretz, & Shaw, 1995) with young people aged between 16 and 29, in two low-income communities in the city of Recife in the northeast of Brazil ($N = 120$). My experience of living in Brazil for over 17 years and knowledge of cultural norms facilitated the establishment of access through local contacts. Young participants were recruited through a local school and via the contacts of a youth community organisation. I used a snowballing method (Atkinson & Flint, 2001) to access a wider sample, based on the criteria of residence in low-income communities. Given the limited data available about young people's perceptions and experiences of safety in the northeast of Brazil, my intention was to facilitate the voices of marginalised young people to be heard and to discuss the issues that they considered important.

Four in-depth focus groups were undertaken in a community organisation and in a school in the two communities, with the aim of exploring issues that residents and young people considered important. Semi-structured interviews were conducted with community activists, high-ranking and low-ranking members of the military and civil police, as well as with members of the public security apparatus (e.g. statisticians, the police ombudsman and policy-makers). Interviews with these groups concerned the changes that occurred with the implementation of the new security intervention, and participants' evaluations of the strengths and weaknesses of this intervention. A total of 185 participants were heard. I also conducted observations of government meetings at the Secretariat for Planning and Management (SEPLAG) in Recife. A thematic approach was adopted to analyse the most recurring emerging topics (Butler-Kisber, 2010).

The genesis of a programme of homicide reduction

In the context of high levels of homicide, Latin American governments have been keen to adopt fast and quick fixes to crime problems, emulating the American experience, which is perceived as best practice (Bailey & Dammert, 2006). In 2007, a violence reduction programme, known as 'Pact for Life' (PPV), was implemented in all of the state of Pernambuco, where Recife is located. The programme is largely founded on the ideas of mainstream managerial criminology, such as rational choice theory and situational crime prevention (Clarke, 1997; Clarke & Felson, 2004), which intensify formal social control (e.g. the use of surveillance and policing). Most importantly, it emulates the COMPSTAT police performance programme used in the 1990s in New York (Macedo, 2012). This approach focuses on the management of information, crime statistics and police targets and has rather problematically been credited with the 'New York Miracle' (Young, 2011) .

In 2007, the governor of the state of Pernambuco, Eduardo Campos, contracted a sociologist from the federal university of Pernambuco, Professor Ratton, to work as his public security advisor. Between March and April 2007, an initial set of consultations and events were organised as part of a forum of public security where the topic of public security was debated and a plan drawn up. Over one hundred project ideas were proposed (PESP-PE, 2007; Ratton, Galvão, & Fernandez, 2014) and categorised into six lines of action. These included improving responsiveness to victims, social prevention, more joined up working, enhanced planning, information management, evaluation and the training of public security staff.

Although investment in public security grew rapidly, many of the projects originally proposed were not implemented, as interviews with public servants confirmed. This critique corroborates the findings of other studies (Macedo, 2012; Portella & Nascimento, 2014). Social crime prevention (e.g. drug rehabilitation programmes) and training of police also received very little attention. Meanwhile, the implemented projects – focused on managing police targets and conducting more arrests – had the effect of expanding the criminal justice system, overcrowding prisons further and exacerbating adversarial police–youth relations.

The hegemonic discourse of success

Although there is a clear disparity in the implementation of projects, with the hard-line of repressive control taking precedence over social approaches, PPV became known as a success. The programme was accredited with reductions in levels of homicide (Ratton et al., 2014) in the state of Pernambuco, where 'between 2000 and 2005 the average homicide rate was 54.13, while between 2006 and 2011 this average fell to 46.67' (Ratton et al., 2014, p. 1). PPV received international awards from the Inter-American Development Bank in 2014 and from the United Nations in 2013 (see GEPE, Governo do Estado de Pernambuco, 2013; Ribeiro, 2014). It has also been promoted as a model for Brazil's federal public security secretariat (SENASP) and other Brazilian states (Macedo, 2012). The intervention was one of the main marketing points of the political campaign of the state governor of Pernambuco Eduardo Campos (2007–2014). Highly publicised reductions in violent crime associated with PPV facilitated Campos' re-election for a second term in office and launched his political career at the national level (Wolff, 2014).

In the narrative of members of the police and public security agents interviewed, two main factors were constructed as the cause of successful reduction of homicides. Those were: (1) the shift to a model of increased management of targets; and (2) the increase in investment in police resources. This is illustrated in the following interview extract with a senior member of the management of the public security secretariat:

To achieve reductions in homicide, having the political will is a start. But an important point is the model of management by results. There is also investment. We increased the public security budget from R$20 million (Brazilian reais) per year to around R$80 million per year. This 80 million is mostly structural investment, such as investing in police stations, appropriate cars for the police, appropriate uniforms, guns, bullet-proof vests, handcuffs. We have also recruited 10,000 new professionals over the last 10 years.

The apparent solution to crime had rather Americanised connotations: increased policing and formal control. Some experts admitted to having travelled to the US and observed the models of policing that (in their view) worked – including ZTP – as shown in an interview with the chief of the Pernambucan civil police:

> Over the years since *Pacto pela vida* started, the prison population has more than doubled from around 15,000 to 30,000 inmates now. Among the *successful* criminological policies in the world, I had the opportunity to visit New York and get to know their *Zero Tolerance* policing, where they had very high incarceration rate. Here it has not been different. [...] I knew it would go well, in six months we went from 50 to 400 captures per month. The secretariat decided this was the secret to success. The secret to success is incarceration. This is our aim. I don't know any other policy in the world that could revert a situation of violence without incarceration.

The punitive approach to crime control has been widely discussed in criminology in recent years (Feeley & Simon, 1992; Garland, 2001; Wacquant, 2003). It is not the aim of this discussion to explore this phenomenon directly. What this article addresses are some of the ways in which this phenomenon has manifested itself in Brazilian discourses about security and some of its social effects. The case of PPV's widening of policing and incarceration, as illustrated by police narratives above, has exacerbated many existing problems in Brazil. For example, the prison population in Pernambuco, as well as in the rest of Brazil, has continuously increased since the 1990s (Carvalho, 2013), even before the implementation of PPV. It is clear that this process has been accelerated during the PPV years.

Nevertheless, there was an overall reduction in the number of homicides in the state of Pernambuco and in Recife between 2008 and 2013 (Ratton et al., 2014), but with more recent fluctuations upwards[2] (Oliveira, 2015). It is difficult, and perhaps impossible, to assess whether this is a direct impact of *Pacto pela Vida* or whether there may be other influencing factors. It is important to note that, although repressive security interventions have been marketed and discoursed as a success, they have had perverse outcomes. The following analysis of young people's perceptions illustrates some of these effects.

Youth perceptions of the effects of the securitisation agenda

The analysis of youth and community residents' perceptions highlights the disparities between hegemonic state discourses of success with the voices emerging from street level. When I started visiting a low-income community surrounding one of the largest prisons in Latin America, in the city of Recife, young people complained about the nature of state intervention in their lives, the lack of public spaces for leisure, inadequate access to housing and public services (e.g. education, health and transport). According to these young people, the State was clearly present in their lives and in their communities. Some of the problems they experienced related to the ways in which the State was present. There were some changes and some continuities in the ways in which the

State and its institutions interacted with young people. For example, many young people complained about increasing stop and search police operations. However, they perceived the kind of policing they experienced to be 'old wine in new bottles'. The police and their institutionally racist practices had not been reformed.

Young people's experiences of being targeted by the military police, and of the increasing use of stop-and-search, were traumatic. Their experiences resonated known problems of coercive rather than consensual policing (Huggins, 1998). The PPV security programme had increased sporadic policing by increasing motorised police patrols and police crackdown operations. However, it had not improved the quality of policing (e.g. the quality of the interactions between the police and community residents) or the level of police accountability.

In the communities studied some young people referred to the police as the *capitão do mato,* a historical character from the time of slavery, who was responsible for capturing fugitive slaves and punishing those who caused disorder or who disobeyed their masters. The analogy said much about the type of policing available for poor black and ethnically mixed communities, as illustrated in the narrative of a young black community resident:

> The military police gave him a *baculejo* (that is a violent stop and search). They looked at his ID card, took 40 *reais* (equivalent to approximately £13 at the time) from his wallet and called him a shameless cripple. He wasn't disabled or anything, but he had a broken leg. (Luther)

The myth of a 'racial democracy', that is the idea that Brazilian miscegenation led to non-racist social relations, has been by and large discredited, disproven and contested by multiple studies that reveal Brazil's profound racial inequalities (Skidmore, 2010, 199–200). The evidence emerging from interviews with members of the police and with residents in low-income communities indicates that both social class and 'race' were mobilising factors in police–community interactions. This is not a surprising finding – it is well backed up by the Brazilian and the international literature (Barros, 2008; Bowling & Phillips, 2007; Wacquant, 2008; Zaluar, 2004) – but nevertheless it is a rather enduring and bleak one. What is distinctive in the evidence presented here is the extent of discrimination, disdain and ethnic and social class divisions in the ways in which community–police relations took form in Recife, despite efforts to implement new security interventions. The new security agenda instituted new modes of police governance, with the creation and regular monitoring of targets. However, no significant effort was directed at reforming the police or changing police practices.

The unequal distribution of policing and disproportionate policing tactics – such as police racial profiling, verbal and physical confrontation with residents of poor communities – generate resentment and hostility towards the methods of the police. As a consequence, trust in public institutions is damaged, with residents refusing to provide information to the police. The approach of increasing policing resources and managing performance targets fails to make the police act fairly, or to enable them to protect the most marginalised citizens.

Negotiating life and criminalisation in a violent city

Young residents experienced an informal curfew, and many refrained from using public space due to fear of crime and fear of being perceived as a criminal. They claimed that using public space after 9 pm, and being black immediately implied criminality to those policing the war on drugs, an issue shown in young people's narratives of their interactions with the police:

> My brother was coming back from a gig at night when one of his mates stole his silver chain, so he decided to call the police. When the police came, instead of treating him as a victim, they accused him of theft and of carrying a firearm. He didn't have a firearm. They shot him but he survived […] My other brother was involved in drug trafficking and he was shot and killed by the police last year. My mother was devastated. (João, 17 years old)

These narratives reveal a great deal about criminalised and marginalised people's struggles in an increasingly penal state. As a number of academics have argued, Brazil has been experiencing a shift towards a crime and security management discourse in which transgressing social boundaries is increasingly seen as a threat (Feltran, 2011; Moore, 2015, pp. 267–268). The use of public space, access to leisure activities and consumer goods by afro-descendants is policed and perceived as a threat to long-standing power relations that had privileged the dominance of white elites, the ones who are perceived and treated as respectable and deserving citizens. For marginalised young people, crossing those boundaries has become increasingly dangerous, increasing their exposure to lethal violence or of being criminalised and eventually spending time in the country's fast growing prison industry.

Young men in the communities expressed some masculine bravado, claiming that despite the risks and dangers of being out at night, they still used public space at night. One of their strategies of survival was to walk in groups. For young women on the other hand, the risk of violence, rape and common knowledge about multiple unsolved rape cases in the community was enough of a threat to inhibit their use of public space at night. Young women expressed feeling incarcerated inside and outside their homes. In addition to the risks outside the home, domestic violence was also rife as illustrated in the following comments by a young female interviewee:

> I don't spend much time out on the streets so I don't know much about the neighbourhood. I know that we have problems with sanitation [and] mudslides in the community during the rainy season so people can lose their homes. There is plenty of drug trafficking and drug use, especially crack cocaine […] now and then you hear of a young person who was killed […] Like a friend of my cousin's, he was killed because of drug debt, that is quite common. There are also cases of men killing their women. Recently a guy shot, killed and cut up the body of his woman because of jealousy.

PPV's focus on homicide reduction and increasing levels of incarceration has side-lined other important crimes in poor communities, including rape, non-lethal violence, violence against women, extortion and crimes committed by state-actors, such as police abuses of force and abuses of human rights in prisons and young offender institutions. Women have specifically been overlooked by the policy and so have the needs of young people. PPV defined and over-enforced the idea of security as the reduction of homicides. This has taken precedence over the overall protection of human rights. Respect and fairness towards people in low-income communities should, but has not, gone hand-in-hand with legitimate policing or democratic police reform.

Most residents in the low-income communities studied did not notice any positive effects of public security interventions at ground level. In sum, the protection of the rule of law has not been the emphasis of programs such as PPV. Changing the focus and methods of security programmes is fundamental to promoting more democratic, just and accountable policing. This needs to start from the training of the police and has to include educative campaigns to increase public support for the rule of law.

Living with organised criminals in a punitive state

Evidence from the case study communities revealed that simply incarcerating members of organised criminal groups did not, according to residents, dismantle extermination groups in charge of the sale of security in these communities. Participants explained that illicit security and extermination groups formed by ex-policemen operated by extorting money from residents in return for their services. Residents were coerced into paying fees and claimed that they would be victimised if they did not, potentially by the same security racketeers. Extermination groups were responsible for informal justice in the community, killing any petty criminals, people who owed money and even drug dealers and users. According to numerous residents, the imprisonment of members of these informal groups did not resolve issues in the community:

> Some people miss the time when Marcos was out because the community did not have problems with drugs. The drugs problem started here in the last 7 or 10 years. But you know he was not arrested because of the community. No one here would have spoken about him (reported him to the police). But his friends are also ex-police officers and they are all being investigated for being part of an extermination group. […] Now everything here is run down, there is crack cocaine everywhere. When Marcos was out, the problem in the community was just homicides between rival security groups. People died because of the competition between extermination groups. One group would start terrorising the community to damage the reputation of the other group, because they wanted to take over the security business, it caused all sorts of fights. (Luther)

Despite increased spending on policing with the implementation of PPV, the monopoly of violence in these communities continues to be fragmented and the marginalised continue to be treated as expendable nonentities victimised both by violent police and by illegal security groups which are themselves often made up of ex-police officers. From inside the prison, members of these groups continued to manage and profit from a parasitic business, which, extorts money from residents in forcibly selling alternative forms of security.

Young people perceived the PPV security programme as a political discourse rather than an intervention that reduced violence. They did not feel safer. They felt increasingly targeted by police on the basis of their social status. When asked what the state should do to reduce violence, the key local demands were social and preventative interventions such as investment in (1) vocational training for the young, (2) better-quality education, (3) access to leisure spaces and cultural activities, (4) improved work opportunities, (5) the demilitarisation and enhanced training for the police to develop dialogue and respect for human rights in their interactions with the public. Residents viewed these as essential to promoting a safer society. Instead, *Pacto pela Vida* focuses on proving more policing (of an unsatisfactory nature), on imprisoning offenders and on measuring and monitoring targets.

Conclusion

Police violence and diverse forms of routine violence have been enduring problems in Latin America, predominantly in the communities most affected by social inequalities.

This study has examined the effects of a managerial homicide reduction programme in one Brazilian city. The data above suggest that the emulation of mainstream criminological theories of crime control from the Global North, based on the idea of managing crime statistics and police performance – without police reform – has produced large-scale perverse effects in the context of countries of the Global South. Theories produced in the North and applied in the South, have failed to take into account: the context of the Global South, the literature emerging from the South, complex diverse harms and the experiences and victimisation of marginalised urban dwellers, women and young people. Methods of crime control cannot succeed if the communities affected and the institutions supposedly delivering change (in this case the police and the criminal justice system) are not understood within Brazil's historical and socio-economic context.

There was a clear dissonance between what high-ranking officials, police, and academics involved with new security interventions claimed as a 'success' (Ratton et al., 2014), and what people in marginalised communities experienced. Poor people in the communities studied felt increasingly trapped, isolated and criminalised by increasing the policing. The police now had targets, and their work and performance was measured on the basis of the volume of drugs and firearms that they apprehended, the number of investigations concluded and sent off for prosecution.

Incarceration rates grew but long-standing ills in the police – including: racism, classism, violent practices and militarised culture – were not addressed or targeted. Both the model and intensity of the use of policing and the growing use of the prison had perverse effects for the communities studied, some of which can be captured by the inability of these methods to maintain order or contain crime, an issue illustrated by the recent prison escapes. This failure is also evident given that homicide rates and levels of violence only declined until 2013. The State has perhaps simply contributed to a fluctuation in levels of violence, but ultimately the State's adoption of securitisation has proven unsustainable. The context in which organised criminals operate and engage with outside communities over, under and through the prison walls epitomises the failures of global North methods of crime control. Security programmes have failed to inhibit diverse forms of violent and organised crime. Moreover, the securitisation agenda promises to exacerbate existing inequalities affecting the most marginalised populations by bringing them into contact with the criminal justice system as suspects and perpetrators rather than as victims.

Notes

1. I have refrained from using italics for the term favela because it has become internationally used and widely known.
2. Homicide rates have been increasing since 2014 again, coinciding with the period since Brazil entered a new economic downturn.

Acknowledgements

I am grateful for the feedback provided by the anonymous reviewers, Fiona Macaulay and Graham Denyer Willis to previous drafts of this work.

Disclosure statement

No potential conflict of interest was reported by the author.

Funding

This work was supported by the Economic and Social Research Council [under grant number ES/J500057/1] and the Arts and Humanities Research Council [under grant number AH/L000717/1].

Notes on contributor

Dr Roxana Pessoa Cavalcanti is a lecturer in Criminology at the University of Westminster. Her research focuses on urban violence, crime and justice in Brazil. She is currently working on a book manuscript based on her PhD research conducted at King's College London (2012–2017).

ORCID

Roxana Pessoa Cavalcanti ⓘ http://orcid.org/0000-0003-3885-8603

References

Alessi, G. (2016, October 13). Entenda o que é a PEC 241 e como ela pode afetar sua vida. *El País.* https://brasil.elpais.com/brasil/2016/10/10/politica/1476125574_221053.html

Amorim, D. (2016, October 27). Taxa de desemprego fica em 11,8% e mantém patamar histórico. *Estadão.* http://economia.estadao.com.br/noticias/geral,taxa-de-desemprego-fica-em-11-8-e-mantem-patamar-historico,10000084713

Arias, E. D. (2006). *Drugs & democracy in Rio de Janeiro : Trafficking, social networks, & public security.* Chapel Hill: University of North Carolina Press.

Arias, E. D., & Goldstein, D. M. (2010). Violent pluralism: Understanding the new democracies of Latin America. In E. D. Arias & D. M. Goldstein (Eds.), *Violent democracies in Latin America* (pp. 1–34). Durham, NC: Duke University Press.

Atkinson, R., & Flint, J. (2001). Accessing hidden and hard-to-reach populations: Snowball research strategies. *Social Research Update, 33,* 1–4.

Azevedo, R. G., & Cifali, A. C. (2015). Política criminal e encarceramento no Brasil nos governos Lula e Dilma: Elementos para um balanço de uma experiência de governo pós-neoliberal. *Civitas - Revista de Ciências Sociais, 15*(1), 105–127.

Bailey, J., & Dammert, L. (2006). Public security and police reform in the Americas. In J. Bailey & L. Dammert (Eds.), *Public security and police reform in the Americas* (pp. 1–23). Pittsburgh,PA: University of Pittsburgh Press.

Barros, R., Carvalho, M. D., Franco, S., & Mendonça, R. (2010). Markets, the state, and the dynamics of inequality in Brazil. In L. López-Calva & N. Lustig (Eds.), *Declining inequality in Latin America: A decade of progress?* (pp. 134–174). New York, NY: UNDP and Brookings University Press.

Barros, G. D. S. (2008). Filtragem racial: a cor na seleção do suspeito. *Revista Brasileira de Segurança Pública, 2*(3), 134–155.

Becker, A., & Müller, M.-M. (2013). The securitization of urban space and the "rescue" of downtown Mexico city: Vision and practice. *Latin American Perspectives, 40*(2), 77–94. doi:10.1177/0094582x12467762

Bourgois, P. I. (2003). *In search of respect : Selling crack in El Barrio* (2nd ed.). Cambridge: Cambridge University Press.

Bowling, B., & Phillips, C. (2007). Disproportionate and discriminatory: Reviewing the evidence on police stop and search. *The Modern Law Review, 70*(6), 936–961.

Butler-Kisber, L. (2010). *Qualitative inquiry: Thematic, narrative and arts-based approaches*. London: Sage.

Carvalho, S. (2013). Theories of punishment in the Age of mass incarceration: A closer Look at the empirical problem silenced by justificationism (The Brazilian case)*. *Open Journal of Social Sciences, 1*(4), 1–12.

Cavalcanti, R. P. (2017, January 25. *How Brazil's far right became a dominant political force, the conversation*. Retrieved from https://theconversation.com/how-brazils-far-right-became-a-dominant-political-force-71495

Cerqueira, D., Ferreira, H., Lima, R. S. D., Bueno, S., Hanashiro, O., Batista, F., & Nicolato, P. (2016). *Atlas da Violência*. Brasil: IPEA & FBSP.

Clarke, R. V. G., & Felson, M. (2004). *Routine activity and rational choice*. New Brunswick, NJ: Transaction.

Clarke, R. V. G. (1997). *Situational crime prevention : Successful case studies* (2nd ed.). New York, NY: Harrow and Heston.

Comin, A. A., Barbosa, R. J., & Carvalhaes, F. O. (2012). *Manufacturing jobs: Economic cycles, job creation and structural change*. Coventry: ESRC Pathfinder Programme on Collaborative Analysis of Microdata Resources, Warwick Institute for Employment Research IER. Retrieved from https://www2.warwick.ac.uk/fac/soc/ier/research/glmf/heeer/manufacturing_jobs_in_brazil_-_comin_js_pdf.pdf

Darke, S., & Garces, C. (2017). Surviving in the new mass carceral zone. *Prison Service Journal, Special Edition: Informal Dynamics of Survival in Latin American Prisons, 229*, 2–9.

Darke, S. (2013). Inmate governance in Brazilian prisons. *Howard Journal of Criminal Justice, 52*(3), 272–284.

Davies, M. (2006). *Planet of slums: Urban involution and the informal working class*. London: Verso.

Davis, D. E. (2013). Zero-tolerance policing, stealth real estate development, and the transformation of public space: Evidence from Mexico city. *Latin American Perspectives, 40*(2), 53–76. doi:10.1177/009458212467761

Denyer Willis, G. (2015). *The killing consensus: Police, organized crime, and the regulation of life and death in urban Brazil*. Berkeley: University of California Press.

Douglas, B. (2015, April 17). Brazil's 'bullets, beef and bible' caucus wants to imprison 16-year-olds. *The Guardian*. Retrieved from http://www.theguardian.com/world/2015/apr/17/brazil-rightwing-caucus-lower-age-criminal-responsibility?CMP=share_btn_tw

Drybread, K. (2009). Rights-bearing street kids: Icons of hope and despair in Brazil's burgeoning Neoliberal state. *Law & Policy, 31*(3), 330–350. doi:10.1111/j.1467-9930.2009.00304.x

Drybread, K. (2014). Murder and the making of man-subjects in a Brazilian juvenile prison. *American Anthropologist, 116*(4), 752–764. doi:10.1111/aman.12147

Emerson, R., Fretz, R., & Shaw, L. (1995). *Writing ethnographic fieldnotes*. Chicago, IL: University of Chicago Press.

Feeley, M., & Simon, J. (1992). The new penology: Notes on the emerging strategy of corrections and its implications. *Criminology; An Interdisciplinary Journal, 30*, 449–474.

Feltran, G. D. S. (2011). *Fronteiras de Tensão: Política e Violência nas Periferias de São Paulo*. São Paulo: Unesp.

Fernandes, F. L. (2013). Youth gang members in Rio de Janeiro: The face of a 'lost generation' in an Age of fear and mistrust. *Bulletin of Latin American Research, 32*(2), 210–223. doi:10.1111/blar.12030

Garland, D. (2001). *The culture of control: Crime and social order in late modernity*. Oxford: Clarendon.

GEPE, Governo do Estado de Pernambuco. (2013, July 23). Governo de Pernambuco recebe prêmio da ONU pelo êxito do Pacto Pela Vida. Retrieved November 1, 2016, from http://www.pe.gov.br/blog/2013/06/27/governo-de-pernambuco-recebe-premio-da-onu-pelo-exito-do-pacto-pela-vida/ .

Gledhill, J. (2013). *The production of insecurity in Brazil and Mexico*. Paper presented at the SLAS 2013 annual conference, University of Manchester, Manchester, UK.

Hagedorn, J., Davis, M., & Ebrary, I. (2008). *A world of gangs: Armed young men and gangsta culture*. Minneapolis: University of Minnesota Press.

Hall, A. (2008). Brazil's Bolsa Família: A double-edged sword? *Development and Change, 39*(5), 799–822.

Huggins, M. K. (1997). From bureaucratic consolidation to structural devolution: Police death squads in Brazil. *Policing and Society, 7*(4), 207–234.

Huggins, M. K. (1998). *Political policing: The United States and Latin America*. Durham, NC: Duke University Press.

Jones, G. A., & Rodgers, D. (2009). *Youth violence in Latin America [electronic resource]*. Basingstoke: Palgrave Macmillan.

Leeds, E. (1996). Cocaine and parallel polities on the Brazilian urban periphery: Constraints on local level democratization. *Latin American Research Review, 31*(3), 47–84.

Macedo, A. d. O. (2012). *"Policia, quando quer, faz!" Analise da Estrutura de Governanca do "Pacto pela Vida" de Pernambuco* (*Masters*). Universidade de Brasilia.

Meirelles, Fernando. (Director). (2002). Film title: City of God. Producers: Andrea Barata Ribeiro, Mauricio Andrade Ramos, Elisa Tolomelli, Walter Salles. Distributors: Miramax Films (US) and Buena Vista International. Date released: 18 May 2002 (Cannes); 30 August 2002 (Brazil).

Molyneaux, M. (2008). The 'neoliberal turn' and the New social policy in Latin America: How neoliberal, how new? *Development and Change, 39*(5), 775–797.

Moore, H. (2015). "Do you have my son?" Criminalization and the production of (un)relatedness in Brazil. In J. Minaker, & B. Hogeveen (Eds.), *Criminalized mothers, criminalizing mothering* (pp. 264–291). Bradford, ON: Demeter Press.

Neri, M. (2009). Income policies, income distribution, and the distribution of opportunities in Brazil. In L. Brainard & L. Martínez-Diaz (Eds.), *Brazil as an economic superpower?* (pp. 221–269). Washington, DC: Brookings Institution Press.

O'Donnell, G. (1993). On the state, democratization, and some conceptual problems: A Latin American view with glances at some postcommunist countries. *World Development, 21*(8), 1355–1369.

Oliveira, W. (2015, March 2). *Pacto pela Vida da sinais de fracasso, Diário de Pernambuco*. Retrieved from http://blogs.diariodepernambuco.com.br/segurancapublica/?p=8014

Padilha, J. (Writer). (2007). Elite Squad. In J. Padilha & M. Prado (Producer). Brazil: Universal Pictures (Brazil), IFC Films (United States).

Pereira, A. W. (2008). Public security, private interests, and police reform in Brazil. In P. R. Kingstone & T. J. Power (Eds.), *Democratic Brazil revisited* (pp. 185–208). Pittsburgh, PA: University of Pittsburgh Press.

PESP-PE. (2007). *Plano Estadual de Seguranca Publica: PACTO PELA VIDA. Recife: Cultura*. Retrieved from http://www.seres.pe.gov.br/index/pacto_pela_vida.pdf

Pinheiro, P. S. (2006). *World report on violence against children*. Geneva. Retrieved from United nations secretary-general's study on violence against children: http://www.unicef.org/lac/full_tex(3).pdf

Portella, A. P., & Nascimento, M. G. D. (2014). Impactos de Gênero na Redução da Mortalidade Violenta: Reflexões sobre of Pacto pela Vida em Pernambuco. *Revista Brasileira de Segurança Pública, 8*(1), 48–68.

Ratton, J. L., Galvão, C., & Fernandez, M. (2014). Pact for life and the reduction of homicides in the state of pernambuco. *Stability: International Journal of Security & Development, 3*(1), 1–15.

Ribeiro, L. M. L. (2014). *Modelo de Gestão por Resultados do programa Pacto pela Vida, Pernambuco, Brasil*. Retrieved from GobernArte: Categoria Governo Seguro: http://publications.iadb.org/bitstream/handle/11319/6564/GobernArte, Categoria governo seguro (Version en Portugues).pdf?sequence=4

Rizzini, I. (1997). Olhares sobre a criança no Brasil: séculos XIX e XX Rio de Janeiro: Ed. Universitária Santa Úrsula/Amais.

Scheper-Hughes, N. (2004). Dangerous and endangered youth: Social structures and determinants of violence. In J. Devine, J. Gilligan, K. A. Miczek, R. Shaikh, & D. Pfaff (Eds.), *Youth violence: Scientific approaches to prevention* (pp. 13–46). New York: New York Academy of Sciences.

Skidmore, T. E. (2010). *Brazil : Five centuries of change* (2nd ed.). New York, NY: Oxford University Press.

Souza, E. R. D., Ribeiro, A. P., & Valadares, F. C. (2012). *Informações sobre os homicídios no Brasil: uma ferramenta para a consolidação da democracia e da cidadania*. Retrieved from http://www.usp.br/

imprensa/wp-content/uploads/5C2BA-RelatC3B3rio-Nacional-sobre-os-Direitos-Humanos-no-Brasil-2001-2010.pdf

UNICEF. (2015). *ECA 25anos: Estatuto da Criança e do Adolescente: Avanços e desafios para a infância e a adolescência no Brasil (online)*. Retrieed from http://www.unicef.org/brazil/pt/ECA25anosUNICEF.pdf

Ventura, Z. (1994). *Cidade Partida*. Sao Paulo: Companhia de Letras.

Wacquant, L. C. J. D. (2003). Toward a dictatorship over the poor? Notes on the penalization of poverty in Brazil. *Punishment & Society-International Journal of Penology, 5*(2), 197–205. doi:10.1177/146247450352004

Wacquant, L. C. J. D. (2008). *Urban outcasts: A comparative sociology of advanced marginality*. Cambridge: Polity.

Waiselfisz, J. J. (2011). *Mapa da Violência: Os Jovens do Brasil (online)*. Retrieved from http://www.cnt.org.br/ImagensCNT/NotC3ADcias/Fevereirode2011/2011mapa_VdolC3AAncia(1).pdf

Waiselfisz, J. J. (2013). *Mortes Matadas por Armas de Fogo: Mapa da Violencia*. http://mapadaviolencia.org.br/

Waiselfisz, J. J. (2014). *Mapa da Violencia 2014: Os jovens do Brasil*. Retrieved from http://www.mapadaviolencia.org.br/pdf2014/Mapa2014_JovensBrasil_Preliminar.pdf

Wolff, M. J. (2014). *Criminal authorities and the state: Gangs, organized crime, and police in Brazil* (PhD). University of New Mexico, USA.

Young, J. (2011). *The criminological imagination*. Cambridge: Polity.

Zaluar, A. (2004). *Integração Perversa: Pobreza e Tráfico de drogas*. Rio de Janeiro: FGV.

Zaluar, A. (2010). Youth, drug traffic and hypermasculinity in Rio de Janeiro. *Vibrant – Virtual Brazilian Anthropology, 7*(2), 7–27.

Struggling for tomorrow: the future orientations of youth activism in a democratic crisis

Tin-yuet Ting

ABSTRACT

Recent protest movements worldwide have painted a picture of youth striving in times of crisis to secure self-determination and justice for more democratic futures. While traditional theory has viewed youth activism as the result of structural strains or collapse of order, recent studies have focused attention upon the role of future orientations merely as movement strategies. What is missing from these accounts, and what this article seeks to address, is the initiatives of youth to carry out their future-oriented agendas and struggles at the grassroots. Drawing upon interview data with young citizens, who took part in recent political activism in response to a democratic crisis in Hong Kong, this article illustrates how young people were involved in political struggles as they enacted their life goals and identities. Rather than static political ideals, these visions of future were constantly reconstituted in the activist practices alongside unfolding crises. This article thus re-theorises youth activism simultaneously as the manifestation as well as the constitution of alternative futures in practice. Moving beyond the notion of youth activism as passive reaction to repression or abstract political anticipation, it leverages for youth agency and everyday experience to understand youth's political imagination and commitment to social transformation.

Introduction

From rebellious students in England to youth discontent in the Arab countries and the wired generation in the globalised Occupy Movement, a plethora of youth activism facilitated by new information and communication technologies has developed in the face of socio-economic dislocations on a global scale (Gordon, 2010; Harlow, 2011; Jeffrey, 2013; Juris, 2012; Lim, 2012). Whereas Hong Kong lacks the tradition of radical protests, the 2014 Umbrella Movement enjoyed considerable support amongst the younger generation in the Asian global city (Ming Pao, 2014; *The Huffington Post*, 2014), where political activism surged alongside a democratic crisis provoked by China's conservative reform to Hong Kong's electoral system (Ortmann, 2015; *The Economist*, 2015; Yuen, 2015). These political neophytes many of whom took part in protest movements for the first time not only extensively engaged in the 79-day, large-scale occupation protest, but also involved in diverse civic-political activities beyond the immediate movement field.

Whereas traditional theory of collective behaviour viewed youth activism as collapsing social and political orders (cf. LeBon, 1895; Smelser, 1962), an alternative strand of social movement studies and futures research has begun to focus attention upon the role of crisis as opportunities for the construction of alternative futures (Juris, 2008; Melucci, 1996; Schulz, 2016a, 2016b; Touraine, 1981). This article seeks to advance this research by addressing the initiatives of youth to carry out future-oriented agendas and struggles at the grassroots. Rather than movement strategies such as meta-narratives and collective action frames (cf. McAdam, 1982; Pratt, 2003; Snow, Benford, Worden, & Benford, 1986), it conceptualises future orientations from a transformative perspective (Stetsenko, 2010, 2015), and explores how assumptions and aspirations about the future (re-)constitute youth's paths to political activism in practice.

In this analysis, this article presents an exploratory study that aims to understand how youth has involved in political struggles as they enacted their life goals and future selves, which were rooted in the everyday domain. Drawing upon interview data with young activists, who took part in the Umbrella Movement, it illustrates that youth participation in political activism was closely linked to the fracture between their orientations towards the future and the democratic ruptures that cloud these assumptions and aspirations. Rather than static political ideals, their future orientations were constantly reconstituted in their activist practices in response to unfolding crises. This article thus conceptualises youth activism simultaneously as the manifestation as well as the constitution of alternative futures. Moving beyond the notion of youth activism as passive reaction to repression or abstract political anticipation, it leverages for youth agency and everyday experience to understand youth imagination and commitment to social transformation.

Approaches to youth activism and crises

Traditional approaches tended to view youth activism as crises of social instability and disorder. In the earliest theory of collective behaviour, collective action was considered the result of irrationality of mobilised masses and their manipulability. Similar to LeBon (1895) classic treatment, which interpreted the crowds of the French Revolution as irrational reversions to animal emotion, this literature regarded social movements and political activism as people induced to lose their ability to think rationally thus driving towards violent action. Then, collective behaviour theory developed in the 1960s conceptualised crowd behaviour as the response of agency of social control and disruptive to the society (Della Porta & Diani, 2006). Rooted in the viewpoint of structural functionality, it interpreted collective action as the consequences of strain within the social system, community, or group (Smelser, 1962). In these views, youth activism was thought of as social crises in themselves. Although being the earliest explanations of collective action, some of these perspectives are still widely accepted by many people worldwide, and prevail in the mainstream media in understanding youth activism against the backdrop of ongoing crises.

The wave of student movements in the 1960s and 1970s in the US and beyond, however, inspired another round of development of social movement theory. As the resource mobilisation theory (RMT) (McCarthy & Zald, 1977) and the political process approach (PPA) (McAdam, 1982) became the most dominant models, conceptualisations of youth activism were altered. Breaking with the traditional collective behaviour theory, which had considered movements and activism as irrational expressions of social dysfunction, RMT and PPA emphasised on the concepts of 'cognitive liberation' (McAdam, 1982), 'collective action frame' (Snow et al., 1986), and 'identity narratives' (Pratt, 2003), and viewed a central part of movements and activism to be 'claim-making' that 'brings recognition as a credible political player with the capacity to make a difference in the next political struggle' (McAdam, Tarrow, & Tilly, 2001, pp. 147–148). As a result, a large part of social movement studies and futures research have been addressed to well-established institutions and political elites (Schulz, 2016a, 2016b), such as movement organisations and activist leaders. In these studies, future visions were treated as recourses ready to be used for mass mobilisation and for the coordination of collective action. They were subsumed under the analytical categories of movement strategies or organisational purposes (Della Porta & Diani, 2006). From these perspectives, youth activism was regarded as calculative, instrumental decisions, in which future orientations became narrative or discursive weapons for mobilisation.

Indeed, dominant approaches to youth activism and the future tended to collapse the individual dimension into the movement realm while undertheorising the former (Melucci, 1996). Whereas much has been said about the role played by elite actors in the mobilisation and organisations of protest movements, less has been known about how youth agency for civic engagement and political participation arises at the grassroots. As Schulz (2016b) critiques, 'this elite orientation ... neglects the initiative of ordinary citizens, social movements, and subaltern networks – grassroots actors with less formal standing and less institutional power but nevertheless with moral standing, imaginative voices, and potential impact' (Schulz, 2016b, p. 9). In particular, extant literature was too strongly tied to the present conditions of 'political opportunity structures' (Tarrow, 1996) or, more recently, 'mediation political opportunities' (Cammaerts, 2012) in situating youth activism in times of crisis, and does not sufficiently engage the future orientations of youth for creating democratic alternatives.

In contrast, scholars and researchers associated with the so-called 'new social movements' seek to address the cultural potential of social movements. Among them, Touraine (1981) conceptualises collective action as a field of tensions where actors confront dilemmas, and where processes of social creativity may occur. He proposes to acknowledge social movements as 'the voice and the eye' of society, in that they produce alternative futures for society. In the same vein, Melucci (1996) recognises social movements as 'prophets' and 'vehicles' of society as they identify existing social problems and formulate alternative futures. With the case of anti-corporate globalisation movements, Juris (2008) examines how networked activists have used e-mail lists, Web pages, and free software to organise actions, share information, coordinate at a distance, and stage 'electronic civil disobedience' to build social laboratories for the production of alternative values and practices based on a cultural logic. Albeit from a different perspective, Schulz (2016c) explores the social construction of future realities during the current wave of global crises since 2011. Crises, in his view, have opened up social imageries and the horizon of the range of options and measures. This strand of research thus starts to shift away from reductionist approaches to recognition of activism in times of crisis as the site for manufacturing future visions, projects, and critical knowledge from below.

More recent research has been carried out on contemporary youth activism but predominantly concentrated on American experiences. While some of these studies examine how youth activist groups engaging youth from marginalised populations like the youth of colour affected by urban inequalities (Clay, 2012), others look at immigrants' activism at local schools (Terriquez, 2011) or student movements that are concerned with school funding, the environmental crisis, the prison industrial complex, standardised testing, corporate accountability, and educational reform (Gordon, 2010; Kwon, 2013; Larson & Hansen, 2005). Despite local variations, a similar trend can be observed in research that examines youth activism in Latin America. These include studies investigating youth activism against poverty and social misery in slums (Silva & de Castro, 2015) or youth activism on body politics and sexual health (Coe, Goicolea, Urtig, & Sebastain, 2015). These studies based on cases of the North and Latin Americas thus focus attention upon local projects and community development with an emphasis on social justice (Kirshner, 2007) in contextualising contemporary youth activism.

While the conditions and contexts of the Americas focus attention on youth activists' social and economic struggles, youth activism in semi-democratic societies or counties in transition may manifest distinguishing patterns (Kirshner, 2007). In contrast to youth activism in the West increasingly characterised by lifestyle politics, identity politics, and consumerist acts (Bennett, 2003), contemporary youth activists in many parts of the world 'are fighting against historical barriers, such as fear-driven political cultures or repressive colonial laws' (Zhang, 2013 , p. 254). Therefore, a more inclusive lens should be extended to societies where high proportion of youth still lives under political repression and exclusion. To better understand how youth in other parts of the world interpret their future in coming to activism, we need to move outside the Western context, where the bulk of research and theorising about contemporary youth activism has occurred. The current case of Hong Kong, where (semi-)authoritarian regime and (neo-)colonialist governance has prevailed particularly regarding the struggle over universal suffrage, thus provides an alternative context to examine the contentious-political experiences and future orientations of contemporary youth activism.

Transformative perspectives of youth activism and the future

In the context of social movement literature and futures research, as discussed, future orientations are not very often conceived of as dynamic processes of mundane everyday life. However, this is perhaps one of the most crucial research sites for the investigation of contemporary youth activism, as it has been observed to be characterised by fragmented and individualised forms of collective action (Bennett, 2012; Bennett & Segerberg, 2011; Bimber, Flanagin, & Stohl, 2005, 2012; Castells, 2012; Juris, 2012; Shirky, 2008). Extending the strand of research which reflects on future visions of the grassroots, this article illustrates the dynamic interplays between youth activism and the future by examining how future orientations enact and shape youth's paths to political activism in times of crisis, and how these future assumptions and aspirations are in turn reconstituted in their activist practices in the present. Towards this end, this article draws insights from research on transformative activist stance (TAS).

Expanding on Vygotsky's (1997, 2004) scholarship, Stetsenko's TAS (2010, 2015) proposes to understand citizens as agentic actors, who seek to contribute to the society in the pursuit of their own visions. In this view, social transformation takes place 'through people's activities and contributions to their communities ... in their day-to-day lives, struggles, and pursuits' (Stetsenko, 2015, pp. 107–108). Rather than co-creators of the status quo, citizens are seen as agents of social change through their own acts and deeds. Yet, instead of pre-existing social transformative practices, 'human being are "always already" constituted by social practices ... as they are carried out and constantly transformed by people themselves in their own pursuits and efforts' (Stetsenko, 2015, p. 108). Therefore, while aiming at transforming the current conditions, youth themselves are changing along with their future visions in fundamental ways within real-world projects and struggles.

From the transformative perspective, youth activism has to do with people collectively participating in and contributing to their world in view of their future goals and purposes; and also through this process they come to realise and reformulate these future orientations in practice. In this view, future orientations are simultaneously a process and outcome of youth activism. On the one hand, acts and deeds for social transformation are impossible without an orientation to the future in terms of people's own commitments and pursuits. In Stetsenko's words, 'we always act in pursuit of goals rather than mechanically react to the world ... contingent on what individuals and communities consider *should be*' (Stetsenko, 2010, p. 11, emphasis in the original). On the other hand, future assumptions and aspirations are 'constantly work-in-progress ... contingent on activist involvements in, and contributions to, collaborative transformative practices' (Stetsenko, 2015, p. 108). In other words, people are the knowers and makers of themselves at becoming through the very acts of their agency and activism for social change. Of centrality to this conceptualisation is the understanding that we constantly construct assumptions and aspirations about the future through immediate experiences and practical activities rooted in concrete historical-material conditions in the real time.

This view is particularly useful for understanding youth activism in times of crisis, as it recognises youth participation in contentious politics as future-oriented commitments and contributions, moving beyond the conventional understanding of youth being passively situated in existing conditions and merely responding to top-down repressions. In the case of Hong Kong, for instance, while some of the youth activists initiated their networked activism by rescuing student protestors from other police violence aiming at 'remediating the future of Hong Kong', others sought to secure their future anticipation of further democratisation in the city, especially regarding the universal suffrage of the Chief Executive (CE). Future orientations are therefore the importance relational quality through which we position ourselves within historically evolved conflicts and struggle for what is ought to be.

Concurrently, this is also a desirable conceptualisation for understanding contemporary youth activism, as it highlights the processes of enactment by considering future orientations as manifested in the forms of day-to-day activities and personal identity. In fact, many youth activists, who took part in the Umbrella Movement, altered their personal life goals and future plans in the course of their movement participation. These shifts in future orientations tended to be expressed in terms of everyday decisions and mundane projects. They include university students who changed their career choices in order to avoid (participation in) potential political suppression, young adults who decided to not have babies or to not invest in Hong Kong properties, and youth who considered emigration as a result of lacking confidence in the future society. Rather than strategies or agendas towards societal or policy change, future orientations are thus considered by this research as the result of dynamic processes in the everyday domain.

From democratic crisis to the Umbrella Movement

While Hong Kong kept its own executive and legal system under the 'one country, two systems' principle, by which it retained a degree of autonomy, the handover of Hong Kong from Britain to China did not provide further impetus for democratisation. After its handover in 1997, the mainland Chinese government reformed the electoral system in order to weaken the pan-democratic camp.

In 2004, the Chinese government demonstrated its opposition to the democratisation of Hong Kong when it ruled out the introduction of universal suffrage for electing the CE before 2012. In 2007, it was finally resolved that universal suffrage should be implemented by 2017. However, pro-Beijing reformers were only willing to allow Hong Kong people a choice between two or three preselected candidates. While this was based on the Basic Law's requirement for the existence of a nominating committee, it ignored the fact that essentially all Hong Kong people should be able to run for office regardless of their political convictions (Yuen, 2015).

The nomination process soon became the focal point of contention. Fearing that the election might turn out to be a 'fake universal suffrage', some democratic supporters in Hong Kong insisted on the introduction of civic nomination, a mechanism that would allow the public to bypass the nominating committee and directly nominate CE candidates, but which has been immediately rejected by the Chinese government. Others would accept a more democratically formed nominating committee, as long as there was reform on its composition and/or a reasonably lower nomination threshold (Yuen, 2015).

Within the democracy movement, the role of political parties had decreased over the years. Instead of party politics, mass protests had become the main arena in the fight for greater democracy. The most well-known example for such an organisation is the Occupy Central with Love and Peace (Occupy Central), which was founded in January 2013 led by academics and professors at local universities. Occupy Central carefully planned its non-violent disobedience movement with workshops and a detailed manual that was posted online. However, this stood in contrast to the younger generation, who were much more aggressive in their position and eventually became the driving force of the Umbrella Movement.

To counter the democracy movement in Hong Kong, on 31 August 2014, the Chinese National People's Congress Standing Committee of the mainland Chinese government issued a 'White Paper' as a decision on election reform for setting guidelines for the 2017 CE election in Hong Kong, in which it asserted full control over political development. By claiming 'comprehensive jurisdiction' over the city, Beijing declared that the nominating committee must be formed 'in accordance with' the existing 1200-strong four-sector election committee, which had been criticised for over-representing the interests of Beijing.

Shortly following the issuing of the 'White Paper', secondary and university students in Hong Kong, led by Scholarism and the Hong Kong Federation of Students, jointly launched a boycott of classes starting on 22 September 2014 against Beijing's decision. As the week progressed, students gave an ultimatum to CE, Leung Chun-ying, to meet with them and to discuss universal suffrage by 25 September. But because there was no willingness to engage in dialogue, students decided to increase the pressure by climbing over the fence to enter the Civic Square – the forecourt of the government headquarters. On 26 September, as the students attempted to enter the square, they were met with a tough response from the police. This in turn mobilised thousands of people to join the protest movement.

On 28 September, the massive rally was met with tear gas and pepper spray, which protesters repelled with their umbrellas, thus giving the movement its name. Upset about the violent response to peaceful protests, more Hong Kong people joined the movement. As the number of people grew, the police used pepper spray and tear gas on a massive scale against the protesters. The violent reaction by the police led to a backlash, as it led to a dramatic increase in the number of protesters who began occupying the streets. Eventually, it was reported that over 200,000 people and the occupation protest spread from Admiralty to other major commercial districts in the city including Mongkok and Causeway Bay. As such, the 79-day Umbrella Movement, the largest and longest episode of collective contention in the history of Hong Kong kicked off.

The study

To examine how youth political activism interacts with future orientations in times of crisis, this research undertook a qualitative study of youth activists in the Umbrella Movement. It adopted an interpretive approach which aims to reconstruct the actual lived experiences that moved the young citizens to take part in political activism. By recognising them as active moral and political subjects, it means to examine the democratic crisis and occupation protest from the alternative perspective of youth who struggled for social justice and human dignity in relation to their future assumptions and aspirations. This thus enabled the researcher to explore the influence of future orientations upon the youth's path to/of political activism through their movement experiences in times of crisis.

This research drew data from interviews with youth activists. It used in-depth interviews to collect empirical material, consisting of the youth activists' personal narratives on their paths to/of networked activism for the Umbrella Movement and beyond. I interviewed 17 youth activists at the ages between 17 and 29, 10 out of whom were male and 7 of whom were female. They were selected because of their self-identified intensive participation in the movement for democracy in Hong Kong, and of their ages within the range of 15–30. According to Cheng and Chan (2016), this range of age reflects the majority of the Umbrella Movement as 53.5% of the movement participants were of the ages between 18 and 29. The age range of 15–30 is also consistent with the definition of youth widely adopted by transnational organisations such as the Commonwealth (The Commonwealth, 2017) as well as national governments such as most of the EU countries (Bendit, 2006; Perovic, 2016), India (*Indiatimes*, 2012), Kenya (Ministry of Home Affairs, Heritage and Sports, 2002), and Malaysia (The Rakyat Post, 2015). Arguably, this definition can better capture the recent global trend in which the ages for youth to complete formal education and enter the labour market have steadily increased in the last few decades (Bendit, 2006; Canadian Youth Foundation, 1995; Cheal, 2003; Yalnizyan, 1998).

All the interviews were conducted in Hong Kong in the summer of 2015. Mostly in public venues such as Cafés and fast food restaurants, they were carried in locations chosen by the informants. The time of each interview lasted between one and a half hours to two hours. They were in-depth interviews guided by four sets of open-ended questions; and each set of these questions was related to one specific thematic area. But these questions were only suggestive, as some of them were not asked in the interviews if the interviewer found them less relevant to the case of the informant; some additional questions were added and probed further when the interviewer considered them to be important and more relevant to the case of the interviewer. In the first part, I asked general questions about the informants' biographical details. The second and the most important part of the interviews revolved around their paths to/of political activism. The third part of the interviews was about their evolving activist identity and life goals. The last part of the interviews was concerned with the impact of movement involvement on their everyday life, as well as their interpretations of the consequences of the Umbrella Movement at the societal level.

The empirical materials drawn from in-depth interviews were examined for the reconstruction of the youth activists' lived experiences and actual practices in the face of the democratic crisis. They were used to interpret the youth's paths to/of networked activism. During this process, a series of key themes emerged. Subsequently, the researcher analysed and interpreted them to construct meaningful historical discourses for answering the specific questions of this research. In presenting the data, while none of the interviewees requested anonymity, all the names were changed so as to protect the anonymity of the youth activists.

Youth activism and future orientations in a democratic crisis

Engaging in the present and changing the future

The outbreak of the Umbrella Movement opened up a series of historically unprecedented opportunities for youth to exercise their social imaginations through direct participation in contentious activities. For many youth interviewees, the initiation of their political activism represented a fracture between their future orientations and the democratic ruptures that cloud these aspirations. The feeling of emergency to rescue student protestors from police violence so as to remediate the future of Hong Kong was a key component of their paths to political activism against the backdrop of the crisis of democracy.

In the evening of 26 September 2014, the last day of the weeklong class boycott cum demonstration in front of the government headquarters, dozens of students climbed over the metal barriers and stormed the empty forecourt of the Headquarters by surprise. While some of them were swiftly arrested by the police, the remaining students were surrounded in the Civic Squire. During the arrest and confrontation, some students were injured and shown with blood on their faces, while others were still trapped in the forecourt overnight. However, this move undertaken by the police dramatically backfired, as it created a 'moral shock' (Jasper, 1997) that helped to mobilise the first wave of political activism among individual actors. Among all the youth activists that I had the chance to talk to, Sally was among the first wave of protestors, who headed Occupy Headquarters immediately after they knew about the arrest of the students. What initiated her prompt involvement were not the ideals of democracy or freedom, but rather her future aspirations for the student protestors who were under attack and arrest. As she recalled in the interview:

> Back then, I did not expect a large-scale protest movement to occur. I decided to go there after watching what the students had been through for simply demanding a fair and just electoral reform for all Hong Kong people ...

> They were just students! If we allow them [the police] to treat the students like that, it will be legit for them to treat any of us like that soon. To me, that was our last chance to make our stance clear – To say 'no' to the authoritarian regime. Otherwise, Hong Kong would go all the way down from there.

Sally's personal experience was not an exception but a recurrent theme among the youth interviewees, who commonly interpreted the police violence to be an attack on Hong Kong's future society. Samantha was another youth activist who read such signs in watching news on social networking sites (SNS). When asked about how she initiated her political activism and why she came to take part in the Umbrella Movement, she reported that:

> After watching the news about the arrest of students and police violence on Facebook, multiple friends of mine who were already there called for more people to support the students on the SNS. They told people to bring water, goggles, and plastic wrap to protect themselves from pepper spray ...

> That was before the idea that we are having a social movement at all. We just went there to help blockade the police and prevent them from approaching the government headquarters where the students were violently suppressed ...

> They were just student! A lot of them were still in school uniforms! That was not the Hong Kong I knew! That was not the Hong Kong we worked hard for! That was not the Hong Kong we desire!

> As [young] adults, we had the responsibility to go protect them because they are the future of Hong Kong. Eventually, they will be responsible for our society. We went to protest our own future, so to speak.

Moreover, while the youth's paths to political activism were informed by embedded visions for the future linked to social justice and human emancipation, they are nonetheless enacted within practical activities in the real world. For instance, Eric originally did not plan to go to the protest movement as he had had a long day and wanted to take a rest at home. He changed his mind only because his friends suggested him to go alone to just take a look. But as he stepped outside the Mass Transit Railway (MTR) station of Central, what was about to happen dramatically changed his view and action towards the movement since:

> I was attacked by rounds of tear gas immediately when I stepped outside the MTR station. I thought to myself – What the hell?! Why do you do that to me?! I didn't do anything! I am just standing and watching. I didn't even yell a single slogan, or demanded anything. Why did you shoot the tear gas at me?! – I felt very innocent and angry ...

I thought to myself – If you can shoot [tear gas] at me without warning today, you can fire at me with a tank tomorrow just like the Forth Indecent in 1989. I believe that was the sentiment that got me and kept me involved …

That was the first night I slept in Admiralty. The next morning I had to go to work. But then I came back almost every day since …

Apparently, Eric's real-time experience of the protest movement informed his future frames of reference which were dramatically connected to the political history of China's 1989 Tiananmen Square Incident, and which escalated into more intensive movement involvement. Rather than static action orientations and activist roles, it was his immediate experience in the Umbrella Movement that modified his future expectation and upscale lifted his level and/or mode of movement involvement.

Struggling at becoming and experiencing failure

While youth activists were with a set of future orientations in coming to political activism, they constantly (re-)negotiate their future assumptions and aspirations in altering their relationships with the outcomes of the crisis of democracy and redefining the meanings of the Umbrella Movement. This becomes more obvious when we look at how the youth's future orientations shifted alongside their embodied experiences of political activism. Sam, for instance, described the shift in his political attitude towards Hong Kong–China integration and his view on the future Hong Kong society after participating in the Umbrella Movement:

After taking part in the movement, my 'illusion' about democratization of mainland China with Hong Kong as a stepping stone simply evaporated. I used to believe that despite a gradual and slow progress, China would become more liberal and democratic one day, and that in this process Hong Kong would serve as the gate through which democracy enters China …

Now, however, I do not have such 'illusion' anymore. Although I might not necessarily agree with everything emerging localism advocates for, I come to believe that a strict separation between Hong Kong and mainland China would result in a better social and political reality for Hong Kong people. Now I come to believe that Hong Kong should become more self-contained and self-sustainable, instead of being more integrated with mainland China …

Actually, this is what Hong Kong was supposed to be under the 'one country, two systems' policy. However, China has distorted the 'one country, two systems' policy once and for all. It has been clear that the Chief Executive of Hong Kong will never be elected by Hong Kong people anymore …

In this movement, I came to realize that the Hong Kong government will only suppress local demands for democracy and justice with violence. In the future, its policy will be merely subjected to the interests of China.

In the same vein, John's shifted from a non-violent peaceful protestor to a potential radical after joining the protest movement, with the emerging assumption that peaceful protests would not be effective in the future in the face of an authoritarian regime:

We were peaceful throughout the occupation project; we did that for months, but we have achieved nothing. After the movement ended, I shift from a peaceful, non-violent stance to a more radical stance for the democracy movement …

Now, I start to think about whether the independence of Hong Kong would be a way out. I used to identify myself as a Chinese and thus never thought about that. But now I start to think that the Beijing authority is hopeless and that Hong Kong should go for independence like Singapore did.

This shift took place mainly because I witnessed too many outraged incidents in the movement – So many peaceful protestors were beaten by the police even though they were just demonstrating peacefully.

For many youth activists, the dramatic historical event represented life-changing moments not only limited to rising civic awareness and changing political attitude but also including shifts in patterns of their actual behaviours oriented towards the future. For instance, Sunny, whose father and aunt were policeman and policewoman, respectively, came to alter his career choice from preparing himself to join Hong Kong Police to a refusal to join the police force. This shift in his future career plan had everything to do with his direct experience of participating in the Umbrella Movement, particularly with regard to police violence on the ground.

What I experienced in the movement entirely altered my views on the Hong Kong Police. I used to consider the Hong Kong Police to be professional and fair … But all I saw was multiple innocent citizens, who simply bypassed the streets, were under attack. They [the policemen] were supposed to control themselves and remain calm when they were on duty, so that they could do their job properly. But in this movement, a lot of them act biasedly against peaceful protestors only because the protesters were expressing anti-government opinions …

If you ask me now, I definitely will not join the police force anymore after my university graduation, which will happen next year. Maybe I will consider joining other disciplined services, such as Fire Services Department, which will be less likely involved in political repressions. I think this way I can then truly serve the Hong Kong society.

For Sunny, his vision of future well-being with his potential ability to become a civil servant in disciplined services other than the police force stands in sharp contrast to his interpretation of the future Hong Kong society, in which, in his future assumption, will only end up in more and more political suppression and repressive violence, and in which the police force will be always required to act biasedly against dissidents who, however, behave in a civil manner.

Sunny was by no means alone in altering his concrete future plan. Catharine also changed her mind on her mundane life goals after joining the protest movement:

During the Umbrella Movement, I came to realize that there were a lot of things that are 'bigger' and more meaningful than my own personal goals.

I used to desire for a middle class lifestyle. For example, I wished that I could have my own property, you know, those with a club house. Although I'm now single, I also wished that my children will study in 'superior' schools.

But after the Umbrella Movement, I lowered all my expectations for the future. Now, I only desire a simple life. I don't need my own property; I don't mind staying in public housing as long as I have a place to live. I thought I wanted to have two to three kids. But now, I will rather have no kids, if the social and political situation of Hong Kong remains the same. As long as we don't get these societal problems solved and democracy fixed, all my future expectations of buying an estate and having kids will be hanging forever.

Indeed, many youth activists reported to have experienced worries and insecurities about their futures in parallel to the future of Hong Kong. Migration was thus another recurrent theme among the youth interviewees. Kate's statement effectively illustrates such processes:

> Now I'm very disappointed about Hong Kong. I used to plan to stay in Hong Kong for the rest of my life, since my family and friends are all here. But after witnessing what the government did to its own people, more and more I consider spending my life somewhere else.

> Actually, since I'm planning to study aboard in the close future, I've been thinking about if I should stay in a foreign country after my graduation.

> I don't think the Hong Kong government will change for good. You see?! Not even such a large-scale protest movement could achieve that. There's nothing we can do about it, no matter how many Umbrella Movements we are going to undertake. I think I am giving up, just like many people around me.

Similarly, Zak, who was a young lawyer, considered emigration to be a long and difficult journey, and yet he might still go for it:

> After the Umbrella Movement, I seriously consider to move to another country. I never thought about migrating to another country before, due to my occupation. You know, you got your license and professional networks in Hong Kong. If you move to another place, you might not be able to be a lawyer anymore. You need to start all over again, from your license to connections. Also, usually you don't earn as much elsewhere as in Hong Kong. That's why this is not common among my people.

> However, the cost-effectiveness of migration has risen for me now, due to the deteriorating governance in the city, where the authoritarian regime only serves the interests of big business and mainland China. Nowadays, I have been paying close attention to potential countries and firms overseas that I might be able to work for.

> Hong Kong has reached a dead end … If the Umbrella Movement can't change it, nothing can. During the movement, laws were arbitrarily interpreted by the government and selectively executed by the police. This was very disrespectful and harmful to our profession. One day, the value of my profession and thus my career will go down …

> Will Hong Kong become just like China one day? Are we going to be discriminated and threatened if we work as defence lawyers for those who protest against the government? I only see a dark future ahead.

Zak was acutely aware of the future cost of migration. Yet, by extending his future visions in a do-or-die manner, with overseas freedom at one pole and political sanction in Hong Kong at the opposite, Zak considered migration to be a painful but perhaps necessary move.

Conclusions

This article has briefly discussed the case of Hong Kong as an example of future orientations that shape youth activism in times of crisis. Drawing insights from research on activist transformative stance, it foregrounds the importance of future orientations as loci for youth activism in response to social and political dislocations. In this view, future assumptions and aspirations are generative of youth activism within particular historical moments.

They inform grassroots resistance of young as well as their civic-political engagement in the long run. Yet, rather than predefined ideologies or unconscious by-products of material conditions, they are realised in people's direct engagement in meaningful activities out of the world while seeking to transform it.

Whilst acknowledging that not all young people with strong social imaginations became interested in contentious politics or participate in wider public activities that responded to the surging democratic crisis, it has been suggested that for those who did, the role of future orientations is critical in shaping their paths to/of activism. For the young people with stronger commitments to intervene the status quo, they undertook collective action in seeking to transform the existing conditions of the society. In many of these cases, it was neither an immediate threat to the youth's socio-economic status nor a political ideal of democracy that ignited their political activism. Rather, they variously voiced a desire for alternative futures in combating the status quo through direct engagement in the present. In some cases, not only did the young people take part in the historically unprecedented protest movement, but they also continued to participate in diverse civic activities and even formal politics after the Umbrella Movement ended. This is particularly reflected in the results of the 2015 District Council Election (*The Economist*, 2015; Time Out, 2015) and the more recent 2016 Legislative Council Election.

While the future orientations of many youth activists were reconfigured in their immediate encounters in the movement, they should be seen more as individual lifestyle perspectives that are strongly informed by the youth's everyday life and day-to-day experience. Unlike those who had been recruited by traditional social movement organisation as dutiful members, youth activists interviewed rarely direct their future plans towards policy change. Rather, they focused on struggling in real-world projects that organise their lives through the prism of a vision for the future. For them, emphasis was placed upon the shifts in their life goals so as to secure decent personal futures, as social change was regarded as less effective and likely than individual change.

This article contributes to the literature by examining the interplay between youth political activism and the future, particularly in the face of a democratic crisis. It has illustrated several ways in which perceptions of the future affect youth civic-political participation, and how future goals and identities are themselves (re-)constituted within political activism. These insights can inform scholarly discussion and debate about recent youth engagement in the civil society and contentious politics, as they capture the notion of future self being an unfolding process, thereby conveying that it is not something predefined but rather enacted through direct civic-political participation. This approach represents a step forward in overcoming the rhetoric and stereotype that interpreted youth activism as passive reaction to repression or abstract political anticipation. Instead, it refocuses our attention upon youth agency and everyday experiences that are likely to become essential for examining contemporary social struggles and should be included as an important site for further research.

Disclosure statement

No potential conflict of interest was reported by the author.

Funding

This work was supported by the Horowitz Foundation for Social Policy under the 2014 Horowitz Foundation Grant Award; and the Chiang Ching-Kuo Foundation for International Scholarly Exchange (USA) under Doctoral Fellowships DD031-A-14.

Notes on contributor

Tin-yuet Ting is Research Assistant Professor of Sociology in the Department of Applied Social Sciences, The Hong Kong Polytechnic University. His research focuses upon the intersection of social movements, digital media, globalisation, and youth citizenship.

References

Bendit, R. (2006). Youth sociology and comparative analysis in the European Union member states. *Papers: Revista de Sociologia, 79*, 49–76.

Bennett, W. L., & Segerberg, A. (2011). Digital media and the personalization of collective action: Social technology and the organization of protests against the global economic crisis. *Information, Communication & Society, 14*(6), 770–799.

Bennett, W. L. (2003). Communicating global activism: Strengths and vulnerabilities of networked politics. *Information, Communication & Society, 6*(2), 143–168.

Bennett, W. L. (2012). The personalization of politics: Political identity, social media, and changing patterns of participation. *The ANNALS of the American Academy of Political and Social Science, 644*, 20–39.

Bimber, B., Flanagin, A., & Stohl, C. (2012). *Collective action in organizations: Interaction and engagement in an era of technological change.* New York, NY: Cambridge University Press.

Bimber, B., Flanagin, A. J., & Stohl, C. (2005). Reconceptualizing collective action in the contemporary media environment. *Communication Theory, 15*(4), 365–388.

Cammaerts, B. (2012). Protest logics and the mediation opportunity structure. *European Journal of Communication, 27*(2), 117–134.

Canadian Youth Foundation. (1995). *Youth employment.* Ottawa: Canadian Youth Foundation.

Castells, M. (2012). *Networks of outrage and hope: Social movements in the internet age.* Oxford: Polity.

Cheal, D. (2003). Finding a niche: Age-related differentiations within the working-age population. In D. Juteau (Ed.), *Social differentiation: Patterns and processes* (pp. 81–116). Toronto: University of Toronto Press.

Cheng, E. W., & Chan, W. (2016). Explaining spontaneous occupation: Antecedents, contingencies and spaces in the Umbrella Movement. *Social Movement Studies, 16*(2), 222–239.

Clay, A. (2012). *The hip-hop generation fights back: Youth, activism and post-civil rights politics.* New York, NY: NYU Press.

Coe, A., Goicolea, I., Urtig, A., & Sebastain, M. S. (2015). Understanding how young people do activism: Youth strategies on sexual health in Ecuador and Peru. *Youth & Society, 47*(1), 3–28.

Della Porta, D., & Diani, M. (2006). *Social movements: An introduction.* Oxford: Blackwell.

Gordon, H. R. (2010). *We fight to win: Inequality and the politics of youth activism.* Rutgers, NJ: Rutgers University Press.

Harlow, S. (2011). Social media and social movements: Facebook and an online Guatemalan justice movement that moved offline. *New Media & Society, 14*(2), 225–243.

Indiatimes. (2012, August 2012). So, who's the youth? *Indiatimes.* Retrieved from http://timesofindia. indiatimes.com/life-style/spotlight/So-whos-the-youth/articleshow/15746136.cms

Jasper, J. M. (1997). *The art of moral protest: Culture, biography, and creativity in social movement.* Chicago, IL: University of Chicago Press.

Jeffrey, C. (2013). Geographies of children and youth III: Alchemists of the revolution? *Progress in Human Geography, 37*(1), 145–152.

Juris, J. (2008). *Networking futures: The movements against corporate globalization*. Durham, NCDuke University Press.

Juris, J. (2012). Reflections on occupy everywhere: Social media, public space, and emerging logics of aggregation. *American Ethnologist, 39*(2), 259–279.

Kirshner, B. (2007). Introduction: Youth activism as a context for learning and development. *American Behavioural Scientist, 51*(3), 367–379.

Kwon, S. A. (2013). *Uncivil youth: Race, activism and affirmative governmentality*. Durham, NC: Duke University Press.

Larson, R. W., & Hansen, D. (2005). The development of strategic thinking: Learning to impact human systems in a youth activism program. *Human Development, 48*(6), 327–349.

LeBon, G. (1895). *The crowd: A study of the popular mind*. Atlanta: Cherokee Publishing.

Lim, M. (2012). Clicks, cabs, and coffee houses: Social media and oppositional movements in Egypt, 2004–2011. *Journal of Communication, 62*, 231–248.

McAdam, D. (1982). *Political process and the development of black insurgency 1930-1970*. Chicago, IL: University of Chicago Press.

McAdam, D., Tarrow, S., & Tilly, C. (2001). *Dynamics of contention*. Cambridge, UK: Cambridge University Press.

McCarthy, J. D., & Zald, M. N. (1977). Resource mobilization and social movements: A partial theory. *American Journal of Sociology, 82*(6), 1212–1241.

Melucci, A. (1996). *Challenging codes: Collective action in the information age*. Cambridge, UK: Cambridge University Press.

Ming Pao. (2014, November 2014). Post-Umbrella Movement: Farewell to the political apathy. *Ming Pao (in Chinese)*. Retrieved from http://news.mingpao.com/pns/E5BE8CE99BA8E58298E9818BE 58B95EFBC9AE5918AE588A5E694BFE6B2BBE586B7E6849FE79A84E5B9B4E4BBA3-E4BD9CE88085 EFB995E984ADE78592E38081E8A281E7918BE78699/web_tc/article/20141129/s00012/14171975 42046

Ministry of Home Affairs, Heritage and Sports. (2002). *Kenya national youth policy*. Retrieved from http://www.youth-policy.com/Policies/Kenya20National20Youth%20Policy.pdf

Ortmann, S. (2015). The Umbrella movement and Hong Kong's protracted democratization. *Asian Affairs, 46*(1), 32–50.

Perovic, B. (2016). *Defining youth in contemporary legal and political frameworks across Europe*. Brussels: The European Knowledge Centre for Youth Policy.

Pratt, J. (2003). *Class, nation and identity: The anthropology of political movements*. London: Pluto Press.

The Rakyat Post. (2015, May 2015). New definition of youth age to be implemented in 2018, says Khairy. *The Rakyat Post*. Retrieved, from http://www.therakyatpost.com/news/2015/05/16/new-definition-of-youth-age-to-be-implemented-in-2018-says-khairy/

Schulz, M. (2016a). Social movement and futures research. *World Future Review, 8*(2), 98–107.

Schulz, M. (2016b). Debating futures: Global trends, alternative visions, and public discourse. *International Sociology, 31*(1), 3–20.

Schulz, M. (2016c). Social imagination and the politics of crisis. *Journal of the Brazilian Sociological Society, 2*(1), 46–59.

Shirky, C. (2008). *Here comes everybody: The power of organizing without organizations*. New York, NY: Penguin Press.

Silva, C. F. S., & de Castro, L. R. (2015). Brazilian youth activism: In search of new meanings for political engagement. *Alternatives: Global, Local, Political, 39*(3), 187–201.

Smelser, N. J. (1962). *Theory of collective behavior*. Glencoe, IL: Free Press.

Snow, D. A., Benford, R. D., Worden, S. K., & Benford, R. D. (1986). Frame alignment processes, micro-mobilization, and movement participation. *American Sociological Review, 51*, 464–481.

Stetsenko, A. (2010). Teaching-learning and development as activist projects of historical becoming: Expanding Vygotsky's approach to pedagogy. *Pedagogies: An International Journal, 5*(1), 6–16.

Stetsenko, A. (2015). Theory for and as social practice of realizing the future. In J. Martin, J. Sugarman, & K. L. Slaney (Eds.), *The Wiley handbook of theoretical and philosophical psychology: Methods, approaches, and new directions for social sciences* (pp. 102–116). Hoboken, NJ: Wiley.

Tarrow, S. (1996). States and opportunities: The political structuring of social movements. In D. McAdam, J. D. McCarthy, & M. N. Zald (Eds.), *Comparative perspectives on social movements: Political opportunities, mobilizing structures and cultural framings* (pp. 41–61). Cambridge, UK: Cambridge University Press.

Terriquez, A. (2011). Schools for democracy: Labor union participation and Latino immigrant parents' school-based civic engagement. *American Sociological Review, 76*, 581–601.

The Commonwealth. (2017). *Youth*. The Commonwealth. Retrieved from http://thecommonwealth. org/youth

The Economist. (2015, November 2015). A new force emerges in Hong Kong's politics. *The Economist*. Retrieve from http://www.economist.com/news/china/21679083-participants-huge-pro-democra cy-protests-year-ago-make-mark-neighbourhood-elections-new/

The Huffington Post. (2014, September 2014). Umbrella Revolution protests spread in Hong Kong. *The Huffington Post*. Retrieved from http://www.huffingtonpost.com/2014/09/29/hong-kong_n_ 5899116.html

Time Out. (2015, November 2015). Hong Kong's first election since Occupy: Meet the candidates. *Time Out*. Retrieved from http://www.timeout.com.hk/big-smog/features/74908/hong-kongs-first-election-since-occupy-meet-the-candidates.html/

Touraine, A. (1981). *The voice and the eye: An analysis of social movements*. Cambridge, UK: Cambridge University Press.

Vygotsky, L. S. (1997). *The collected work of L. S. Vygosky*. New York, NY: Plenum.

Vygotsky, L. S. (2004). *Essential Vygosky*. New York, NY: Kluwer.

Yalnizyan, A. (1998). *The growing gap*. Toronto: Centre for Social Justice.

Yuen, S. (2015). Hong. Kong After the Umbrella Movement: An uncertain Future for 'one country, two systems' . *China Perspectives, 1*, 49–54.

Zhang, W. (2013). Redefining youth activism through digital technology in Singapore. *The International Communication Gazette, 75*(3), 253–270.

Resistant identities: culture and politics among Kuwaiti youth

Emanuela Buscemi

ABSTRACT

The present paper investigates the role of youth in contemporary Kuwait, and how their diverse resistance strategies contest and challenge dominant cultural and political paradigms, affecting identity construction and social patterns. It examines the distance between the government and youth, and a growing crisis of representation through the analysis of three main areas of resistant practices enacted by youth, seemingly interdependent and possibly overlapping: political mobilisation, political radicalisation and civic engagement. Political mobilisation concerns the protests staged in Kuwait mainly in 2012; political radicalisation examines political violence and terrorist episodes, while civic engagement investigates examples from an invigorated civil society. The article investigates and addresses youth practices employing classic and alternative social movements literature developed in Latin America and the Middle East, together with original ethnographic data.

Introduction

Twenty-six years after the liberation from the Iraqi invasion, Kuwait is experiencing a severe economic crisis due to falling oil prices and the absence of significant political reforms (Gause, 2015). The National Assembly and the government have been unable to address budget cuts, including a reduction of benefits and welfare provisions, and have been struggling to increase the prices of petrol and other services (El-Katiri, 2016).

Memories of martyrs and atrocities juxtapose, in the national discourse, to the image of a united country, strong in fighting both external and internal pressures, as terrorism, radicalisation and recession. The government, thus, fosters and draws upon the concept of a national community, based upon shared cultural and social values, rooted in its Arab, Muslim and *Khaleeji*[1] identity. The 25th liberation anniversary in 2016, celebrated with military parades and gigantic pictures of the Emir and the crown prince, was marked by the repression operated against political activists and protesters, following Arab Spring-inspired demonstrations, and by an increased government vigilance over the internet and the social media (Buscemi, in press).

The lack of an honest political debate about the Invasion and its impact on the local society, together with a political stagnation, signal the distance the regime has produced in the last quarter of century between the leadership and the youth, failing to address the effects on the population of the nation's most traumatic event in recent history. And, similarly, failing to respond to the related emerging requests for reform.

The present paper investigates the role of youth in contemporary Kuwait, and how their diverse resistance strategies contest and challenge dominant cultural and political paradigms, affecting identity construction and social patterns. Three main areas of resistant practices are hereby addressed, seemingly interdependent and possibly overlapping: political mobilisation, political radicalisation and civic engagement.

The present article draws on original data collected through ethnographic work conducted in Kuwait between February and May 2013,[2] and between January 2014 and June 2016. Real names of research participants have been anonymised to protect their identity. Secondary sources are employed to complement primary data.

Youth, society and culture

Youth and resistance

The present article concentrates on youth and the elaboration of resistant identities and cultures in contemporary Kuwait. Youth is conceptualised here as a social construct and a social category relating to the passage between childhood and adulthood, respectively defined in terms of dependency and autonomy.

International organisations and institutions rely on age-groups to delimit it, and in particular UNESCO individuates the age group 15–24 to best describe youth in relation to education goals (United Nations Secretary-General's Report to the General Assembly, 1981), primarily for statistical purposes. Recent developments in youth studies go beyond the conceptualisation of young people as 'non adults', or a categorisation through the individuation of an age group, to adopt a relational approach (Wyn & White, 1997) that is culturally and historically determined.

Asef Bayat and Linda Herrera contextualise youth in contemporary Muslim countries, as

a kind of Burdeauian «habitus» that consists of a series of dispositions, mental and cognitive structures, and ways of being, feeling, and carrying oneself that are not consciously or rationally designed, yet follow a structure associated with the biological fact of being young. (2010, p. 6)[3]

To account for a multiplicity of languages, contexts and experiences, authors like Bennani-Chraïbi and Farag (2007), and Bonnefoy and Catusse (2013) address youth as *jeunesses*.

Youth characteristics such as negotiation with the older generations, a desire for change, rebellion against the establishment, the crafting of new practices and cultures or subcultures, become relevant when addressing resistance, intended as an oppositional confrontation. Resistance is shaped by 'systems of power [which] set the possibilities for distinct types of resistance to emerge' (Richter-Devroe, 2011, p. 34), as will be examined.

Kuwaiti society and culture

Kuwait is a hereditary Emirate, whose legislation relies on the Constitution approved and promulgated on 11 November 1962 after independence from the British rule the previous year. The resulting hybrid constitutional system concedes extended powers to the Head of State (Emir), in the framework of an absolute form of government.

The executive power is represented by the Emir, an Al-Sabah family member. The Al-Sabah family, ruling Kuwait since 1756, did not seize power by force, but rather through consensus, in consultation with other clans and tribes, to promote stability in the region. This pacific, nonviolent characteristic has defined Kuwaiti politics for much of the country's history (Casey, 2007).

The legislative power is embodied by the National Assembly *(Majlis al-Umma)*, the first established and longest standing Parliament in the Gulf. The local civil society, as a result, has been traditionally vocal and active, and its citizens[4] have engaged in charities and associations, both secular and religiously inspired (Ghabra, 1991). Political debate, however, is mainly channelled through *diwaniyyas*, domestic gatherings for men organised through tribal and sectarian divides, reproducing the existing societal cleavages. *Diwaniyyas*, traditionally led by heads of families or tribes, pre-date the Parliament as *loci* for the articulation of political debate and interests, providing patronage and brokerage (Redman, 2014).The prestige of these gatherings is determined by the role and social status of the host: the highest the social position, the more important the decisions and discussions that will take place in the *diwaniyya*. The most important ministry of the government, a sort of Emir's cabinet, is referred to as *Amiri Diwan*. For the same reason, existing youth *diwaniyya* explicate a more leisurely function.[5]

The National Assembly de facto amplifies the debate among sects and tribes and becomes a site for establishing power relations between conflicting groups and elites, magnifying their opposing interests. Limited access to the main *loci* of political debate is peculiar to three main groups: youth, women and the *bidūn*[6] (stateless). Through the construction of resistant identities, these groups embody the contradictions and limits of a nationalistic cultural order, displaying varied and conflicting social and political practices.

A glance at available statistical data allows to contextualise the situation of youth in the country. The Kuwaiti population is almost four million people, 30% of which are nationals and almost two-thirds are foreigners (Kuwait Central Statistical Bureau). The population is intrinsically young, as 56.7% of Kuwaitis are below 25 years of age.[7]

A generous welfare system provides Kuwaiti citizens with services, jobs and basic necessities, like food, water and electricity, as well as subsidised fuel. In terms of education, scholarships are offered to nationals to specialise in foreign universities, mainly in the United States and the United Kingdom. The increase in government scholarship schemes went from almost 6000 in 1998 to nearly 16,800 in 2013, more than triplicating the award of scholarships in 15 years.[8] As an increasing number of young Kuwaitis live abroad for study purposes, they become exposed to mainly Western concepts and ways of life. A number of these students tend to form a critical diaspora (see pages 5 and 7).

Another useful set of data concerning Kuwaiti youth is the relation with social media. Internet and social media usage is particularly high in Kuwait. According to the Arab Social Media Report 2012, Kuwait showed the second highest figures for Facebook users (as percentage of the population) among Arab countries (Arab Social Media Report, 2012). It is particularly relevant for youth, as the age group 15–29 accounts for over 70% of Facebook users in the region (Arab Social Media Report, 2012). Moreover, Kuwait has the highest Twitter penetration, and in 2012 its tweets amounted to 34% of all tweets in the Arab region (Arab Social Media Report, 2012). In 2012, during the protests, one of the most popular hashtag across the Arab Region was #kuwait (Arab Social Media Report, 2012).

The widespread Internet and social media access (Kaposi, 2014) has proved crucial for youth activists to initially avoid state censorship, both as mobilising tool for protests (Buscemi, 2016), as well as channelling extremist propaganda (Taylor, 2016), representing an alternative venue for political debate and networking.

Resistance theories between the Middle East and Latin America

The theoretical concept of resistant identities can be investigated through an exploration of different theories relating to the three main forms of resistance here analysed: while classical social movements theories apply to political mobilisation and political radicalisation, here within a specific Middle Eastern context, for civic engagement we will employ resistance theories and social movements theories developed both in the context of the Arab World and Latin America.

Political mobilisation, in the form of protests, manifestations and open movements targeting the establishment, can be conceptualised as a form of social movement due to its main characteristics of fluidity, intentionality (the existence of a cause), and the vindication of rights (primarily material interests) resulting in an open conflict (Neveu, 2005). Recent political mobilisation actions have revolved around identities, and the motivations of social movements actors are now conceptualised as a primary interest (della Porta & Diani, 2006). In particular, Alberto Melucci theorised about actors' engagement in attaining profound changes in society, in so doing challenging prevailing notions of politics via an elaboration of their individual identity through collective action (Melucci, 1982, 1989, 1996).

Political radicalisation emerges as deviant mobilisation, especially in its extremist form of terrorism, and revolves around 'intergroup conflict' (Mc Cauley & Moskalenko, 2008). Cultures of radicalisation root in local and transnational oppositional discourses and practices, often based on socio-religious interpretations, as in the case of the Middle East. Islam assumes the role of a mobilising agenda, and its literal application is envisioned as the ultimate goal, thus aspiring to having the state and religion coincide (Bonino, 2016). In regions like the Gulf, moreover, Islam represents a normative framework (Masud, Salvatore, & van Bruinessen, 2009), and its somehow totalising role in shaping society and culture can be manipulated to engender extremisms.

Civic engagement as a third form of youth resistant identity here examined, is conceptualised through alternative social movements theories developed in the contexts of the Middle East and Latin America. Asef Bayat and Linda Herrera refer to *subversive accommodation* as

> maneuvering within the constraints and making the best of what is available [...], extending between accommodation and subversion [...]. Youth operate within and thus use the dominant (constraining) norms and institutions [...] to accommodate their youthful claims, but in so doing they creatively redefine and subvert the constraints of those codes and norms. (2010, p. 18)

Moreover, 'social nonmovements' as the cumulative actions of individual actors (Bayat, 2009), become an analytical and methodological theory to address locally grounded social change, as well as actors and forms of engagement and agency typical of non-Western geopolitical and social contexts, contributing a new perspective and lexicon to the classical theories of social change and social movements. Bayat's theory relies heavily on the assumption that everyday challenges to the status quo in the form of mundane practices of daily life encompass a certain degree of creativity whose transformative effects are not immediately foreseen (Bayat, 2009).

The three forms of resistant identities here examined all share some common elements. First of all, the role of Islam as a 'crucial mobilizing theory and social movement frame' (Bayat, 2009, p. 7), both as founding theory or as a background element in more secular tendencies. Moreover, the role of the quotidian (de Certeau, 1984) as a common denominator of political actions through radicalisation, mobilisation or civic engagement. Thirdly, culture as a form of agency.

Alternative epistemological practices and creative participatory relations have been investigated in Latin America by Sonia Alvarez, Evelina Dagnino and Arturo Escobar, leading to the conclusion that all culture has a political nature: 'seek[ing] to redefine social power [...], deploy[ing] alternative conceptions [...] that unsettle dominant cultural meanings' (Alvarez, Dagnino, & Escobar, 1998, p. 7), in Latin America as in the Middle East. Culture is, thus, conceived as a process of meaning production, and as such as an integral part of social practices and movements, acquiring political meaning by challenging dominant political cultures.

The combination of these theories, and the deriving conceptualisations of nation, identity and social movements' practices, will provide the necessary theoretical framing for investigating alternative forms of cultural production and generation of symbols in Kuwait.

Political mobilisation

Resistance to the invasion and early 2000s campaigns

The first manifestation of resistant identities in Kuwait addressed in the present article is political mobilisation. The widespread resistance to the Iraqi invasion in 1990, both manifest and as underground movement, served as a pivotal moment for the formation of a sense of engagement and active patriotism (Badran, 1998) which shaped subsequent political forms of activism. After the liberation in 1991, women and youth campaigned for the extension of the suffrage and for political and social reforms. It was only in 2005 that the vote was granted to women, although the first women MPs would not be elected until 2009.

The beginning of a new millennium, thus, saw an increasing politicisation of the civil society with recurrent manifestations and protests. Youth, disaffectioned with the status quo and pursuing change through political reforms, targeted the establishment and challenged the prevailing political and social norms through a series of street actions (Diwan, 2014).

In 2006, youth activists launched the *Nabiha Khams* ('We want it to be five') electoral redistricting reform movement to contrast vote-buying and corruption. The movement, essentially liberal, attracted activists from different backgrounds and affiliations. It was promoted by young activists who had been politicised in university elections both locally and abroad (Albloshi & Alfahad, 2009), many of whom had been involved in the campaign for the extension of the suffrage. Protests were organised through a dedicated website and the extensive use of text messaging, while the orange colour was adopted in internet communication and worn in protests.[9] Innovative communication techniques had been previously used during the women's marches, together with more traditional methods like seeking the support of key *diwaniyya* leaders and the unofficial support of members of parliament through their own *diwaniyyas* (Gause, 2013). Once the electoral reform plan was approved, the campaign subsided. Although the redistricting did not have the expected political outcomes in terms of eradication of corruption, the movement signalled the renewed political mobilisation of young people and women, and was to gain momentum in the following years, capitalising on alternative emerging venues for participation and on new acquired mobilisation skills (Buscemi, 2016). Moreover, the reformed electoral law resulted in the first four women elected as members of Parliament in the following elections.

In 2009 a new campaign directed to the Prime Minister Sheik Nasser Al Mohammad Al Sabah, a key member of the ruling family, erupted in a series of protests sparked by corruption allegations[10] involving members of the parliament and high government representatives. Youth mobilised in the streets (Diwan, 2014) urging the Prime Minister to resign. The *Irhal* ('Leave') campaign was fuelled by document leaking through the social media and prompted youth political action: 'The ruling family came to power by negotiation [...], now they want everything. [They behave] as a royal family'.[11]

'A nation's dignity' and innovative mobilisation strategies

When corruption allegations reached members of the Parliament and cabinet figures in 2011, they ignited a series of protests inspired by the events of the Arab Spring taking place in Tunisia and Egypt. Widespread demonstrations involving tens of thousands of protesters from different political and religious affiliations were organised under the 'A Nation's Dignity' (*Karamat Watan*) campaign[12] in landmarks and symbolic national areas of the country, requesting a democratisation of the rule of law as well as political reforms for the introduction of political accountability.[13] Twitter was the main means of communication employed by activists to circumvent government censorship and facilitate the organisation of the protests,[14] also serving for live communications with foreign media and human rights organisations (Buscemi, in press).

Innovative mobilisation strategies envisaged by young protesters enhanced the visibility of the campaign, as mixed overnight sit-ins in front of the National Assembly,[15] or the desecration of national symbols. The latter was epitomised in the brief storming of the National Assembly by Kuwaiti youth[16] on 16 November 2011, claiming it as 'the house of the people'. A hunger strike ensued, followed by a declaration released by the protesters arrested during the storming, claiming they were detained without trial.[17] The declaration circulated over the Internet and social media in Arabic and English, to attract international sympathies in an attempt to globalise the local protests.[18] The presence of international journalists and the critical reports issued by human rights organisations[19] contacted by young protesters and human rights activists[20] catapulted Kuwait's protests in the context of the Arab Spring events. Moreover, the extensive use of the English language proves the activists' wider aspirations[21] and accounts for the increasing use of bilingualism in everyday Kuwait (Holes, 2011).

An innovative use of sarcasm and irony followed the storming of the Parliament, in the course of which protesters stole the speaker Marzouq Al-Ghanim's hammer (Darwish, 2011), traditionally used to moderate parliamentary sessions. The hammer was reproduced in several larger copies and displayed during rallies, sit-ins, house gatherings, public and private gardens, and posted on the social media, reiterating the intention to recur to street protests in case of unaccomplished reforms.[22]

The use of multiple symbolic spaces as protest sites added an innovative element in a street confrontation with the government that, unlike in other countries, did not identify the movement with a physical public space, as Tahrir square in Cairo, or Pearl Roundabout in Manama (Bahrein). Activists sought iconic traditional landmarks for manifestation locations, evoking symbols of national unity, like the National Assembly building, Herada and Safat squares in the city centre, the coastline Gulf Road, or the Kuwaiti Towers, mobilising memory and visions of a shared past in the course of the biggest and widely attended protests in the country's history, however never attempting to over-throw the regime, but only to reform it. Preoccupied with its youth activism, the establish-ment acted on various levels: extending material and financial benefits for the citizens, repressing dissent with censorship and incarceration, and launching a National Youth Project (NYP) designed to open an institutional dialogue with the youth.[23] The NYP, a tem-porary advisory board initiated by the Emir, was aimed at promoting youth initiatives and suggestions under the motto 'Kuwait's listening'. It had a short life, lasting throughout 2012–2013, and its initiatives and policy recommendation had limited effects on local legislation.

Innovative mobilisation strategies, the use of sarcasm and irony, the evocation of sym-bolic and historical landmarks as protest sites, the bilingual communication tactics, the activation of international channels and contacts, and the capacity to amplify the protests on multiple levels, all prove the rupture with the status quo and the desire for change enacted by Kuwaiti youth in devising inventive and provoking practices and method-ologies, all above examined as youth characteristics. While wearing the traditional *abaya* female attire and *dishdasha* men's garments, youth challenged prevailing social norms with mixed night sit-ins and mixed marches, in the course of manifestations that signalled the visibility not only of youth but of women, too, especially young women.

While youth activists took on the memory of the resistance to the invasion, often nar-rated by their parents or grandparents,[24] during the campaign for the extension of the suf-frage and the *Nabiha Khams* manifestations they became familiar with movements organisation and mobilisation, and in the course of the *Irhal* campaign they channelled popular indignation towards corrupted members of parliament and cabinet, defying the Emir's reiterated decision to reconfirm the prime minister.

With *Kharamat Watan* youth threatened to shake the system from its foundation, attracting international attention and placing Kuwait on the map of the Arab Spring-inspired protests. This mobilisation actions underline the desire to redefine identities, whether the protesters', the citizens' or the country's, in a framework that confirms both Alberto Melucci and Della Porta and Diani's theories concerning social movements, motiv-ations and identity (della Porta & Diani, 2006; Melucci, 1982, 1989, 1996).

Political radicalisation, islamic extremism and political violence

The second main manifestation of conflicting resistant identities is political radicalisation. The progressive islamisation of Kuwait's society from the end of the 1970s[25] originated from the attempt, on the part of the leadership, to counter the rising Arab nationalism in the form of progressive, secular and liberal ideologies, and as a strong opposition in the Parliament. The formation of religious groups springing from the Muslim Brotherhood or the Salafi movement alternatively, promoting a new Islamic recuperation of tradition under the provisions of *sharia*, led to the Islamists' control not only of the Parliament, but of a whole array of crucial institutions for the social and economic development of the country, among which charities, mosques, students' and teachers' associations at Kuwait University (at the time the only university in Kuwait), Islamic banking and professional societies (Al-Mughni, 2010).

Conservative laws were passed, mainly regarding the role of women in society and the preservation of traditional values in gender roles, increasingly targeting the youth population. Among these laws, one forcing early retirement upon working mothers after 15 years of service, and measures to impose gender segregation in public schools and universities.[26] After the liberation, Islamists have been a major political driving force in the National Assembly, attempting but not succeeding in introducing *sharia* as official rule (al-Mdaires, 2010). Kuwait has progressively shifted towards a more sustained islamisation, also to ensure stability and continuity for the ruling *élite*. Islamist groups have gained support among the local population, insisting on the primacy of Islam in all spheres of life, reinstating traditional attire, campaigning about traditional values and the importance of the family as a cornerstone of society.

Some groups and individuals have been politically radicalised in their support of extremism and political violence. In the 1990s, *Al-Qaeda* gained prominence among local extremists. Some Kuwaiti citizens were reported to be close collaborators of the terrorist group leader, while others were allegedly active militants.[27] Moreover, one of the group key figures was Abu Ahmed Al-Kuwaiti, a Kuwait-born militant of Pakistani origins.[28] The Islamist radical political groups gained global visibility after 9/11, and the Syrian civil war produced further radicalisation in the region, resulting in an increased political activism of cells and groups based in Kuwait,[29] and in political violence.

On 26 June 2015, a prominent Shia mosque in Kuwait city was bombed during the Friday prayer in the holy month of *Ramadan*.[30] The attack, in which 27 people were killed and over 200 injured, was claimed by ISIS militants,[31] and was perpetrated by a young Saudi extremist. It raised a number of questions regarding the Islamic State and its strategy to infiltrate local ethnic and social cleavages to recruit new young members in the Gulf countries.[32]

Following this attack, on 25 February 2016, a Kuwaiti 20-year-old man hit and killed a policeman and wounded five more who were patrolling one of the main roundabouts of the city during the national day celebrations. The attacker, who had been planning the killing for days, claimed to be affiliated with ISIS. The incident was initially reported as a terrorist attack, although the young man's family later released a statement clarifying that he suffered from mental health issues. Moreover, last June 2016 the Ministry of Interior claimed to have foiled some terrorist plots[33] involving Kuwaitis, among which a young boy. Another violent episode occurred on 10th October 2016, when a suicide attack failed as an explosive loaded truck attacked a vehicle from the United States army.[34]

These violent events all involved young nationals or other young Gulf citizens mobilised and radicalised to ISIS, in a process involving, as has been analysed above, extremist interpretations of Islam as 'mobilizing theory and social movements frame' (Bayat, 2009, 7). Political radicalisation is rooted also in local cleavages and politics of ethnic stratification whereby the establishment has, over the years, promoted, coopted or marginalised groups or sections of the populations over others for its perpetuation in power (Buscemi, 2016). This peculiar political culture resonates in the words of a university professor I met in Kuwait:

> I started writing in a newspaper, and my writing got a little bit of attention [...] when I started writing about *Hezbollah*. And it was very disturbing, because I come from [a] Shia family, and so, if I come from [a] Shia family, I have to support [them], right or wrong. And so this created a buzz within the community, and the international institutions started hearing of this [...]. People [were] reacting to the articles [...], but there were some aggravations.[35]

The woman, who is also a political activist and a human rights advocate for the *bidūn*, received death threats for her political positions. Moreover, some male members of her family were harassed in *diwaniyyas*, and threatened to lose their businesses. The words from the interview underline the profound cleavages in the Kuwaiti society, and how the local political culture can translate into further divisions among the population.

The same divisions surface in the case of local involvement with the conflict in Syria, either through recruits or financing (Dickinson, 2013). News have reported arrests of Kuwaitis supporting terrorist attacks in Syria or through terrorist groups based in Syria; some other Kuwaiti youths have been repatriated from Syria for their involvement in acts of political violence or ISIS-related illicit political activities in third countries.[36] Moreover, Kuwaitis are fundraising for the Syrian conflict, with Shia and Sunni donating for opposition factions.[37]

According to American sources, Kuwait is one of the main countries through which fundraising for terrorist groups in Syria is channelled,[38] through *diwaniyyas*, local charities and online methodologies, with some MPs openly admitting to actively finance Syrian rebels.[39] Unlike other Gulf countries, Kuwait has decided not to provide military support to Syrian rebels, provoking the discontent of many citizens.

Ethnic and social cleavages reproduce intergroup conflict (Mc Cauley & Moskalenko, 2008) as a main mechanism for the perpetration of political violence, while youth, actively involved in attacks, external support or fundraising activities, is being radicalised locally and through international networks. For extremist groups, as examined above, Islam, or better, its deviant versions, assume the role of 'mobilizing agenda' (Masud et al., 2009), shaping beliefs and actions.

Resistance through civic engagement

The third main declination of resistant identities in Kuwait is civic engagement. Historically, and arguably to support projects of nation building and regime perpetuation (Buscemi, 2016), civil society has been relatively more lively in Kuwait than in other Gulf countries (Gause, 2013). The recent emergence of groups, collectives, associations, platforms, active in civil society through engagement in culture, arts, environment and preservation, architecture, solidarity with deprived groups, however, is marked by a conscious choice to operate outside official channels of participation and refusing to seek government sponsorship. Informality allows for flexibility and adaptability of these fluid civic structures, while avoiding state censorship.

Civil society groups are mainly composed of youth and women previously socialised to volunteerism through human rights organisations, both local or international, high school and/or university clubs and elections, religious community groups, or by joining groups in the diaspora, being exposed to new ideas and activism when studying abroad, or attending local private schools (Buscemi, in press). As government repression turned harsh, with the detention of protestors, increased censorship over the internet, traditional and social media, stripping nationals of their citizenship and cracking down on freedom of expression (Human Rights Watch, 2015), activists turned to civil society and renewed forms of civic engagement, or reactivated already existing ties.

Rhoda, an entrepreneur, private sector employee and human rights activist, explains the reason of her engagement in society:

> Since I was little, I'd think of everything in Kuwait critically, and I hear how people always complain [...]. In university I decided I needed to do something about it instead of just complaining and thinking «I wish this was different». I noticed a lot of minority groups that are oppressed in Kuwait. I feel like that was a push for me [...] do something and change things [...]. Just bring[ing] it all together.[40]

Urban projects, gardening communities, art collectives, design forums, itinerant markets, mixed cultural *diwaniyyas*,[41] organic lifestyle social gatherings, charities, literary groups, have become a feature of Kuwaiti social and cultural life. The relevance of these projects invests also the political arena, although in a more nuanced, less confrontational attitude, circumventing the government restrictions and pushing the boundaries for a more active and conscientious citizenship. These experiences and experiments draw upon a heightened 'sense of community'[42] while 'creating a dialogue and ruffling some feathers'.[43]

Civic engagement, like the previous two forms of resistant identities, is rooted in identity, in the necessity for Kuwaiti youth and women to overcome disconnection and to forge alternative cultural and political practices. As Salwa, a food writer, explains:

> I had this idea of accumulating all the recipes from my childhood into a book [...], then I decided to explore the different food venues. [It] was [...] lovely [...] for me to find a way creatively to negotiate my first culture. [...] what definitely motivates me is the need to connect. [...] this is still part of me, and I need to find a way [...] to bridge the gap in a creative way.[44]

Through multiple individual or collective projects, youth engages in fostering community while re-signifying belonging and citizenship, often operating outside formal channels but reinvigorating a pre-existing culture. It is precisely through this *subversive accommodation* (Bayat & Herrera, 2010) that youth tries to affect social change while recuperating a sense of community by affinity. The sum of individual actions aims at promoting reform in society and awareness raising, challenging the establishment in the quotidian, as Bayat identified with his theory of *social nonmovements*. As Hala, a designer and co-founder of a cultural platform, points out:

> I feel like we are reviving something that always existed, Kuwait always had culture. [...] we're just reviving an existing instinct in the youth [...] and creating acceptance again for it in society. [...] we have to also value the tradition itself, but not be constrained by it.[45]

Conclusions

Kuwaiti youth, caught between conflicting local social requests and wider aspirations, instilled by modernity and its declinations, have developed forms of resistant identities, among which political mobilisation, political radicalisation and civic engagement have been examined in the present article. The three features are characterised by a shift of political socialisation and activism, and the extension of political debate to more informal venues of participation, beyond the Parliament and the *diwaniyyas*, the aggregating role of social media, and the elaboration of new projects of participation in society and resistance to the establishment, marking a disaffection towards traditional politics in Kuwait and its canons. A great motivation and a large part of the recent cultural antagonistic production lies in Islam as founding element of identity building (Wadud, 1999), socialisation and cultural reference for nation and institutional building. Islam does not work as a strong, founding motivation only for radical Islamism or for visible, openly confrontational social movements' struggles, but is also the driving force for re-signifying collective identity through processes of creative cultural transgression.

Emblematic of the distance between the establishment and Kuwaiti youth was the participation of the country in the 2016 Rio Olympic Games. As Kuwait had once more been suspended by the International Olympic Committee (and other international sports federations) over state interference on sports organisations, its young athletes competed under the IOC flag, the only country to have been suspended, among representatives of countries at war, or which had been sanctioned, or among those refugees that the Kuwait government did not allow in the country.[46]

Notes

1. *Khaleeji* is the common Arabic adjective and noun referring to the Gulf.
2. The earlier interviews were co-conducted with Samyah Alfoory.
3. The authors, however, identify an age group marked by the birth year, namely between 1979 and 1993, as the youth on which they focus their research.
4. Citizenship is passed through patrilinearity, through the father's line. Alternatively, foreign women married to nationals can apply for it and receive it after a number of years.
5. Interview with Khaled, 25th January 2015, Kuwait.
6. Figures about *bidūn* presence in Kuwait are variable. According to Claire Beaugrand, they represent around 10% of the local population, estimating their number in about 100,000 people (Beaugrand, 2018).
7. Author's personal elaboration on 2013 data. See http://gulfmigration.eu/
8. Author's elaboration on UNESCO data (UNESCO UIS). www.uis.unesco.org
9. Interview with Lina, Kuwait, 6 May 2013.
10. http://www.al-monitor.com/pulse/politics/2012/10/kuwaiti-youth-look-forward-to-new-political-epoch.html
11. Interview with Sama, Kuwait, 23 April 2013.
12. Interview with Lina, Kuwait, 6 May 2013.
13. Interview with Seema, Kuwait, 20 April 2013.
14. Interview with Sama, Kuwait, 23 April 2013.
15. http://www.reuters.com/article/us-kuwait-politics-sitin-idUSBRE89F0HI20121016
16. http://studies.aljazeera.net/mritems/Documents/2011/12/12/2011121271015281734Kuwait_The%20dilemma%20of%20the%20Popular%20Movement%20and%20Political%20Power.pdf
17. https://globalvoices.org/2011/12/05/kuwait-a-new-prime-minister-and-detainees-bailed-out/
18. Interview with Lina, Kuwait, 6 May 2013.
19. https://www.hrw.org/world-report/2012/country-chapters/kuwait
20. Interview with Sama, Kuwait, 23 April 2013.
21. Interview with Ghadir, Kuwait, 15 May 2013.
22. Interview with Lina, Kuwait, 6 May 2013.

23. http://www.huffingtonpost.com/magda-abufadil/abdulaziz-sadeq-spearhead_b_1714192.html

24. Interview with Hala, 22 February 2015.

25. This *islamisation* was officially declared by government decree in 1978 as the application of Islam and its principles to all spheres of active life.

26. The segregation measures were later mitigated with the institution of private universities.

27. http://edition.cnn.com/2016/01/08/politics/guantanamo-detainee-released-kuwait/

28. http://www.bbc.com/news/world-south-asia-13300680

29. http://www.agsiw.org/biduns-in-the-face-of-radicalization-in-kuwait/

30. http://english.alarabiya.net/en/News/middle-east/2015/06/26/Explosion-hits-mosque-in-Kuwait-during-Friday-prayers-.html

31. http://www.aljazeera.com/news/2015/06/isil-claim-responsibility-kuwait-shia-mosque-attack-150626124555564.html

32. http://www.thearabweekly.com/Top-Stories/978/In-Kuwait%2C-ISIS-tried-to-exploit-vulnerabilities

33. http://www.nytimes.com/2016/07/04/world/middleeast/kuwait-isis-shiite-muslims.html?_r=0

34. http://english.alarabiya.net/en/News/middle-east/2016/10/10/US-embassy-Troops-in-Kuwait-came-under-terrorist-attack.html

35. Interview with Eman, 7 May 2015.

36. http://timesofindia.indiatimes.com/india/Kuwait-arrests-man-suspected-of-funding-ISIS-sympathisers-in-India/articleshow/53571994.cms

37. http://foreignpolicy.com/2013/12/04/shaping-the-syrian-conflict-from-kuwait/

38. Matthew Lewitt and Lori Plotkin Boghardt, 'Funding ISIS', 2014. http://www.washingtoninstitute.org/policy-analysis/view/funding-isis-infographic Matthew Lewitt, 'Terrrorist Financing and the Islamic State', 2014. https://www.washingtoninstitute.org/uploads/Documents/testimony/LevittTestimony20141113.pdf Lori Plotkin Boghardt, 'The Terrorist Funding of Disconnect With Qatar and Kuwait', 2014, The Washington Institute. http://www.washingtoninstitute.org/policy-analysis/view/the-terrorist-funding-disconnect-with-qatar-and-kuwait

39. http://www.newsweek.com/2014/11/14/how-does-isis-fund-its-reign-terror-282607.html?piano_t=1

40. Interview with Nura, Kuwait, 29 January 2015.

41. These alternative *diwaniyyas* adopt the name of the traditional domestic male gatherings, but are very different in nature: not gender segregated, open and conducted in semi-public venues like professionals' studios, following schedules that are not regular, they are rather cultural meetings and informal discussions.

42. Interview with Seema, Kuwait, 5 February 2015.

43. Interview with Sondus, Kuwait, 11 April 2015.

44. Interview with Salwa, Kuwait, 28 January 2015.

45. Interview with Hala, Kuwait, 9 May 2015.

46. https://www.washingtonpost.com/news/worldviews/wp/2015/09/04/the-arab-worlds-wealthiest-nations-are-doing-next-to-nothing-for-syrias-refugees/?utm_term=.cf3460d7f848

Disclosure statement

No potential conflict of interest was reported by the author.

Notes on contributor

Emanuela Buscemi is a doctoral candidate in Sociology at the School of Social Science of the University of Aberdeen, Scotland, and a research associate at CEFAS – *Centre Français d'Archéologie et de Sciences Sociales*, Kuwait. She is a former instructor of the American University of Kuwait (AUK).

References

Albloshi, H., & Alfahad, F. (2009). The orange movement of Kuwait: Civic pressure transforms a political system. In M. J. Stephan (Ed.), *Civilian jihad: Nonviolent struggle, democratization, and governance in the Middle East* (pp. 219–233). New York, NY: Palgrave Macmillan.

al-Mdaires, F. A. (2010). *Islamic extremism in Kuwait: From the Muslim brotherhood to Al-Qaeda and other Islamist political groups*. Oxon: Routledge.

Al-Mughni, H. (2010). The rise of Islamic feminism in Kuwait. *Revue des mondes musulmans et de la Méditerranée [Journal of Muslim Worlds and the Mediterranean]*, 128, 167–182.

Alvarez, S. E., Dagnino, E., & Escobar, A. (Eds.). (1998). *Cultures of politics, politics of cultures: Re-visioning Latina American social movements*. Boulder, CO: Westview Press.

Badran, M. (1998). Gender, Islam and the State: Kuwait women in struggle. In H. Y. Yazbeck & J. Esposito (Eds.), *Islam, gender and social change* (pp. 190–208). New York, NY: Oxford University Press.

Bayat, A. (2009). *Life as politics: How ordinary people change the Middle East*. Cairo: The American University in Cairo Press.

Bayat, A., & Herrera, L. (2010). *Being young and Muslim: New cultural politics in the global South and North*. Oxford: Oxford University Press.

Beaugrand, C. (2018). *Stateless in the Gulf: Migration, nationality and society in Kuwait*. London: I.B. Tauris.

Bennani-Chraïbi, M., & Farag, I. (Eds.). (2007). *Jeunesses des sociétés arabes. Par delà les promesses et les menaces* [Youth in Arab Societies: Beyond Promises and Threats]. Paris: Au lieux d'être.

Bonino, S. (2016). Violent and non-violent political Islam in a global context. *Political Studies Review*. Retrieved from http://journals.sagepub.com/doi/abs/10.1177/1478929916675123?journalCode=pswa

Bonnefoy, L., & Catusse, M. (Eds.). (2013). *Jeunesses arabes. Du Maroc au Yémen: loisirs, cultures et politiques* [Arab Youth. From Morocco to Yemen: Leisure Time, Cultures and Politics]. Paris: La Découverte.

Buscemi, E. (2016). *Abaya* and yoga pants: Women's activism in Kuwait. *AG About Gender – International Journal of Gender Studies*, 5(10), Retrieved from http://www.aboutgender.unige.it/index.php/generis/issue/view/17

Buscemi, E. (in press). Reclaiming space(s): Kuwaiti women in the protests. In R. Stephan & M. M. Charrad (Eds.), *Women rising: Resistance, revolution and reform in the Arab spring and beyond*. New York: New York University Press.

Casey, M. S. (2007). *The history of Kuwait*. Westport, CT: Greenwood Press.

Darwish, B. (2011, November 21). Hooligans Tarnishing democracy. *Kuwait Times*. Retrieved from http://news.kuwaittimes.net

de Certeau, M. (1984). *The practice of everyday life* (Rendall S. Trans). Berkeley, CA: University of California Press.

della Porta, D., & Diani, M. (2006). *Social movements: An introduction* (2nd ed.). Malden, MA: Blackwell.

Dickinson, E. (2013). Shaping the Syrian conflict from Kuwait. *Foreign Policy*, December 4. Retrieved from www.foreignpolicy.com

Diwan, K. S. (2014). Breaking taboos: Youth activism in Gulf states. *Atlantic Council Issue Brief*. Retrieved from http://www.atlanticcouncil.org/publications/issue-briefs/breaking-taboos-youth-activism-in-the-gulf-states

Dubai School of Government (2012). Social media in the arab world: Influencing societal and cultural change? *Arab Social Media Report* 1(2). Retrieved from www.arabsocialmediareport.com.

El-Katiri, L. (2016). Vulnerability, resilience and reform: The GCC and the Oil price crisis 2014–2016. Columbia Center on Global Energy Policy. Retrieved from http://energypolicy.columbia.edu/sites/default/files/energy/Vulnerability%2C%20Resilience%20and%20Reform%3A%20The%20GCC%20and%20the%20Oil%20Price%20Crisis.pdf

Gause, G. F. I. I. I. (2013). "Nabiha 5": A Kuwaiti youth movement for political reform. AUB Background Paper. Retrieved from https://www.aub.edu.lb/ifi/public_policy/arab_youth/Documents/background_paper/20130314ifi_wps_Gregory_Gause.pdf

Gause, G. F. I. I. I. (2015). Sultans of swing? The geopolitics of falling oil prices. Brookings Doha Center Policy Briefing. Retrieved from https://www.brookings.edu/wp-content/uploads/2016/06/Falling-Oil-Prices-English.pdf

Ghabra, S. N. (1991). Voluntary associations in Kuwait: The foundation of a new system? *Middle East Journal, 45*(2), 199–215.

Holes, C. D. (2011). Language and identity in the Arab Gulf. *Journal of Arabian Studies: Arabia, the Gulf and the Red Sea, 1*(2), 129–145.

Human Rights Watch. (2015). World report of 2015: Events of 2014. Retrieved from https://www.hrw.org/world-report/2015.

Kaposi, I. (2014). The culture and politics of internet use among young people in Kuwait. *Cyberpsychology: Journal of Psychosocial Research on Cyberspace, 8*(3). Retrieved from https://cyberpsychology.eu/article/view/4318/3368

Kuwait Central Statistical Bureau. Population estimates in mid-year. Retrieved from www.csb.gov.kw

Masud, M., Salvatore, A., & van Bruinessen, M. (2009). *Islam and modernity. Key issues and debates.* Edinburgh: Edinburgh University Press.

Mc Cauley, C., & Moskalenko, S. (2008). Mechanisms of political radicalization: Pathways toward terrorism. *Terrorism and Political Violence, 20*, 415–433.

Melucci, A. (1982). *L'invenzione del presente: movimenti, identità, bisogni individuali.* Bologna: Il Mulino.

Melucci, A. (1989). *Nomads of the present.* London: Hutchinson Radius.

Melucci, A. (1996). *Challenging codes.* Cambridge, UK: Cambridge University Press.

Neveu, É. (2005). *Sociologie des mouvements sociaux* [Sociology of Social Movements]. Paris: La Découverte.

Redman, J. C. A. (2014). *The diwaniyya: Guestroom sociability and bureaucratic brokerage in Kuwait* (Doctoral dissertation). University of Utah.

Richter-Devroe, S. (2011). Palestinian women's everyday resistance: Between normality and normalisation. *Journal of International Women's Studies Special Issue, 12*(2), 32–46.

Taylor, E. (2016). The internet in the Gulf countries: How issues of internet access and cybercrime impact the region. London: Chatham House. Retrieved from https://www.chathamhouse.org/sites/files/chathamhouse/events/2016-01-12-internet-in-the-gulf-countries-meeting-summary.pdf

UNESCO UIS. International student mobility in tertiary education. Retrieved from www.data.uis.unesco.org

United Nations Secretary-General. (1981). Report to the general assembly, A/36/215. Retrieved from www.un.org

Wadud, A. (1999). *Qu'ran and woman. Rereading the sacred text from a woman's perspective.* New York, NY: Oxford University Press.

Wyn, J., & White, R. (1997). *Rethinking youth.* Crows Nest: Allen and Unwin.

Between rap and jihad: spectacular subcultures, terrorism and visuality

Uliano Conti

ABSTRACT
This article underlines the importance of terrorist jihadist online communication. The visual expressions of sociocultural identity are a trademark of jihadist terrorist groups. This paper also shows that subcultural perspective constitutes a privileged point of view for the analysis of the phenomenon of Western-born jihadist terrorism. In scientific literature there is a lack of empirical research on the visual dimension of jihadist terrorism in a subcultural perspective. In this perspective, the article analyses the subcultural identity of a Western-born jihadist terrorist, the former rapper Deso Dogg, also known as Abu-Maleeq. This paper proposes an original analysis of terrorist group membership, analysing through visual sociology the YouTube videos of Deso Dogg – Abu-Maleeq. The visual jihadist representation is based on the repetition of semantic elements. This result confirms the importance of the semantic coherence of communication, namely the Hebdigian homology. Furthermore, terrorist communication assigns new meanings to traditional cultural elements. This result confirms the relevance of the subcultural practice of *bricolage*. In conclusion, the article allows an original perspective for the study of terrorist communication and underlines the importance of Hebdigian perspective for the understanding of what processes turned troubled Western youth into terrorists.

1. Terrorism, subcultures, visuality

Deso Dogg, alias Abu-Maleeq, born in Berlin, former rapper; L Jinny, alias Jihadi John, born and raised for a few years in Kuwait, former rapper; Mc Kahlif, alias Al Italy, born and raised for a few years in Morocco, former rapper; Omar Abdel Hamid El-Hussein, born in Denmark of Jordanian-Palestinian parents, former member of the gang *Brothas*; Michael Adebowale, born in London of Nigerian parents, former member of the gang *Woolwich boys* and Bastian Vasquez, alias Abu Safiyya, born in Norway of Chilean parents, are all examples of young people who have grown up in Western cities, like the Italians Giuliano Ibrahim Delnevo and Maria Giulia Sergio, alias Fatima Az Zahra, listening to rap music and smoking marijuana, just like many other thousands of young people in cities around the world. These dynamics, coupled with their *status* as second-generation immigrants

(Baba Faye, 2011),[1] are not the reason they are considered famous. What singles them out is the fact they have all since enrolled as terrorists in extremist jihadist groups.

Scientific literature considers terrorism from different perspectives (Victoroff, 2005). It tries to understand if terrorists may be considered as individuals suffering from psycho-pathologies. Some studies on groups such as *Hezbollah* claim that no psychopathological disorders emerge among their members (Crenshaw, 1981). The viewpoint concentrating on the psychopathological characteristics of terrorists has been criticised (Ferracuti, 1982; Victoroff, 2005). For example, noticing the prosociality of terrorists, Della Porta (1988) has refused the lone wolf stereotype. The sociopath or the mentally ill may exist among terrorists, but terrorists are not, by fact of their political violence, necessarily socio-pathic or mentally ill (Ferracuti, 1982; Orsini, 2009).

Attention has also been focused on socio-demographic factors which could favour the growth of terrorist groups. Using variables ascribable to education and socio-economic condition as explanatory factors, referring to European groups of the Sixties and Seventies, it appears that disadvantaged socio-economic conditions are not explanatory factors for why people join terrorist groups (Orsini, 2012). However, when we examine the case of Palestinian groups of the Eighties, poverty assumes an active role in the choice to join ter-rorist groups. Since the end of the Nineties, in the analyses of explanatory factors, scholars refer to a wide socio-demographic range: in fact there are women, professionals, university students among terrorists (Victoroff, 2005). Some studies look at the dynamics of group processes. In this perspective, the main character of terrorism is that it is a group phenom-enon based on indoctrination and on communication processes of reciprocal influence among people (Sageman, 2004).

Terrorism has traditionally used communication as a tool in its struggles (Lombardi, 2015). Hatred on the web has been studied with particular attention to the contents and language used by the Al Qaida websites and web platforms (Roversi, 2006). Lombardi (2015) underlines the role of ISIS communication in promoting processes of self-indoctri-nation as a result of a process of radicalisation or, expressed in other words, of the Islami-sation of radicalism: adhesion to the terrorist group is seen as a falsely religious veneer covering radical and violent behavioural aptitudes (Roy, 2015).

Web platforms such as YouTube are an important piece of the ISIS communication strategy. The themes are the promotion of terrorist activities and the recruitment. Many propaganda videos are created with very good graphics and in colour spreading the world vision of the terrorist group (Lombardi, 2015). A strong link between visuality and extremist propaganda exist: 'The domain of ideology coincides with the domain of signs (semiology) as they equate with one another. Whenever a sign is present, ideology is present too. Everything ideological possesses a semiotic value' (Volosinov, 1973, p. 79). The analysis of the videos allows us to study the jihadist extremism and to further identify visual narratives like those of violence. An exemplary case of violence transmitted via the web is represented by the decapitation video, like that of the reporter James Foley. This video was broadcast online and then continued on social networks and in online maga-zines (Vergani & Bliuc, 2015; Vergani & Zuev, 2015). With regard to the narrative regime, a study needs to be considered upon the use of YouTube by jihadist groups. Vergani and Zuev (2015) analyse videos on YouTube on the part of jihadist groups made by jihadist groups depicting the conflicts in Chechnya and Xinjiang: the analysis of the videos allows us to identify the visual narratives of war, of victimisation, of violent brotherhood (Vergani & Zuev, 2015).

Web platforms are not the only media channel used by terrorists. ISIS uses social network channels as a means of communication, along with websites and web platforms. The ISIS communications strategy integrates multiple media channels (Lombardi, 2015). It includes social networks such as Twitter and Facebook. Images, photographs and videos play a fundamental role. The different channels of communication have in common a stylistic coherence between graphics, photos and videos and a narrative regime which also calls for video scripts created according to cinematographic or television series standards (Lombardi, 2015). Among the languages that human beings use, the ones of a visual nature are particularly relevant with regard to the topic in question.

The studies dedicated to the role of images in the terrorist communication (Lombardi, 2015; Vergani & Zuev, 2015) adopt a semiotic and interpretivist intellectual stance in the analysis of images. This is coherent with the fact that the studies on the visual dimension of social phenomena have traditionally used a qualitative research strategy (Chalfen, 1987; Margolis & Pauwels, 2011; Palumbo & Garbarino, 2006). Looking at the factors that have come to light as explanatory with regard to terrorism, we note the recent attention given to the subcultural group membership (Reem & Pisoiu, 2014; Sageman, 2004). The youths previously mentioned here are all attackers and former members of spectacular subcultural groups (Hebdige, 1979, 1988). Before joining terrorist groups, they were members of subcultures. Some of them were members of non-criminal spectacular subcultures like hip hop, others belonged to criminal spectacular subcultures such as gangs. After having been a part of subcultures, occidental youths of various cultural origin, as well as native Europeans, tend to choose a form of authoritarian communitarianism as a way to develop their own adult identity (Touraine, 1997). The subcultural perspective helped establish an original point of view for the analysis of the home-grown European jihadist terrorism.

Studies underline the importance of style and sociocultural identity for the members of subcultures. The outfits they wear are one fundamental way of expressing this identity. Visual signs expressing subcultural identity such as their way of dressing, physical appearance, makeup, hairstyle, personal objects and gadgets, circulate through the media (Hebdige, 1979, 1988).

2. British subcultural perspective, jihadist terrorism and spectacularity

In order to consider the issues of jihadism terrorism, communication and visuality when using the concept of subculture, it is possible to look at one theoretical approach: the so-called subcultural approach of British origin from the Birmingham Centre for Contemporary Cultural Studies. This approach used a Neo-Gramscian perspective in a project of class analysis sympathetic with the symbolic resistance of working class youth (Hall & Jefferson, 1976; Williams, 2011). An important point drawn by the British approach holds that the problems experienced by the subcultural members are magically resolved (Hebdige, 1979, 1988) in spectacular expressions of style. The subcultural groups' counter-response to mainstream culture is centred around age and social class and expresses itself in the creation of alternative spectacular styles such as mods, punk and skinhead (Cohen, 1972). Such alternative styles are attempt to resist bourgeois hegemony. Resistance is carried out through the meaning of signs (Hebdige, 1979, 1988). The spectacular stylistic expressions of resistance are conceptualised as bricolage (i.e. the way in which traditional meanings are radically subverted) and as homology (i.e. the symbolic coherence among values, lifestyle, music and subjective experience). Homology is a structural resonance 'between the different elements making up a socio-cultural whole' (Middleton, 1990, p. 9). Hebdige cited Willis's (1978) use of the term homology to identify:

> The symbolic fit between the values and lifestyle of a group, its subjective experience and the music forms it uses to express or reinforce its focal concerns [...]. The internal structure of any particular subculture is characterized by an extreme orderliness: each part is organically related to other parts and it is through the fit between them that the subcultural member makes sense of the world. (Hebdige, 1979, p. 113)

The term *bricolage* is intended as follows:

> Together, object and meaning constitute a sign, and, within any one culture, such signs are assembled, repeatedly, into characteristic forms of discourse. However, when the bricoleur re-locates the significant object in a different position within that discourse, using the same overall repertoire of signs, or when that object is placed within a different total ensemble, a new discourse is constituted, a different message conveyed. (Hall & Jefferson, 1976, p. 177)

Notions such as homology and *bricolage* (Hebdige, 1979) are still usefully applicable to the contemporary terrorism. In the studies on European jihadist terrorism Pisoiu (2012) feels that the terms *bricolage* and homology can be used. The meaning of traditional cultural elements is subverted into an extremist jihadist sense. For example, *nasheeds* are traditional chants focusing on the lyrics and battle-*nasheeds*,[2] chants with highly militant lyrics, play a central role within the musical genre pop-jihad (Danschke, 2013, p. 15). In conclusion, the studies on terrorism underline the importance of the processes of indoctrination and mutual influence among people. These processes are articulated also through the media. In the ISIS communication strategy, images play a privileged role: videos, photographs, photomontages, magazines, online games are based on visual language. One gap may be identified in the literature under consideration. In the analyses of the visuality and of the visual semantic elements of terrorist communication, spectacular subcultural perspective has not been held in sufficient consideration. The sense of belonging to a subculture is an important characteristic in the recruitment of youths within terrorist groups. In essence, terrorist groups may be studied as criminal subcultural groups. There is a lack of analysis of the visual aspects of terrorist communication considered in a subcultural perspective. With regard to the current literature on terrorism, it is clear that to gain a clearer picture the scientific community needs to take into account the visual expressions of subcultural identity.

3. Web and jihadist terrorist subculture. methodology and visual research tools

In the last years, the debate on subcultures has been considered in relationship to computer-mediated communication (Castells, 1996; Robards & Bennet, 2011). Membership in spectacular subcultural groups, whether they are criminal or non-criminal, manifests itself in forms of online and offline aggregation. In this regard, the ecosystem of media communication is an area of inquiry. Those who belong to deviant or criminal subcultures express themselves using computer-mediated communication including photographic images and videos.

In order to analyse youth subcultural identity expressions and sense of group membership, computer-mediated communication should be given adequate consideration. The relationship between subcultures and computer-mediated communication is deep, so much so that some speak of an online community as an electronic network of communication with a shared purpose (Jenkins, 2006). In the last decade, many scholars go beyond the online–offline dichotomy, considering these two dimensions as closely related (Davis, 2010). Some studies (McArthur, 2009), instead of separating online and offline, study the close relationship between virtual and real, showing that participating in online communities can facilitate face to face interaction.

Considering the use of web platforms, some scholars speak of digital subcultures (McArthur, 2009). The web is considered a *medium* which, on the one hand, keeps barriers between groups and reinforces subcultural membership. On the other hand, the web also provides platforms that allow crossover among styles and cultural identities. In this final sense, interpretation of the subcultural issue comes close to a post-subcultural interpretation. In this regard, some studies emphasise the characteristics of hybridisation of subcultural groups (Torkelson, 2010). Robards and Bennet (2011) with particular reference to social network sites study the post-subcultural direction, which has involved subcultural studies.

Research tools are essential to analyse the contexts where the visual expressions of subcultural identity are manifest. We can consider visual sociology for the analysis of the online expressions of the identity of the members of subcultural groups. Visual research tools allow us to analyse online expressions of subcultural identity. Recognising some procedures for online visual analysis is useful to understanding what kind of semiosis the images generate. Three sites (contexts) and three modalities will be considered for interpretation of images (Rose, 2001). The sites that generate the meaning of an image are: production of the image; the image itself and the context in which the audience sees the images. Each of these sites contributes to generating the meaning (see Table 1). Specific modalities of semantic generation exist in each site, which are:

- Technological: We are referring to the kind of *apparatus* which contributes to the form of the image. The *medium* itself, understood as a technological device, whether we are dealing with a smartphone or television, contributes to generating the meaning.
- Compositional: This modality refers to image signifiers that include colour, spatial organisation of the subject matter, framing, perspective.
- Social: This modality concerns the economic, social, cultural and political relationships that surround an image. Online images are in relation to the off-screen dimension.

In the analysis of the visual sign three characteristics can be distinguished, also called functions (Eco, 1984, 2009):

- Expressive: This characteristic regards the meaning generated by elements such as image perspective and subject pose (relationship of the sign with the expressions, which make the signifier).

Table 1. Sites and modalities for visual analysis.

Context (sites)	Production	Image and relative functions (characteristics)	Audience
Semantic generation (modalities)			
Technological (*medium*)	How the medium allows us to express ourselves: technological possibilities of image production	Syntactic: relationship between media devices and images (ex. *software* to create image collections) Semantic: 'the *medium* is the message' Expressive: visual properties of the *medium*	How the *medium* is used as a technological artefact
Compositive	Composition characteristics possible thanks to the medium as a technological artefact	Syntactic: photo sequence, video editing Semantic: theme, captions, text of the images Expressive: subject's pose and position, colours, perspective, framing …	How the composition is decoded (how the recipient interprets the image)
Social	Social cultural group which produces the images (how the author imagines the recipient)	Syntactic: languages of a sociocultural group Semantic: *issues* of a sociocultural group Expressive: visual expressions particular to a sociocultural group (style)	Audience as a more or less stable sociocultural group

Note: Our elaboration from Eco (1984, 2009) and Rose (2001).

- Semantics: Pertains to the meaning generated by the theme of the image, from the captions or from the words of the music which accompany the images (relationship of the sign with possible meanings). The visual empirical basis is driven by the use of a system of signs, that is to say, a code, which enables a process of significance to be achieved.
- Syntactic: concerns the meaning generated by the juxtaposition and sequence of images (relation of the sign with other signs of the code).

3.1. Case study: between rap and jihad

The youths previously mentioned, like other members of criminal or non-criminal subcultures, express their own sociocultural identity through styles and visual forms, namely principally through images of the self. *Homo sapiens* in fact is not just *homo loquens* but *pluriloquus*, and he is *signans*, indeed *plurisignans, polysemicus* (De Mauro, 2008).[3] We can analyse the images of the self, which circulate on web platforms. The images are also among the tools of recruitment, leveraging emotional dimensions.

The visual communication of Deso Dogg – a rapper who became a terrorist – on YouTube is a case for analysis. Deso Dogg appears in music videos as a rapper. He also appears, more recently, in jihadist propaganda videos, with the name of Abu-Maleeq. There are about 260 online videos, distributed in about 13 pages of YouTube. Not all videos are relevant to the topic in question. In some cases the video consist in news broadcasts. Generally, the jihadist videos are executed in a professional manner. The main targets are youth from the West, in particular young people who come from families of foreign origin. The objectives are indoctrination, recruitment and self-recruitment. Many videos concentrate on the figure of the enemy, who is to be totally destroyed. Videos portray the enemy radically and violently. The enemies are Occidental politicians and citizens, everyone who ISIS considers as a target to strike. The violent portrayal of the enemy emerges as an important context of meaning in ISIS group identity (Sontag, 2003).

As a technological tool YouTube presents peculiar characteristics. YouTube is a structure for the disintermediation and for the distribution of contents and permits media expressivity (i.e. the possibility for those who consume media products to produce them in turn). Other web platforms such as Flickr, Facebook and Instagram allow you to create photo collections. These platforms are well known for their recreational aspects. In spite of this, on Instagram user profiles which refer to jihadist themes are only marginally present. A slight thematisation of jihadism is witnessed, where images of ritual ceremonies and similar are presented together with graphically appealing combat images. The examples in Figures 1–3 show frames taken from a YouTube video. In many propaganda videos, we note the attention to graphics which are created and processed with professional software, and at the same time the use of simple, understandable, static shots as in the case of the medium static shot. In order to be forms of association with low barriers for expressiveness, jihadist online communities express themselves in an accessible way out of necessity.

From an expressive point of view, as represented in Figure 2 with reference to the speech of Abu-Maleeq on YouTube, we note the static pose, the use of medium close-up and stationary shot. This expression of solidness immediately recalls the visual format used by Bin-Laden. From a semantic point of view, the videos of battle-*nasheed* are a *bricolage*. Videos combine traditional cultural elements with pop militant lyrics understandable by young native Europeans. From a syntactic point of view, many jihadist

Figure 1. Deso Dogg alias Abu-Maleeq (photo taken from a musical album cover).

Figure 2. Frames from a jihadist video on YouTube: Deso Dogg alias Abu-Maleeq holds a speech.

videos juxtapose traditional cultural elements with contemporary terrorist issues. Figure 3 shows a frame of a jihadist propaganda video: the image represent some medieval-style knights before the part dedicated to the statements of Abu-Maleeq begins. These juxtapositions are rather frequent in propaganda and are based on the result of analogous editing and effect of the association of ideas, which dates back to Ejzenštejn. The combination between images of medieval-style knights and the speech of Abu-Maleeq is an example of *bricolage*.

In many videos Deso-Dogg appears as gangsta rapper. Videos have titles such as *Gangsta Inferno*, *Willkommen in meiner Welt* (literally: Welcome to my world). The *topoi* of the hip-hop subculture, in particular of the gangsta rap genre, emerge: life in the ghetto, weapons, drugs, hate for police, loyalty to the crew, women seen as sex objects, money. In the rap videos Deso-Dogg shows the style and the outfit of a rapper. He wears oversize pants and hooded sweatshirt. In some videos Abu-Maleeq appears dressed according to the style and the outfit of jihadism. He wears camouflage or black clothes. He shows the black flag of ISIS. The camouflage suit is a dress often worn by rappers and the ISIS uniform is over-sized as the rapper's outfit. Abu-Maleeq adds traditional elements, like *kefiah*, to this look. The *kefiah* evokes the Palestinian groups of the Eighties. The megaphone is another traditional element which appears near Abu-Maleeq. This object evokes Abu-Maleeq's communicative power and his propaganda commitment. The megaphone, a material object, is a symbol of Abu-Maleeq's tangible engagement as a propagandist. In some videos Abu-Maleeq talks about his past as gangsta

Figure 3. A frame of a jihadist propaganda video. The image represents some medieval-style knights before the part dedicated to the statements of Abu-Maleeq begins.

rapper. Past life is described as impure. The adhesion to the jihadist group allows a puri-fication from drugs, alcohol and a rash sexual conduct. In the jihadist video women never appear. There are only young males of foreign parental origin. In a video message, Abu-Maleeq appears seated in a hysterical position and behind him there are some young boys (see Figure 2). They symbolise the new generations and the jihadist tension towards the education of Western youth. In this perspective, the Hebdigian *bricolage* – intended as mix of traditional cultural elements and contemporary identity features – pre-sents new characteristics. First, traditional elements such as *kefiah* are combined with new elements like the ISIS flag. Secondly, semantic elements of rapper's life, such as dresses and outfit, are joined to new elements, such as the jihadist uniform. We can therefore talk about double *bricolage*: *bricolage* between a traditional subculture and a new subcul-ture and *bricolage* between personal past and personal present. On the one hand, tra-ditional cultural elements belonging to Deso Dogg's hip-hop subculture are combined with new elements of the Abu-Maleeq's jihadist subculture. In the meantime elements of rapper's past life are combined with elements of the present life of Abu-Maleeq. Double *bricolage* is a dialogue between normative codes and individual characters and make the jihadism understandable for European youth. Double *bricolage* favours dynamics of identification.

The concept of homology is also a useful interpretative key to jihadist videos. From social networks like Twitter and Facebook, websites and other online platforms such as YouTube there emerges a stylistic coherence (homology) between video, graphics and photographs. A common feature among the videos is the regime of narration that provides script muck like to that of a cinematic production or from a serial television programme. The stylistic coherence and the regime of narration are conscious choices made by terrorists following the criteria of marketing. Hebdigian homology concretises in visual isotopies. In general terms, isotopy is 'a «reduntant set of semantic categories that make possible the uniform reading» of a story (Greimas, 1970, p. 188) or, in other words, the repetition of any semiotic unit (Kerbrat-Orecchioni, 1976). Coherence between semantic elements unifies the videos in a single coherent narration. The elements often present are the following. Abu-Maleeq appears as gangsta rapper or as a jihadist. The identity of the recruiter is always present. He is located in a peripheral spatial *locus*: he is isolated in the ghetto with his crew or he is located in the Syrian war scenario, far away from the West. The recruiter is never placed in a mainstream site, is always elsewhere. Signs of non-involvement – whether with regard to the gangsta rap subculture and with regard to the signs of jihadism – to Western mainstream culture are constant. A stable element is the concrete physical position of Deso-Dogg – Abu-Maleeq. The position is that of the one speaking to the public, both as rapper and as a jihadist recruiter. It is a protagonist's position. It is a single person who speaks to the undifferentiated and unknown mass of the web. The physical positioning of Abu-Maleeq is hieratic and static. Body movements are few and decisive. The facial expression is imperative. The gaze is quiet and turned to the camera. He represents calmness, strength and determination.

In brief, the ISIS visual representation is based on the repetition of semantic elements (isotopies), on the semantic coherence of communication (homology), and on the mix between traditional cultural elements and contemporary elements (*bricolage*). Jihadist terrorism gives new meanings to signs and objects. The signs of the subculture are mixed with the signs of jihadism. The analysis of YouTube videos allows us to identify a double *bricolage*: between rap culture and jihadist culture and between personal past as a rapper and present as a terrorist.

4. Final conclusions and directions to future works

The above-mentioned literature proposes the subcultural perspective for the study of jihadist terrorism. In the British studies, the spectacular signs and the visual elements of the group identity assume a privileged cultural role. Visual styles and expressions of subcultural identity are a trademark of jihadist terrorists. The paper allows an original way for studying terrorism, accordingly to a subcultural perspective, and for understanding the sense of belonging and the sociocultural identity of young Western foreign-fighters and European native-born jihadists. The article indeed combines the analysis of terrorism in a subcultural perspective with the visual analysis of the spectacular subcultures. In this way, the paper enhances the studies on jihadist terrorism. Such studies did not take into adequate consideration the subcultural visual elements. Visual elements are indeed not merely communicative features, but signs of the jihadist subculture and of terrorist sense of belonging. In order to develop an original perspective for the analysis of terrorism, a case study is considered. Deso Dogg – Abu-Maleeq was born in Europe, as many other young Western foreign-fighters. He does not accept the mainstream European culture and adhere to a spectacular subculture and later to ISIS.

Visual sociology is the means to analyse the subcultural identity of Deso Dogg – Abu-Maleeq and allows us to study terrorist subcultural memberships in an original way. The contemporary subculture of the European jihadist terrorists is the result of a mix of Western subcultures and non-Western subcultures. Hundreds of young foreign-fighters have grown up in Europe, not in Syria or Iraq. European peripheries are characterised by problems of unemployment and discrimination and by peculiar subcultural styles of life and widespread model well reflected by the hip-hop music genre. Youth groups experience weak family ties, lack of attention for future, lack of interest in education, minimal adult supervision over young males, weak social control, and widespread indifference towards others (Banfield, 1968; Lagrange, 2010). This is the scenario of the processes of jihadist radicalisation. In this perspective, it will be preferable to analyse terrorist jihadist subculture with regard to the European sociocultural context, instead of considering terrorist subculture only as a stranger cultural element, alien from Western sociocultural context. In the future, studies on jihadist terrorism will have to pay attention to elements of Western culture underlying the relevance of visual dimensions of terrorist phenomenon.

Notes

1. For Baba Faye (2011) the terms children of immigration include categories as children rejoined to family, children from migrant couples, children from mixed couple.
2. Deso Dogg, whose original name was Denis Cuspert, was a German rapper. He became a terrorist and a *nasheed* music singer. He joined ISIS in Syria.
3. Human being uses spoken language in many ways. Moreover, human being creates and interprets meanings through multiple semantic activities, for example, through glances, posture and body movements.

Disclosure statement

No potential conflict of interest was reported by the authors.

Notes on contributor

Uliano Conti Ph.D. is Research Fellow at University of Perugia, Department of Philosophy, Social Sciences and Education. He was visiting researcher at Arizona State University (U.S.A.) and Loughborough University (U.K.). He has been working for years with visual sociology. His research topics are methodology, visual sociology and subcultural theory. He teaches Social Research Methodology at the Bachelor's Degree program in Sciences for Investigation and Security and Method and Techniques of Social Inquiry at the Master's Degree program in Management of Social Risks at the University of Perugia.

References

Baba Faye, A. (2011). *Identità e appartenenza: l'impatto biculturale nei figli dell'immigrazione.* [Identity and membership: the cultural impact of sons of migration]. In L. Meglio (Ed.), *I colori del futuro. Indagine sul tempo libero e la quotidianità dei giovani immigrati di seconda generazione in Italia* [The colours of the future. A research on everyday life and free time of second generation migrants] (pp. 23–30). Milano: FrancoAngeli.
Banfield, E. C. (1968). *The unheavenly city: The nature and the future of our urban crisis.* Boston, MA: Little.

Castells, M. (1996). *The rise of the network society* (Vol. 1). Oxford: Blackwell.

Chalfen, R. (1987). *Snapshot versions of life*. Madison: University of Wisconsin Press.

Cohen, S. (1972). *Folk devils and moral panics: The creation of the mods and rockers*. London: MacGibbon and Kee.

Crenshaw, M. (1981). The causes of terrorism. *Comparative Politics, 13*(4), 379–399. doi:10.2307/421717.

Danschke, C. (2013). "Pop Jihad": History and structure of salafism and jihadism in Germany. *ISRM working paper series, 2*.

Davis, J. (2010). Architecture of the personal interactive homepage: Constructing the self through MySpace. *New Media & Society, 12*(7), 1103–1119. doi:10.1177/1461444809354212.

Della Porta, D. (1988). Recruitment processes in clandestine political organizations: Italian left-wing terrorism. In B. Klandermans, H. Kriesi, & S. Tarrow (Eds.), *From structure to action: Comparing social movement research across cultures* (pp. 155–172). Greenwich, CT: JAI Press.

De Mauro, T. (2008). *Lezioni di linguistica teorica*. Roma-Bari: Laterza.

Eco, U. (1984). *Semiotica e filosofia del linguaggio* [Semiotics and philosophy of language]. Torino: Einaudi.

Eco, U. (2009). *Cultura y semiótica* [Culture and semiotics]. Madrid: Circulo de Bellas Artes.

Ferracuti, F. (1982). A sociopsychiatric interpretation of terrorism. *Annals of the American Academy of Political and Social Science, 463*, 129–140.

Greimas, A. J. (1970). *Du sens* [On sense]. Paris: Seuil.

Hall, S., & Jefferson T. (Eds.) (1976). *Resistance through rituals: Youth subculture in post-war Britain*. London: Routledge.

Hebdige, D. (1979). *Subculture. The meaning of style*. London: Methuen .

Hebdige, D. (1988). *Hiding in the light: On images and things*. London: Routledge.

Jenkins, H. (2006). *Fans, bloggers, and gamers*. New York: New York University Press.

Kerbrat-Orecchioni, C. (1976). Problématique de l'isotopie[The problem of the isotopy], *Linguistique et sémiologie. Travaux du Centre de Recherches Linguistiques et Sémiologiques de Lyon, 1*, 11–34.

Lagrange, H. (2010). *Le déni des cultures* [The denial of cultures]. Paris: Seuil.

Lombardi, M. (2015). *IS 2.0 e molto altro: il progetto di comunicazione del califfato*[Isis and the communication project of the caliphate]. In M. Maggioni, & P. Magri (Eds.), *Twitter e jihad: la comunicazione dell'ISIS* [Twitter and Jihad: The communication of ISIS] (pp. 91–132). Novi Ligure: ISPI.

Margolis E., & Pauwels, L. (Eds.). (2011). *The SAGE handbook of visual research methods*. London: SAGE Publications.

McArthur, J. A. (2009). Digital subculture: A geek meaning of style. *Journal of Communication Inquiry, 33*(1), 58–70. doi:10.1177/0196859908325676.

Middleton, R. (1990). *Studying popular music*. Philadelphia, PA: Open University Press.

Orsini, A. (2009). *Anatomia delle Brigate Rosse. Le radici ideologiche del terrorismo rivoluzionario* [Anatomy of the red brigades: The religious mind-set of modern terrorists]. Soveria Mannelli: Rubbettino.

Orsini, A. (2012). Poverty, ideology and terrorism: The STAM bond. *Studies in Conflict & Terrorism, 35* (10), 665–692. doi:10.1080/1057610X.2012.712030.

Palumbo, M., & Garbarino, E. (2006). *Ricerca sociale. Metodo e tecniche* [Social research. method and techniques]Milano: FrancoAngeli.

Pisoiu, D. (2012). *Islamist radicalisation in Europe. An occupational change process*. Milton Park: Routledge.

Reem, A., & Pisoiu, D. (2014). Foreign fighters: An overview of existing research and a comparative study of British and German foreign fighters. *Zeus Working Paper, 8*, 3–19.

Robards, B., & Bennet, A. (2011). My tribe: Post-subcultural manifestations of belonging on social network sites. *Sociology, 45*(2), 303–317. doi:10.1177/0038038510394025.

Rose, G. (2001). *Visual Methodologies: An Introduction to the interpretation of visual materials*. London: Sage.

Roversi, A. (2006). *L'odio in Rete. Siti ultras, nazifascismo online, jihad elettronica*. [Hate on the Web. Ultras Websites, Online Nazism, Electronic Jihad]Bologna: il Mulino.

Roy, O. (2015). *La peur de l'islam. Dialogue avec Nicolas Truong* [The fear of Islam. dialogue with Nicolas Truong]. La Tour-d'Aigue: Ed. de l'Aube.

Sageman, M. (2004). *Understanding terror networks*. Philadelphia: University of Pennsylvania Press.

Sontag, S. (2003). *Regarding the pain of others*. New York, NY: Picador, Ferrar, Strauss and Giroux.

Torkelson, J. M. (2010). Life after (Straightedge) subculture. *Qualitative Sociology, 33*, 257–274. doi:10.1007/s11133-010-9153-1.

Touraine, A. (1997). *Pourrons-nous vivre ensemble? Égaux et différents* [Can we live together? Equality and difference]. Paris: Fayard.

Vergani, M., & Bliuc, A. M. (2015). The evolution of the ISIS' language: A quantitative analysis of the language of the first year of Dabiq. *Sicurezza, Terrorismo e Società, 2*, 7–20.

Vergani, M., & Zuev, D. (2015). Neojihadist visual politics: Comparing Youtube videos of North Caucasus and Uyghur Militants. *Asian Studies Review, 39*(1), 1–22. doi:10.1080/10357823.2014.976171.

Victoroff, J. (2005). The mind of the terrorist: A review and critique of psychological approaches. *Journal of Conflict Resolution, 49*, 3–42. doi:10.1177/0022002704272040.

Volosinov, V. N. (1973). *Marxism and the philosophy of language*. New York, NY: Seminar Press.

Williams, J. P. (2011). *Subcultural theory: Traditions and concepts*. Cambridge, MA: Polity Press.

Willis, P. (1978). *Profane culture*. London: Routledge and Kegan Paul.

'Squashing the Beef': Combatting Gang Violence and Reforming Masculinity in East London

Gary Armstrong and James Rosbrook-Thompson

ABSTRACT

The article draws on the findings of two years' ethnographic fieldwork in exploring how gang activity in Newham, East London is combatted by faith-based organisation, Targeted Against Gangs (TAG). More specifically, the authors examine how TAG seeks to reform the identities of young male gang members according to the principles of what we have called 'Pentecostal realist masculinity'. The characteristics of this reformed masculinity include an awareness of the racial (and racist) dynamics of criminal and wider society, a focus on individuals thriving within fraternal networks, and the desire to channel creative energies into legitimate entrepreneurial activities. Though this strategy did not mount a direct challenge to the racist societal structures it identified, it was effective in reducing levels of gang violence in East London.

Introduction

Street gangs in London represent a serious problem for both the Metropolitan Police Service (MPS) and governmental institutions at national and local levels.[1] In 2007, youth gangs became the focus of a Home Office specialist subgroup, the *Tackling Gangs Action Programme*, while in the aftermath of 'riots' in summer 2011, incumbent London Major, Boris Johnson, vowed to tackle 'gang violence' through Operation Shield, a scheme modelled on policies pioneered in the USA and centring on community mobilisation and harsh punishments for recalcitrant gang members. In Newham, East London, MPS officers facing some of the capital's most notorious 'gang nominals' – those suspected by police of gang involvement – have turned to faith-based intervention in attempting to make the streets safer for the borough's residents and visitors. The work of the organisation it turned to, Targeted Against Gangs (TAG), is the focus of this paper. More specifically, we examine how its attempts at intervention and rehabilitation involve the cultivation of 'Pentecostal realist masculinity'.[2]

We begin by surveying the literature on youth street gangs and masculinity, before evaluating faith-inspired interventions designed to rehabilitate young men embroiled in gang activity. We then use the findings of two years' ethnographic fieldwork to explore how TAG both diagnoses and attempts to reform the masculine identities of gang members. The desired outcome, what we have called Pentecostal realist masculinity, retains but redirects the emphasis on individualism and fraternity in the direction of legal and potentially lucrative niches in a racist society. In doing so, it does not mount any fundamental challenge to racist and racialised social structures, but is undoubtedly effective in reducing levels of Serious Youth Violence (SYV).

Gang membership: a crisis of masculinity?

Notions of masculinity have been central to attempts to frame and make sense of gang activity in theoretical terms. The oldest theory of gang membership, social disorganisation theory (Thrasher, 1927), posits that young men are driven onto the street by a breakdown of traditional societal institutions such as the school, church and family. Shaw and McKay (1931, 1942) sought to develop Thrasher's theoretical model, arguing that levels of disorganisation were highest in urban neighbourhoods where parents lacked any firm 'functional authority' over their children, and particularly their sons. This sees the emergence of criminal traditions which are transmitted from generation to generation via processes of socialisation, often involving role models.

In studying the youth gangs of late Victorian Manchester, Davies (1998) notes how for working-class young men the link between violence and masculinity was drawn and cemented by observing the actions of role models. These (not mutually exclusive) figures included the breadwinner, whose status accrued from providing economically for their family, and the 'hard' man or 'man's' man whose actions were defined by toughness; he possessed a heroic capacity for both demanding physical labour and the consumption of alcohol (often a precursor to, or accompanied by, fighting). The status of breadwinner was unattainable for many young men in Victorian Manchester; they played second-fiddle to their fathers in terms of both income and, relatedly, household authority. The role of hard man was, therefore, the only masculine ideal available to them. Similarly, Miller (1958, p. 9) places great emphasis on the link between toughness and masculinity in his exploration of the relationship between gang delinquency and 'lower class culture'. Indeed, masculinity is one of the 'qualities or states' that define the 'toughness' so valorised by 'lower class' groups: '"masculinity," symbolised by a distinctive complex of acts and avoidance (bodily tattooing; absence of sentimentality; nonconcern with "art," "literature," conceptualization of women as conquest objects, etc.)'.

As the reader will notice, many of these studies follow the basic arc of Merton's (1938) analysis, namely that it is the 'strain' between a universally accepted set of goals and differential access to the resources needed to realise such goals that leads to the formation of delinquent subcultures. Realising that they are unable to pursue such objectives through officially, socially sanctioned channels, young men express their 'status frustration' by 'striking out' against middle-class value systems, entering collectives where violence, destruction and instant gratification are endorsed. A similar approach, the theory of differential opportunity (Cloward & Ohlin, 1960), sees gang members 'waging war' on a system they blame for their own social failure through outbursts of anger, bravado and the cultivation of fearsome reputations.

More recent research has questioned whether the vocabulary of strain, opportunity, etc. is fit for the post-industrial conditions today's gang collectives respond to and forge an existence within. Hobbs' (2013) work in the East London borough of 'Dogtown' stresses the area's fragmented, diverse, post-industrial character in modifying and recoding older scripts of masculinity. As Fraser (2015) points out, processes of globalisation have led to these characteristics being reproduced in urban settings around the world. Though, at bottom, young men's recruitment by gangs is an expression of 'defiant individualism' (Sanchez-Jankowski, 1991) involving cultures of machismo, physical strength (Young, 1999) and an expression of marginalised masculinity (Horowitz, 1983; Majors & Billson, 1992; Rios, 2011; Vigil, 2007), other features relate more closely to specific local conditions.

Fraser (2015, p. 51) describes this process in the case of Glasgow, where deindustrialisation has meant that older, 'industrial masculinities no longer tallied with the economic realities of the new service economy'. This leads to a negotiation between old and new – in the worst case prompting the emergence of a 'tormented habitus' – with neoliberal motifs like the individual being pitted against working-class communities which until recently had been so clearly defined. Elsewhere this confrontation between old values and new circumstances has led to the former being recast and redeployed. In the north-east of England, for example, young men reimagine 'grafting' as a criminal apprenticeship while still cleaving to traditional notions of respect (Nayak, 2006).

Combatting gang masculinities through faith: deflecting the crisis?

In the United States and Latin America, faith-inspired intervention programmes have addressed a clutch of 'gang-related' issues including drug and alcohol addiction (Brennerman, 2011; Leon, 1998; Sanchez-Walsh, 2003; Wolseth, 2008). These are designed to combat criminal behaviours through a combination of religious practice, prescribed patterns of scripture-inspired interaction and techniques of self-monitoring. The 12-step model of Alcoholics Anonymous (AA) – beginning with the admission of addiction and culminating with the assistance of fellow group members – directly informs the work of organisations such as *Criminal and Gang Members Anonymous*. The model is premised on the drawing out of latent religiosity in offenders as well as explicit negotiations of (hyper)masculinity (Flores & Hondagneu-Sotelo, 2013, p. 4). According to their proponents, programmes incorporating the 12 steps have enjoyed considerable success (Toft, 2000).

Flores (2014) has documented the work of faith-based intervention programmes, both Jesuit and Pentecostal, in the context of Chicano gang membership in Los Angeles. Though denominational differences are important in directing the path to 'recovery', the result – ideally – is the same: a 'reformed barrio masculinity'. Integral to the development of the latter is an unashamed acknowledgement that young men come from a 'street background' but reorient 'masculine expressions away from the street and toward conventional social spheres, such as the church, household, and workplace' (2015, p. 13). Faith-based programmes facilitate this process of reformation by occupying a third space between gangs and mainstream society.

However, such interventions have also been subject to criticism. It has been claimed that they serve to reinforce neoliberal policies at state and federal level (which champion 'entrepreneurial values' and 'individual responsibility') by forcing subjects to accept fault and accountability (Bourgois & Schonberg, 2009). Others have argued that such methods disempower adherents by forcing them to follow a linear narrative of recovery from a regrettable past, to existential crisis, to clean future (Carr, 2010; Flores & Hondag-neu-Sotelo, 2013), thereby extending and reinforcing state power.

Aside from pointing to the basic contradiction between its rhetoric of 'freedom' and its ascetic codes (O'Neill, 2011; Pine, 2008), commentators have noted Pentecostalism's per-petuation of patriarchal ideals. In the majority of Pentecostal churches in the United States, leadership positions can only be occupied by men. It might be argued, therefore, that the church's appeals to recovering gang members are predicated on trading one male code of honour for another (Leon, 1998; Sanchez-Walsh, 2003). These young men may be encour-aged to forgo extreme acts of machismo (such as street violence), but do so in exchange for the less exaggerated masculine dominance of the household – or, in other words, the privileges of so-called soft patriarchy (Wilcox, 2007). Interestingly, some researchers have praised this adaptation of masculinity because of its facilitation of upward social mobility through the deflection of resources from the street to the domestic family unit (Brusco, 1995).

As already alluded to, Pentecostalism's persistent focus on the individual has led to claims that it chimes with, and possibly even vindicates, the neoliberal paradigms of gov-ernance and security which so many have blamed for widening inequality and deepening injustice. Indeed, it is easy to see the parallels between Pentecostal efforts to convert indi-viduals rather than tackle wider societal ills (Lancaster, 1988) and neoliberal security regimes which promote qualities such as 'choice', 'character' and 'self-discipline' (O'Neill & Thomas, 2011). This is ironic given the reality that neoliberal policies – including the cur-tailment or elimination of social services, suppression of wages and funding cuts in areas such as state education and healthcare – result not just in the suffering of individuals but in the atrophying of the 'social body' (O'Neill, 2013). Structural conditions most notably evident in economic policies can see public spaces become unsafe and levels of civic par-ticipation (particularly among young people) drop accordingly. In fact, it is this retreat from public space which has arguably strengthened the appeal of 'privatised' Pentecostal fra-ternities as well as the 'private' street gangs that cause such consternation (Montenegro, 2001; O'Neill, 2011).

Settings and method

The research described here took place between 2011 and 2013 in the east London Borough of Newham (LBN). In the contemporary Newham setting, gangs are one of the main con-cerns of those tasked with policing, community relations and all manner of related public-spirited interventions (see Armstrong, Giulianotti, & Hobbs, 2016). Situated north of the River Thames, around five miles from the City of London, Newham is one of the poorest boroughs in the UK. It is also the second most diverse in terms of the ethnicity of its residents. According to the results of 2011 Census, 29.0% of Newham's estimated 307,000 population is White (16.7% White British, 0.7% White Irish, 0.2% Gypsy or Irish Tra-veller, 11.4% Other White), 4.6% of mixed race (1.3% White and Black Caribbean, 1.1% White and Black African, 0.9% White and Asian, 1.3% Other Mixed), 43.5% Asian (13.8% Indian, 12.21% Bangladeshi, 9.8% Pakistani, 1.3% Chinese, 6.5% Other Asian), 19.6% Black (12.3% African, 4.9% Caribbean, 2.4% Other Black), 1.1% Arab and 2.3% of other ethnic heritage.

An ethnographic approach was adopted, with observation, participant observation and in-depth interviews used in combination (O'Reilly, 2011; Venkatesh, 2008). The fieldwork was carried out within three institutions, all of which had a stake in combatting gang-related activity in Newham: the local council, MPS and TAG. The nature of the problem was defined in different ways by different organisations, and it is the approach and methods of TAG that receive attention here.

Knocking on heaven's door: TAG

Beginning life in 2007, the 'Gangsline', a 24-hour helpline for youth 'gang' members or those fearful about the involvement of friends or family members in youth gang-related activity, evolved over the following two years into TAG. TAG sought to reach youths involved in a life of drugs, guns and knife crime through messages of hope derived from Pentecostal Christianity. This faith was most evident in the phone and face-to-face conversations of its founder, former gang member Sheldon Thomas (ST), which were smattered with words such as 'bred' (short for brethren) and 'bless' (the sign-off: God bless). The organisation thus grew from an information/advice service – primarily a phone-line which also produced leaflets distributed in fast-food outlets and wherever its outreach workers could find groups of young people 'hanging out' – to an intervention-based organisation that was both reactive (with a specialist Outreach Response Team) and proactive in utilising its knowledge and expertise.

From its inception, TAG sought to address the root causes of gang membership, a task which ST believed required an understanding of psychosocial issues including family breakdown, anger problems, the consequences of rejection, emotional hurt, unresolved conflict, a (missing) sense of belonging and the despair of struggling parents. In founding Gangsline/TAG, ST was seeking to offer credible support through programmes and workshops that focused on developing the unrealised talents of gang members. The interventions were structured according to curricula and programmes based in conflict resolution and counselling delivered over a 12-week period. All aimed to equip individuals with the necessary tools to bring about responses to emotional, physical, financial and spiritual factors which – ideally – would allow an individual to break free from distorted thinking and destructive life cycles.

The TAG mission was underpinned by a faith-based framework that focused on notions of personal responsibility, morality, positive thinking and self-esteem. Its training programmes did not follow a set format and its curriculum was delivered in diverse settings to individuals or groups. Sessions were adapted in order to meet the needs of young people – predominantly young men – at times too frightened or lacking the confidence to leave their known and 'safe' environment. ST led the sessions and utilised his major strengths of articulacy and charisma. It was speeches delivered by ST at conferences addressing youth offending in London that had seen him approached and contracted by both local government officials and MPS personnel over the years 2008–2011 to conduct various forms of interventionist work with young offenders.

ST's diagnosis of the gang problem emphasised the role of institutional failure in the kind of social disorganisation which drove young men into the clutches of gangs. The institution he singled out for most blame was the family. As he stated in conversation with one of the authors after an intervention session, with his audience having dispersed:

> I would put family breakdown as a major cause. It's not parenting *per se*, some of their homes are nice and some have a good family network, but it's too female-centred for many of these

boys. There's a common denominator in many of these boys' lives, and that is the absence of a father. A good father would make all the difference and go a long way to stopping all this.

It was the absence of bonds in the familial sphere, particularly between boys and their fathers, which made young men amenable to gang membership. It was not that a masculine ideal embodied by a father was somehow unattainable (Davies, 1998), the problem was rather the lack of any stable and positive male presence. Another commonality ST identified was domestic violence, with boys having been party to such violence as both witness and victim. As he commented during a training session with police, youth workers and youth offending teams:

> It's not just absent fathers, it's worse. It's a carousel of abusive men. They're seeing Mum, a man living with her for a few months, knocking her and probably the boy about. Then he's gone. After a while another one comes along – same thing, same pattern. This is experienced as normal for these young men ... Now are you beginning to see where the anger, depression, trauma, et cetera is coming from? These boys are ripe for recruitment by local gangs. They suddenly feel they're protected and that they belong. ... The bravado covers up lots of serious trauma.

This deficit in terms of family structure related to one element of Pentecostal realist masculinity. The Pentecostal church could provide surrogate social bonds which previously would have been proffered – at a considerable cost – by gang membership. Like Pentecostal-based interventions elsewhere, a 'doctrine of separation from community life' was at work here (Wolseth, 2008). Indeed, it was TAG's intermediate position between gangs and wider society which proved so propitious. Interestingly, however, for many of those TAG reached out to, rehabilitation involved a return to, rather than discovery of, the religious life. Most young men ST dealt with had attended church regularly as youngsters, so involving themselves in religious life represented a gathering up of slackened spiritual reins, as opposed to being something wholly new. Entering the function room of a Methodist church in Newham which he used to stage intervention sessions, ST explained how many of the teenage boys TAG worked with in this area knew the location well: 'They once came here as little kids on Sunday mornings, dragged by their Mums.'

Membership of an alternative group offered more effective insulation from the inequities of a heavily racialised and racist society. Indeed, another characteristic of Pentecostal realist masculinity was a sense of fraternity which was cognisant of wider racial and racist societal dynamics. For ST, talking about gangs meant talking about 'race', and any reformed or reoriented masculinity would be a racialised one. Just as gangs provided refuge and solidarity amid a racist society (Flores, 2014), having exited gang life one must forge a sense of manhood which took account of racial dynamics. As he commented after a meeting with a group of gang nominals:

> Forget the 'Big Man' gangster stuff around here, because once you have a gun, you are your own man and no one gives you orders. Guns come from all over down this end: Bosnians, Lithuanians, white criminal networks. Black guys don't have structures like them. Neither do they have the markets for the straps (guns) so they have to buy second-hand. A 9 mm cost £300, a Glock £450, a MAC 10 £800, an Eagle Eye £600. The ammo (ammunition) comes with the guns. The thing is, there's no target practice or training ... that's the reason why these black youths can't really shoot straight; they buy a piece (gun), and use it the next day but can't control it and that's how innocents get killed or maimed. These black kids

need telling they are not 'gangsters', because unlike their white counterparts, they don't make money. White gangs don't live with their Mums. White gangsters don't live in blocks with piss-filled lifts and their children don't go to no-hope comprehensive schools ...

The disorder wrought upon black communities by economic and social dislocation was reflected in the structure – or, more specifically, the lack of structure – of their gang collectives. These collectives were predominantly male, with the lack of positive role models for young men being a large factor in the lives of gang members. Leaving gang life behind meant no longer being a dupe within criminal networks that ultimately served to enrich other people. Pentecostal realist masculinity recognised the importance of being a breadwinner, but also the futility of seeking an income through gang membership. Part of the appeal of gang life was a vague, superficial and ironic notion of 'fighting back' against racial others who, in reality, exploited gang collectives. Moving beyond this mentality involved realising the hopeless position of black street gangs and identifying niches of legitimate opportunity within societal structures, niches insulated by Pentecostal fraternities.

In pursuing this line of reasoning, ST's appeals to young people shared the characteristics of other Pentecostal-inspired interventions. They sought to reorient masculine identities by harnessing existing propensities to individualism, entrepreneurship and notions of manhood. Indeed, two of ST's most compelling appeals centred on the possibility of making money through legal channels, and parlaying masculine capital amassed in gang life within the sphere of the wider community. In this way, the fraternal networks of Pentecostalism could facilitate the forging and sharpening of individual identity in extending legitimate and potentially lucrative opportunities. So in leaving behind the 'ghetto mentality', young men could transpose rather than relinquish certain strains of their masculinity. Being part of a religious community did not mean setting aside one's individual (and largely acquisitive) objectives, and ST often underscored this fact by pointing to the futility and inefficiency of gang members' current schemes. The street-corner drug market required some twelve hours on duty each day, he explained to those gathered before him, which entailed making oneself available until the early hours. The business also called for constant vigilance; rival dealers would 'rob' their adversaries of drug monies at knife- or gunpoint, well aware that no complaint to police would ensue. The ideal response to such an affront was violence, but not all possessed the resources, capability or desire needed for summary retribution. The young men, usually by now chastened into admitting that they had earned only a few hundred pounds in recent months, were told that this amounted to perhaps half the national minimum wage, before occasional taxation rates of 100% were factored in. If this was a business model, it had no future. There had to be a better way.

ST took the opportunity of a gathering of young men at the Methodist church to explain the wider context and implications of gang membership. Six young black men sat around a table in the meeting room of the church complex with ST. Hailing from three different areas of the borough and representing three named 'gangs', they had all participated in the sale of drugs on the street and in altercations with one another's peer groups wherein weapons were used. Two had stabbed rivals; two had suffered stab wounds in similar circumstances. The meeting place carried no territorial threat or controversy. Like faith-inspired attempts to rehabilitate gang members in Los Angeles

(Flores, 2014), the choice of venue and status of ST as former gang member (of considerable clout) positioned TAG advantageously between gangs and wider society.

To help matters ST had met all concerned on streets in the vicinity and walked with them to the venue. Once in the room they were soon at ease with ST who had spoken with them personally over the previous six months during street-based 'outreach' work which saw him drive around various neighbourhoods and alight to talk with groups of teenage boys and young men stationed on street corners. Obtaining the mobile phone numbers of certain key players, in the weeks ahead he was able to get those now gathered to attend the meeting at the appointed time and place. Now they had arrived, ST began by asking all present for a basic level of respect, which required them to turn their mobile phones to silent and avoid answering any calls for the duration of the meeting. Then, after thanking them for attending, ST launched into a narrative as to his '*ting*' (purpose). 'This may sound superficial, but in truth why I'm here is as much about stopping innocent people getting killed as about youse.' This led to him probing what they consider to be future ambitions. The issue of respect was raised with a new dimension offered. ST explained: 'What you call "respect" is actually not about fighting … the respect a man gets in life … is based in how you can help people. You've got to put down noise (fracas between members of rival groups) and guns and get off the road. In a few years, you'll be lucky to have wives and kids (one individual in the room has a child – he is aged 17). Who's gonna' pay for your kids food and school? Are you going to settle down with a girl with that life? Are you gonna' be 29-years-old sticking up people (robbing people at knife- or gunpoint), thinking you're bad? (All nod approvingly.) And that's why I'm here; squashing the beef' (reducing the sources of conflict).

The enormity of the task was brought home as Asa, a member of a gang called the Beckton Boys, explained that the problem was their Woodgrange equivalents.[3] According to Asa, who was the victim of a recent beating at the hands of youths from the Woodgrange district, they must strike up the first apology to end matters: 'They rushed (collectively attacked) me first – they have to say sorry.' The ensuing silence was again broken by ST, who asked, looking around the room: 'How do we stop all this?' One youth ventures the following argument, stating: 'If we (Beckton) come off, the rest have to do the same. Trust is needed. We need to know we're all on the same ting'. Another youth, hitherto silent, chipped in: 'There's six groups (named "gang" entities) on Newham – so which crew do we start with? I agree, I don't want my kids going down this road, and I don't want my daughter taking a bullet from a stray shot.'

The youngsters around him were implored to divert their resources into family life. Their current endeavours, he explained, were destined to flounder or fail; legitimate revenue streams would be more lucrative. They already possessed the means to be successful. What was required was a reappraisal of methods and priorities. Having been deflected into alternative social spheres, masculine energies could be directed towards profitable, and importantly legal, notions of manhood. Conscientiousness would secure such an elevated status and, consequently, material betterment. Aware of Asa's skills in penning lyrics for YouTube rapping clips, ST outlined a business model whereby Asa's undoubted ability as a 'lyricist' could be promoted by those in rival areas of the borough who had other skills and the collective product transported by those from yet another area – in a sense, a collaborative business model where everybody involved wins, i.e. makes money from the enterprise. This was a familiar enough strategy but one inflected by the post-industrial conditions of contemporary East London and the platforms available to young people via internet-enabled devices. That said, it was the more tangible networks represented by religious groups which could give youngsters the edge and keep things on a virtuous footing.

Before the group departed, ST asked them to come again, to bring their friends, but warned that if anyone in the interim 'beefs' (continues gang-based vendettas) they were not to come back. The words seemed to register and the departing Asa stated aloud: 'I'm squashing the beef'. A couple of others nodded slowly in approval but said nothing. All present were asked to clasp their hands together in prayer and close their eyes while ST asked for God's blessing on all in the room and all the things they held sacred. His closing word of 'Amen' was repeated by all eight of his listeners. These young men then went their separate ways.

In watching ST stage interventions, the central elements of Pentecostal realist masculinity were possible to discern. As we have seen, a number of existing predispositions were retained but redirected. An acquisitive streak was not discouraged. It could be harnessed along with the forging and sharpening of individual identity within fraternal Pentecostal networks, with a young man's creativity now channelled into legitimate expressive activities. These networks replaced the gang and compensated for a deficit in terms of family structures. Pentecostal realist masculinity also represented a more mature approach to the racial and racist dynamics of wider society. The notion that gang membership struck a blow against exploitative racial others was hopelessly naïve. Indeed, black street gangs were often the unwitting dupes of criminal networks headed up by these 'others'.

Conclusion

To outsiders, the recruitment of ST and TAG by Newham Council and the MPS may seem to represent a desperate plea for divine intervention; one might reason that the shortcomings of 'official' approaches to gangs were made plain in the shift towards a faith-based scheme. However, understanding this as a move from rational to irrational approaches would be wide of the mark. TAG's Pentecostal realism was effective because of the position it carved out between gangs and wider society, together with the fact it could accommodate a modified masculinity and an entrepreneurial spirit.

When framed in terms of the short-term objectives of TAG, local police and Newham Council, the cultivation of Pentecostal realist masculinity undoubtedly worked. TAG's work with the borough's street gangs saw offenses classed as SYV decrease by more than 25%. The borough commander was open in attributing this significant reduction to TAG and, more specifically, ST. Criticisms of other faith-based gang intervention and rehabilitation programmes, that they tend to work with the grain of neoliberal tenets (Lancaster, 1988), largely hold for TAG's work. It promised converts a greater appreciation of society's power dynamics and how these were spun around fundamentally racist social structures. The challenge it posed to these structures was indirect, recognising the almost irresistible pull of individualist identities and reorienting them towards legal and potentially lucrative societal niches. However, the most important thing for ST and TAG was that fewer young men were dying on the streets of East London. And, when dealing in matters of life and death, one works with short time horizons. What mattered was that which could be achieved in the here and now. Finding God could work in the rehabilitation of gang members, but only if the search had a certain worldly resonance.

Notes

1. The constant – and unresolved – issue in all multi-agency approaches to the issue of SYV/ gangs was agreeing on what constituted a 'gang'. There were academic and police attempts at definition but none that were universally accepted nationally or specifically in the Newham context. For TAG, it was less important whether a group self-identified as a 'gang' than if its affiliates engaged consistently in SYV.
2. The man credited with organising the first institutionalised practice of Pentecostalism, William Seymour, the son of former slaves, learned the doctrine that glossolalia (or speaking in tongues) was evidence of a Christian being infused with the Holy Spirit from white preacher Charles Parnham. Seymour was given permission to listen to Parnham's lectures, but only through an open door while sat in the corridor of a Bible School in Houston, Texas. Though Parnham was initially supportive of Seymour's attempts to spread the word of Pentecostalism, as a sympathiser of the Ku Klux Klan he disapproved of the co-presence of whites and blacks at religious gatherings, and the two became dissociated, forming the (black) Church of God in Christ and the (white) Assemblies of God, respectively.
3. Taking their name from a district of Newham, in 2012 the 25 young men who gathered under the banner of 'Woodgrange' attained London-wide notoriety via a YouTube video titled 'Who's That Click'. The five-minute clip showed the gang rapping and subtly insulting neighbouring groups. The video had been viewed more than 250,000 times. It was eventually taken down from the website following an appeal to YouTube by Newham Police in conjunction with Newham Council.

Acknowledgements

The authors are indebted to Sheldon and Michelle Thomas and all the sessional workers who facilitated this research and provided answers to our questions. We thank also the young men who tolerated our presence while listening to the words of the TAG workers. Finally, we are grateful to the anonymous reviewer who, along with Charalambos Tsekeris, provided valuable feedback on an earlier draft of this paper.

Disclosure statement

No potential conflict of interest was reported by the authors.

Notes on contributors

Gary Armstrong is Reader in Sociology at Brunel University. He has written extensively on surveillance, football hooliganism, and sporting cultures in a range of settings including Liberia and Malta. His most recent book (co-authored with Dick Hobbs and Richard Giulianotti), *Policing the 2012 London Olympics: Legacy and Social Exclusion*, was published by Routledge in 2016.

James Rosbrook-Thompson is Senior Lecturer in Sociology at Anglia Ruskin University. He is an urban sociologist whose research interests include 'race' and ethnicity, citizenship and belonging, youth delinquency, and sport. He is currently writing a book (with Gary Armstrong) about life on a mixed-occupancy housing estate in London.

References

Armstrong, G., Giulianotti, R., & Hobbs, D. (2016). *Policing the 2012 London Olympics: Legacy and social exclusion*. London: Routledge.
Bourgois, P., & Schonberg, J. (2009). *Righteous Dopefiend*. Berkeley, CA: University of California Press.

Brennerman, R. E. (2011). *Homies and Hermanos: God and gangs in Central America*. Cambridge, MA: Oxford University Press.

Brusco, E. E. (1995). *The reformation of Machismo: Evangelical conversion and gender in Colombia*. Austin, TX: University of Texas Press.

Carr, E. S. (2010). *Scripting addiction: The politics of therapeutic talk and American sobriety*. Princeton, NJ: Princeton University Press.

Cloward, R., & Ohlin, L. (1960). *Delinquency and opportunity*. New York, NY: Free Press.

Davies, A. (1998). Youth gangs, masculinity and violence in late Victorian Manchester and Salford. *Journal of Social History, 32*(2), 349–369.

Flores, E. O. (2014). *God's gangs: Barrio ministry, masculinity and gang recovery*. New York, NY: New York University Press.

Flores, E. O., & Hondagneu-Sotelo, P. (2013). Chicano gang members in recovery: The public talk of negotiating Chicano Masculinities. *Social Problems, 60*(4), 1–15.

Fraser, A. (2015). *Urban legends: Gang identity in the post-industrial city*. Oxford: Oxford University Press.

Hobbs, D. (2013). *Lush life: Constructing organized crime in the UK*. Oxford: Oxford University Press.

Horowitz, R. (1983). *Honor and the American dream: Culture and identity in a Chicano community*. New Brunswick, NJ: Rutgers University Press.

Lancaster, R. N. (1988). *Thanks to god and the revolution: Popular religion and class consciousness in the new Nicaragua*. New York, NY: Columbia University Press.

Leon, L. D. (1998). Born again in East LA: The congregation as border space. In R. S. Warner & J. G. Wittner (Eds.), *Gatherings in diaspora* (pp. 163–196). Philadelphia, PA: Temple University Press.

Majors, R., & Billson, J. M. (1992). *Cool pose: The dilemmas of Black manhood in America*. New York, NY: Simon and Schuster.

Merton, R. K. (1938). Social structure and anomie. *American Sociological Review, 3*, 672–682.

Miller, W. (1958). Lower class culture as a generating milieu of gang delinquency. *Journal of Social Issues, 14*, 5–19.

Montenegro, S. (2001). *Jóvenes y cultura política en Nicaragua: La generación de los 90*. Managua: Editorial Hispamer.

Nayak, A. (2006). Displaced masculinities: Chavs, youth and class in the post-industrial city. *Sociology, 40*(5), 813–831.

O'Neill, K. (2011). *City of god: Christian citizenship in postwar Guatemala*. Berkeley, CA: University of California Press.

O'Neill, K. (2013). LEFT BEHIND: Security, salvation, and the subject of prevention. *Cultural Anthropology, 28*(2), 204–226.

O'Neill, K., & Thomas, K. (Eds.). (2011). *Securing the city: Neoliberalism, space and insecurity in post-war Guatemala*. Durham, NC: Duke University Press.

O'Reilly, K. (2011). *Ethnographic methods*. London: Routledge.

Pine, A. (2008). *Working hard, drinking hard: On violence and survival in Honduras*. Berkeley, CA: University of California Press.

Rios, V. M. (2011). *Punished: Policing the lives of black and Latino boys*. New York, NY: New York University Press.

Sanchez-Jankowski, M. (1991). *Islands in the street: Gangs and American urban society*. Berkeley, CA: University of Berkeley Press.

Sanchez-Walsh, A. (2003). *Latino pentecostal identity: Evangelical faith, self, and society*. New York: Columbia University Press.

Shaw, C. R., & McKay, H. D. (1931). *Social factors in Juvenile delinquency* , 2: 13. Washington, DC: Government Printing Office.

Shaw, C. R., & McKay, H. D. (1942). *Juvenile delinquency and urban areas*. Chicago, IL: University of Chicago Press.

Thrasher, F. (1927). *The gang: A study of 1,313 gangs in Chicago*. Chicago, IL: University of Chicago Press.

Toft, D. (2000). Recent research offers compelling support for the effectiveness of Twelve Step-based treatment. *The Voice* (summer).

Venkatesh, S. (2008). *Gang leader for a day*. London: Penguin.

Vigil, J. D. (2007). *The projects: Gang and non-gang families in East Los Angeles*. Austin: University of Texas Press.

Wilcox, W. B. (2007). *Soft patriarchs, new men: How christianity shapes fathers and husbands*. Chicago and London: University of Chicago Press.

Wolseth, J. (2008). Safety and sanctuary: Pentecostalism and youth gang violence in Honduras. *Latin American Perspectives, 35*, 96–111.

Young, J. (1999). *The exclusive society: Social exclusion, crime and difference in late modernity*. London: Sage.

Disadvantaged students and art school: the outcasts on the inside between acquiescence and contestation

Anna Uboldi

ABSTRACT
This research explores the educational experiences from a qualitative perspective with in-depth interviews and focus groups with disadvantaged young pupils. The research takes place in two secondary art schools in Milan. I define art in the space of educational choices, in a Bourdieusian perspective. This type of school is an ambivalent practical lyceum. I study the meanings of this choice, the educational representations and attitudes of the students as well as the ambitions for the future. I investigate the school choice, the learner identity and the creative aspiration as classed concepts by means of cultural capital and habitus tools. The social class determines the way in which students orient themselves towards creative educational routes and professional future careers. A research of mediocrity and modesty characterises their dispositions towards school and art. The educational artistic experience is considered as a merely autotelic practice without value and relevance to their life. The disadvantaged young students are incomplete neo-liberal subjectivities and their life projects are undefined in terms of tools, aims and trajectories. In sum, I examine the role of secondary art school to reproduce the social disadvantages in terms of educational and professional aspirations.

1. Introduction

In this essay, I will investigate the educational experiences of students from a disadvantaged social background. My focus is on state and private art schools. Art school, with its practical dimension, is a choice that condenses, almost paradoxically, senses of limits and aspirations. I will argue how these pupils, and their educational experiences, can be interpreted in terms of 'outcasts on the inside' (Bourdieu et al., 1993, 602).[1]

I will draw on some of Bourdieu's observations to understand the situations of 'elimination with sweetness' experienced by 'newcomers' and generated by the period spent in the school system (Bourdieu et al., 1993, 600). This reference does not relate, therefore, to an elimination in the strict sense of the term, to those school drop out situations.

I will examine those upper secondary school experiences where the school path prefigures the probability of a self-exclusion from future educational routes, and from the field of creative economy.

It can be assumed that self-exclusion refers to specific dynamics generated by the encounter and interaction between class habitus and school field (Bourdieu & Passeron, 1964).

These considerations are based on my PhD research conducted in two Italian art schools. I will study the educational experiences in the artistic field, viewed as a specific context of study in which definite educational dispositions and creative aspirations converge. Specifically, I will examine the experiences of working-class students with a low family cultural capital.

2. The literature on disadvantaged students

The theoretical framework consists of studies initiated by Bourdieu. They convey a vivid picture of the condition of students coming from disadvantaged social classes (Bourdieu et al., 1993). Bourdieu's work explains how the social class differences act in school dynamics and lead to cultural and social reproduction (Bourdieu & Passeron, 1964,1970).

In particular, the concept of symbolic violence allows one to reflect on the role played by the neo-liberal school rhetoric on the formation of different learning identities. Bourdieu refers to a specific form of violence acting at a symbolic level and operating with the acquiescence of the people. Bourdieu explains it as a: 'violence which is exercised upon a social agent with his or her complicity' (Bourdieu & Wacquant, 1992, p. 167). Symbolic violence is thus the interiorisation of categories of thought by dominated social agents.

In addition, the cultural capital theory is also crucial. Bourdieu (1979a, 1979b) explains social divisions through capitals playing in social fields: economic, cultural, social and symbolic capitals.[2] From this perspective, I have taken the idea of cultural capital and habitus[3] as heuristic tools (Bourdieu, 1974, 1980). I have studied the incorporated cultural capital investigating knowledge, perceptions and meanings of school life (Bourdieu, 1989; Bourdieu & Passeron, 1964), educational career and future and artistic/aesthetic experiences of the interviewees. Finally, I have considered the class habitus as a deeper level to understand dispositions, feelings of familiarity or extraneousness and emotions related to these dimensions. The class habitus is used to study the relationship between the self and the social structure.

I have applied exclusively the institutional and incorporated forms of cultural capital[4] (Bourdieu, 1979a). Following Holt (1998), I have considered the objectivated form of cultural capital as less relevant to understand the distinction dynamics in contemporary Italian society.

A second essential reference concerns the line of research initiated by the work of Willis. It explores forms of symbolic domination through which the subordinate social classes reproduce their own position, cultivating a specific relationship with academic knowledge. However, the students I have interviewed, though characterised by some forms of disaffection and a certain degree of discontent with school, cannot be considered as simple profiles of new 'lads'.[5]

Overall, these represent two basic perspectives of study which, despite their differences, allow us to consider how young people live, adopt and distance themselves from their class position (Mac an Ghaill, 1996). Skeggs explains:

class is made through cultural values premised on morality, embodied in personhood and realised (or not) as a property value in symbolic systems of exchange. The processes I describe work simultaneously across different sites and are solidified, concretised, condensed into bodies and personhood at different moments, generating different compositions and volumes of exchange-value. (Skeggs, 2005, p. 969)

In line with Skeggs's complex considerations, and by bringing them back to a more prag-matic level, it is possible to consider the educational field as a privileged site to observe those class dynamics intervening in the construction of individual subjectivities.

The theoretical reference perspective is, therefore, cultural class analysis (Savage, 2000). It allows me to consider social class as an implicit and tacit dimension, deep-rooted in ways of acting and feeling, in the practical sense of the individuals.

In short, several new sociologists of education have focused their attention (Archer & Yamashita, 2003; Evans, 2006; Gillborn, 2010; Ingram & Bradley, 2013; Lehmann, 2009; Stahl, 2015) on the educational problems experienced by pupils with a low family cultural capital.

These are important reference works in which I can, however, identify some gaps. In fact, research has mainly moved in two directions: on the one hand, analysis has been carried out on extreme experiences of educational and social marginalisation. On the other hand, it has been building up a trend that explores the underlying dynamics of the first form of social mobility represented by educational success. These two research areas are critically important, but nevertheless bring to light only the two extremes of edu-cational and social reproduction processes.

Less attention has therefore been devoted to unproblematic educational experiences marked by traits of ordinariness. However, it is clear that, beyond the specific topics of analysis, this heterogeneous ensemble of studies provides the necessary tools to explore the most diverse educational experiences of disadvantaged youths (Archer & Yamashita, 2003; Ball, Maguire, & Macrae, 2000; Ingram, 2009; Reay, 2005; Roberts & Evans, 2013). A research interest in 'ordinariness', as a characteristic dimension of disad-vantaged classes, has developed only recently, under the impetus arising from the work of scholars such as Savage, Bagnall, and Longhurst (2001), Stahl (2015) and Weis (2004).[6]

Within this general frame, I intend to refer to some recent works developed in sociology from the English-speaking world and, above all, to the contributions of Stahl (2015) and Allen (2014). These studies allow the investigation of the link between social identity and learning identity as well as to explore how young people experience school in a world marked by deep social divisions and a pervasive neo-liberal rhetoric. The first refer-ence point is the research carried out by Allen (2014), investigating the effects of market ideology on aspirations of female students in British art schools. It is one of the few studies on the educational world of creativity, in addition to the research on fashion design schools by McRobbie (2005). The second reference point is the research undertaken by Stahl (2015) on the impact of neo-liberal ideology on young Australian students from dis-advantaged social backgrounds. In the light of the profound social changes which have occurred in recent decades, the author offers some suggestions for further consideration, allowing Willis's and Bourdieu's theories to be updated. In this direction, Stahl develops the concept of egalitarianism as a central feature of the habitus of low-social-class students. However, these studies represent only the necessary starting reference points to analyse disadvantaged young people who refuse to follow both purely professional paths and more traditional upper secondary educational courses.

3. The research: data collection and analysis

The data presented comes from an extensive qualitative doctoral research carried out in art schools in Milan, in the two years 2014–2015. I selected two schools, one state and one private, with very different positions in the city and socio-demographic characteristics of the students. The first school is private and located in a residential area which has pupils from the neighbouring bourgeois areas. The second school is a state school in a multi-ethnic part of the city, which has pupils who live in the north-west outskirts of the city.

I used in-depth interviews and focus groups with the pupils, aged between 16 and 21, and in-depth interviews with their parents. In this article, only the data on the focus group and the interviews with the pupils with a low cultural capital will be examined. The selection of the students took place in three phases, between September 2014 and June 2015. At first, an informative questionnaire was given out in all the classes to collect informed consent and socio-personal details. In the second phase, I selected the students for the focus groups (for a total of 7 focus groups with 8 students each). Lastly, I identified the students for the 30 in-depth interviews. The focus groups and the in-depth interviews were carried out in the schools and during school time, in appropriately arranged spaces. This choice allowed me to complete the interview data with ethnographic observations made during the lessons and everyday school life.

The interviews were carried out using the timeline (Bagnoli, 2009), as a projective stimulus to foster biographical reflection. The timeline is a graphic instrument supporting the conversation where interviewees are asked to complete in pen on a sheet of paper a timeline showing the times and dates of greatest significance for their school and family experience. This instrument makes starting a reflection on the biographical experience easier, for the interviewee, and also makes the organisation of the conversational flow easier. This solution, therefore, allows giving a first-time imprint on the interview, where the introductory reconstruction of the crucial points and transitions forms an interpretative frame within which the interactive dynamic can be deployed.

The choice of the form of interview was dictated by the need for the initial theoretical approach, full of hypotheses and concepts, to have the same serendipity as empirical reality. In essence, I tried to use a plan of an interview able to reflect some theoretical questions trying to avoid remaining trapped in what Bourdieu et al. (1993) defines as scholastic *doxa*. The attempt to make empirical reality and a theoretically aware gaze interact therefore took shape in the choice of a conversational interview with a low level of structuring. I tried to avoid the risk of falling into the transformation of the interview situation into a mere school test. I used the timeline as an instrument to control the interview but also as an opportunity for a first free articulation of the youngsters' experience. In short, through this form of interview, I tried to put into practice, in a pragmatic and simple dimension, the principles of Bourdieu's 'structuralist constructivism' (1997), combining theory and practice in the creation of an interactive dialectic theoretically based and guided but open to empirical reality (Burke, 2016; Kloot, 2016).

The 30 students interviewed were then divided into two macro-groups, distinguishing between more or less privileged. In forming the two groups, the level of education and of the occupational class of both parents were taken into account, ordered according to the principle of dominance.[7]

In the examination of the written interviews, I used a free software of qualitative textual analysis (QDA Miner 4 lite) for preliminary work on the areas and categories of analysis. I subsequently proceeded with a manual analysis of the contents of the texts of the interviews, vertically and horizontally. In this way, I was able to enter the narrations trying to keep the specificity of each single educational path, together with the need to develop a ranking that classified and explained the differences found.

4. Theory and practice as forms of classification: art school in the educational field

The 'artistic lyceum' – a type of upper secondary school specializing in art – is a particular school because it goes beyond the line of division between manual work and intellectual activity. It also alludes to some forms of artistic culture, which appear to be still related to the sphere of high culture, albeit in a veiled relationship that is, in some respects, diluted and moderated by the mostly practical nature of school experience.

Therefore, almost paradoxically, art school is the first institution which creates a basic barrier, giving the right to enter or banning the entrance to the world of art. The art world is a social field in which exclusive and elitist characters persist (Allen & Hollingworth, 2013; Banks & Oakley, 2016; Burke & McManus, 2011; Abbing, 2002; McManus, 2006; McRobbie, 2005). However, it represents, in the education field, an upper secondary school of the second class, with a strong and purely technical imprint and appealing to working-class students.

It is, therefore, possible to consider how art school, with its unique combination of practical and intellectual knowledge, comes into play in class dynamics. These students are in fact different from the 'lads' studied by Willis. They seem to choose the path of upper secondary school as a way to aim at something better, to improve their class condition. Nevertheless, they cannot even be considered to be pure 'class defectors' (Bourdieu, 1979b).

They seem to have established, at the same time, not only a sense of limits, with respect to what they can aspire to, but also a basic attitude that is far, or perhaps just different from, educational and artistic cultures. They seem to have incorporated, and finally reproduced, the same division between manual and intellectual tasks identified by Willis in England in the 1970s, albeit in a peculiar manner. It appears as if these dimensions address those 'forms of classification' analysed by Bourdieu, that 'receive a first objectification in pairs of opposite adjectives' and that 'are always indebted to their ideological effectiveness to the fact of recalling [...] the most fundamental oppositions of the social order: that between dominated and dominants' (Bourdieu, 1979b, p. 469).

4.1. The 'street artist' students and their school contestation

The symbolic ambivalence of art school is to be found in the words of some interviewees. They argue that their decision was made within a space of possible choices where technical and vocational schools were the first options. In doing so, the art school represents a challenge to their destiny, marked by judgments made by school and by categories of their families' perceptions.

For example, one student describes his decision as made at his own initiative, in contrast both with his parents' wishes, who would have liked him to attend a technical school, and with the viewpoint of his teachers.

> I chose it because I like drawing even if my teachers did not approve of it! This was one more reason to show them that they had it all wrong! (Focus group, state upper secondary school)

Another pupil, Luca, talks at length about the deep disappointment he experienced following his teachers' negative judgment and about his decision to act against the assessments made by the 'adult world':

> The first crucial moment in my life is related to the final examinations in eighth grade [...] It was then that I found out how full of shit the adult world is! [...] it has been crucial for me because thanks to this I was able to say 'I'm going to do what I want' without receiving orders from anyone. That's why I went for this school, although some people might have thought that the level of study required was too high for me ... that I wouldn't have made it at any sort of level [...] anyway this was my choice ... to show other people and myself that I can do what I have in mind. (Luca, 16 years old)

Students like Luca regard art school as a second chance, as a chance to redeem themselves as students. However, many of the young people surveyed have had and still have a complex and problematic relationship with education. What emerges from their words is a profound ambivalence (Reay, 2005) towards the world of school. This ambivalence is defined by feelings of attraction and attitudes of a haughty distance, or even mistrust, towards rules, knowledge and education. Moreover, Luca's accounts convey a deep ambivalence with regard to the sense of failure related to his own school experience:

> This will be the basis that will shape me and determine what I will do in the future, so, if I fail here, I will fail in my life, too ... anyway, I am not interested in making a point out of this. (Luca, 16 years old)

According to Reay, the fear of failure expressed by this young student can be interpreted in terms of emotional capital. Therefore, some of the observations made by Reay with regard to British university students from a disadvantaged background could be applied to the students I interviewed, lacking that 2002 typically bourgeois sense of entitlement.

Their educational involvement seems to recall the pattern 'going beyond and then fail. This sense of failure is not merely academic. It involves the individual in a much more holistic sense, to the extent that it seems that they feel they fail as adequate persons' (Reay, 2005, p. 103).

A form of 'resigned disenchantment, disguised in self-confident, casual nonchalance' (Bourdieu et al., 1993, p. 603) recurs in their narratives and, in particular, in their descriptions of school days, mostly spent away from classrooms and focusing on the extensive use of recreational areas, such as school playgrounds. The school playground is a liminal zone, characterised by substantial freedom, where you can find students smoking, but also doing artistic activities, such as in painting or making graffiti at any time. As explained by Willis, fighting to claim spaces of symbolic autonomy can be considered as a small form of everyday resistance to school authority. However, an ambivalent attitude towards education can be found in the words of the young people interviewed. This ambivalence differs from the forms of rebellion studied by Willis and seems to be close to some of the attitudes towards school and legitimate culture adopted by disadvantaged youth as observed by Weis (2004) in America in the 1980s.

Moreover, with respect to the students I interviewed, the relationship with the culture of the school bears a particular connotation because it is closely linked to artistic practice. It is a moment and a way of partial reconciliation with the school (Stahl & Dale, 2013). As explained during the interviews, the only reason they felt motivated to attend school on a daily basis was to dedicate themselves to artistic practice. The rejection of the school system does not correspond to a radical closure, whereas participation in school life, even if *sui generis* and as a way to claim their own time and space (Weis, 2004), is considered relevant. As Luca explains:

> It's important because it shapes you for the rest of your life I mean, a man without culture, in my opinion, is not a man so … […] but I'm a little bit unconventional here because I am not a hundred per cent sure that school is useful at all …. (Luca, 16 years old)

It is, however, a complex relationship where the desire to be distant from the rules and the legitimate culture remains relevant, even if it does not lead to a clear opposition.

The interviewees experience different forms and degrees of alienation from school (Reay, 2009). For example, a sense of extraneousness with respect to some contents of legitimate culture and to the school experience itself can be detected in the words of the students interviewed.

> I realised that the guys here are treated … as if they are nothing […] here we do not learn anything, they force us to do things that are absolutely unnecessary, that are useless […] so, I think that today almost everyone has a degree and I believe I will never get one. (Valerio, 21 years old)

These narratives recall some considerations made by Reay. In analysing the class dynamics involved in the making of a learning identity, Reay observes that it is necessary to consider those 'small and mundane class injuries that permeate […] the interactions between teachers and pupils. Class identifications, visceral aversions and feelings of inferiority and superiority are aspects of the daily routine of school life' (Reay, 2005, p. 917). From their narratives there emerges a sense of uselessness of their own school experience; an attitude that recalls the 'class injuries' perpetrated by the school system and according to which the school is set up as 'a place [where] too often they are seen, and see themselves as worthless' (Reay, 2009, p. 27). For example:

> When it comes to art, I give everything I have. And it is hard to realise that all the things you work so hard on have no power. And, since they are powerless, they avoid power because they are you, but you are not worth anything, and your things are worth nothing. As with Van Gogh and his paintings. They were great masterpieces. And you, just like them, you are worthless as a student, as an artist. (Piero, 16 years old)

> Art is my personal thing […] art has made me visible to the world … to the people around me … and it is just you in the end[…] look, being here, attending something useless, like school, is already too much for me. (Focus group, state upper secondary school)

These students show a strong interest in art practice; however, it is experienced as an instrument of resistance to education, which is considered too stringent. It seems to be some sort of tactic, a mediator instrument between messages coming from different cultural worlds, such as the school and the disadvantaged background which they come from. It is, therefore, a way to reconcile a potentially dual and divided habitus (Ingram, 2011; Stahl, 2013).

> So it's like I'm ... as if, on the one side there are disadvantaged people and on the other those who are ok and I'm right in the middle. (Focus group, state upper secondary school)

In this way, it is possible to retrieve some suggestions developed by Archer with regard to performances of style of English students. Archer explains how students' involvement in these creative practices 'can be read as attempts to generate capital and to claim recognition and value through alternative means within schools' (Archer, Hollingworth, & Halsall, 2007, p. 226). There are expressions of opposition to school that contribute to reproducing a disadvantaged condition. These attempts to build value within scholastically weak subjectivity become, thus, resistant 'to class injuries' experienced in school and, in particular, to those feelings of nothingness and worthlessness that seem to have marked their school experience.

Art becomes a *limen* in which to play with one's student identity and where to renegotiate one's school and social failures. They are forms of reproductive contestation, where the act of embracing art seems to lead to a certain marginalisation by the school system, considered as distant and different from one's authentic subjectivity. Art is outlined as a tactic, an opposition to a fate which has already been preordained: both in the choice of upper secondary school, opposed to vocational school, and in the vision of the future, where subordinate and repetitive jobs are feared, and where, at the same time, ambitious projects are rejected. For example, with his words this student expresses his anger at the issues in his life; an anger that expresses his own perception of art:

> Honestly, right now ... All I would like to do would be to get up. take these desks and then break them all apart. And once I have done that, I would leave this entire pile of wood right there, in the middle of the room. And this is what I call art ...
>
> Well yes.
>
> I would spear the chair in the desk, break everything and apply a heart made of chalk. I don't know why I do art, guys ... It's all very confused in my mind. (Focus group, state upper secondary school)

Prefiguring oneself as an artist becomes a way of dreaming of a future that is different from the one that has been prescribed, without having to convert one's own class identity to the values of a bourgeois world.

In conclusion, these students seem to identify the profile of outcasts from the inside. In this context Bourdieu says: 'obliged by negative sanctions from the school to give up to educational and social aspirations [...] they treat without conviction an education that they know without future' (Bourdieu et al., 1993, p. 603).

4.2. The 'scholastic' students and the reproductive acquiescence

The profile of 'scholastic'[8] students is attributed to young people with a good educational path. They seem to quietly adhere to academic values. They are neither overly committed to the study nor show signs of disaffection. The dimension of ordinariness seems to mark their experience in art school and, eventually, their own learner identity[9] (Brown, 1987).

The decision to pursue an artistic path is set up as a choice among many, often not animated by a particular artistic passion, and especially not intended to remedy a difficult educational career. Art is merely a school subject, to which to devote effort and attention but without any cult of the gift or artistic love. These pupils are 'scholastic' connoisseurs of art. From their narratives, a marked interest characterised by the register of the 'didactic' as 'an expression of monopolizing power of scholastic study' (Bourdieu & Passeron,1964, 176) emerges:

> I mean, I like it ... but I don't see it as a passion and so yes ... it stops here at school [...] I don't know a lot (she laughs) about these e things. (Teresa, 17 years old)

These words recall Bourdieu's considerations on the subject. He explains how the most hard-working student can simply learn the contents, even the most amateurish ones, but nevertheless he remains stuck in one 'good cultural will' (Bourdieu & Passeron, 1970, p. 42) and, thus, within a didactic and notional vision. In addition, what distinguishes their learning identities is a particular orientation towards modesty and mediocrity, in the valorisation and search for ordinariness.

It is a characteristic trait of the working-class condition that, as Stahl (2015), Brown (1987), Sayer (2005) and Savage et al. (2001) put it, has different facets. Based on Stahl, I can observe how, in these students, egalitarianism becomes a fundamental means to give a meaning to their role in the school. In their narratives, what Stahl defines an 'anti-aspirant egalitarianism' can be identified, which leads them to pursue educational mediocrity and to refuse success, as a characteristic middle-class value (Sayer, 2005).

As Reay explains, the creation of biographies marked by 'ordinariness' seems to be defined as a means to maximise the same ability to negotiate potential failure. As a matter of fact, expressions of 'normality' and quiet involvement often recur in the considerations made by the students I interviewed:

> Q: What kind of student are you?
> A: Well I get fairly good grades at school, huh ... oh well ... that's normal ... [...] all in all, I do not see myself as different ... There is nothing particularly abnormal about myself as compared to other students ... . (Giulia, 18 years old)

> Q: And how has your educational path been?
> A: Well, I must tell you ... then ... oh I generally get ... fairly good grades [...] There is nothing I am particularly proud of, but that's quite normal, I have nothing to be proud of but there is also nothing not to be proud of. That's it. (Erica, 18 years old)

> Q: What is your attitude towards school?
> A: Normal, in the sense I cannot say 'going to art school is my passion' ... but I cannot even say: 'I hate going to school' ... usually I do it because it is right [...] At the moment, this is what I have to do at the end of the day and I just do it. (Teresa, 17 years old)

In these students, mediocrity is a way to balance their class identity within the school context (Brown, 1987). In conclusion, following Aggleton's (1984) considerations, I can observe how active adhesion to the school *ethos*[10] (Bourdieu, 1989) activates the dynamics of reproductive acquiescence, resulting in the reproduction of class disadvantage.

4.3. Dispositions towards the future: unfulfilled dreams and aspirations

Lastly, it is appropriate to examine the effects of symbolic domination taking shape when defining aspirations. The starting point is the considerations of Bourdieu, who explains the class nature of dispositions towards the future arguing that 'the relationship with the possible is a relationship with powers' (1980, p. 102).

Firstly, in the educational and professional aspirations of the students I interviewed, I can identify a 'modest' disposition, a levelling. For example, a very general definition of a life project, implying having an acceptable profession and a family, emerges from the words of this girl:

> I don't know ... when I'm 26, 27 years ... maybe then I will think about having ... a family, about something (she laughs) and ... maybe even an ordinary job ... maybe I will start my own business ... (she laughs). (Francesca, 16 years old)

For many of these young people, studying art is a choice made in a *doxic* opposition, or in a partial indifference, to the logic of the market; a sterile way that, in their opinion, will lead them to an uncertain future. I can read in these experiences a common 'cut off destiny' (Bourdieu & Passeron, 1964, p. 229).

These young people do not seem to interpret their artistic skills as something that can be profitably employed in their life. The art school is considered a path to a *cul de sac* that precludes many other routes, in particular those leading to the most traditional university courses.

> I am not cut out for this [the reference is to university] because I realise that without a solid basis it is very difficult ... I realise that it's not something that I care about so much as to say: 'okay, in the summer I will study a subject that I have never studied before to pass the test' ... that's the way it is. (Erica, 18 years old)

Moreover, the purely autotelic definition of art (Holt, 1998) is reflected in their educational and professional aspirations, which are predominated by a sense of disorientation about the future. Therefore, these young people tend not to take into account any creative profession because they are perceived as distant from their daily experience and as hard goals to reach.

> Q: Why? What do you think you'll be doing in the future?
> A: Well, I am thinking about living in another country. I do not know, for a couple of years, and then the best thing for me to do would be to open a business with my friends ... a restaurant or a bar ... something to be able to work in good company if I really have to do it (he laughs). I have been working in a restaurant for two years and I like cooking! (Andrea, 20 years old)

> I would like to work in the art field but, I don't know, I wouldn't mind working as a barman. It doesn't matter! That's it! In the end, if you have a family, it's fine, you can say that you are happy to work as a cleaner to give money to your son ... That's it. What I want to say is that it doesn't matter if I don't become an artist. (she laughs). (Francesca, 16 years old)

> Q: And how do you see yourself in the future?
> A: I see myself ... not as a painter but I don't know ... maybe I would see myself doing something different ... working as a make-up artist. I wouldn't see myself as a sculptor or a painter, I mean, as a person that earns money by selling works of art. (Giulia, 18 years old)

Their own artistic skills and competences seem to be confined to very practical and manual terms. For example, several girls mentioned the idea of becoming a professional make-up artist. During one of the interviews Giulia told me that her dream would be to work at La Scala theatre as a make-up artist. However, after a few months, during our second conversation, she talked to me about the difficulties she was encountering, about having been rejected from a vocational make-up artist school and about her decision to look for a similar position in retail as a sales assistant for make-up products. Giulia is still convinced that art, viewed as the ability to work as make-up artist, is her path. It is curious that her secondary school teachers suggested she attend a vocational school for hairdressers. Fate, or 'call to order, that is, the probable' (Bourdieu, 1997, p. 86), to some extent, seems to repeat itself and Giulia appears to have accepted it, even after five difficult years in secondary school.

Although, when defining professional projects, art is rejected or considered in very practical terms, it is mainly in the educational aspirations that it adds instability and insecurity to the lives of these students (Atkinson, 2010, p. 198). Indeed, the continuation of studies is not considered as inevitable and is characterised by the absence of a clear and strong plan.

> If I go to university … I don't know … otherwise I'm going to take courses that last a year, but they are expensive and then I will have to see (she laughs) courses in cinema makeup … I have no other idea […] I can't study design or something similar … it's not my real passion … I'd do it just to earn money, but I won't find it easy … , but I still have to look at what I can do. (Sonia, 18 years old)

> I don't know. I'd like to become a student at the art academy, well I hope I'll be able to. Otherwise I wouldn't mind doing a course … who knows?! I mean, maybe in five years I will change my mind completely and I'll end up abroad (he laughs). (Piero, 16 years old)

These students seem to lack planning skills, enabling them to link their present to their future goals. The future is, indeed, imagined in confused and abstract terms. Not only their preordained jobs have very general traits, as noted by Willis (1981), but university is also seen as a very remote option, and defined in a very vague way. In essence, what prevails is not a definite rejection but a sense of disorientation, well exemplified by the recurring expression: 'I don't know'. For example:

> Eh … I don't know about that … I cannot imagine a future … in a job … I don't know how … I don't know what I will do, I cannot see myself … (she laughs). (Marta, 19 years old)

> Good question! (she laughs) I think I will continue to study but I have not decided what yet … I really don't know because even if I think about university I see so many potentially interesting options, but I cannot see myself fully interested in any of them. I see so many things but none of them is what I really want to do. I still need to clear my mind […] I can say psychology and cinema make-up, but I wouldn't exclude journalism … really I am not oriented toward a specific thing. (Erica, 18 years old)

> I don't know why I don't really like Brera (art academy in Milan) […]; I do not know. There is no particular reason why I decided not to continue … . (Valerio, 21 years old)

> I don't know which faculty to choose at university or if I go to university, I hope to go … but, I am not fully convinced of what I have to do yet, because I don't know … no one has ever told me how it works, what university is like, what I could do. (Luca, 16 years old)

Finally, some of them questioned the usefulness of university education when confronted with the imperative need to work:

> I think that university is useful on the one hand. But on the other, it is not because you spend five years of your life studying instead of working. And perhaps, once you have worked for five years you can become head, rather than being unemployed with a piece of paper (academic certificate)! (Focus group, state upper secondary school)

In a similar way, this other student seems to assume a fatalistic attitude of self-exclusion and, from his words, it emerges how freedom of choice is 'conditioned by the realms of impossibility. He is aware of what is not possible. His imagination about the future is open and closed in a single paragraph' (Ball et al., 2000, p. 133):

> Q: So are you planning to go to the academy?
> R: Well, the idea has always fascinated me and I think it's something that I might do, sooner or later, maybe in a few years' time … but, I am in no rush, because I think these things are a bit … it's something that comes naturally, that I do just for myself, because, as I said before, working as an artist it's difficult […] impossible even …. (Andrea, 20 years old)

The new creative economy seems to be defined as something that 'is not for them' (Bourdieu, 1979b), job options in these fields are in fact considered and immediately rejected (Atkinson, 2010). The artistic disposition remains, therefore, part of school subjects or future practical hobbies and does not seem to be able to guide their educational or professional continuation. In this sense, facing the absence of certainty and secure plans, the future is clearly seen as a burden rather than an opportunity to explore new chances. In conclusion, these young people seem, paraphrasing Bourdieu's words, 'to accept without drama or revolt' their own exclusion; and, eventually, as taught by the French sociologist, they show how the class ethos is at the basis of the same 'principle of the level of professional aspiration' (Bourdieu & Passeron, 1964, p. 253).

4.3.1. Between reflexivity and pragmatic fatalism: the attitudes regarding the future

These students do not have a highly individualised subjectivity; their narratives reveal a lack of reflective capacity (Leccardi, 2006). It can be observed how 'the reflexive self' is a 'very specific class formation' (Skeggs, 2004). Considerations about the future, particularly possible obstacles and difficulties, reveal a deep interiorisation of the sense of limits. They do not show an absence of aspirations but, nevertheless, seem to implicitly recognise the limits that come between their daily life experience and the highest educational and professional routes (Archer, 2010).

The definition of basic objectives, such as obtaining a job or an academic qualification, is thus accompanied by the identification of obstacles, in which the identification of material problems prevails, as already noted by Nilan and Threadgold (2009). These obstacles go beyond their skills, commitment and devotion to the effort and mainly refer to external difficulties linked to socio-economic conditions.

Therefore, in their narratives I can detect a high perception of risk and a low propensity to individualisation, considered as the reflective ability to elaborate biographical projects. In the words of these young people, realistic and disillusioned attitudes predominate:

> Eh I am afraid to think about what will happen when I leave here, because it is difficult for young people to find a job … and because of what my parents tell me. That it would be

better to get a degree, because this way I will have something, but I do not know ... It saddens me to think that I might have to do something that I do not like very much ... I do not want to end up doing something that I am not interested in! (Teresa, 17 years old)

Q: What obstacles do you foresee?
A: A lot (he laughs) and I don't know ... because I want to go away and the idea of going away and then coming back here and maybe not being able to do anything for a couple of years. It's this possibility that scares me a lot (he laughs). But I think that everyone can find a job, even if it is not what really suits you ... maybe you can find something ... but I am working right now because I like it, because I can concentrate more on ... but studying ... I'm not good at studying (he laughs). (Focus group, state upper secondary school)

But I would not see myself so very different from how I am now [...] I'll always be the same, lacking interest in studying, and yet wanting to create something, to assimilate and then reproduce and work. (Andrea, 20 years old)

Instead of going to university, which is probably what I don't want to do, because I will waste time and money [...] this is what I fear[...] I know that I should study, plan what I want to do, but the problem is that I don't know what I want do [...]. This is what I lack, I have no certainties, and so I don't want to. (Filippo, 17 years old)

In the words of the last two students, I can see some fragments of the symbolic violence exercised by school. The reference to the practical dimension of doing, creating, assimilating and producing is in contrast with the theoretical and intellectual reference.

This contrast is explained by a disciplined view, which seems to have assimilated the educational values. Indeed, the path taken by these students is recognised as wrong; a way that is disrespectful of the imperative of creating one's own biography, according to the neo-liberal precepts. Their words might, therefore, be a small example of how neo-liberalism has become a pervasive form of symbolic violence. Following some suggestions from the works of Atkinson (2010), Skeggs and Loveday (2012) and Reay, I can see the effects of the interiorisation of symbolic domination exercised by the school system. These young people seem to regard and to interpret themselves from the point of view of those who dominate, of a neo-liberal doxa (Bourdieu, 1998). A symbolic domination that works through the same processes of individualisation, and that seems also traceable in the strong sense of individual responsibility perceived by these students for their weakness and failure related to their learning and social identity.

Nevertheless, these young people seem distant from those highly reflective subjectivities, characteristic of the era of individualisation, able to interpret themselves as active builders and entrepreneurs of their present and future condition (Ball et al., 2000). For example, these students have no aim, except in abstract and generic terms:

I don't know what I will do, I don't know what I will be ... . and I haven't got long-term projects yet ... my only goal would be to travel because I don't find what I'm studying here interesting ... it's not my nature ... so, sitting down and reading for hours ... or writing these things ... they aren't for me. I know it's the right path for a ... that it's a correct path to follow and it should be carried out for my ... I'm not liking it perhaps because I didn't like the schools I went to ... because I didn't particularly like what I studied, because of the relations with my teachers ... in other words, because of everything. (Valerio, 21 years old)

And what work do you dream of doing?

Hum (he laughs) no ... no, I think that my highest working aspiration would be to have a studio where I can carry out my work [...] and to start my own business with my friends ... I am not a person with high expectations (he laughs). (Andrea, 20 years old)

To summarise, the narratives of these pupils give a realistic view of their lives, of the world they can be content with. As noted by Stahl, they are subjectivities that can be 'happy with less', permeated by a sense of modesty that eliminates any ambitious imagination about the future. Based on Ball, I can see in them a sense of 'lethargy, fear, passivity and reactivity. There are plans, ideas, possibilities that remain in the not yet [...] a form of social minimalism [...] there is a sense of unfulfilled possibilities [...] futures are vague, late, difficult to think' (Ball et al., 2000, pp. 108–110).

In their narratives, I observe that they are aware of a difficult future due to unemployment and to the economic crisis. The attitude of fatalism and resigned acquiescence towards this socio-economic situation goes beyond their possibilities and hopes of control (Farrugia, 2013). In conclusion, these students can be considered as the new outcasts from the inside, whereas the exclusion exercised by the school system seems to lead to, or better to convince them of, precarious, uncertain and nebulous destinies (Marks, 2003).

As explained by Kenway and Kraack (2004), disadvantaged young people nowadays experience a very different situation from the industrial world studied by Willis; it is a situation that leads them to reshape and redefine themselves through forms of involvement in the educational world but, at the same time, even towards the same resigned acceptance of uncertainty. An open future that is experienced with a meaning of negativity. In conclusion, the students I interviewed seem distant from the precepts of neo-liberalism, which encourage them to 'make an enterprise of themselves' (Apple, 2006, p. 63).

With their pragmatic realism and with their dreams, which have been interrupted in their preliminary reflexive elaboration, these young people mostly appear as imperfect neo-liberal subjects (Skeggs, 2004), lacking a strong spirit of initiative and enterprise. Paraphrasing Evans, I can see how these students are characterised by 'passive forms of individualisation in which the goals are weakly defined and the strategies to achieve them remain uncertain' (Evans & Heinz, 1994, p. 15).

In this way, it is possible to agree with France, Evans (2002), Roberts (2007), Furlong and Cartmel, (2006), Nilan and Threadgold (2009) and Farrugia (2013) in assuming that the reflective capacity is primarily a social class resource. As Roberts (2007) explains, a 'structured individualism' seems to mark the biographical experiences of students with a low family cultural capital. These young people, in fact, exercise a certain reflexivity, and yet always within a structure of opportunities defined by the class system and by the characteristics of the labour and school market. As discussed above, the students I interviewed are reflexively involved in biographical choice processes; however, their own future orientations seem to still reflect their class memberships.

5. Conclusions

In this essay, I have investigated the experience of students with a low cultural capital at art school. These experiences appear to share some common traits of an ordinary, insecure, fatalistic and yet pragmatic habitus. The latter seems to attenuate their deep individual differences and to reveal, on the other hand, the same class condition. As Skeggs explains well:

> What is significant in the use of culture as a resource in the self-making is how different forms of subjectivities are made available to different groups; subjects with or without value; different forms of subjectivity and thus shape and unfold class differences. (Skeggs, 2005, p. 975)

Therefore, a common fatalistic *habitus* polishes the differences in school abilities, bringing both the most diligent and the most rebellious towards the perspective of an uncertain future. In these students, I cannot observe a clear absence of aspirations and a linear formation of an anti-school culture. However, there are ambivalent processes of identification and de-identification from their class condition (Reay, 2001). This dynamic reveals a perception of deep insecurity and disorientation around their aspirations (Allen, 2014).

Therefore, I have studied their learning identities, exploring the feelings of alienation and affinity experienced while at school. As Bourdieu explains, 'in all the activities in which one expresses the relationship that a group of students establishes with their studies, there emerges [...] the fundamental relationship that their social class has with society, success and culture' (Bourdieu & Passeron, 1970, p. 44).

What has emerged is a profile of students involved in relationships of dependence, both of opposition and of acquiescence, on the school system, its legitimate representatives and their own judgments. This peculiar involvement in the game played by school seems to lead them out of it, or at least to its margins. The future educational pathways are perceived as uncertain and unlikely. In addition, these students view the artistic sphere itself as external and distant from their everyday experience in the family. Art thus becomes a pure manual skill, a school notion or even, in some cases, an emblem of unreal aspirations of rebellion against the 'order of things' (Bourdieu, 1979b).

To summarise, I can refer to some considerations by Reay who explains how, due to the symbolic violence carried out by neo-liberalism, disadvantaged young people are characterised by a

> concentrated ambivalence. The ambivalent nature holds together opposing affective orientations toward the same object [...] Although they are involved in discourses of individualisation as part of a series of self-protective tactics, they are the victims of neoliberalism, not its beneficiaries. (Reay, 2013, p. 43)

A *habitus* of outcasts shapes the lenses used by these young students to navigate the world. They seem to show a 'counter habitus' (Stahl, 2014) when compared to the neoliberal dictates. The ideas of flexibility and self-employment are in contrast with a lack of tools capable of neutralizing the negative aspects of risk taking, related to the exploration of opportunities.

In conclusion, it can be observed how this study leaves many spaces open and unexplored. It raises questions, for example, on other art schools. In addition, the role of teachers, dedicating specific attention to them, could be explored in greater depth.

Lastly, at the interpretative level, the dimension of gender has partly remained in silence in the analysis proposed. This is a conscious decision and dictated mainly by the need to limit the most significant dimensions for the response to the initial questions of the research, according to the path shared by other scholars (Ball et al., 2000; Burke, 2016; Reay, Ball, & David, 2005). However, it is clear that the models of gender are interwoven with class belonging in forging specific social and learning identities. The analysis of this topic, however, would have required extending the initial cognitive questions and modifying the outlines of the interview. The interview data collected do not allow precisely identifying differences of gender in the relation that the students have with the world of school.

Nevertheless, the results of the research raise new questions on the different nuances of gender of the class habitus observed. In this direction, feminist-inspired sociology of education offers some lines of potential development of work (Allen, 2014; Mac an Ghaill, 1996; Skeggs, 2004; Walkerdine & Ringrose, 2006). Based on the work of Mac an Ghaill, we could, for example, reflect on which forms of masculinity have been developed by the students, who differ from the 'lads' of Willis but also from that new expression of neo-liberal and bourgeois masculinity, represented by 'the muscular intellectual' (1996). We could investigate if and how the different models of gender, male and female, are translated and take shape in the learning identities of the young people who look at creative fields (Allen, 2014). These are questions which remain open and require studies.

Notes

1. All quotations from Bourdieu's books are my translations.
2. The economic capital is related to material and financial assets. The social capital concerns the social relationship and the resources linked to forms of affiliation to a social group. The symbolic capital refers to the effects of any form of capital. Finally, Bourdieu distinguishes three forms of cultural capital (Bourdieu, 1979a, 1979b).
3. The habitus is a basic notion in Bourdieu's framework. It refers to tacit ways of acting, thinking and evaluating interiorised through everyday life (Bourdieu, 1994).
4. To define working-class students with a low family cultural capital, I acted in two ways. First, I selected those students whose parents have low qualifications (low upper secondary school and upper secondary vocational school). Then I studied the habitus and the incorporated cultural capital by analysing interview narratives.
5. The term 'lad' is used by Willis (1981) to identity a group of working-class students with a counter-culture characterised by a rejection of scholastic values. It is a slang expression retrieved by Willis from the same students.
6. One of the few exceptions has been the work of Brown (1987).
7. The employment class was attributed to the family corresponding to the highest class between the occupations of the two parents, independently of the fact of whether the employment that that of the mother or of the father, instead of considering only the father's.
8. Scholastic is used as a generic adjective to depict students abiding to school rules.
9. The term 'learner identity' (Reay, 2010) indicates forms and ways of involvement in school world by pupils. These ways contribute to shaping specific students' social identities.
10. The term 'ethos' is used by Bourdieu (Bourdieu & Passeron, 1964, 1970; Bourdieu, 1989) to indicate the sphere of values and tacit beliefs.

Acknowledgements

I would like to express my gratitude to the young students who took part in this research. I would also like to thank the editors and the anonymous reviewers for your helpful comments. I am grateful to Prof. Mario De Benedittis for the encouragement and also to Prof. Marcello Maneri, Prof. Alan Warde and Prof. Carmen Leccardi for the advice and careful observations to my PhD research thesis and to my first Professor of Sociology, Prof. Gianmarco Navarini.

Disclosure statement

No potential conflict of interest was reported by the author.

Notes on contributor

Anna Uboldi is a PhD scholar in Applied Sociology at the University of Milano Bicocca. Teacher assistant at the University of Milano.

References

Abbing, H. (2002). *Why are artists poor?* Amsterdam: Amsterdam University Press.

Aggleton, P. (1984). *Rebels without a cause*. London: The Falmer Press.

Allen, K., & Hollingworth, S. (2013). Social class, place and urban young people's aspirations for work in the knowledge economy: 'sticky subjects' or 'cosmopolitan creatives'? *Urban Studies, 50*(3), 499–517. doi:10.1177/0042098012468901

Allen, K. (2014). Blair's children: Young women as 'aspirational subjects' in the psychic landscape of class. *The Sociological Review, 62*, 760–779. doi:10.1111/1467954X.12113

Apple, M. (2006). *Educating the 'Right' way. Markets, standards, God, and inequality*. London: Routledge.

Archer, L, Hollingworth, S., & Halsall, A. (2007). 'University's not for Me – I'm a Nike Person': Urban, working-class young people's negotiations of 'style', identity and educational engagement. *Sociology, 41*(2), 219–237. doi:10.1177/0038038507074798

Archer, L. (2010). Making jobs 'thinkable': Engaging with the complexity of young people's career aspirations. Retrieved from http://hdl.voced.edu.au/10707/269150

Archer, L., & Yamashita, H. (2003). Knowing their limits'? Identities, inequalities and inner city school leavers' post-16 aspirations. *Journal of Education Policy, 18*(1), 53–69. doi:10.1080/0268093032000042209

Atkinson, W. (2010). *Class, individualization and late modernity. In search of the reflexive worker*. London: Palgrave.

Bagnoli, A. (2009). Beyond the standard interview: The Use of graphic elicitation and arts-based methods. *Qualitative Research, 9*(5), 547–570. doi:10.1177/1468794109343625

Ball, S., Maguire, M., & Macrae, S. (2000). *Choice, pathways and transitions post-16*. London: Routledge.

Banks, M., & Oakley, K. (2016), The dance goes on forever? Art schools, class and UK higher education. *International Journal of Cultural Policy, 22*(1), 41–57. doi:10.1080/10286632.2015.1101082

Bourdieu, P., Accardo, A., Balazs, G., Beaud, S., Bonvin, F., Bourdieu, E., ….Waser, A.-M. (1993). *La misère du monde*. Paris: Éditions de Seuil.

Bourdieu, P. (1974). Avenir de classe et causalité du probable. *Revue française de sociologie, 15*(1), 3–42. Retrieved from http://www.persee.fr/doc/rfsoc_0035-2969_1974_num_15_1_2234

Bourdieu, P. (1979a). Les trois états du capital culturel. *Actes de la recherche en sciences sociales, 30*, 3–6. doi:10.3406/arss.1979.2654

Bourdieu, P. (1979b). *La distinction. Critique sociale du jugement*. Paris: Minuit.

Bourdieu, P. (1980). *Le sens pratique*. Paris: Minuit.

Bourdieu, P. (1989). *La Noblesse d'état. Grandes écoles et esprit de corps*. Paris: Minuit.

Bourdieu, P. (1994). *Raisons pratiques. Sur la théorie de l'action*. Paris: Seuil.

Bourdieu, P. (1997). *Méditations pascaliennes, éléments pour une philosophie négative*. Paris: Seuil.

Bourdieu, P. (1998). *Contre-feux. Propos pour servir à la résistance contre l'invasion néo-libérale*. Paris: Liber.

Bourdieu, P., & Passeron, J. C. (1964). *Les héritiers. Les étudiants et la culture*. Minuit: Paris.

Bourdieu, P., & Passeron, J. C. (1970). *La réproduction. Éléments pour une théorie du système d'enseignement*. Paris: Minuit.

Bourdieu, P., & Wacquant, L. (1992). *Réponses. Pour une anthropologie réflexive*. Paris: Seuil.

Brown, P. (1987). *Schooling ordinary kids*. London: Routledge.

Burke C. (2016). *Culture, capitals, and graduate futures: Degrees of class*. London: Routledge.

Burke, J. P., & McManus, J. (2011). Art for a few: Exclusions and misrecognitions in higher education admissions practices. *Discourse: Studies in the Cultural Politics of Education, 32*(5), 699–712. doi:10.1080/01596306.2011.620753

Evans, G. (2006). *Educational failure and working class white children in Britain*. New York, NY: Palgrave MacMillan.

Evans, K., & Heinz, W. (1994). *Becoming adult in England and Germany*. London: Anglo-German foundation.

Evans, K. (2002). Taking control of their lives? Agency in young adult transitions in England and the New Germany. *Journal of Youth Studies, 5*(3), 245–269. doi:10.1080/1367626022000005965

Farrugia, D. (2013). Young people and structural inequality: Beyond the middle ground. *Journal of Youth Studies, 16*(5), 679–693. doi:10.1080/13676261.2012.744817

Furlong, A., & Cartmel, F. (2006). *Young people and social change*. Milton Keynes: Open University Press.

Gillborn, D. (2010). The white working class, racism and respectability: Victims, degenerates and inter-est-convergence. *British Journal of Educational Studies, 58*(1), 3–25. doi:10.1080/00071000903516361

Holt, D. (1998). Does cultural capital structure American consumption? *Journal of Consumer Research, 25*, 1–25. doi:10.1086/209523

Ingram, N., & Bradley, H. (2013). Banking on the future: Choices, asporations and economic hardship in working- class students experience. In W. Atkinson, M. Savage, & S. Roberts (Eds.), *Class inequality in Austery Britain* (pp. 51–69). London: Palgrave.

Ingram, N. (2009). Working-Class boys, educational success and the misrecognition of working-class culture. *British Journal of Sociology of Education, 30*(4), 421–434. doi:10.1080/01425690902954604

Ingram, N. (2011). Within school and beyond the gate: The complexities of being educationally suc-cessful and working class. *Sociology, 45*(2), 287–302. doi:10.1177/0038038510394017

Kenway, J., & Kraack, A. (2004). Reordering work and destabilizing masculinity. In N. Dolby, G. Dimitriadis, & P. Willis (Eds.), *Learning to labor in new times* (pp. 81–94). London: Routledge Falmer.

Kloot, B. (2016). Narrative inquiry as a method for embedding Bourdieu's tools. In C. Costa, & M. Murphy (Eds.), *Theory as method in research* (pp. 132–151). London: Routledge.

Leccardi, C. (2006). Redefining the future: Youthful biographical constructions in the 21st century. *New Directions for Child and Adolescent Development, 113*, 37–48. doi:10.1002/cd.167

Lehmann, W. (2009). University as vocational education: Working-class students' expectations for university. *British Journal of Sociology of Education, 30*(2), 137–149. doi:10.1080/01425690802700164

Mac an Ghaill, M. (1996). Sociology of education, state schooling and social class: Beyond critiques of the New right hegemony. *British Journal of Sociology of Education, 17*(2), 163–176. doi:10.1080/0142569960170203

Marks, A. (2003). Welcome to the new ambivalence: Reflections on the historical and current cultural antagonism between the working-class male and higher education. *British Journal of Sociology of Education, 24*(1), 83–93. doi:10.1080/01425690301910

McManus, J. (2006). Every word starts with Dis. The impact of class on choice, application and admis-sions to prestigious higher education Art and design courses. *Reflecting Education, 2*(1), 73–84. Retrieved from http://ualresearchonline.arts.ac.uk/645/

McRobbie, A. (2005). *British fashion design. Rag trade or image industry?* London: Routledge.

Nilan, P., & Threadgold, S. (2009). Reflexivity of contemporary youth, risk and cultural capital. *Current Sociology, 57*(1), 47–68. doi:10.1177/0011392108097452

Reay, D. (2001). Finding or losing yourself? Working-class relationships to education. *Journal of Education Policy, 16*(4), 333–346. doi:10.1080/02680930110054335

Reay, D. (2005). Beyond consciousness? The psychic landscape of social class. *Sociology, 39*(5), 911–928. doi:10.1177/0038038505058372

Reay, D. (2009). Making sense of white working class educational under achievement. In K. P. Sveinsson (Ed.), *Who cares about the white working class?* (pp. 22–28). London: Runnymede Perspectives. Retrieved from: http://www.runnymedetrust.org http://www.runnymedetrust.org

Reay, D. (2010). Identity-making in schools and classrooms. In M. Wetherell, & M. C. Talpade (Eds.), *The SAGE handbook of identities* (pp. 277–295). London: Sage.

Reay, D. (2013). 'We never get a fair chance': Working class experiences of education in the twenty-first century. In W. Atkinson, M. Savage, & S. Roberts (Eds.), *Class inequality in Austery Britain* (pp. 277–294). London: Palgrave.

Reay, D., David, M., & Ball, S. (2005). *Degrees of choice: Class, race, gender and higher education*. London: Sage.

Roberts, K. (2007). Youth transitions and generations: A response to Wyn and Woodward. *Journal of Youth Studies, 10*(3), 263–269. doi:10.1080/13676260701204360

Roberts, S., & Evans, S. (2013). 'Aspirations' and imaginated futures: The im/possibilities for Britains' young working class. In W. Atkinson, M. Savage, & S. Roberts (Eds.), *Class inequality in Austery Britain* (pp. 33–50). London: Palgrave.

Savage, M., Bagnall, G., & Longhurst, B. (2001). Ordinary, ambivalent and defensive: Class identities in the northwest of England. *Sociology, 35*(4), 875–892. doi:10.1177/0038038501035004005

Savage, M. (2000). *Class analysis and social transformation*. Buckingham: Open University Press.

Sayer, A. (2005). *The moral significance of class*. Cambridge: Cambridge University Press.

Skeggs, B. (2004). Exchange, value and affect: Bourdieu and the self. *The Sociological Review, 52*(2), 75–95. doi:10.1111/j.1467-954X.2005.00525.x

Skeggs, B. (2005). The making of class and gender through visualizing moral subject formation. *Sociology, 39*(5), 965–982. doi:10.1177/0038038505058381

Skeggs, B., & Loveday, V. (2012). Struggles for value: Value practices, injustice, judgment, affect and the idea of class. *The British Journal of Sociology, 63*(3), 472–490. doi:10.1111/j.1468-4446.2012.01420.x

Stahl, G., & Dale, P. (2013). Success on the Decks: Working-class boys, education and turning the tables on perceptions of failure. *Gender and Education, 25*(3), 357–372. doi:10.1080/09540253.2012.756856

Stahl, G. (2013). Habitus disjunctures, reflexivity and white working-class boys' conceptions of Status in learner and social identities. *Sociological Research Online, 18*(3), 1–12. Retrieved from http://www.socresonline.org.uk/18/3/2.html. doi:10.5153/sro.2999

Stahl, G. (2014). The affront of the aspiration agenda: White working-class male narratives of 'ordinari-ness' in neoliberal times. *Masculinities and Social Change, 3*(2), 88–118. doi:10.4471/MCS.201446

Stahl, G. (2015). *Aspiration, identity, neoliberalism: Educating white working class boys*. London: Routledge.

Walkerdine, V., & Ringrose, J. (2006). Femininities: Reclassifying upward mobility and the neo-liberal subject. In C. Skelton, B. Francis, & L. Smulyan (Eds.), *The sage handbook of gender and education* (pp. 31–46). London: Sage.

Weis, L. (2004). *Class reunion*. London: Routledge.

Willis, P. (1981). *Learning to labour*. New York, NY: Columbia University.

Aspiring workers or striving consumers? Rethinking social exclusion in the era of consumer capitalism

Lara Monticelli ⬤ and Simone Baglioni

ABSTRACT
This study is part of a special issue aimed at investigating young people's trajectories in troubled and challenging times. The paper tackles the topic by providing the results of an in-depth qualitative and exploratory study conducted on young unemployed people in the Italian city of Turin – the industrial 'capital' of the Sixties, now undergoing a massive wave of deindustrialization. Interviews were gathered in 2010, when the Great Recession was severely affecting young people living in Southern European countries like Greece, Italy, Spain and Portugal. The article proceeds along two levels of analysis. The first focuses on the subjective experience of unemployment and job precariousness seen through the eyes of young people, aware of living in exceptionally hard and uncertain times. The second focuses on the broad mechanisms leading to social exclusion paying particular attention to deprived experiences of consumption. Findings reveal that while work has not lost its material and symbolic meaning, a great importance is attributed to experiences of consumption, as a way for young people to socialize with peers.

1. Social exclusion: a literature in need of renewal

Finding a definition of 'social exclusion' is far from being an easy task. The term is widely used in a wide range of areas in the social sciences: economics, sociology, criminology, policy studies and international relations, as well as official policy reports and a variety of claims produced by politicians, governmental agencies and international institutions.[1] Social exclusion is usually defined as being a multidimensional concept that refers to deprivation in economic, political, relational, spatial and material spheres of life (Byrne, 2005; Hills, Sefton, & Stewart, 2009; Levitas, 1996). The effort of defining what is social exclusion has often been accompanied by the attempt to relate it to the concepts of poverty and relative deprivation (Church et al., 2000; Lister, 2004; Sealey, 2015; Sen, 2000).

Among the most recent critical reviews of how the concept of social exclusion is applied in contemporary social sciences and policy-making, the contribution of Clive Sealey (2015) is particularly insightful. Two aspects of Sealey's analysis are relevant for this study. Firstly, his discussion of the linguistic meaning of 'social exclusion' which connects the concept to issues of power. Exclusion, in fact, can be used either with an active or a passive meaning, but 'the idea of active exclusion […] is that it makes evident that the conditions of disadvantage are caused by the lack of power which individuals have, rather than the expression of their deviant agency' (Sealey, 2015, p. 611). In Sealey's words, the excluded people's powerlessness is 'caused by active agents with a specific zero-sum game assertiveness to power, and the maintenance of such power' (Sealey, 2015). Secondly, his argument about the nature of social exclusion as a longitudinal (i.e. cross-time) evolving process, an ongoing self-reinforcing vicious circle, rather than a static outcome (Sealey, 2015, pp. 606–607). This point helps to understand that there is a difference, in substantive and qualitative terms, between poverty – a static condition (which may be the cause or the consequence of social exclusion), and social exclusion itself – a process.

The definition provided by Pierson (2003, p. 7) is in this sense clarifying:

> Social exclusion is a process that deprives individuals and families, groups and neighbourhoods of the resources, economies and political activity of society as a whole. This process is primarily a consequence of poverty and low income, but other factors such as discrimination, low educational attainment also underpin it. Through this process people are cut off from their institutions and services, social networks and developmental opportunities that the great majority of society enjoys.

The concept of social exclusion thus implies that the 'excluded' cannot access the 'normal areas of participation of full citizenship' (Percy-Smith, 2000). Social exclusion is often conceived as an 'umbrella concept' (Byrne, 2005) whose features can be inductively derived in opposition to what is considered 'social inclusion', i.e. an array of entitlements, material possessions and social roles that are usually recognized as part of a 'normal life'.

Among the studies reviewed, the conceptualization of social exclusion and spheres of socialization proposed by Paugam and Gallie's book 'Welfare regimes and the experience of unemployment in Europe' (2000) proves to be particularly illuminating when investigating young unemployed and precarious people. In the book, the authors build on classical sociological thinking to divide social integration (which we understand to mean social inclusion) into three spheres. The primary sphere includes family ties, the secondary sphere friends and acquaintances, and the third sphere refers to connections generated by participation in collective organizations with formalized goals and objectives (e.g. associations, political parties, voluntary organizations, etc.). According to this model, as the level of social exclusion increases, socialization shrinks to the primary sphere, i.e. it is limited to family and close friends. This is due to a combination of limited economic, cultural and social resources. Thus, Paugam and Gallie's approach allows for an understanding of social exclusion as a multidimensional phenomenon that can be discerned by analysing people's breadth of socialization across the three spheres.

In parallel with the flourishing of studies deploying the concept of social exclusion over the last two decades (Berghman, 2006; Byrne, 1997, 2005; Hills, 2002; Labonte, 2004; Pierson, 2003; Sen, 2000), more recent contributions have stressed the need to renew and actualize the notion itself and to link it more explicitly with the latest developments in contemporary capitalism and to the effects of the Great Recession on the underprivileged segments of society (Winlow & Hall, 2013). In other words, to connect it more explicitly with the dynamics of power that constitute the preconditions for the persistence and reinforcement of social exclusion itself. Following this line of thought, the traditional

Marxian interpretation according to which job insecurity and unemployment are instrumentally used by the owners of capital to maintain a permanent 'reserve army of workers' – keen to re-enter the labour market at the first opportunity, no matter the conditions (Byrne,1997) – has been integrated with critical viewpoints arguing that it is necessary to rethink the classic academic discourse on deprivation and social exclusion.

Among this strand of studies, based on the idea that, in contemporary post-industrial societies, the condition of workplace insecurity is being normalized and that the positive symbolism associated with a 'a job for life' is slowly but relentlessly vanishing (Doogan, 2015), Winlow and Hall (2013) posit that unemployed and deprived people nowadays constitute a 'reserve army of consumers' rather than one of workers (Winlow & Hall, 2013, p. 107). Building their argument on ethnographic studies conducted in North-East England (Hall, Winlow, & Acrum, 2008; Winlow, 2001; Winlow & Hall, 2006), the authors describe how 'those who do not possess the resources to indulge legally in hedonistic consumption with any degree of regularity, continue to imagine and mentally calibrate their social value in relation to it' (Winlow & Hall, 2013, p. 107). In their recount, instead of assuming a contentious attitude towards the wealthy social classes, contemporary working classes – the 'precariat' (Standing, 2011, 2014) – are craving to live 'the good life', i.e. the life as it is portrayed by dominant neoliberal ideology, by consumerist culture and by the social imaginary created by the mass media. The consumption of leisure and 'secondary' goods, like branded clothes or technological items, becomes a relevant aspect of life because of their symbolic value. Therefore, consumption is a crucial experience for the formation of identity and self-identification processes, especially among adolescents and young adults. This argument constitutes the core message of their book – influenced, in particular, by the thoughts of Slavoj Žižek and Jean Baudrillard. Neoliberal ideology is so pervasive that it manages to 'overdetermine' the 'socially excluded ones' and their aspirations, leaving very little, if any, room for solidarity, political mobilizations and emancipatory (re)actions (Winlow & Hall, 2013, pp. 143–151).

Winlow and Hall's work is not the first attempt at investigating social exclusion in relation to consumption and, specifically, to the lack of it. Contemporary philosopher and sociologist Zygmunt Bauman has made substantial contributions to the understanding of the 'homo consumens' in his work on the socialization mechanisms in post-industrial and post-modern societies (Bauman, 2005, 2007, 2011). For example, in his book 'Workers, Consumerism and the New Poor', Bauman illustrates how the 'producer society' has been replaced by the 'consumer society' (Bauman, 2005). If in the former, the vocation towards production can be fulfilled only through a collective endeavour (the act of goods' production), in the 'consumer society' the act of consumption reduces the individual to an atomized, lonely, isolated actor that builds her or his own identity around it. In other words, according to Bauman's interpretation, socialization occurs nowadays through acts of consumption rather than through work. In his words:

> work has lost its privileged position – that of an axis around which all other effort at self-constitution and identity-building rotate. But work has also ceased to be the focus of particularly intense ethical attention in terms of being a chosen road to moral improvement, repentance and redemption. (Bauman, 2005, pp. 32–33)

In contrast with this perspective in which individual agency is left with little room to manoeuvre and in which work has lost its intrinsic value, the literature produced by social movement and political participation scholars analyses the rise of new waves of mobilization and the attempts of contemporary young workers to self-organize and to raise the voice as a reaction to rising precariousness (Bassoli & Monticelli, 2017; Chabanet & Faniel, 2012; Choi & Mattoni, 2010; Corbetta & Colloca, 2013; Della Porta, Hanninen, Siisianen, & Silvasti, 2015; Giugni, 2010; Mattoni & Vogiatzoglou, 2014; Monticelli & Bassoli, 2016).

2. Aim and objectives

The aim of this article is to investigate, through a qualitative and exploratory analysis, the importance attributed to consumption of both primary and secondary goods among unemployed and precarious youth, as well as the connection between unemployment, lack of consumption and the perception of social inclusion/exclusion.

Concerning the consumption aspect, the analysis has been inspired by Winlow and Hall's critical appraisal (2013), as well as Bauman's work introduced earlier (Bauman, 2005, 2007, 2011). This focus on consumption as a meaningful experience in young people's lives is supported by aggregate data which show that despite a deterioration in employment opportunities, people do not stop purchasing and 'consuming' goods. Figure 1 compares the increase in consumption of a number of young people in Europe who are 'Not in Education nor in Employment or Training' (NEET)[2] (in percentage) with household expenditure on leisure activities and goods (still in terms of percentage on overall household expenditure). The data in Figure 1 show that despite the growing number of young NEETs, particularly following the effects of the economic and financial crisis in 2008, expenditure on leisure remained stable over time. Moreover, data for Italy[3] show that when comparing two years, 2005 and 2012, respectively before and after the financial crisis of 2008/2009, the expense for leisure increases from 2.7% to 3.3%, while in the same period the youth unemployment rate rises from 17.7% to 25.4% (Eurostat). The data thus suggest that economic hardship has not affected the importance that leisure consumption is given in people's lives.

By interviewing a sample of long-term unemployed and precarious youth living in the Italian city of Turin during the Great Recession, it is possible to discern, through their own recounts, how exclusion from the labour market has affected the patterns of consumption of both primary and leisure goods, and how this deprivation has changed their perception of social exclusion and isolation.

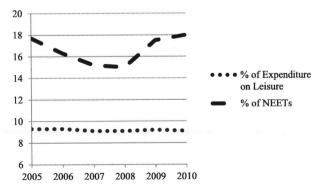

Figure 1. Percentages of expenditure on leisure among NEETs in Europe. Source: Eurostat.

3. Methods, sample and context

This study is based on a qualitative analysis of 19 in-depth interviews with young unemployed and precarious people living in the Italian city of Turin. Inspired by Grounded Theory (Glaser & Strauss, 1967), the authors used interviews to inductively unfold the multidimensional features of subjective experiences of unemployment. From this, they developed theoretical assumptions (Mattoni, 2014) about the role of work and consumption in the formation of trajectories of emancipation. In accordance with the tradition of qualitative research, the interview process was perceived as an interactive exercise. The authors are aware that the findings presented in this article are their own reflection of the interviewees' words, the reflection of two academic researchers who, nonetheless, have observed and been part of the discussed milieu for a long time.

Interviews have been conducted following a loosely structured topic-centred interview schedule (Mason, 1996) based on sensitizing concepts, i.e. concepts suggesting 'directions' where to look for an empirical phenomenon rather than prescriptive instructions on what to see (Blumer, 1954, p. 7; Bowen, 2006). The interview schedule allowed to investigate unemployment against various aspects of life such as social and political embeddedness (questions focusing on social dimensions, civic and political engagement), well-being and sense of belongingness to a given community, economic-financial situation, experiences with labour market policy and institutions, and future perspectives in life.[4]

The interviewees consisted of 7 women and 11 men whose age ranged from 19 to 35 (see Appendix), most of them with educational attainment limited to compulsory or secondary levels (only two interviewees had a tertiary education degree). The choice of this age range is justified by the willingness to include individuals who recently concluded the cycle of compulsory education and were trying to enter the labour market for the first time, as well as those who already had some experience of precarious work (and/or unemployment). Moreover, taking into consideration this wide age range allowed the authors to interview people coming from a variety of different households. Although the majority of the interviewees had a partner, only few of them lived with her/him or as an independent household, while most were still living at home with parents or close relatives. In sum, the selected age range allowed to gain a holistic perspective on the experience of precarious work and unemployment among young adults in Italy.

Fifteen of the interviewees were born in Italy, three in Romania and one in Nigeria (cfr. more detailed information in the Appendix). Young unemployed and precarious workers were primarily recruited at the job desk of a social enterprise in Turin, after which a snowballing technique was used to enlarge the sample. Interviews took place in the premises of the social enterprise itself and in public spaces like cafés, and in one case, upon his demand, the interviewee's flat. Interviews, lasting between one-and-a-half and two hours, were all recorded and transcribed. Transcriptions were analysed manually by both authors. Each of them reflected on the data while refining the sensitive concepts used in the preparation of the interview schedule. They shared their reciprocal thinking and exchanged views on each other's interpretative notes. Finally, they elaborated the conceptualizations and understanding of unemployment and consumption as discussed in the paper.

This study was conducted in 2010, a critical socio-economic juncture in which the economic and financial crisis started in 2008 was still peaking in Italy, with dramatic consequences on the country's rate of unemployment, especially among young people.[5] Unemployment had become a salient issue in the public debate and, as such, something that people experiencing it would be more prone to speak about (Gallas, 1996; Monticelli, Baglioni, & Bassoli, 2016). Nevertheless, the authors did experience a certain degree of reluctance to accept to be interviewed among the people at the job desk. It therefore took six months to collect a satisfactory number of interviews. The resulting fieldwork brought to an in-depth disclosure of interviewees' perceptions and experiences of a jobless life in hard times. This provided with a reliable basis for an interpretive, data guided analysis of the consequences of unemployment on a group of young people's well-being and sense of belonging in contemporary Western European society.

This study has to be considered in connection with the context in which it was developed, the city of Turin. The city was chosen because it is emblematic of the economic and industrial dismantling occurring in the country and therefore of the declining living conditions among blue-collar workers' families. Interviewees, in fact, come mainly from a working class milieu and represent the social group that – due to fewer educational and relational resources – benefited less from the 'tertiarization' of the economy. Turin has for more than a century been the core of Italian manufacturing industry, hosting the headquarters of the largest national carmaker, FIAT. For decades, it attracted manpower from the poorest Southern Italian regions, and established its role as a centre of the industrial engine, while promoting a model of social integration based on the cities' dualist catholic-communist tradition of civic engagement, associational life and strong unionization (Bassoli & Theiss, 2014). However, in the nineties, the country's economic and industrial landscape started to change under the pressure of globalization and the implementation of neoliberal economic policies (Dunford & Greco, 2006). The waves of deindustrialization, outsourcing and deregulation of the labour market reshaped the contours of the labour market. Employment opportunities and social cohesion deteriorated into one of scarce opportunity and social isolation. While the current economic reshaping of the city is creating new opportunities of employment, it has mainly been captured by those endowed with more education and relational resources, leaving low-skilled workers struggling to find employment opportunities (Berta, 2006; Gallino, 2003).

Many of the young unemployed in the sample are daughters and sons of the generation that, during the economic boom that followed the Second World War, migrated from the rural and underdeveloped south to the northern regions, mainly Lombardy, Emilia-Romagna and Piedmont. During the nineties, as a consequence of deindustrialization and the outsourcing of manufacturing, many of the blue-collar workers were gradually dismissed and found themselves in a condition of extreme precariousness and at risk of remaining stuck in a condition of permanent unemployment. The story of these interviewees, as it will become clear in the next section, is thus the reflection of a historical, cumulative and inter-generational cycle of social exclusion.

4. 'A man is nothing without a job': the material and symbolic value of work among unemployed youth

The interviews allowed to gather a large amount of empirical material, in the form of long transcriptions.[6] The quotes reported in this section can bring a deeper understanding of the meaning and features of (or lack of) work and the role that consumption plays in processes of social exclusion.

The first topic extrapolated from the interviews is that, as described in other studies focusing on the precarization of employment relations in Italy (Barbieri & Scherer, 2009; Fullin, 2004), work trajectories are reported as being discontinuous and 'de-standardized' (Elzinga & Liefbroer, 2007), thus leaving little room for developing an independent life and for planning the future. While irregular jobs and fragmented work experiences are sometimes instrumental to pay for further education, more often they are the beginning of non-standard, 'trapped' trajectories of work. As outlined in several analyses of young Italian people's transitions to the labour market, individual trajectories usually follow the typical 'Mediterranean' model characterized by precariousness at the end of studies, prolonged co-habitation within the parents' household and a late departure from it.

> Since the secondary school, I've started working ... I started working with an informal contract at 'Orto Gallery' that are stalls selling cheap jewelry ... I was employed irregularly but I was still a student so I did not care and having some money in the pockets was good [...]. At the end of the school I worked in a self-service restaurant near Piazza Carlo Alberto, there as well I was employed informally ... but working there was not worth the effort, I used to work for eight-nine hours per day for three hundred Euros per month. I worked a few days there but then I felt ill because of the stress. After that I worked in a show room of electronic goods as a secretary.
>
> *For how long have you worked there?* For 4 months more or less.
>
> *Which contract did you have?* I was employed irregularly at the beginning and I earned six hundred Euros then she [*the employer*] wanted to put me under an apprenticeship contract but I refused because of the little amount of money that implied. (Woman, 20 years old)

Many recounts reflect the 'yo-yo transition model' described in the literature: instead of linear advancements in the job market, every slight improvement in terms of job quality and workplace is often followed by a period of unemployment or by a recoiling in terms of contract or tasks (Biggart & Walther, 2006; Du Bois-Reymond & López Blasco, 2003). The idea mentioned earlier that social exclusion derives from a self-reinforcing cycle of negative episodes, rather than being a static 'snapshot' condition, emerges bluntly from the interviews. Moreover, the Marxian concept of a 'reserve army of workers' really comes to mind when reading the words of this young woman employed through occasional contracts as a shop assistant during periods of peaking sales across the year:

> I worked with an apprenticeship contract at the Decathlon [*a sportswear chain*] for two months, January and February, I was a cashier during sales. It has been a nice experience like the one I had at Zara in July and August for the summer sales. (Woman, 20 years old)

Together with job precariousness, the importance of having a job to plan an adult life and to emancipate from the family is expressed with special emphasis among the youngest interviewees:

> For me it is imperative, we can say vital, to be independent economically, I do not want to escape from my family but I think that when you are twenty-five years old it is legitimate to have your own flat, your own life, and because I am unemployed I cannot do it and this is something making me suffer. (Man, 25 years old)

In contrast to the literature which suggests that work has lost its centrality in the production of social meaning and individual identity (Southwood, 2011; Winlow & Hall, 2006), interviewees portray the importance of having a job, linking it with the need to 'give a sense', a 'mission', to their everyday life, otherwise regarded as boring and depressing. The 'positive symbolism' (Winlow & Hall, 2013, p. 106) attached to employment expressed by the interviewees, in spite of its contractual or remunerative quality, seems to contradict Winlow and Hall's argument.

> I miss my job. Now, once I have accompanied my child to school at nine o'clock, if you have a job interview or something do to it's ok but otherwise you don't have a busy day, I miss my job … I feel meaningless … I would like to do something, but I can't … I am born to manage or to organize things … […]

> *So without a job you found yourself in a new world?* Yes, you feel … . [in a world] that does not belong to you, it does not belong to you. (Woman, 35 years old)

Together with a sense of fulfilment at the idea of being employed, the youngest interviewees describe the psychological effects deriving from parents' and relatives' expectations and pressures.

> Not having a job is psychologically hard to bear, it is not a good situation, I feel like a guest in my parents' house, not because I don't like them, but because I think that the time [for leaving the parents] has come … .I can't bear this situation, I am stressed and my parents too are stressed as they are worried about my future. I would not say there is a constant conflict among us but there is tension, I can feel some tension … […] moreover with a girlfriend things get worst when you are unemployed because … well, because when you have a job it is a different social life. Let me phrase this better: having a job makes you more confident, it gives you self-esteem, you believe in yourself […] being twenty-five years old and having a partner for four years and still not being able to move and live together is a strong constraint on a relationship. (Man, 25 years old)

> I spend my days on Facebook. They have invented this damn computer … what should I do, I drop my CV around, or take documents to my solicitor or to the tribunal. (Woman, 21 years old)

Both material and symbolic significances are at stake. A job is still conceived as one of the main pillars of life:

> A man is nothing without a job. (Woman, 20 years old)

> It is terrible, it is terrible, as I was used to work since I was in my early twenties … I got used to waking up early to go to work … at least I could enjoy that: to be alive in the morning and not to sleep over … I miss that. (Woman, 35 years old)

> I miss the most important part of one's life, a job … actually the most relevant thing in our life is a good health … and I have that … so I miss the second most relevant thing in life … a job, to understand what we want to make out of our life we need a job, [to elaborate] a minimal capacity of planning, a future, ways out … . (Man, 35 years old)

Interviewees describe their 'ideal' job as one with two main characteristics: fulfilling personal aspirations and providing a sense of long-term stability. Previous studies conducted on Italian graduates' school-to-work transitions have underlined that the strategy implemented, once in the labour market, is 'open and circular' (Franchi, 2005), often subject to iterative adjustment processes in which young people juggle and struggle to find a compromise between the need to find stable and remunerative employment, and the desire to match it with personal aspirations and vocations (Monticelli, 2014). In this case, despite interviewees' educational attainment levels being in line with the Italian average (Appendix), the authors found that they almost systematically end up downgrading their expectations due to the impossibility of fulfilling them.

> Personally, I would wish myself to find a job that I like to be satisfied with myself, this is what I miss. I feel realized in my sentimental life, I found the person of my life with whom I made a child, hence I miss a job and with a job other projects that go with it like a new flat ... I miss a job to be satisfied ... it would be enough to be satisfied, only that.

> *Where do you see yourself in five years' time?* Where? I hope not here [she laughs] in the same situation because at forty years it would be even more a critical situation ... at that age, one will have to content oneself with an ordinary job of cleaner ... but with which satisfaction or enthusiasm can you keep on going? And maybe you find yourself crying and saying 'I don't feel realized in my life and would like to go back'. (Woman, 35 years old)

> In a year time, I hope to have a permanent job. In ten years, I would like to have a family to give my children what I haven't got, from nesting to bigger things. I do really hope that in ten years all this will happen. (Woman, 20 years old)

In sum, analysing young people's perception of their condition of unemployment suggests that, although employment patterns have dramatically changed in post-industrial societies, work has not yet lost its centrality in life. On the contrary, it is still perceived as an essential vehicle of agency, the one allowing young people to move towards an independent, adult life. Moreover, having a job is considered fundamental since it helps shaping and presenting one's own personality and identity while relating to other people, as exemplified by this quote:

> [*While I was studying*] when I met someone the question was 'What do you do in your life?' and the answer 'Well, I study, actually I am going to graduate soon' and the reply 'Oh nice, interesting' ... now when they ask me 'What do you do in your life? Do you work?' and I say 'No, I am looking for a job' 'Ah', that's all, the conversation stops there. (Woman, 25 years old)

In the next section, deprived experiences of consumption deriving from the lack of financial resources are interpreted in relation to socialization mechanisms and social exclusion.

5. A reserve army of consumers? Experiences of consumption and patterns of socialization

The second central theme arising from the interviews, together with the material and symbolic meaning attached to work, is the relationship between unemployment, consumption and social exclusion. Consumption, similarly to work, holds a symbolic value as well. According to Winlow and Hall (2013), the 'ideological incorporation' of what constitutes the 'good life and confers social status' (p. 109) is deeply rooted in people's mind. So deeply that even the least wealthy social classes conceive the possession of certain status-goods as a priority (Winlow & Hall, 2013). In Baudrillard's words (1998, p. 81): '(consumption) is something enforced, a morality, an institution. [...]. The consumer society is also the society of learning to consume, of social training in consumption [...]. That is to say there is a new and specific mode of socialization ... '.

To what extent is this true among the interviewees of this study? What the authors found is that not having the economic resources to go out for a drink, to a club or to the gym is indeed perceived as a missed opportunity to socialize, thus reinforcing the cycle of social exclusion:

> You know there is always this situation when I have to ask my mother to buy a pair of jeans, or shoes. [...] I would like to go swimming, to go to the gym but obviously these are things you need money for and I cannot afford them now so I have no hobby. (Woman, 25 years old)

> No, I don't go to places like pubs and clubs because as you say I don't have the money for it. My friends used to go to these clubs and found a girlfriend there … but you know, I don't have these [*gesture for money*] and so cannot afford going there. [...] I don't practice any sport, I don't have the money for that either. (Man, missing age)

> It is normal, when you are in your twenties, to desire buying a nice shirt when you see it in the windows but I cannot afford it, I cannot afford spending even fifteen Euros … .but when you go for job interviews you meet these ladies who look like a model from 'The devil wears Prada'[7] and they look at you … they humiliate you. (Woman, 20 years old)

Among the oldest interviewees, the comparison with the life *before* unemployment highlights the changes occurred in everyday life experiences, especially referring to consumption patterns:

> *Where did you have to cut expenses in your family budget after becoming unemployed? Did you change your way of life or do you manage to get on with the same life?* No, I would not say we are able to live the same life, in fact before we could afford going out in the evening or we used to have a pizza on Saturday night somewhere, now we never go out and if we have a pizza then we bake it ourselves or there is always the frozen pizza to eat at home. Also, buying clothes has changed, before I used to go to the market to buy them, which was not such a luxury habits, now I do not go anymore … even buying knickknacks at the market as I did sometimes has become unaffordable, so for sure we cut these expenses. (Woman, 35 years old)

In a few cases, deprivation also affects the consumption of primary goods, so that the interviewees are forced to procure food for them and their offspring at local charities or at the local church. These are cases of profound and deep material destitution, in which the family of origin is also living under similar conditions of poverty and thus cannot provide any help. Social exclusion deriving from material deprivation seems thus to be not only a cumulative process taking shape across along the span of a lifetime, but appears to be also an inter-generational phenomenon. All four types of capital (financial, cultural, human and social) identified by Pierre Bourdieu (2003) as elements that lead to social reproduction of inter-generational inequalities can be recognized. In other words, the interviews show that social exclusion is a process taking shape within and between generations.

> I cannot count on my parents' support as my mother is the only one working at home, and it is already difficult for them to live with her salary and having two more people to feed [*herself and her son*] would make the situation even harder … .I look for my food at the church or in various associations [*charities*] … three to four times per month and I eat something with that. [...] I don't eat meat, I eat pasta, what should I say … luckily my son eats at school, he can eat meat there and for dinner having a dish of pasta is ok for him. In any case I always manage to get something [to eat] from somewhere … an acquaintance, someone from the San Vincenzo charity that calls me when she has cooked the spezzatino [*stewed meat*] and can give me some

of it … eventually she can give me a couple of steaks […] sometimes they also have five or ten Euros for me. […] I am nine months behind with my rent … . for an overall amount of nine thousands Euros.

You said you have four brothers, you have a boyfriend, couldn't you borrow some money from them? Oh, my God … it would be like taking the bread out of their mouth! Absolutely no!

*So … It's out of the question, they cannot give me money … .. (Woman, 34 years old)

Moreover, in support of Paugam and Gallie's (2000) 'three-tiered' social integration model, interviewees show levels of socialization limited primarily to the sphere of family and relatives, and seldom to friends and acquaintances, while only one interviewee described a socialization pattern which included the third sphere (associations and collective action).

My friends are all gone … my school friends, my university friends, we don't see each other anymore … I go out with my boyfriend and his family members, his sister, his brother in law, they are more or less of our age … I like them. (Woman, 25 years old)

The opportunities to hang out with friends and acquaintances are very limited, although it remains unclear whether this is caused by the lack of monetary resources, of social capital or by some kind of self-inflicted stigma that prevents to look for socialization opportunities. When speaking about 'spaces' for socialization, they only refer to their home or their parents' one. Again, in line with Paugam and Gallie's assumptions, one interviewee says:

With friends one [*an unemployed person*] has to say no to many things, instead of seeing them four times a week you see them once, maybe twice, to see them you are forced to move, to go in clubs … .of course one does not take a drink but fuel does cost and it is rare that when we go out with friends we do not go in a club or similar place. (Man, 35 years old)

We don't have friends [*she refers to herself and her husband*] apart from my two brothers that are more or less of our age with their girlfriends, so we used to go out with them and their friends but for me these were not 'my friends', and I did not like them … .so basically we are alone, we spend our evenings among ourselves, you and me, me and you … always like that and at 35 years old you feel like an old person. (Woman, 35 years old)

However, the picture emerging from the interviews is quite different from Winlow and Hall's recounts from North-East England (Hall et al., 2008; Winlow, 2001; Winlow & Hall, 2006). 'They want big screen TV, flash cars, new clothes, foreign holidays rather then forge new solidarities, to elevate themselves above those around them', report the authors in their recent book which attempts to describe how consumerist ideology is nowadays shaping people's desires and aspirations (Winlow & Hall, 2013, p. 108). In this case study, a reference to a comparable ambition for luxury consumption is hard to find. Nonetheless, the issue of consumption appears to be articulated and expressed along two thematic lines: the first one concerns consumption of goods as a primary need and a necessity (especially when related to food and shelter), the second one relates to secondary-leisure goods as a tool that eases socialization mechanisms among young people and helps with the formation of one's own personality and identity. The interviewees can be divided into two ideal-typical groups: on the one side those who cannot count on the support of their relatives (parents and partners) and thus struggle even to buy food and other primary goods; on the other side, those who are still living with their parents, who can still afford, although in a limited manner, secondary goods and leisure opportunities.

6. Concluding remarks and perspectives for further research

In this article, the authors discussed the perception of social exclusion among a group of young unemployed and precarious people living in the Italian city of Turin. A former economic and industrial centre, the city has dramatically changed its economic profile due to post-industrialization dynamics. The manufacturing industry has shrunken and a tertiary sector has developed to replace it. Therefore, working opportunities in the city do not appeal to all but to the segment of young people with higher cultural and educational resources. The others, primarily young people from blue-collars families, have limited income and scarce opportunities to plan for the future and foresee a passage into an adult, independent life.

A wealth of literature has investigated the effect of unemployment and precariousness on peoples' lives, with specific attention paid to the detrimental consequences of joblessness on well-being, sense of belonging to communities, capacity to plan ahead and transitioning to adulthood. This study contributes to the debate by investigating how unemployment affects socialization patterns through deprived experiences of consumption.

Succinctly put, the in-depth interviews reveal that employment is still considered a formative experience of life and that young unemployed people express regret and suffering for not having a job. Moreover, they feel that their jobless status jeopardizes their social 'value' and their social standing in society. What is not found in their discourses, though, are references to unemployment as a stigma. Perhaps the chronic Italian (and Southern European) double-digit rate of youth unemployment has changed ordinary people's perceptions, and therefore a jobless status has ceased being interpreted, at least among the interviewees, as a stigmatizing condition. Still, from an individual viewpoint, unemployment continues to be a situation which causes anxiety and a pessimistic outlook. Furthermore, the interviews tell a story of social exclusion as a longitudinal, intergenerational process – one in which deprivation is in some cases 'inherited' from parents who have been unable themselves to navigate the changed economic landscape.

Despite expressing feelings of powerlessness, the young people interviewed were striving to maintain their capacity and agency to deal with challenging circumstances, albeit they did not take any form of public stance, and did not engage in collective action to affect the political arena. In the future, though, the claims of this youth could perhaps take the shape of a collective voice and gain political visibility if it was mobilized by civil society associations, social movements and political leaders. At the moment of writing, there is anecdotal evidence suggesting that this may already be underway, given the recent election in June 2016 of the 31-year-old mayor of Turin, Chiara Appendino, from the populist Five Star Movement.

Turning to consumption, interviewees also evidenced the ordinary features of young people living in a modern society by attributing value to consumption as a way of gaining social status and socializing with friends and acquaintances. Socialization occurs mainly with family and relatives – the primary tier of socialization – and when it moves beyond it, it is inextricably related to experiences of consumption: drinking a beer or going to the restaurant or the club. Hence, limited economic resources due to joblessness become inhibitors of social life and contribute to a perceived sense of social exclusion.

In contrast to the accounts about unemployed and deprived people in the UK (Hall et al., 2008; Winlow, 2001; Winlow & Hall, 2006) although, in this case study consumption does not seem to be perceived as having a symbolic value *per se*. One could hypothesize that the phenomenon of 'ideological incorporation' (Winlow & Hall, 2006) is therefore not as ingrained in the imagination of unemployed Italian young people as it is in the British case. Indeed, interviewees in this study perceive experiences of consumption instrumentally – as a *means* to socialize.

To conclude, consumption of leisure goods appears to be intrinsically intertwined with socialization and, ultimately, subjective feelings of social inclusion and integration. Despite the existence of an extensive network of third-sector voluntary organizations, cultural-political associations (like ARCI – Italian Recreational Cultural Association) and autonomous 'centri sociali' (occupied spaces by grassroots activists) in Turin, interviewees were all unaware that these spaces and organizations could provide opportunities for 'un-commodified' and politically engaged moments of socialization. Investigating the reasons behind this distance is certainly worth further and more in-depth analysis.

Notes

1. See Sealey (2015) for a review.
2. The definition of NEET provided by Eurostat is: the indicator young people neither in employment nor in education and training, abbreviated as NEET, corresponds to the percentage of the population of a given age group and sex who is not employed and not involved in further education or training. The numerator of the indicator refers to persons meeting these two conditions: they are not employed (i.e. unemployed or inactive according to the International Labour Organisation definition); they have not received any education or training in the four weeks preceding the survey. The denominator is the total population of the same age group and sex, excluding the respondents who have not answered the question 'participation to regular education and training'. In the case of the data presented, the age range considered is 20–34.
3. Available at: http://ec.europa.eu/eurostat/.
4. Interview schedule available on request.
5. Longitudinal series available at http://ec.europa.eu/eurostat/statistics-explained/index.php/Unemployment_statistics.
6. Interviewers' questions, comments and notes have been italicized and out in parentheses throughout the quotes.
7. 'The Devil Wears Prada' is a 2006 American movie in which a young woman, after graduating, starts to work for a famous fashion magazine in New York.

Acknowledgements

The data analysed in this paper are the result of the research project YOUNEX – 'Youth, Unemployment, and Exclusion in Europe: A Multidimensional Approach to Understanding the Conditions and Prospects for Social and Political Integration of Young Unemployed'. The authors are grateful to Matteo Bassoli who helped collecting the interviews during the fieldwork in 2010 and to all the members of the international research consortium.

Disclosure statement

No potential conflict of interest was reported by the authors.

Funding

This work was supported by Seventh Framework Programme [Grant Agreement no. 216122].

Notes on contributors

Lara Monticelli is post-doctoral research fellow at Scuola Normale Superiore di Pisa (Italy). Her research is centred on the study of political participation in its various forms, social movements, prefigurative politics and alternative, sustainable lifestyles.

Simone Baglioni is Professor of Politics in the Yunus Centre for Social Business and Health at Glasgow Caledonian University (UK). He is the coordinator of the EU Horizon 2020 project SIRIUS and the principal investigator in the 'TransSol' and 'Fab-Move' projects dealing with social innovation and collective actions issues.

ORCID

Lara Monticelli http://orcid.org/0000-0003-2108-6352

References

Barbieri, P. & Scherer, S. (2009). Labour market flexibilisation and its consequences in Italy. *European Sociological Review, 25*, 677–692. doi:10.1093/esr/jcp009

Bassoli, M. & Monticelli, L. (2017). What about the welfare state? Exploring precarious youth political participation in the age of grievances. *Acta Politica*, 1–27. Advance online publication. doi:10.1057/s41269-017-0047-z

Bassoli, M., & Theiss, M. (2014). Inheriting divisions? The role of the catholic and leftist affiliation in local cooperation networks: The case of Italy and Poland. In S. Baglioni & M. Giugni (Eds.), *Civil society organizations, unemployment and precarity in Europe* (pp. 175–203). Houndmills: Palgrave Macmillan.

Baudrillard, J. (1998). *The consumer society: Myths and structures*. London: Sage.

Bauman, Z. (2005). *Work, consumerism and the new poor*. Maidenhead: Open University Press.

Bauman, Z. (2007). *Consuming life*. Cambridge: Polity Press.

Bauman, Z. (2011). *Collateral damage: Social inequalities in a global age*. Cambridge: Polity Press.

Berghman, G. (2006). Social exclusion in Europe. Policy context and analytical framework. In G. Room (Ed.), *Beyond the threshold. The measurement and analysis of social exclusion* (pp. 11–28). Bristol: Policy Press.

Berta, G. (2006). *L'Italia delle fabbriche: ascesa e tramonto dell'industrialismo nel novecento*. Bologna: il Mulino.

Biggart, A., & Walther, A. (2006). Coping with yo-yo-transitions: Young adults struggle for support, between family and state in comparative perspective. In C. Leccardi & E. Ruspini (Eds.), *A New youth? Young people, generations and family life* (pp. 41–62). Abingdon: Routledge.

Blumer, H. (1954). What is wrong with social theory? *American Sociological Review, 19*(1), 3–10.

Bourdieu, P. (2003). Cultural reproduction and social reproduction. In C. Jenks (Ed.), *Culture: Critical concepts in sociology* (Vol. *1*, pp. 63–100). London: Routledge.

Bowen, G. A. (2006). Grounded theory and sensitizing concepts. *International Journal of Qualitative Methods, 5*(3), 12–23. doi:10.1177/160940690600500304

Byrne, D. (1997). Social exclusion and capitalism. *Critical Social Policy, 17*(1), 27–51. doi:10.1177/026101839701705002

Byrne, D. (2005). *Social exclusion* (2nd ed.). Maidenhead: Open University Press.

Chabanet, D., & Faniel, J. (Eds.). (2012). *The mobilization of the unemployed in Europe: From acquiescence to protest?* New York: Palgrave Mcmillan US.

Choi, H. L., & Mattoni, A. (2010). The contentious field of precarious work in Italy: Political actors, strategies and coalitions. *Journal of Labor and Society, 13*(2), 213–243. doi:10.1111/j.1743-4580.2010.00284.x

Church, A., Frost, M., & Sullivan, K. (2000). Transport and social exclusion in London. *Transport Policy, 7* (3), 195–205. doi:10.1016/S0967-070X(00)00024-X

Corbetta, P., & Colloca, P. (2013). Job precariousness and political orientations: The case of Italy. *South European Society and Politics, 18*(3), 333–354. doi:10.1080/13608746.2013.769791

Della Porta, D., Hanninen, S., Siisianen, M., & Silvasti, T. (2015). *The new social division. Making and unmaking precariousness.* Basingstoke: Palgrave Mcmillan UK.

Doogan, K. (2015). Precarity – Minority condition or majority experience? In D. della Porta, S. Hanninen, M. Siisianen, & T. Silvasti (Eds.), *The New social division. Making and unmaking precariousness* (pp. 43–62). Basingstoke: Palgrave Macmillan UK.

Du Bois-Reymond, M., & López Blasco, A. (2003). Yo-yo transitions and misleading trajectories: Towards integrated transition policies for young adults in Europe. In A. Lòpez Blasco, W. Mcneish, & A. Walther (Eds.), *Young people and contradictions of inclusion. Towards integrated transition policies in Europe* (pp. 19–41). Bristol: Policy Press.

Dunford, M., & Greco, L. (2006). *After the three Italies: Wealth, inequality and industrial change.* Malden, MA: Blackwell.

Elzinga, C. H. & Liefbroer, A. C. (2007). De-standardization of family-life trajectories of young adults: A cross-national comparison using sequence analysis. *European Journal of Population/Revue Européenne de Démographie, 23*(3–4), 225–250. doi:10.1007/s10680-007-9133-7

Franchi, M. (2005). *Mobili alla meta. I giovani tra Università e lavoro.* Roma: Donzelli Editore.

Fullin, G. (2004). *Vivere l'instabilità del lavoro.* Bologna: Il mulino.

Gallas, A. (1996). Politische Wirkungsmöglchkeiten von Arbeitlosen. In F. Wolski-Prenger (Ed.), *Arbeitlosenarbeit. Erfahrungen. Konzepte. Ziele* (pp. 169–186). Opladen: Leske und Budrich.

Gallino, L. (2003). *La scomparsa dell'Italia industriale.* Torino: Einaudi.

Giugni, M. (Ed.) (2010). *The contentious politics of unemployment in Europe: Welfare states and political opportunities.* Basingstoke: Palgrave Mcmillan UK.

Glaser, B., & Strauss, A. (1967). *The discovery of grounded theory.* Chicago, IL: Aldine.

Hall, S., Winlow, S., & Acrum, C. (2008). *Criminal identities and consumer culture: Crime, exclusion and the new culture of narcissism.* Devon: Willan.

Hills, J. (2002). Does a focus on 'social exclusion' change the policy response? In J. Hills, J. Le Grand, & D. Piachaud (Eds.), *Understanding social exclusion* (pp. 226–243). Oxford: Oxford University Press.

Hills, J., Sefton, T., & Stewart, K. (2009). Conclusions: Climbing every mountain or retreating from every foothills? In J. Hills, T. Sefton, & K. Stewart (Eds.), *Towards a more equal society?* (pp. 341–360). Bristol: Policy Press.

Labonte, R. (2004). Social inclusion/exclusion: Dancing the dialectic. *Health Promotion International, 19*(1), 115–121. doi:10.1093/heapro/dah112

Levitas, R. (1996). The concept of social exclusion and the new Durkheimian hegemony. *Critical Social Policy, 16*(46), 5–20. doi:10.1177/026101839601604601

Lister, R. (2004). A politics of recognition and respect: Involving people with experience of poverty in decision-making that affects their lives. In J. Andersen & S. Birte (Eds.), *The politics of inclusion and empowerment* (pp. 116–138). Basingstoke: Palgrave Macmillan UK.

Mason, J. (1996). *Qualitative researching.* London: Sage.

Mattoni, A. (2014). The potential of grounded theory in the study social movements. In D. della Porta (Ed.). *Methodological practices in social movements research* (pp. 21–42). Oxford: Oxford University Press.

Mattoni, A. & Vogiatzoglou, M. (2014). Italy and Greece: Before and after the crisis: Between mobilization and resistance against precarity. *Quaderni: Communication, Technologies, Pouvoir, 84,* 57–71. doi:10.4000/quaderni.805

Monticelli, L., Baglioni, S., & Bassoli, M. (2016). Youth long-term unemployment and Its social conse-
quences in Italy: 'In a world that does Not belong to Me'. In C. Lahusen & M. Giugni (Eds.),
Experiencing long-term unemployment in Europe. Youth on the edge (pp. 139–169). Basingstoke:
Palgrave Mcmillan.

Monticelli, L. & Bassoli, M. (2016). Precarious voices? Types of 'political citizens' and repertoires of
action among European youth. *PArtecipazione e COnflitto* (PACO), *9*(3), doi:10.1285/
i20356609v9i3p824

Monticelli, L. (2014). *Scalatori o Prigionieri del Mercato del Lavoro? Uno Studio sulle Traiettorie
Occupazionali dei Giovani Laureati Italiani* (Unpublished doctoral dissertation). Università degli
studi di Brescia, Italy.

Paugam, S., & Gallie, D. (2000). Oxford: Oxford University Press.

Percy-Smith, J. (ed.) (2000). *Policy responses to social exclusion. Towards inclusion?* Buckingham: Open
University Press.

Pierson, J. (2003). *Tackling social exclusion*. London: Routledge.

Sealey, C. (2015). Social exclusion: Re-examining its conceptual relevance to tackling inequality and
social injustice. *International Journal of Sociology and Social Policy, 35*(9/10), 600–617. doi:10.1108/
IJSSP-05-2014-0040

Sen, A. (2000). *Social Exclusion: Concept, application, and scrutiny*. Social Development Papers
No. 1. Asian Development Bank. Retrieved from: https://www.adb.org/sites/default/files/
publication/29778/social-exclusion.pdf

Southwood, I. (2011). *Non stop inertia*. Alrlesford: Zero Books.

Standing, G. (2011). *The precariat: The new dangerous class*. London: Bloomsbury.

Standing, G. (2014). *A precariat charter: From denizens to citizens*. London: Bloomsbury.

Winlow, S., & Hall, S. (2006). *Violent night: Urban leisure and contemporary culture*. Oxford: Berg.

Winlow, S., & Hall, S. (2013). *Rethinking social exclusion: The end of the social?* London: Sage.

Winlow, S. (2001). *Badfellas: Crime, tradition and new masculinities*. London: Bloomsbury.

Appendix. List of interviewees (age, sex and household features)

Age[a]	Sex	Education	Household[b]	Partner	Place of birth	Additional info
19	M	Compulsory + professional training	(3) Divorced mother (employed), older brother (unemployed)	Yes	Italy	Private house
20	M	Compulsory + professional training	(4) Parents, (housewife, employed), older sister (unemployed)	No	Italy	/
21	M	Compulsory	(8) Parents (employed), 2 older sisters (single unemployed mother, employed), 2 younger brother (student), 1 nephew (toddler)	Yes	Italy	/
19	M	Compulsory	(5) Mother (housewife), younger brothers (student), partner	Yes	Italy	The father lives on his own
29	M	n.a.	Living with his cousin	Yes	Romania	None
20	F	Tertiary	(4) Parents (both employed), younger sister (student)	Yes	Italy	Mortgage
21	F	Secondary	(4) Parents, (housewife, on unemployment benefit), older brother(unemployed)	Yes	Italy	Mortgage
30	F	Compulsory	(3) Living with friends	No	Nigeria	Precarious housing conditions
35	F	Compulsory	(2) Single mother	Yes	Italy	Social housing
26	M	Compulsory	He lives between Turin and his hometown	Yes	Italy	/
34	M	Secondary	(3) Parents (pensioners)	No	Italy	/
24	M	Compulsory	(2) Brother	No	Italy	Rented flat

(Continued)

Appendix. Continued.

Age[a]	Sex	Education	Household[b]	Partner	Place of birth	Additional info
19	M	Tertiary	(4) Parents (employed), partner	Yes	Romania	/
n.a.	M	Secondary	(5) Parents (housewife, social assistance), older brother (part-time employed), younger sister (unemployed)	No	Italy	Rented flat
25	M	Secondary	(3) Parents (housewife, pensioner), younger sister (student)	Yes	Italy	Private house
25	F	Secondary	(3) Partner, his parents	Yes	Italy	/
32	M	Secondary	(2) Wife (employed)	Yes	Romania	/
35	F	Secondary	(3) Partner (employed), son (student)	Yes	Italy	Rented flat
23	F	Primary	(3) Husband (unemployed), son (toddler)	Yes	Italy	/

[a]At time of interview (2010).
[b]The number in parenthesis refers to the number of household members.

Youth in the age of anxiety: the case of a southern European location

Valerie Visanich

ABSTRACT
This paper examines the sociological implications of personal anxiety for youth in tertiary education. The arguments brought forward are positioned broadly within a discourse on individualisation – on how youth today are devising their lives on their own free-will and experiencing anxiety due to self-reliance. Various socio-economic and cultural conditions have a direct impact on their degree of anxiety. This paper focuses on three of them – changes in the educational system, employment prospects and personal debts. This paper analyses increased anxiety in youth, outlined by various studies, and how it transcends in southern Europe. The data drawn on for this paper are taken from interviews conducted in Malta. The implications brought forward include the need for a more detailed exploration of the familial support network and its work in reducing anxiety. Youth experience a kind of 'institutional individualisation' – Their reflexive deliberations leading to angst are cushioned by their familial support network.

Introduction

In recent years, young people in Western societies are arguably having more autonomy in designing their own life and navigating their life trajectories in a highly individualised way, compared to their predecessors. Nevertheless, the increased self-reliance is also producing anxiety in taking responsibility for actions and failures. In liberal democracies today, in the so-called crisis of youth, within a risk and individualised society, is central to debates about youth. Even though most of these studies on the process of individualisation in the west have come to take centre stage in debates, its application in the life domain of youth in a southern European context is more or less absent in the social sciences. This article tackles this shortcoming.

This article assesses how the individualisation process transcends in the life experiences of young people in a location in the European south. Reference is made to studies and statistics on various southern European countries. The intention is to provide a contextual framework of structural conditions that influence the degree of anxiety amongst youth. The framework of this study can be applied to any other given location that is also in ambivalence between modernity and tradition.

In particular, this paper draws data from one southern European country, the small island state of Malta, a location that is still relatively traditional due to its' somewhat strong Catholic morality and kinship ties, making it an ambivalent location (Mitchell, 2002). The Catholic Church has considerable political, social and cultural influence and a central role in the provision of non-state social welfare. Nevertheless recent reforms, such as the legislation of divorce and granting more LGBTIQ rights indicate a more liberal society (Briguglio, 2016).

The isle of Malta is far too small to be considered as a model of southern Europe. Far from generalising by using Malta as a case study, this paper provides insights on a location in southern Europe which shares common cultural particularities but disparate economic conditions – an example of this is economic development in the last three decades of the twentieth century. One pertinent distinction between youth in Malta and in other southern European countries is the fact that Maltese youth do not pay fees for their under-graduate studies.

The data drawn on for this paper are taken from in-depth interviews with young people who have had opportunities for tertiary education. This is to make sense of youth whose life chances included opportunities for tertiary education and who, presumably, have more bargaining power in designing their life on their own free-will. The point to such analysis is two-fold. First, my purpose is to contribute to the discussion on the reflexive deliberations of youth and their anxiety in contemporary society. This is supplemented by reference to individual biographies in Malta. Second, this article concludes by empha-sising the importance of the extended family and its central role in the life of youth in southern Europe that cushions some of the consequences of their individualised life experiences. The very idea of 'institutional individualisation' in this article goes beyond the welfare-institutional order (Frericks, Höppner, & Och, 2016) influencing youth. It refers to the support structures of youth within the southern European conditions, in par-ticular those in Malta, and how such structures cushion the harsh effects of living a 'life of one's own'.

Discourses on youth anxiety

In recent years, discourse on anxiety in the so-called risk society has been prominent in social sciences on the situation of youth today (Beck, 1992; Giddens, 1991). However, anxiety amongst youth is not a contemporary phenomenon. In his book *The Student in the Age of Anxiety*, Ferdynand Zweig (1963) highlighted some of the constraints experi-enced by university students in the 1960s. He referred to the stress of university life and the anxiety youth experience in relations to work prospects and personal relations.

Youth, as a definitive autonomous stage of life, gained its prominence in the mid-twen-tieth century particularly with the emergence of the social category 'teenager' (Savage, 2008). However, the attribution of adolescence predates the Second World War. In order to describe the intermediate transitory phase between childhood and adulthood, Stanley Hall (1904), a psychologist, coined the term 'adolescence'. In his two-volume work, Hall (1904) presented a detailed account of this stage of life clearly defined by age, extending over the period of 14–24 years. During this life course of 'storm and stress', individuals experience biological development during puberty as well as socially constructed developments that typify this stage. In addition, Hall (1904) considered adolescents as being particularly influenced by their peers and the print media. To some degree, the risk behaviour is associated with identity exploration and the desire for new intense experiences in sensation seeking. He argued that this life stage needs to be lengthened and marked by specific rites of passage in order to provide young people with a refuge within the industrial society. Such refuge during times of anxiety is more than ever required especially in late modernity, in the individualised life domain.

Nevertheless in sociological literature, youth is not only studied in terms of anxiety but also as a time for increased exploration and self-focus. Jeffrey Arnett's conceptualisation of 'emerging adulthood' looks at youth as a liminal stage when individuals are enjoying not having full adult responsibilities. Young people free themselves from the normative expectations of childhood dependency and move into exploring the variety of possible life directions. For Arnett (2001) young people in their early twenties tend to be more committed to move out of the family home, establish stable relationships and choose their adult identity. However, typically young people do not regard themselves as adults but more as individuals making long-term commitments and decisions (Arnett, 2001).

The individualisation process in the life domain of youth

The process of individualisation refers to increased freedom of choice yet at the same time increased risks (Archer, 2000, 2003; Bauman, 1996; Beck, 1994; Beck & Beck-Gernsheim, 2008[2002]; Giddens, 1991). Life biographies are said to be witnessing a threat in predictability and certainty when individuals are now the directors of their own life;

> Individualisation liberates people from traditional roles and constraints in a number of ways … women are cut loose from their 'status fate' of compulsory housework and support by a husband … . (Beck & Beck-Gernsheim, 2008[2002], pp. 202–203)

Therefore the concept of individualisation is seen as contradictory – while it provides choice for individuals, nonetheless it produces anxiety and uncertainty. This need to be contextualised within socio-economic conditions of the *laissez-faire* ideology in late modernity in countries where neo-liberal policies are embraced and applied, by the removal of regulations and restrictions on trade (Bauman, 1998; Kamenetz, 2007; Sennett, 1998).

Within a global neo-liberal climate of competition and diminishing job security as well as increasing flexible short-term contract jobs, young people are anxious and find it a must to spend more time in education and equip themselves with a couple of degrees. Irrespective of the fact that Beck and Beck-Gernsheim (2008[2002]) deny the connection between individualisation and neo-liberalism, there is a close affinity between the two (McGuigan, 2010). In a neo-liberal society, the focus is on the individual rather than on society as a whole. By using the paradox of 'institutional individualism' Beck and Beck-Gernsheim (2008[2002]) and Zygmunt Bauman (2008) referred to the way legal norms of the welfare state are making individuals rather than groups dependent on institutions – neo-liberal politics encourages individuals 'to devise individual solutions to socially generated problems and to do it individually, using their own skills and individually possessed assets' (Bauman, 2008, p. 4). Although short-term contracts may seem that they are promoting opportunistic bargaining, youth tend to suffer from both economic and psychological effects (Heery & Salmon, 2000). In the name of individual 'sovereignty', neo-liberal mechanisms build an arena where individuals compete with one another in the fight for economic security. This Darwinian conflict is fuelled by threats of restructuring and fear of job loss. In effect, increase in involuntary job contracts in the Western society brought about an increased risk of unemployment and reduced earnings (Heery & Salmon, 2000). Consequentially, this results in anxiety amongst youth.

Education, employment and debt

At the end of the twentieth century, more attention was paid to the preparation of youth and their eventual entry into the labour market (Roberts, 1995). Up until the 1980s, having no academic qualifications did not hinder finding work in places like in Britain – The labour market absorbed virtually all persons and opportunities for the unqualified and unskilled were easily available (Bynner & Côté, 2008).

This situation shifted with changes in the educational system and credentials – 'youth have had little choice but to seek post-secondary educational credentials in the hope of gaining an advantage in access to better-paying jobs' (Bynner & Côté, 2008, p. 260). As a result, young people have to finance their own education with the consequence of entering into significant debts before joining the workforce (Kamenetz, 2007). Moreover, the workforce is much more 'flexible' than ever before. The decline in career-long employment is replaced with contingent contracts and a mobile workforce. Changes in the external labour market and national systems of employment regulation are causing greater insecurity amongst employees (Heery & Salmon, 2000).

Although short-term contracts may seem that they are promoting opportunistic bargaining for employees, workers tend to suffer both from economic and psychological effects (Heery & Salmon, 2000). The replacement of stable jobs with flexible labour mainly in the form of fixed contracts is the result of neo-liberal consumer choice (Bauman, 1998).

The southern European context

Beck (1992) argues that processes of reflexive modernisation 'tend to dissolve' traditional conditions of industrial society. Individuals are increasingly released from these conditions of 'conscience collective' such as class, gender and family relations (Beck, 1992, p. 87). However, the situation in southern Europe is not as straightforward as explained by Beck.

Southern European countries such as Cyprus, Spain, Portugal, Greece, Italy and Malta, have certain characteristics which distinguish them – not only their geographic proximity, but also their common historical and cultural legacies (Gal, 2010). Such common cultural characteristics include the influence of religion (in particular Catholicism) in all aspects of social life as well as the central role of the family and the presence of 'familism' (family solidarity and dependency).

The importance given to kinship networks changes the understanding of the functioning of the welfare state. Gøsta Esping-Andersen (1990) was one of the first scholars to speak about the particularities of countries like Spain, Italy and Greece in the conservative welfare regime, as opposed to countries like Germany, Austria and the Netherlands.

José Pereirinha (1997) maintained that Esping-Andersen's (1990) model on the decommodification of welfare services contains two limitations when applied to southern European countries. Primarily, such model excludes the informal labour market which has a significant presence in the south. Also, it ignores mechanisms of social solidarity and the informal institutions, such as the Catholic Church and its various organisations that work to combat poverty and social exclusion in society. Thus, Pereirinha (1997) supported the argument that studies on the welfare state cannot rely exclusively on the state and the market but need to address the role of the civil society, families and the voluntary sector.

Malta's welfare model is considered as a hybrid model which does not fit neatly in one particular model of welfare outlined by Esping-Andersen (Briguglio & Bugeja, 2011). Unlike other western countries moving further away from the welfare state, towards a more neo-liberal market oriented model, social welfare provisions in Malta are not yet an endangered or contested concept (Briguglio, Bugeja, & Vella, 2016).

Albeit these common cultural conditions, it is pertinent to note out disparate economic conditions of such countries. For example, Malta has not undergone economic crisis like Greece, Italy, Spain and Cyprus. On contrary, GDP growth rate in Malta from 2000 until 2016 averaged at 0.80% reaching an all-time high of 4.40% in the first quarter of 2014 (trading economics, 2017).

The case of Malta

Malta's specific characteristics, not only as a southern European country, but also as a small island state should be taken into consideration here. Similar to other small states, Malta's peculiarities include its openness to international trade and high dependence on imports due to their small economic size (Briguglio, 2014). The vulnerability of Malta to external events is in its 'suddenness of impact, in the intensity of effect and in the rapid speed of penetration'. (Baldacchino, 1998, p. 225).

Malta's economic development reached a surge in the last three decades of the twentieth century, especially with the development of the welfare state, the national health services and the implementation of subsidised housing. It is also worth noting Malta's social wage, comprising of universal benefits like free healthcare and free education. Maltese students at the University of Malta do not pay fees for their undergraduate studies but are given universal maintenance grants as well as receive a stipend during their course of studies. Such local peculiarity, therefore, tends to encourage young people into post-compulsory education.

However, this initiative is not completely reaching its objectives because the number of Maltese youth entering university (26%) is lower than the EU average (European Commission, 2013). The EU targets are for these figures to climb to 30% by 2020. Furthermore, the early school leaving rate of Maltese students is the second highest rate in the EU at 20.8% (European Commission, 2013).

The situation of youth unemployment is also less problematic in Malta (6.9%) when compared to the EU average rate of 18.6% and other southern European countries like Greece (50.4%), Spain (43.9%) and Italy (36.9%) (Eurostat, 2015). The *European Economic Forecast* (2016) reports that Malta's continued economic growth and job creation are accountable for the low rate of unemployment. Such economic conditions have a significant influence on the degree of anxiety experienced by youth in Malta because it smoothens the transition from education to work.

Apart from economic conditions, it is worth noting recent changes in Malta indicating a more liberal society, which can be interpreted as the weakening of the Church's influence (Briguglio, 2016). Civil society organisations have been pertinent in a number of campaigns promoting civil activism, such as the 'Yes' movement for the legislation of divorce. This movement emerged victorious in the 2011 referendum and this led to the legislation of divorce in Malta in October 2011. Another recent move towards a liberal society was the legalisation of same-sex unions, following the enactment of Civil Union Act in 2014. It has been argued that in the space of six year, the institutions of marriage was challenged in Malta, not because of marital breakdown, but due to the rejection of traditional codes of sexual behaviour, especially by youth (Abela, 2013).

Furthermore, in recent years there has been an increasing diversity in family life in Malta, partly due to immigration flows contributing to growing numbers of intercultural marriages – thus the traditional family is no longer the only family form (Abela, 2016). Young people in Malta are increasingly identifying themselves with some aspects of global youth culture, such as consumerism and social media (Cassar, 2016).

The study

The significance of this article is that it questions the extent of personal anxiety in the life domain of youth in tertiary education. The research uses a qualitative approach, extending over a period of approximately 24 months, between 2010 and 2012, employing 12 in-depth interviews with Maltese youth. The aim of drawing from this research is not to generalise on southern European youth in general, but to give insights on the life experiences of a social group of youth and their experienced anxieties.

Young participants were deliberately selected for their specific particularities of being in tertiary education. The selection of participants also included taking into consideration variables like age and gender. A balanced amount of males and females participants were chosen, between the ages of 21 and 26 years. A Purposive sample was used to select participants. My personal network was used to handpick participants that fit this criterion through sound judgement. After contacting them by phone and explaining my research, participants agreed to meet and were interviewed about their lived experiences. All participants whose interviews I am drawing here were white, heterosexuals and living in Malta. They all had post-compulsory education, therefore their interpretations are in no means a normalised experience for all young people of the same age group. Interviews were conducted in person.

All ethical procedures have been followed and participants recruited were informed of their rights to view transcripts, their right to withdrawal and of having their names changed to safeguard their anonymity.

The process of transcription was followed by a thematic analysis, which pinpointed, examined and recorded patterns in the data. Various valid themes emerged from the data analysis process, including on participants' life chances and future plans of this social group of youth. Such analysis may be useful and dealt with elsewhere. However, this article focuses on three themes centred on anxiety amongst youth – on the changes in the educational system, employment prospects and rise in personal debts.

Findings: uncertainties and reflexive decisions

High unemployment and austerity measures in southern European countries give rise to increased social disintegration and anxiety. Greece is an example of this in which 'no other European state has undergone such pain in the last fifty years or more' (Featherstone, 2014). The economic and political crisis in Greece is producing self-suffering (Tsekeris, Kaberis, & Pinguli, 2015). Consequentially, the worsened socio-economic conditions are pervasive in the everyday life of individuals (Economou, Madianos, Peppou, Patelakis, & Stefanis, 2013).

However, for participants in this study, their primary causal factor for anxiety was the experience of uncertainty when choosing their career paths rather than fear of unemployment as in other southern European countries. One explanation for this is the high employment rate of tertiary graduates in Malta which stands at 93% and amongst the highest in the EU (European Commission, 2013). Participants emphasised their deliberate reflexivity in choosing what they want to do in their life, where to study and which career to pursue. They were also aware that the process that offers such choices also creates risks and consequentially anxiety. In a similar manner to what Beck and Beck-Gernsheim (2008 [2002]) argued, 'your own life – your own failure', social problems become linked to psychological dispositions like guilt and anxiety. In line with Bynner and Côté (2008), participants felt pressured by the educational system to obtain higher educational qualifications with the hope of gaining an advantage in access to better-paying jobs.

Jane, a 24-year-old participant, said that she felt the need to increase her marketability by studying for a Master's degree. Equally worried about the lack of predictability, Maria, a 21-year-old participant, maintained that 'I am really anxious about my future. The fact that I won't have things planned out really scares me.' Shouldering individual responsibility made her anxious about the future.

The increased importance to qualifications, especially a university degree, is now a universal goal for young people with similar life chances as the research participants. Participants felt that a university degree was part of their trajectory into adulthood even though they were unsure what to do in their life. For instance, Lara, a 23-year-old student emphasised this;

> I am studying but I don't know for what. It was just a normal process that I had entered university after obtaining my Advanced Levels. But still, I don't know what I want to do in life and which job to go for.

Jane maintained that she had more alternatives today compared to her parent generation. Her ambition was to be a psychologist. Regardless of Jane's perceived advantageous position in having the ability to devise her own life-plan, she also felt anxious about her future and in a liminal stage as an emerging adult. In a powerful discourse about the shift in females' life chances, Jane compared her situation with her grandmother's. She said that she has more things to think about, more stress to deal with and more uncertainty about what to do.

> Life was simpler. Although I think today women have more opportunities but I think life was simpler. Women had fewer anxieties. They only thought about marriage. So advancement has also brought about negative consequences like anxiety. A woman used to think about marriage and childcare whereas today she needs to balance the family with a career. Sometimes when I'm very anxious, by the way I'm a feminist, but sometimes I say it was better when we were simpler.

Jane felt anxious with no certainty or permanence in her chosen career path. Her 'do-it-yourself biography', albeit exciting, is contradictory, especially in line with the changes in the educational system and credentials. Her decision to further her studies had also a significant impact on her free and leisure time. The concept of work–life balance and the support structures in place such as by family members are important considerations when studying leisure patterns amongst youth (Clark & Cassar, 2013).

It can be argued that liberating conditions from traditional stereotypical roles created a contradictory situation. In particular, young female participants maintained that they are faced with greater individual choice but they also have to shoulder new responsibilities and deal with more anxiety. Despite the progress made toward the equalisation of sexes in Malta, as a southern European location, young females are not completely released from traditional gender roles. Besides their reflexive deliberations, most female participants spoke about the need to juggle work and family in the future. Albeit the rapid increase in the rate of women working, there is still a considerable division of gender roles in the Maltese family (Abela, 2016). It is not the case, as the Beck and Beck-Gernsheim (2008[2002]) asserted, that 'in education young women increasingly face the same demands and opportunities as men and not least for this reason they develop increasingly similar expectations and demands for their career' (Beck & Beck-Gernsheim, 2008[2002], p. 66).

Cushioning anxiety

The socio-economic and cultural conditions of the research location need to be taken into consideration when analysing the debt situation of youth. The stress and anxiety of young participants are, in part, being cushioned by a number of socio-economic and cultural factors.

First, none of the research participants took up loans to finance their undergraduate degrees because of the free tertiary educational system in Malta.

Second, financial difficulty and debts linked to unemployment is one causal factor for anxiety amongst youth. The low rate of youth unemployment, as already explained, is cushioning financial anxiety. This makes the transition from school to work a smooth move towards financial autonomy.

Third, participants emphasised the centrality of the community, family-oriented principles and family obligations in their everyday life. Robert Putnam (1995) emphasised the important of a 'community' with a close network of social relations, in what he refers to as social capital 'features of social organisation such as networks, norms, and social trust that facilitate coordination and cooperation for mutual benefit' (Putnam, 1995, p. 67). The concept is beneficial because of three elements – confidence, reciprocity and networks (Putnam, 1995). These tie in with the need to cultivate connections in Malta through the close network of social relations (Baldacchino, 2013). Moreover, such networks and the family cushions youth's transition into adulthood. This needs further elaboration to make sense of participants' responses.

High intensity of kinship networks

The significance of the kinship network in the southern region is different to the more central and northern European countries – what Reher (1998) refers to as the 'weak' family link of the northern European nuclear setting compared to the 'strong' family ties of the Mediterranean region. An example of this is the difference in family obligation in care for intergenerational relations and the way the family organises support for its most vulnerable members (Cliquet, 2003; Viazzo, 2010). Similarly in Malta, the extended family occupies a central role in the provision of support for all members – an example of this is in the way the extended family organises innovative rotating care patterns to accommodate vulnerable, especially elderly, family members (Innes, Abela, & Scerri, 2011).

It has been argued that societies with traditional strong family ties, characterised by the extended family setting, are more willing to accommodate for the needs of vulnerable members in the family (Cliquet, 2003; Reher, 1998). These usually include dependent members like young people who are financially dependent on their parents. In Greece, for instance, young people living in the climate of high unemployment, rely on their parents for financial support – a situation that can change, according to Greek youth, through solidarity, cooperation and volunteerism (Tsekeris, Pinguli, & Georga, 2015).

Parents are also willing to provide financial support to buy various consumer goods. Financial anxiety is also fuelled by the culture of consumerism (Kamenetz, 2007). Youth are especially seduced by the all-embracing Western consumer culture that incorporates even disaffection and rebellion into capitalism itself – what Jim McGuigan (2009) refers to as 'Cool Capitalism'. One participant enthusiastically referred to the culture of conspicuous consumption, yet she spoke about her limited budget since she is still financially dependent on her parents. Most of the respondents embraced the mantra of 'never spend beyond my budget'. Even though most participants considered themselves easily seduced by consumer goods, they proudly declared that they kept their feet firm on the ground and never stretched out for something that they cannot afford. David summarised this by saying 'I am not ready to buy stuff just to be like others and end up with loans.' Such characterisation has affinities with the principle to 'save up for a rainy day' as one of the traditional fundamental values of the Maltese society.

Mark, in particular, was trained during childhood to be financially responsible. He declared that he doesn't have any financial problem;

> I don't really have a problem. My mother … because of the fact that she brought us up in the absence of my father, always taught us to save money … I spent some time working part-time and managed to save up some money so if I want to buy a car I won't have to borrow or rely on anyone because I have my money.

Even though participants said they would not spend beyond their means, they referred to need to take up bank loans in the near future, especially when buying their own property. It is typical for young people in Malta to buy a property rather than rent it. It is often the case therefore, that the financial situation of young people becomes dire when they take their first home loan; usually after starting working full-time. In view of this, most participants were aware that they don't afford to fully enter independent living before having a full-time job.

Nevertheless, participants referred to the way the close-knit family environment in Malta is at times sheltering youth from the preoccupations of future financial debts. Despite the fact that most of the time parents cannot afford to financially support their children into buying a property, they tend to find ways to ease the financial burden and reduce anxiety. Jane referred to a typical solution that some parents are adopting;

We thought of redesigning again my mother's house cause my brother is an architect and we were planning to reconstruct the house so I will have the upper floor and he will have the lower floor. But that is a future plan.

Leaving parental home

Hedonistic consumerism coupled with student loans to finance higher education, credit card debt and the high cost of housing are resulting in a gloomy life situation for most Western young people (Kamenetz, 2007). It comes to no surprise that young people are leaving their parental home at a later age or even return back living with their parents after college due to financial difficulty – a trend which gave youth today the name of a boomerang generation.

Youth's financial situation is one of the main reasons why they are delaying leaving parental home according to the 'Youth in Europe' survey (Eurostat, 2009). This is a case in countries like Italy (Ferrera, 1996; Reher, 1998; Rosina & Fraboni, 2004). Culturally, Maltese youth share similar tendencies to other southern Europeans. The average age of leaving parental home in Malta is 30.1 years; one of the highest in the EU28 (Eurostat, 2013). Empirical evidence showed that this delay in Malta can be explained in three ways, due to financial, cultural and geographical conditions.

First, the lack of financial stability, mainly due to extending years in training is delaying having a full-time job and transitioning into independent living. This is resulting in lengthening the years of financial dependence on parents.

Second, the high intensity of kinship network, interlaced with a Catholic mentality, reinforces the tendency of moving out of parental home upon marriage. Southern European young adults give importance to the attitudes and values of their parents, particularly when leaving parental home and making their family formation choices (Di Guilio & Rosina, 2007; Esping-Andersen, 1990; Ferrera, 1996). Compared to most northern European countries that witnessed an increase in youth's formation of informal unions, for southern European youth leaving the parental household usually coincides with marriage (Reher, 1998; Schröder, 2008). Di Guilio and Rosina (2007) refer to the way Italian parents are deeply involved emotionally in the lives and decisions of their adult children, including in their choices on marriage and cohabitation – it is also a case that 'children ... avoid choices which openly clash with the values of parents' (Rosina & Fraboni, 2004, p. 162).

Malta's high institutionalisation of marriage plays a crucial role in youth's decision to lengthening their years living at their parental home. All participants were still living with their parents during the time of interview. This was not solely a financial decision for them, but a cultural one. Most participants felt obliged to respect their parents' values and leave home upon marriage. Two respondents maintained that their parents would not be pleased if they decided to live on their own before getting married. Elena said that her mother warns her that she will not accept her back home if she decides to leave; 'my mother ... she always says that once we leave, she won't accept us back home.'

Third, due to the smallness of the Maltese islands the scope of living on campus does not make sense because of the short distances. David spoke about this peculiarity;

In Malta, due to the short distances, even if you opt to leave, your bond with the extended family remain strong and if something happen to you, you can easily go back home.

As a general rule, most participants in this research had no interest to live on their own but hoped to remain in partial dependence as long as possible. They felt free from normative expectations of childhood dependency and in a stage of exploring the variety of possible life directions. In line with Arnett (2001), they were in a stage of emerging adults, choosing their adult identity by making long-term commitments and decisions. Participants admitted that they were living comfortably at their parental home, being financially and emotionally supported. Anthony's reply is an exemplary reply of their unwillingness to move out;

> I still live with my parents and I will leave when getting married. The reason is that my parents never restricted me in anyway. If I want to go back home at five in the morning, they don't restrict me not to. I don't see why I should leave. Water and electricity bills are sent to my father and I am happy as it is.

Discussions

Institutional individualisation and anxiety

From this research, it was possible to discern a number of patterns in the ways participants dealt with their anxiety. This article referred to the role of the family and support network, in a time of increased emphasis on self-reliance. Recent literature on the life experiences of young people, in the Anglo-American context, refers to an individualisation boost (Beck & Beck-Gernsheim, 2008[2002]). Notwithstanding the credibility of Beck and Beck-Gernsheim's argument, this study has shown that this process is not consistent with the cultural variables in a southern European context. Anxiety amongst youth in Malta is cushioned by the family support network – this supports youth both financially and emotionally and as a result it reduces anxiety. Furthermore, the very fact that Malta did not undergo an economic crisis, just like other southern European countries, as well as the low rate of youth unemployment, are also attributable factors towards the degree of anxiety experienced.

There is a kind of 'institutional individualisation' in the life domain of youth in Malta – a balanced view between contextual support structures and reflexive deliberations. This concept builds on the study on institutional individualisation in the welfare-institutional order (Frericks et al., 2016) and looks into youth's informal support network in southern Europe and how this is cushioning anxiety. Young people in southern European countries have more freedom in devising their own life, yet the family support structure is influential in their decisions. Similar to the concept of 'structured individualisation' (Nagel & Wallace, 1997; Furlong & Cartmel, [1997]2007), a balanced view of the structure-agency relation is needed when examining the life experiences of youth.

This paper suggests the need for a more nuanced exploration of the changes in the life experiences of young people in other locations in southern Europe, to build a better understanding of the complex relationship between structural constraints and individual agency. The framework set out here can be broadened and applied to explore other instances where youth's choices are continuously influenced by other contextual factors and in other locations. It would also be useful to explore the application of individualisation to young people with diverse life conditions and chances to assess how the process of individualisation transcends to other social groups who may not have opportunities for tertiary education.

Conclusion

Studies on the state of anxiety in youth have been central in youth studies especially in Sociology and Psychology. The significance of this article is that it positions such discussion within the discourse on individualisation to provide a credible explanation of the situation of the life situation of youth today. It focuses on how this transcends in southern Europe, in the life domain of youth in tertiary education by exploring their degree of reflexive deliberations as well as anxiety. The peculiar socio-economic and cultural characteristics of the South were taken into consideration here. This paper focuses on three of such peculiarities – in the educational system, employment prospects and personal debts.

A number of implications were brought forward in this discussion. The familial support network plays a crucial role in reducing anxiety, both through financial and emotional support. Youth experience a kind of 'institutional individualisation' in which their reflexive deliberations, leading to anxiety, are cushioned by their family especially during the lengthening years of living at their parental home.

Acknowledgements

The author would like to thank Jim McGuigan for his helpful support throughout the writing of this study.

Disclosure statement

No potential conflict of interest was reported by the author.

Notes on the contributor

Dr Valerie Visanich is a lecturer at the Department of Sociology, University of Malta. Her main fields of interest are sociology of culture and art and youth studies. She is chair (2017–2019) of the European Sociological Association, Research Network Sociology of Art (RN2). She is also the co-founder and chairperson of the Malta Sociological Association.

References

Abela, A. (2013). Divorce in Malta. In R. E. Emery (Ed.), *Cultural sociology of divorce: An Encyclopaedia* (Vol. 2, pp. 748–752). Thousand Oaks, CA: Sage.

Abela, A. (2016). Family life. In M. Briguglio & M. Brown (Eds.), *Sociology of the Maltese Islands* (pp. 18–46). Luqa: Miller.

Archer, M. (2000). *Being human: The problem of agency*. Cambridge: Cambridge University Press.

Archer, M. (2003). *Structure, agency, and the internal conversation*. Cambridge: Cambridge University Press.

Arnett, J. (2001). *Adolescence and emerging adulthood: A cultural approach*. Upper Saddle River, NJ: Pearson Prentice Hall.

Baldacchino, G. (1998). Far better to serve in heaven than to reign in hell: Malta's logic of relating to the European Union. In G. Baldacchino & R. Greenwood (Eds.), *Competing strategies of economic development from small islands* (pp. 213–238). Charlottetown: Institute of Island Studies, University of Prince Edward Island.

Baldacchino, G. (2013). *Social class in Malta: Still our daily bread*. Centre for Labour Studies, Biennial Report 2011–2013, University of Malta. Retrieved from https://www.um.edu.mt/__data/assets/pdf_file/0010/191197/biennial_doc_2012.pdf

Bauman, Z. (1996). From pilgrim to tourist – or a short history of identity. In H. Stuart & P. Du Gay (Eds.), *Questions of cultural identity* (pp. 18–26). London: Sage.

Bauman, Z. (1998). *Globalization – The human consequences*. Cambridge: Polity Press.

Bauman, Z. (2008). The absence of society. In Joseph Rowntree Foundation, *The social evils series*. York: Joseph Rowntree Foundation.

Beck, U., & Beck-Gernsheim, E. (2008[2002]). *Individualization*. London: Sage.

Beck, U. (1992). *Risk society: Towards a new modernity*. London: Sage.

Beck, U. (1994). The reinvention of politics: Towards a theory of reflexive modernization. In U. Beck, A. Giddens, & S. Lash, (Eds.), *Reflexive modernization. Politics, tradition and aesthetics in the modern social order* (pp. 1–55). Cambridge: Polity.

Briguglio, L. (2014). *A revised vulnerability and resilience framework*. Retrieved from https://www.um. edu.mt/__data/ … /Small_states_Competitiveness_and_resilience.pdf

Briguglio, M. (2016). Political parties and social movements. In M. Briguglio & M. Brown (Eds.), *Sociology of the Maltese Islands* (pp. 324–337). Luqa: Miller.

Briguglio, M., & Bugeja, I. (2011). Exploring Malta's welfare model. *Bank of Valletta Review, 43*, 12–27.

Briguglio, M., Bugeja, I., & Vella, M. G. (2016). Social policy, poverty and social exclusion. In M. Briguglio & M. Brown (Eds.), *Sociology of the Maltese Islands* (pp. 374–390). Luqa: Miller.

Bynner, J., & Côté, J. (2008). Changes in the transition to adulthood in the UK and Canada: The role of structure and agency in emerging adulthood. *Journal of Youth Studies, 11*(3), 251–268.

Cassar, J. (2016). Youth. In M. Briguglio & M. Brown (Eds.), *Sociology of the Maltese Islands* (pp. 69–82). Luqa: Miller.

Clark, M., & Cassar, J. (2013). *Leisure trends among young people in Malta*. Office of the Commissioner for Children and Agenzija Zghazagh, Malta. Retrieved from https://www.academia.edu/29766207/ Clark_M._and_Cassar_J._2013_._Leisure_Trends_Among_Young_People_In_Malta._Malta_ Office_of_the_Commissioner_for_Children_and_AC4A1enzija_C5BBgC4A7aC5BCagC4A7

Cliquet, R. (2003). *Major trends affecting families*. New York, NY: United Nations.

Di Guilio, P., & Rosina, A. (2007). Intergenerational family ties and the diffusion of cohabitation in Italy. *Demographic Research, 16*(14), 441–468.

Economou, M., Madianos, M., Peppou, L. E., Patelakis, A., & Stefanis, C. N. (2013). Major depression in the era of economic crisis: A replication of a cross-sectional study across Greece. *Journal of Affective Disorders, 145*(3), 308–314.

Esping-Andersen, G. (1990). *The three worlds of welfare capitalism*. Princeton, NJ: Princeton University Press.

European Commission. (2013). *Education and training monitor 2013*. Retrieved from http://ec.europa. eu/dgs/education_culture/repository/education/library/publications/monitor13_en.pdf

European Commission. (2016). *European economic forecast winter 2016*. Retrieved from http://ec. europa.eu/economy_finance/publications/eeip/pdf/ip020_en.pdf

Eurostat. (2009). *Youth in Europe, A statistics portrait*. European Commission, Luxembourg: Publications Office of the European Union.

Eurostat. (2013). *What it means to be young in the European Union today*. Retrieved from http://ec. europa.eu/eurostat/documents/2995521/6783798/1-16042015-AP-EN.pdf/5d120b02-c8df-4181-9b27-2fe9ca3c9b6b

Eurostat. (2015). *Euro area unemployed at 10.1%*. May 2016. Retrieved from http://ec.europa.eu/ eurostat/documents/2995521/7545626/3-01072016-AP-EN.pdf/4281f757-75ef-4463-a15c-ca9f968b8513

Featherstone, K. (2014). *The political challenges of institutional reform in Greece. Policy Network*. Retrieved on 23 November 2016. http://www.policy-network.net/pno_detail.aspx?ID= 4578&title=The-political-challenges-of-institutional-reform-in-Greece

Ferrera, M. (1996). The 'southern model' of welfare in social Europe. *Journal of European Social Policy, 6*(1), 17–37.

Frericks, P., Höppner, J., & Och, R. (2016). Institutional individualisation? The family in European social security institutions. *Journal of Social Policy, 45*(4), 747–764.

Furlong, A., & Cartmel, F. ([1997]2007). *Young people and social change*. Berkshire: Open University.

Gal, J. (2010). Is there an extended family Mediterranean welfare states? *Journal of European Social Policy, 20*(4), 283–300.

Giddens, A. (1991). *Modernity and self-identity. Self and society in the late modern age.* Cambridge: Polity.

Hall, S. G. (1904). *Adolescence: Its psychology and its relations to physiology, anthropology, sociology, Sex, crime, religion and education.* New York, NY: D Appleton and Company.

Heery, E., & Salmon, J. (Eds.). (2000). *The insecure workforce.* London: Routledge.

Innes, A., Abela, S., & Scerri, C. (2011). The organisation of dementia care by families in Malta: The experiences of family caregivers. *Dementia (Basel, Switzerland), 10,* 165–184.

Kamenetz, A. (2007). *Generation debt.* New York, NY: Riverhead Books.

McGuigan, J. (2009). *Cool capitalism.* London: Pluto Press.

McGuigan, J. (2010). *Cultural analysis.* London: Sage.

Mitchell, J. (2002). *Ambivalent Europeans, ritual, memory and the public sphere in Malta.* London: Routledge.

Nagel, U., & Wallace, C. (1997). Participation and identification in risk societies: European perspectives. In J. Bynner, L. Chisholm, & A. Furlong (Eds.), *Youth, citizenship and social change in a European context* (pp. 42–55). Aldershot: Avebury.

Pereirinha, J. (1997). Welfare states and anti-poverty regimes: The case of Portugal. In M. Rhodes (Ed.), *Southern European welfare states, between crisis and reform* (pp. 198–239). London: Frank Cass.

Putnam, R. D. (1995). Bowling alone: America's declining social capital. *Journal of Democracy, 6*(1), 65–78.

Reher, D. S. (1998). Family ties in Western Europe: Persistent contrast. *Population and Development Review, 24*(2), 203–234.

Roberts, K. (1995). *Youth and employment in modern Britain.* Oxford: Oxford University Press.

Rosina, A., & Fraboni, R. (2004). Is marriage losing its centrality in Italy. *Demographic Research, 11*(6), 149–172.

Savage, J. (2008). *Teenage: The creation of youth 1875–1945.* London: Pimlico.

Schröder, C. (2008). The influence of parents on cohabitation in Italy: Insights from two regional contexts. *Demographic Research, 19*(48), 1693–1726.

Sennett, J. (1998). *The corrosion of character. The personal consequences of work in the new capitalism.* New York: W.W. Norton.

Trading Economics. (2017). *Malta GDP growth rate.* Retrieved from http://www.tradingeconomics.com/malta/gdp-growth

Tsekeris, C., Kaberis, N., & Pinguli, M. (2015). *The Self in crisis: The experience of personal and social suffering in contemporary Greece,* GreeSE Paper No.92, Hellenic Observatory Papers on Greece and Southeast Europe, London School of Economics: London.

Tsekeris, C., Pinguli, M., & Georga, E. (2015). Young people's perception of economic crisis in contemporary Greece: Crisis observatory, A social psychological pilot study. *Hellenic Foundation for European and Social Policy, 19.*

Viazzo, P. P. (2010). Family, kinship and welfare provision in Europe, past and present: Commonalities and divergences. *Continuity and Change, 25*(1), 137–159.

Zweig, F. (1963). *The student in the age of anxiety.* New York, NY: Free Press of Glencoe.

Imagining the future in a difficult present: storylines from Spanish youth

María Luz Morán ⓘ and Laura Fernández de Mosteyrín ⓘ

ABSTRACT
This paper examines Spanish juveniles' effort to imagine the future in times of uncertainty. The breakdown of youth strategies to adulthood exacerbates the disarticulation of imagined futures. 'Presentism' is further intensified by the 2008 crisis, making it difficult for youth to 'find their place in the world'. Our evidence comes from biographical narratives collected in the form of 'letters' written by Spanish university students. Borrowing from literature on youth transitions, temporal sociology and situated culture, we develop a narrative analysis which shows how, in the process of imagining their future, Spanish youth are reconsidering their expectations and generating new solutions. Their accounts show how they manage to connect their individual experiences with the collective, generational dimension.

Introduction

The aim of this article is to show how young Spaniards represent their future in a context characterised by a far-reaching economic, social and political crisis that has had a particularly marked impact upon them.[1] This crisis, together with the imposition of a hegemonic discourse – an 'ideational regime' (Somers, 2008) – in relation to it has modified their transitions to adult life to the extent that many of the strategies that they had designed and implemented to culminate their socio-political integration have become obsolete in the course of just a few years.

On the basis of these premises, we develop three hypotheses. First and foremost, we consider that the breakdown suffered by the strategies of young people exacerbates the disarticulation of their imagined futures, something that has already been described in various studies on the consequences of the greater complexity of their transitions to adulthood and the acceleration of the rhythms of life. Second, the crisis increases tensions among young people when they seek their forward projection into the future to 'find their place in the world', so that they are forced to devise new stories about the possibilities, fears and hopes of adult life. Finally, although writing a piece about one's future is undoubtedly an individual endeavour, imagining the future is not. It is a relational process by which individuals establish a dialogue with others and with the broader cultural framework. According to Swidler, culture is imagined before it can be put to work:

[...] cultural imagery is used somewhat the way bats use the walls of caves for echolocation. Bats know where they are by bouncing sounds off the objects around them. Similarly people orient themselves partly by bouncing off the cultural alternatives made apparent in their environments. (Swidler, 2001, p. 30)

As a result, analysing these stories provides important insights into their new common strategies for culminating their socio-political integration and into some of the ways in which they construct and put into practice their citizenship.

Analytical framework

Our study connects with two lines of research. First, we share the premise that transitions to adult life are increasingly disjointed and individualised, as numerous studies of European youth have long noted (Biggart, Furlong, & Carmel, 2008; Côté, 2014; Furlong, Cartmel, & Biggart, 2006), and as has been corroborated for the Spanish case, albeit that it presents some specific characteristics of its own (Jiménez Roger et al., 2008; López Blasco, 2005). One of the main distinctions was the intergenerational pact, established since the early 1990s between young people and adults, by which the former agreed to delay their emancipation and prolong situations of semi-dependency. In return, families increased their investment in their children's education to improve their conditions of joining the labour market. Young Spaniards adopted an individualistic and meritocratic discourse that expressed their confidence in the fact that their efforts and qualifications would be recognised when they entered the adult world, although they admitted that 'they were playing with marked cards' as far as their social origin and gender were concerned. Until the outbreak of the crisis, the two main consequences of this pact were a reduction in social unrest and the relative absence of pressure to draft any specific youth policies. However, its negative effects soon became apparent, most notably (besides its obvious demographic consequences),[2] the over-qualification and the self-marginalisation of young people from institutional politics.[3]

In recent years, different trends – the rapid increase in youth unemployment, the reduction in the number of young people in skilled jobs, the rise in their rates of emigration, etc. – confirm the abrupt termination of this pact.[4] Despite the diversity of young people's trajectories, the suffering of this 'unfulfilled promise' constitutes a genuine generational experience, although it is Spain's middle-class youth who have been affected most. It is worth recalling briefly some of the changes wrought by the crisis in addition to those of the already disjointed transitions to adulthood. It has meant having to face an extraordinarily complex situation, full of contradictions and often indecipherable. Conscious of the inadequacy of their resources for adopting individual strategies in a changing and threatening environment, they give voice to their tensions generated by their incessant struggle to adapt and to 'reinvent' themselves. This gives rise to processes of biographical and social introspection in which they confront the harsh reality of their broader environment. Specifically, this sense of unease results in the loss of security previously provided by the spaces of their daily lives, requiring them in turn to think about 'life somewhere else'.

Second, our study makes an argument for the relevance of young people's imaginaries of the future to understand these transformations. Studying young people in a situation of crisis forces us to examine their autobiographies and their life trajectories, which means making a case for a 'temporalised sociology' (Baert, 1992) as the most appropriate analytical perspective for understanding the role of individualisation, self-reflection and agency in present-day societies (Baert, 1992; Bertaux, 1979; Carpentier & White, 2013; Giddens, 1990; Martuccelli, 2002). Although to date the subject has not received a lot of research attention, given that imagining a future of some kind is a basic element of social life, we believe that it should be considered an empirical category of analysis.

> Looking at our empirical data it can hardly be denied that almost everything human beings seem to do when they relate to each other is actually based on the reflected or non-reflected assumption that there will be a future. Future confers on our everyday life a longitudinal dimension, allowing us to picture our life beyond the present moment. (Cantò-Milà & Seebach, 2015, p. 199)

Accordingly, we recognise that, in present-day societies, the growing sensation of being surrounded by risks and uncertainties, the acceleration in the processes of economic, social and technological transformations and the consequent growth in the speed of the rhythms of life render the idea of the future as 'undesirable' in itself:

> The consequence of living in a high speed society (…) is that the future is, so to say, burned up: it folds back into the present, it is absorbed within it and is consumed before it can really be conceived. The present in its turn becomes 'all there is' (…). (Leccardi, 2014, p. 42)

It is, therefore, quite easy to understand that young people constitute a key group for analysing the traits and consequences of these transformations. At a stage in their life-course when they are called upon to make constant individual choices, given that they are 'travellers without a map' (Bontempi, 2003), it is important to study the obstacles they face in being able to anticipate their future: 'Contrary to the vision of first modernity, there is less and less room for an image of the future as controllable' (Leccardi, 2008, p. 123). The difficulty of projecting oneself forward into the future on the basis of an unstable present explains why they develop two extreme types of defensive strategy. On the one hand: 'A new figure emerges from this scenario: that of the hyper-activist individual able to construct his/her own biography, willing to explore and re-explore the present so greatly emphasised by the acceleration society' (Leccardi, 2014, p. 49). On the other hand, others are unable to see beyond the here and now, quite simply they are paralysed: 'As a result, they sometimes refer to the future in conditional terms; the idea of planning for the future is replaced by expectation, by the idea of waiting invested in dreams or illusions' (Machado Pais, 2003, p. 123). A dichotomy that Machado Pais sums up in two ways of *defuturising* the future: (1) through 'utopianisation': a fantasy or totally open future; and (2) through 'atopianisation': the reduction of the future to ordinariness, or simply an absent future.

Fieldwork and methodology

Our article is based on a research study analysing the impact of the crisis on the civic ties of Spanish young people, who find themselves 'exposed to the elements' with little to protect them. Our study population is made up of university students – male and female – between the ages of 20 and 25 in their final year of either an undergraduate or postgraduate degree course at a public university. We selected this group because graduating was at the crux of the aforementioned generational pact – it was the maximum aspiration of young Spaniards since it assured them a ride on the 'social elevator'. Moreover, we focused on students who were about to achieve this objective because it is a key moment for taking decisions about the future. We are, nevertheless, aware that middle-class youth are over-represented, so we will avoid making any generalisations on the basis of our results.[5]

As for the methodology adopted, we seek to examine the students' imagined futures through their stories, on the understanding that autobiographical narrative is the most appropriate method to ensure the emergence of the tensions and contradictions between what is desired, what is possible and what is inevitable. Thus, we have adhered to some of the proposals for the analysis of the 'situated culture', in line with those who believe that narratives allow us to verify the articulation of the structure, the agency and the cultural frameworks (Tavory & Eliasoph, 2013; Wagner-Pacifici, 2009).

> Future projections often take a narrative form that ties into familiar modes of storytelling [...] or social drama [...], which serve as templates for future action. (Mische, 2009, p. 701)

In this article we undertake a 'textual experiment'. In two different waves, conducted in 2013 and 2014, we asked the young students to write letters to a real or fictitious correspondent chosen by themselves, explaining 'how they were getting on in life' and, above all, what their plans were in the short and medium terms. We provided each of them with the research project's email address and waited for their letters to arrive. We received a total of 63.[6] We believe that, as the crisis has given rise to notable processes of self-reflection, the letter represents a particularly suitable genre (Siess, 2010). Moreover, we have been able to experiment with a new source that might contribute to the debate concerning the limits of interviews and life histories in sociological analyses (Cotts & Swidler, 2009; Lamont & Swidler, 2014).

To analyse the content of this material, we employ the concept of 'storyline' (Edley & Whetherell, 1999) to capture the way in which the genre (structure) and the content (agency) of the narrative of future plans entail a reflective and rhetorical work. This, in turn, enables us to understand the forward projections and the dilemmas that define the actors/narrators. We understand the narrative as a cultural solution to the problem of how to translate knowing into telling. Insofar as it is not so much a form of representation but 'a manner of speaking about events, whether real or imaginary' (White, 1980. p. 7), it is an instrument that unites the real with the imaginary and with desire. Hence, it is a suitable strategy for capturing 'wishful thinking'.

In short, our research focuses on the study of images of the future:

> (...) the concrete pictures, which people trace when they imagine and speak of the/their future. Images of the future are always concrete pictures of that which the individuals hope, fear, wish, envisage or forefeel that will come (...). (Cantò-Milà & Seebach, 2015, p. 202)[7]

Analysis of results

Thus, we identify the main storylines used by our young students when presenting their images of the future by first differentiating between the 'utopianisation' and 'atopianisation' of the future (Machado Pais, 2003). Based on these sequences, we then examine the strategies they imagine for achieving their desired goals using the two poles on the hyper-activity/paralysis continuum (Leccardi, 2014).[8]

But, first, we need to discuss a number of prior concerns. Above all, we fully recognise the specific characteristics of our study material: the letters are 'fictitious' because their authors know they will not be read by the person to whom they are addressed but rather by researchers. However, although young people rarely write letters, practically all the letters received conform to their stylistic conventions, confirming that the letter remains a basic genre of linguistic behaviour stabilised by social custom, at the same time as being a type of unilateral verbal interaction with clear links to oral dialogue and conversation (Van Dijk, 1978).

Most of the letters are addressed to acquaintances (friends or relatives) with whom the writers are not in frequent contact, and so they are personal letters that use the conventional forms of introduction and expressions of affection ('I haven't heard from you in ages', 'Hope everything's going well', 'I've got lots of news to tell you'). The emotive nature of their letters is emphasised by resorting to a range of devices ('Hi Auntie Evaaaaa!', 'Lots of hugs and kisses'). Only a few adopt the format of a brief biography, similar in that respect to a letter of motivation attached to an application for a job or scholarship, a genre that the students seem to dominate.[9] All adhere to standard rules of language use,[10] and the division into the three canonical parts – presentation, body and farewell – is clearly marked.

The students write in the first person singular and use their own names.[11] They talk about their lives and their dreams, although in the body of the letter the collective dimension usually emerges. But they do not necessarily switch from using 'I' to 'we', though impersonal and ambiguous formulations are frequent when referring to the context in which they live their lives: 'You know that things are pretty screwed up for everyone; wages falling every day, decent jobs impossible to find, workers' rights being constantly cut (…)' [L61. Male]. When the crisis opens the narrative, the incorporation of the generational dimension is inevitable: 'In short, the outlook in Spain is disastrous, and we, the country's youth, are coming off really badly' [L12. Woman].

Whatever the case, the crisis is omnipresent and references to it run through many of the stories: 'It marks everyone's mood; it's in the very air' [L26. Woman]. Some letters open with it and others conclude with it; but for everyone, regardless of their situation, the crisis represents an unexpected transformation that forces them to reflect, to question what they used to take for granted and, in most cases, to take decisions in a context that they are unable to control. Compared to the youth of a decade ago, the sense of taking responsibility for the difficulties they have to face has disappeared. There are no accounts of personal failings or personal errors; rather they stress the efforts being made by both them and their families who, moreover, they do not blame for their situation.[12] Given this new context, the breakdown in the generational pact is perceived in arguments that can be classified in three basic types. First and foremost, some take the attitude that continuing to depend on their families is the only way to get a better education, 'clarify their thinking' or, simply, the only resort open to them until things improve.

> I guess I'll have to continue to fall back on Mum and Dad and hope they'll continue to support me for a couple of years at least; but not sit around doing nothing, of course, and try to stay patient. [L22. Woman]

> Huh!! To be honest with you, the master's really just to have something to keep me occupied. That way I don't have to hear that nagging voice in my head all the time, because all you want

to do is work and they don't let you, but then it's thanks to my parents that I can do this, because if not who knows where I would be. [L49. Male]

The main change, however, is that, in contrast with the hedonistic perspective associated with this prolongation of youth (Gil Calvo, 2009), the major personal costs are now being recognised. This is particularly visible among women:

> I panic to think how much longer I'll have to depend on my parents, how old I'll be when I can think about becoming a mother and if one day I'll be able to go on a good holiday with my friends as we've planned to do so many times. [L12. Woman]

The second consequence is admitting that they will not be able to live like their parents and recognizing, therefore, that they will have to lower their professional expectations and accept their over-qualification as a permanent condition. It is simply the price they have to pay for their independence and personal fulfilment. Finally, an entirely new element is that of their having to start thinking about going to live their lives somewhere else, in a foreign country. Whether it is to fulfil their professional or personal expectations, emigration – dreamed or feared – appears in a large number of their letters.[13]

> The only thing I know is that rather than continuing to live in my parents' house in Spain doing nothing, I'd sooner be in England working as a waitress. At least there I won't feel I'm useless and a nuisance. [L29. Woman]

> We are convinced that we are going to have to go abroad, there is no future here. (…) We have it all planned out, we're going to go to South America. We've been told there is plenty of growth and there is work in our field. We know it won't be easy being there alone, surrounded by strangers, but it'll be much harder living at home until we're forty without work. We already want to get out and live on our own. [L3. Male]

Future as storylines

> The problem is that as things stand I simply cannot imagine any future. I live a day at a time because I can't afford myself the luxury of thinking beyond that. [L28. Woman]

The main dimensions of these narratives – the switch between individualisation and collective reflections, the rupture of the generational pact and the omnipresence of the crisis – are characterized by a logic that essentially turns the focus on the present, thus confirming Leccardi's thesis. The provisional nature of all that they experience means that any forward projection is replaced by constructions of the future based on hopes and expectations. And this generates the dichotomy proposed by Machado Pais: the 'utopianisation' (openness and fantasy) and 'atopianisation' (banalised version of an impossible future) of the imaginaries of the future.

Both processes are evident in a narrative analysis of the letters because these young people are facing a cultural problem: how to imagine their future. They try to overcome the awkwardness of having to do so using different storylines and, by focusing their stories on specific aspects and by ignoring others, they provide evidence of their priorities, expectations, desires and strategies.[14] The rhetoric they employ when imagining and communicating their future to their audience includes their dilemmas, assertions, emotions and metaphors that construct a biographical 'journey' from the past or from the present forwards. By systematising these sequences, we are able to explore our hypotheses in greater depth.

Among our 63 stories, the distribution of the sequences shows a balance between both types, although there are significant differences by gender. The stories of the women are more open to the future, but, while the men resort more frequently to fantasy, they are also well grounded in the present and centre on the provisional nature of everyday life.[15]

Atopianisation: reconsidering expectations when placed under pressure

The 'defuturising' of the future through 'atopianisation' conceals a reconsideration of expectations that brings into confrontation the present and its structural conditions. Here, we include two types of sequence: those in which the future is absent and those centred on the banal or ordinary. They are the stories in which the future is neither an objective nor a desire, and the authors fail to identify any specific strategies for achieving their expectations. Priority is given to the provisional and to day-to-day survival. In the same story, the two categories, that of the no-future and the immediate, intersect. When the writers try to imagine the former, it appears only fleetingly before they swiftly return to everyday life or to the realisation that what they hope for is not going to materialize.

The future is absent from the stories that look back to the past. They begin by looking at the origin and the development of their professional expectations and dreams, but rather than ending in the future, they end in the present. Frequently, the future is omitted altogether; but it also usually appears not as an illusion, but as something remote and fleeting, like a chimera or an impossible dream as 'I cannot afford to' [imagine the future]' [L29. Woman]. Attempting to imagine the future requires a rhetorical effort between wanting to and being able to, and for this reason, the accounts in which the future is absent are brief and sad, without any hope or expectations of personal or professional growth. The future does not exist and, in those instances in which the writers employ the future tense, it is limited to finding a job.

> Things aren't going too well for me at the moment (…) I'm still out of work. I'm not yet ready to take a job doing something I haven't been trained for, so I'm thinking of studying something else (…) but I don't want my parents to have to face the financial burden of that. But haven't you been listening to the news, the whole country's in the same situation, and I'm no exception (…). If it hadn't been for this devastating crisis, my future over the next five years would have been quite clear, I'd have graduated, I'd have started working (…) perhaps begun travelling and discovering the world (…) I'd be independent and I'd be learning what life is really like (…) those plans were brought to an abrupt halt when I was in the middle of my degree, luckily my parents weren't hit as hard by the crisis as other families, but I began to see that the future would not be what I expected (…). I realized I was not the only one worried about their future, right? As I was saying, I've been thinking about continuing with my studies, but if that doesn't work out (…) I'll have to start thinking about going abroad (…). All of this is conjecture, but the truth is I have to start taking some decisions quickly (…). Being realistic, tomorrow I'll keep sending off my CV and flicking through the pages of language books so that I don't feel I'm wasting my time, I hope things turn out well for you and that you don't have to make the same short-term decisions as me. [L19, Male]

A different strategy is that of focusing on day-to-day affairs. Those who opt for this sequence present a vision focused on the material questions in their daily lives, without mentioning any personal or professional projects. Stories of a banal future report details related to minor issues: the chaotic situation in their faculty, household chores in the family home, their friendships, their pets or their sporting activities. They recognise that they do not give much thought to the future, preferring to improvise and concentrate on the here and now. But these stories are not necessarily devoid of any reflection, and they may be sprinkled with allusions to social indifference or they may propose strictly individual solutions that show that the authors have reconsidered their expectations in the light of collective or generational reflections. The women in our study mix the banal future with the absent future more readily; on many occasions, their narratives focus almost obsessively on their education and on their professional careers: they concentrate on their present achievements without looking to the future.

Paradoxically, one of the primary examples of this inability to foresee a future is a letter addressed to the writer's 'past me'. In a quite remarkable exercise of rhetoric, the letter discusses a dilemma about what the young student hoped for, found and imagined. Finally, the future does not exist; it is uncertain and impossible to imagine:

> You might not know me, but I know you. How's everything going? (…). I used to be like that, full of hope, full of plans and dreams (…). Then you start growing up (…) you begin to imagine your future: you dream that when you graduate it will be easy to find a job (…). You're 30 years old, you have a relatively clear idea of your future, a steady job doing what you spent so many years studying for – not to mention the effort and the money, but you enjoy it and it gives you a sense of fulfilment. What's more, you own a house, you have a beautiful, intelligent girl who knows you well and, yet, still loves you and, in short, you're happy. What more could you ask for? (…). But then you wake up and have to face the harsh reality of things (…) and you begin to be filled with self-doubt and fear. You are just about to graduate, an uninspiring present and an uncertain future. You feel that all your efforts and the money that your parents (…) that the hopes and dreams you had years ago were abandoned along the way and you feel that the more you open your eyes to it (…) the harder it is not to be a complete pessimist. Your expectations about your future have gone up in smoke (…). You try to get yourself a job (…). You watch the news, you read the papers, you go out on to the street, you talk with people … and the more information you obtain and the more experiences you share, the more disgust and shame you feel for the world in general and for the country that you live in, in particular. In the end, you think about emigrating (…) you don't know whether in the long run it will help you get a decent job but at least it will be valuable learning experience. And you find yourself with this dilemma (…). And at the end of the day, you climb into bed, with that double feeling of shame on the one hand (…) and that perhaps you have the dubious honour of belonging to the first surplus generation in the history of this country (…). [L47. Male]

Written between the past and the present, his only way of imagining the future is to write to himself to lead by example and recount what he hoped to have achieved by the age of 24 and the situation in which he actually finds himself. His expectations have not been fulfilled and he knows it affects his whole generation. His hopes of finding work have been reduced to getting a precarious job and the possibility of emigrating. There are more individualistic and much more mundane stories, but this one reveals our three fundamental hypotheses: the difficulty of imagining the future, the centrality of the crisis and the interaction between the individual and the collective.

Utopianisation: continuing to wish and hope despite the crisis

In contrast to the above narratives, we have interpreted other sequences as expressing an open or fantasy future, characterized by wishes and hopes, and by a concerted effort to focus on the medium and long terms. Their fundamental characteristics are that they contain some type of forward projection, and include dreams, wishes and intentions that look beyond the next few months or their lives as students. The open future is seen with hope, but this might be with either illusion or with uncertainty, because the writers may be realistic and accept the difficulties they face. Consequently, they outline strategies-solutions, usually of an individual nature, but which allow them to tell a story with a projection of the future. Although they provide details of their immediate plans (finishing education, taking a trip …), the long term is open; it exists and it does not seem problematic.

These stories are not told without any thought having been given to them; they include references to the collective situation and mention the authors' frustrated hopes. Even so, they manage to maintain and make explicit their individual dreams, however modest or ambitious. These letters focus on personal growth and on the individual's professional/vocational projection; they sketch out concrete strategies with an eye on the future, in many cases tinged with hyperactivity. However, there are few visions in the letters of an open future for the whole generation. Although they value the collective situation and recognize the structural problems, the solutions tend to be solely 'theirs'.

In any case, open futures are very common in this category, especially among women:

> As you know, I'm just finishing my course and I'm really stressed out this month (…). But at the same time I'm really happy because of what that means. First, I get to graduate (…). You do know that the future of psychology graduates these days is not altogether clear, don't you? (…). Actually, I'm very excited because me and some friends are thinking of setting up something ourselves (…). Although I haven't told you yet, there's also a chance I might do a PhD (…) I have lots of ideas and I think there are lots of things I can do. But I'm not going to get stressed out, I'll just see how things pan out when I finish my master's (…). In the near future, I see myself above all in Madrid, working in a company, a school, a nursing home, a private hospital, some sort of association or whatever (ha, ha) and combining that it with a few hours of individual therapy each week. I am at a really great stage in my life and I'm not going to give up fighting to achieve my goals because I've invested a lot of time, money and enthusiasm in this. Besides, ever since I was little, I knew I wanted to be a psychologist and I've always worked towards that dream. I hope my enthusiasm rubs off on you, because I know in these times people are losing hope, but it is the vehicle that can carry us towards our dreams. [L 21, Woman]

By means of a highly individualistic story, focused on her future career, she constructs a sequence with a tone full of wishful thinking and euphoria. And although she recognises the difficulties and the uncertainty, neither the strategy nor the solution she provides are strictly individual. Her professional expectations and the adjustments she has to make illustrate how the crisis has marked the decisions and future of her generation.

Finally, the fantasy future is the least frequent, especially among women. This narrative option is built on goals that are not easily achievable, with the authors outlining what are ambiguous but highly enthusiastic images of what it is they hope to achieve. Above all, they are free of the constraints of work/professional expectations and focus on self-fulfilment and hedonism.

> As for my life, I can't complain, I do what I like and I'm in control of things as far as that's possible (…). And now with all that's going on, I have to choose my future, I've had it all thought out for some time (…) we're going to set up as restaurant consultants (…) but I'm not sure if that's what I want to do, (…). I don't want to keep on doing that (…) I really need to go and live abroad. I need to discover the world (…). I want to travel around the world (…). I'd like to buy a car or a motorbike and start travelling around the world, really getting to know places (…). I think I need to experience this for my future life, with this experience I know that I'll be a better

person and that I'll have a real sense of self-fulfilment (…). When I get back from this incredible trip – in two or three years I hope- I'd love to live in Paris, doesn't bother me where I'd be working (…). It'd be a tragedy if I didn't achieve this, it would mean that I'd put money and possession before my personal fulfilment, forcing me into a life of mediocrity and unhappiness (…). Ah, we'd be backpacking, so we can forget about any luxuries on the trip, we have no money. [L17. Male]

In the narratives of both open and fantasy futures, the possibility of a medium-term future is present. The dream is combined with the realisation that, in the face of great uncertainty, they must develop strategies to overcome the obstacles they are sure to encounter.

Hyperactive youth

The crisis has forced these young people to reconsider the promise of the professional and personal security of their life trajectories founded on high professional qualifications. On the verge of finishing their studies, they have to take decisions in a new context of uncertainty. Returning to the two poles of Leccardi's continuum of hyperactivity/paralysis, it is clear that virtually all the letters tend towards the former. Although the authors do not know how to represent their future in the short term, they neither want to nor are they able to remain inactive. Thus, the image that is most frequently repeated, almost mantra-like, is that of keeping busy:

One thing I'm quite clear about: I'm not going to spend all day in bed, not looking for work because of the crisis, gazing out of the window all day long. (…) you've got to keep busy. My plan is simply to keep some order in my life. Get up early and get out and look for work. And I don't mean sending out thousands of CVs. (…). Sport is the answer: laziness is not going to get the better of me. I'll take charge of the housework: if I'm going to be living with my parents, I have to give something back. (…). As things stand, I know there are no guarantees, but at least I'm not going to bore myself to death and stay in bed until noon. [L31. Male]

Their narratives reveal, though not all of them explicitly, that they cannot afford to stand around doing nothing, possibly because their own personal investment and that of their family has been so great, and because they are aware that they have greater resources than their peers. Therefore, the majority express their hyperactivity with an optimistic tone, either to persevere in their education – studying languages, another master's, etc. – or to explore new possibilities that are beginning to be more highly valued, such as entrepreneurship.

I think that with my qualifications it shouldn't be difficult to find a job, but it's going to be difficult because things are not easy right now, but if you keep on looking, sending out your CV, trawling the internet, you'll find something, or at least I hope so. [L11. Woman]

I don't let it get me down. I know that sooner or later everyone gets what they deserve. I believe in luck in the short term. [L51. Male]

In contrast, another significant number of letters recognizes their fears. Although they cannot sit around doing nothing, they simply admit that they are frightened:

In short, many frustrated dreams that leave the door open to a constant feeling of tension and anxiety. And even still, I want to make the most of this chance to appreciate the value of things and to learn how to be active. I am not thinking of sitting around with my arms folded, I have set myself the goal of becoming a teacher and that's what I intend to do. [L12. Woman]

Finally, we find a small group of 'hyperactive but annoyed' letter writers. They are the ones who, although they opt for the same strategies, openly link their personal situation to a collective discourse of criticism of the situation and, above all, to a discourse of resistance:

> I live in hope that things will change. At least I have that to hold on to. I want to finish my degree, keep trying to make a living and to find work in my field. Yet, well, as things stand, it's a lot to ask for. But as I say, I live in hope. Hope for a better world, hope to switch on the news and not to have to be told that people are going hungry and that one in three Spanish children are on the poverty line.

> The outlook is bleak, for sure; but hey, I'll keep fighting for my future. Because it's mine and no one can take it away from me (…) As long as I can I will keep fighting. [L46. Woman]

Conclusions

'Utopianisation' and 'atopianisation' are rhetorical strategies adopted by young people for imagining the future; they are ways of imagining their biographies in the light of broader contextual changes. Therefore, in reconsidering their expectations, boosting them by means of self-realisation or reducing them to the ordinary details of their daily lives, all the young people's stories share certain traits which can be put forward as findings:

- The epistolary genre of our 'textual experiment' has proven to be particularly well-suited for revealing the complexity of these self-reflection processes. Thinking about the future is a rhetorical struggle between reality and desire: 'I'd like to but I can't now'; 'what I really want is'. Having to compose a story presents them with the dilemma of not wanting to talk about the future or not allowing themselves to do so when it involves their dreams and possibilities. Hence, it arouses the continuous interplay between objections and contradictions that emerge in their stories.
- The crisis has forced these young people to self-reflect on their past and future expectations. Still, most of their accounts show that they face their social environment, and that they are able to think collectively. In most cases, their strategies are individual but their problems are collective. Writing their narratives has meant reflecting individually on their own past and future hopes. But the omnipresence of the crisis in their stories shows that these expectations come into conflict with their broader environment and that they are able to think in terms of their generation.
- The analysis of our letters confirms Leccardi's and Machado Pais' arguments. But there are some fresh findings that can be explained by the impact of the crisis – that has emphasised the dislocation of their imagined futures – but also by the breakdown of the generational pact, especially relevant among these university students. Their narratives are 'presentist', as the future tends to fade away. Besides, 'utopianisation' and 'atopianisation' are rhetorical ways of thinking their biographies. We found that a similar number of young people choose one of the two future models, although there are some gender differences. Moreover, we have detected further nuances in each of them. In the 'atopies', future may be merely missing or reduced to the ordinary. In the utopia –which are much more common among males- open futures prevail, while fantasies are much rare and rather modest.
- The changes of their transitions and the impact of the crisis have forced them, almost without exception, to set up new strategies in order to overcome the obstacles of the

present, turning them into 'hyper activists' of the future. Two main reasons explain this reaction: (a) the investment in their educational training has been so high that there is no 'turning back'; (b) although this is an unfavourable context, they are aware that have greater abilities than other Spanish youth. Therefore, there are no 'paralysed young people' among our university students.

All in all, further research on this subject may contribute to dispel the prevailing bewilderment among recent research on the Spanish youth: the change from apathy and hedonism to the 'outraged generation', some innovative labour experiences, new forms of consumption … In our opinion, it implies at least considering the images of the future among other groups of young people, and also going deeper in gender differences.

Notes

1. In the second quarter of 2016, 46.5% of Spaniards aged between 16 and 25 were unemployed. (Survey of Active Population, INE, 2016).
2. In 2015, the average age at which Spanish women had their first child was 31.20 years (INE).
3. This marginalisation was however compatible with minority political activism in alternative politics and protest movements. See López Blasco (2005) and Jiménez Roger et al. (2008).
4. We have analysed this phenomenon in more detail in Benedicto et al., 2014.
5. The replication of this study with other groups of young people remains pending.
6. Thirty-four letters were written by men and 29 by women enrolled in university courses in Barcelona, Madrid, Salamanca, Badajoz and Granada. Two letters were written by students while abroad (Sweden and Mexico).
7. We processed our data with qualitative software assistance, but instead of sorting out pieces of texts we treated each letter as a single unit and analysed it in its own context. Following a systematisation of sequences by type ('atopic' and 'utopic'), we looked at how the authors presented themselves, their feelings, emotions and attitudes towards the future, and how the storyline evolved: expectations, experiences, the role of the crisis in the narrative and the strategies for the future.
8. Although we assume there are different dimensions (age, type of college degree, family of origin …) that might work in their imagination of future, in this paper we are just concerned with types of sequence and distribution by gender.
9. Two letters are addressed to their 'future me'.
10. Only one letter uses particularly colloquial language littered with swear words: '(…) you're swanning around France with a fucking great job while things back home are getting worse and worse (…)' [L27. Male].
11. With the exception of one letter writer who adopts a pseudonym (Popeye).
12. Only one letter writer reports having ignored the advice from her family:

     The truth is, if I look at the situation people of my age find themselves in, I feel quite thankful. When I finished high school, despite my mother's opposition, I decided to sit the entrance exam to a military academy. I got the place I wanted and now I'm an officer in the Spanish army. [L53. Woman]

13. For these university students, their previous Erasmus experiences and knowledge of languages normalise the possibility of their having to emigrate.
14. In analysing the narratives, we have only considered the type of future (open or closed) that is presented. In this paper, we do not consider other dimensions.
15. We detected 32 tales of 'utopianisation' and 31 of 'atopianisation'. Among women, there were 17 'utopian' and 12 'atopian' from a total of 29 narratives. Among men, the distribution was 15 'utopian' and 19 'atopian' from a total of 34 pieces.

Acknowledgements

We appreciate the work and support of our research partners. An early version of this piece was presented at the XX Conference of the Spanish Federation of Sociology (FES, Gijón, July 2016).

Disclosure statement

No potential conflict of interest was reported by the authors.

Funding

This paper is a result of two research projects. The first study, funded by the Spanish Institute for Youth (INJUVE), has already been published (Benedicto et al., 2014). The second study, 'Redefining citizenship: the impact of socioeconomic crisis in the social basis of the Spanish Welfare State', was funded by the Spanish National R&D and Innovation Plan (MINECO. CS2012-30773).

Notes on contributors

María Luz Morán is Professor of Sociology at the Universidad Complutense of Madrid (Spain). Her recent research focuses on the representations of citizenship among Spanish young people, and on the impact of socioeconomic crisis on the legitimisation basis of the Spanish Welfare State. Results of her research have been published in various scholarly journals, including European Societies, Revista Española de Investigaciones Sociológicas, Revista de Estudios Sociales and Revista Internacional de Sociología.

Laura Fernández de Mosteyrín is a Lecturer at Universidad A Distancia de Madrid (Spain). Her recent research focus is on cultural dimensions of youth politics. Results of her research have been published in scholarly journals including Revista de Estudios Sociales and Revista Política y Sociedad.

ORCID

María Luz Morán ⓘ http://orcid.org/0000-0001-7310-8037
Laura Fernández de Mosteyrín ⓘ http://orcid.org/0000-0002-6040-2832

References

Baert, P. (1992). Time, reflectivity and social action. *International Sociology, 7*(3), 317–327. doi:10.1177/026858092007003004

Benedicto, J., Fernández, L., Gutiérrez, M., Martín, E., Morán, M. L., & y Pérez, A. (2014). *Transitar a la intemperie. Jóvenes en busca de integración* [Transiting out in the open. Young people in search of integration]. Madrid: Instituto de la Juventud (INJUVE). Retrieved from www.injuve.es/observatorio/valores-actitudes-y-participacion/transitar-a-la-intemperie-jovenes-en-busca-de-integracion

Bertaux, D. (1979). Écrire la sociologie [Writing Sociology]. *Information sur les Sciences Sociales, 18*(1), 7–25. doi:10.1177/053901847901800102

Biggart, A., Furlong, A., & Carmel, F. (2008). Modern youth transitions: Choice biographies and transitional linearity. In R. Bendit & Han-Bleibtreu (Eds.), *Youth and the future: Processes of social inclusion and patterns of vulnerability in a globalized world* (pp. 55–72). Opladen: Barbara Budrich.

Bontempi, M. (2003). Viajeros sin mapa. Construcción de la juventud y trayectos de la autonomía juvenil en la Unión Europea [Travelers without a map. The building of youth and the paths of youth autonomy in the European Union]. *Revista de Estudios de Juventud. Edición Especial 1* (*Jóvenes, Constitución y Cultura Democrática*), 24–25.

Cantò-Milà, N., & Seebach, S. (2015). Desired images, regulating figures, constructed imaginaries: The future as an apriority for society to be possible. *Current Sociology, 63*(2), 198–215. doi:10.1177/0011392114556583

Carpentier, N., & White, D. (2013). Perspective des parcours de vie et sociologie de l'individuation [Life trajectories perspective and sociology of individualization]. *Sociologie et Sociétés, 45*(1), 279–300. doi:10.7202/1016404ar

Côté, J. (2014). Towards a new political economy of youth. *Journal of Youth Studies, 17*(4), 527–543. doi:10.1080/13676261.2013.836592

Cotts, S., & Swidler, A. (2009). Hearsay ethnography: Conversational journals as a method for studying culture in action. *Poetics, 37*, 162–184. doi:10.1016/j.poetic.2009.03.002

Edley, N., & Whetherell, M. (1999). Imagined futures: Young men's talk about fatherhood and domestic life. *British Journal of Social Psychology, 38*, 181–194. doi:10.1348/014466699164112

Furlong, A., Cartmel, F., & Biggart, A. (2006). Choice, biographies and transitional linearity: Rec-conceptualising modern youth transitions. *Papers, 79*, 225–239. doi:10.5565/rev/papers/v79n0.834

Giddens, A. (1990). *The consequences of modernity*. Cambridge: Polity.

Gil Calvo, E. (2009). Trayectorias y Transiciones. ¿Qué Rumbos? [Trajectories and transitions. Which paths?]. *Revista de Estudios de Juventud, 87*, 15–29. Retrieved from http://www.injuve.es

INE (2016). *Encuesta de población activa*. Segundo trimestre 2016 [Survey of Active Population]. Retrieved from http://www.ine.es/dyngs/INEbase/es

Jiménez Roger, B., Martín Hernández, A., Navarrete, J., Pinta, P., Soler i Martí, R., & Tapia, A. (2008). *La emancipación precaria. Transiciones juveniles a la vida adulta en España a comienzos del siglo XXI* [Precarious emancipation. Youth transitions to adulthood in Spain at the beginning of the 21st century]. Madrid: CIS.

Lamont, M., & Swidler, A. (2014). Methodological pluralism and the possibilities and limits of interviewing. *Qualitative Sociology, 37*, 153–171. doi:10.1007/s11133-014-9274-z

Leccardi, C. (2008). New biographies in the 'risk society'? About future and planning. *Twenty-First Century Society, 3*(2), 119–129. doi:10.1080/17450140802062078

Leccardi, C. (2014). Young people and the new semantics of the future. *SocietàMutamentoPolitica, 5*(10), 41–54. doi:10.13128/SMP-15404

López Blasco, A. (2005). Familia y transiciones: Individualización y pluralización de formas de vida [Family and transitions: Individualisation and pluralisation of lifestyles]. In A. López Blasco, L. Cachón, D. Comas, J. Andreu, J. Aguinada, & L. Navarrete (Eds.), *Informe de Juventud en España 2004* (pp. 21–150). Madrid: INJUVE.

Machado Pais, J. (2003). The multiple faces of the future in the labyrinth of life. *Journal of Youth Studies, 6*(2), 115–126. doi:10.1080/1367626032000110264

Martuccelli, D. (2002). *Grammaires de l'individu* [Grammars of the individual]. Paris: Gallimard.

Mische, A. (2009). Projects and possibilities: Researching futures in action. *Sociological Forum, 24*(3), 694–704. doi:10.1111/j.1573-7861.2009.01127.x

Siess, J. (2010). Introduction. La lettre, laboratoire des valeurs? [Introduction. The letter, the value's laboratory?]. *Argumentation. Analyse du Discours, 5*, 1–10.

Somers, M. (2008). *Genealogies of citizenship: Markets, statelessness, and the right to have rights*. Cambridge: Cambridge University Press.

Swidler, A. (2001). *Talk of love: How culture works*. Chicago: University of Chicago Press.

Tavory, I., & Eliasoph, N. (2013). Coordinating futures: Toward a theory of anticipation. *American Journal of Sociology, 118*(4), 908–942. doi:10.1086/668646

Van Dijk, T. (1978). Toward a model of text comprehension and production.. *Psychological Review, 85*(5), 363–394. doi:10.1037/0033-295X.85.5.363

Wagner-Pacifici, R. (2009). When future meets the present. *Sociological Forum, 24*(3), 705–709. doi:10.1111/j.1573-7861.2009.01128.x

White, H. (1980). The value of narrativity in the representation of reality. *Critical Inquiry, 7*(1), 5–27. Retrieved from http://www.jstor.org/stable/1343174?seq=1#page_scan_tab_contents

Young individuals as microcosms of the Portuguese *crisis*

Magda Nico

ABSTRACT

The Portuguese *crisis* affected the country's collective identity, and 'the timing of life' at which it struck individual lives in this case is also significant. Quantitative figures show that young people were particularly affected by this *crisis*. However, a long-run qualitative approach provides a multilayered and quite complex view of what this *crisis* is embedding in young people's lives and minds. In qualitative research on 'middle class' transitions to adulthood carried out in 2009, 52 young adults were interviewed about their educational, residential, occupational and romantic lives. In a follow-up study, these individuals' trajectories, plans and expectations are now updated; their past and present confronted; and effects of the *crisis* on their lives questioned. The discussion is held in the form of a critical approach to the theories of individualisation, and goes to the heart of the 'generation in itself' vs. 'generation for itself' and 'biographies of choice' vs. 'discourses of choice' debates.

The *crisis* in Portugal can be seen as a historical landmark that affected the path taken by the country's collective and generational identity (Nico, 2013). The 'crisis period' actually refers to an accumulation of (interacting) financial, economic and political events. As Amaral and Lopes (2016) put it, 'the great recession of 2008/2009 has had a huge impact on unemployment and public finances in most advanced countries, and these impacts were magnified in the southern Euro area countries by the sovereign debt crisis of 2010/2011'. This was followed by a political change in government in Portugal from the Socialist Party to the Social-Democratic Party, an intervention by the Troika and a range of austerity measures taken partly, albeit not exclusively, at its urging. In this article, the concept of *crisis* is necessarily imprecise, as the period studied covers 2009 (first round of interviews) to 2016 (second round), and thus includes many of the aforesaid structural and contextual events. It is also imprecise because it does not perform the role of premise, conclusion or explanatory variable in this research. It is spread – variability spread depending on other life circumstances and conditions – right across the seven years of this research's observation window. This variability and sub-jectivity is what drove the research.

The timing of life at which it strikes also significantly changes the effect a *crisis* can have on people's trajectories and how they understand them. Young people, or people about to lead adult lives, have always been particularly vulnerable to distresses in labour market dynamics, and this *crisis* was far from an exception. That young people and young adults were thus particularly and negatively affected by the *crisis*, and more specifically by the austerity measures taken in its name in the past few years, is as far as static quantitative figures have been able to go in informing us about unemployment rates (Figure 1, as an example), the increase in the young NEETS category, and the duration and persistence of precarious ways of living and working. However, long-run and qualitative accounts of the same reality give a both more accurate and more complex view of what this *crisis* may have been embedding in young people's lives, minds, ideals and dreams (Nico, forthcoming).

Researchers carrying out qualitative and biographical research in 2009 on the – rather broadly defined – 'middle class' transitions to adulthood were somewhat surprised by these historical circumstances. Fifty-two young adults aged between 26 and 32 were inter-viewed about their educational, residential, occupational and romantic lives in an attempt to map and typify transitions to adulthood as socially stratified phenomena (Nico, 2011). The *crisis* itself did not play the role of a protagonist in the interviews and trajectories at that point. As a concept, in 2009 the *crisis* had only taken on an abstract outline. Its effects were not yet felt or imagined, but merely speculated on and not concretely experi-enced. This serendipity effect of the *crisis*, the Troika intervention and the measures taken by the government in response, inspired a follow-up study which involved mobilising a multiplicity of life course research instruments (biographical interview, life calendar, focus of control exercise, past reality checks) to re-interview the 2009 participants. This took place in 2016 – seven politically dense years after the first interviews, and in a new political context. New compared to the previous one, in which the government had been led by the centre-right PSD (Social-Democratic Party), which many would character-ise as conservative in values and neo-liberal in its views of the economy and welfare; and also compared to the last three decades, in that the 2016 scenario represents the first time since the democracy-seeking revolution of 25 April 1974 that the country's centre-left parties have agreed to agree on important social issues related to inequalities, poverty and the population's well-being.

Focusing mainly on the second part of this ongoing study, this article will begin by pre-senting the research design, methodology and data used and suggesting that the eclectic and macro nature of life course methods advocate them as a privileged way of collecting

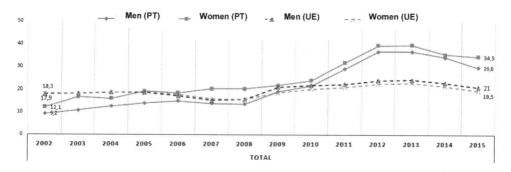

Figure 1. Unemployment rate among 15–24 year olds, by gender, in Portugal and UE28 (2002–2015) Source: EU Labour Force Survey (in Carmo and Matias, 2016).

qualitative data on real people and their real lives. I subscribe to the view of Thomas and Znaniecki when they say that

> the superiority of life records over every other kind of material for the purpose of sociological analysis appears with particular force when we pass from the characterisation of single data to the determination of facts for there is no safer and more efficient way of finding, among the innumerable antecedents of a social happening, the real causes of this happening than to analyze the past of the individuals through whose agency this happening occurred. (Thomas & Znaniecki, 1918, pp. 294–295)

This is achieved by attempting to recover the 'historicality of the individual' (Abbott, 2001) and by looking at individuals as 'microcosms' of societal phenomena (Bertaux & Delcroix, 2000) or historical landmarks. Individuals are the walking *crisis*; they are its crystallisation on the time–space axis. This attempt is valid for both the first and second parts of the research, but goes in the opposite direction to that taken in the post-modern approach to narratives, where 'any intention of interpreting society "as it really is"' is abandoned, 'shifting to post-modern or narrative approaches, in which the interview text replaces society as the focus of study' (Thompson, 2004, p. 238).

At the intersection of youth with the importance of temporality in the research design, and within the framework of our research, there are three studies of note. One of these was an absolute pioneer in longitudinal research, which combined historical time with individual time, analysing the social trajectories of individuals from their childhood during the Great Depression until they reached adolescence, 'tracing step by step the ways in which deprivation left its mark on relationships and careers, life styles and personalities'. In this work by Elder (1994) we find the theoretical and methodological sustenance for the study of individual trajectories as bearers of national history. This is also what we are seeking to do in the present study (albeit with an interval which is much shorter, but which Rindfuss (1991) says is demographically much denser: that of the transition to adult life). The other two projects were also conducted on a large scale, attracted great attention and are again Anglo-Saxon. Despite being longitudinal, they are more contemporary, both theoretically and methodologically, differing from that of Elder mainly with regard to their theoretical stance. While Williamson's (2004) work, which revisits a group of troubled youths in a Welsh community 20 years on, is admittedly 'grounded theory' and a 'personalised' investigation as a consequence of the relationship the researcher developed and maintained with the participants, the study 'Inventing Adulthoods' took place over a 10-year period within a territorially dispersed project undertaken by a large and dedicated team, and followed strong theoretical direction in both its hypotheses and its analysis (Henderson, Holland, McGrellis, Harper, & Thomson, 2007/2009; Thomson, 2009; Thomson et al., 2002).

Following this presentation of the details of the research design and instruments and the arguments behind them, two sets of results will be discussed. One has to do with the most relevant changes and continuities in the values and practices of these individuals across the past seven years, asking how they identify and perceive their 'strategic adaptation' (Elder & Giele, 2009, p. 14; Giele &, Elder 1998, pp. 9–10) to economic and political circumstances. To this end we used the whole life calendar, biographical interviews and especially the innovative 'past reality check' data collection and production instrument. The aim was to analyse the process of subjective and objective life course change; the main result showed the very small extent to which work ethics and life values have been affected, in the sense of corrupted, by the unfavourable economic scenario. The second has to do with the interviewees' recent life story and how it relates with the *crisis*, and the extent to which individuals saw their life events as satellites of the contextual *crisis*. This used the updated life calendar, the biographical interview and the innovative 'locus control' exercise instrument, in which interviewees are able to identify key moments in life and correlate them to some extent with the *crisis*. Counter-intuitive results were found in relation to the ahistorical understandings of their biography.

The conclusion will sum up these results, calling attention to how qualitative understandings of highly quantifiable phenomena – such as financial or economic *crises* – are necessary if one is to grasp the nuances of a historically situated biography, which vary and oscillate from the identity to the explanatory natures of narratives, or in other words, between 'realist' and 'neo-positivist' approaches to life stories (Miller, 2000, p. 13).

Methodology and data

Albeit using new data gathered by different data collection and co-production instruments, the 2016 follow-up project is a natural continuity of the epistemological premises considered in the 2009 research. The 2016 methodological design follows the same epistemological statement, as it goes to the heart of the qualitative and longitudinal concerns and debates about the collection, interpretation and validity of data at specific historical moments. Its instruments are deeply grounded in the four well-established principles of life course research – agency, linked lives, timing of lives and cultural and historical location (Elder, 1974, 1985; Elder, Johnson, & Crosnoe, 2002; Giele et al., 1998); it combines elements of qualitative and biographical approaches with quantitative-oriented instruments of inquiry and the co-construction of life stories, such as the life calendar (Nico, 2016a). Most of all, it advocates the need to resort to qualitative data in order to fully understand how much of the *crisis* is embedded in young peoples' lives and minds, and to longitudinal data capable of confronting and comparing past and current interpretations of the courses of lives. Only by doing so can sociological flesh be put onto the statistical bones produced by statistics institutes and used and abused by the media and political discourse.

The earlier part of this research followed the premise that transitions to adulthood are a moving target, especially vulnerable to rapid social change and severe economic oscillations; and also that as an object of study, such transitions are particularly vulnerable to the biographical turns in the social sciences, as well as to the acritical affiliation with certain individualisation theories (namely Beck, 1992) to which some authors have been calling attention (Roberts, 2012). Trying to avoid some of the 'fetishism of the present' linked to this vulnerability, in which 'youth as a concept prompts researchers to often focus only on the "here and now" rather than taking a longer-term process view' (Goodwin & O'Connor, 2015, p. 39), the research approach was more easily integrated into the life course perspective than into youth studies as such, highlighting and using the concept of generation more than that of age group. The latter thus became more of an operationalisation tool than a thematic in itself.

One important argument underlying the research was based on a critical approach to the theory of individualisation. This is frequently used as a 'package', in which all contemporary changes in a life course, such as deinstitutionalisation, destandardisation, pluralisation and differentiation, are understood as moving in the same direction or at the same pace, independently of the social and geographical coordinates at which the individuals are situated (Brückner & Mayer, 2005; Nico, 2015). As such, in the 2009 and 2016 projects, as far as possible the different dimensions of the life course were analysed through different lenses, avoiding any self-contamination and reciprocal bias of the results (Nico, 2014; Nico & Caetano, 2017).

In the first part of the project, whose fieldwork was conducted over the course of 2009 – before the effects of the *crisis* (and the ensuing austerity measures) were concrete and visible in people's lives – 52 biographical interviews combined with life calendars were applied to 'missing middle' class young people in Portugal (Roberts, 2011). This set of interviewees encompassed a significant, but not statistically representative, variety of individuals in terms of educational attainment, residential status and family social background. The sample was also gender-balanced. The major concern was to identify and map different trajectories towards adulthood, along with the social backgrounds and contexts that shaped and determined them (Nico & Caetano, 2017; Nico & de Almeida Alves, 2017).

The second, still ongoing, part of the study is recovering the contacts made in 2009. The approach has been direct and the agreement to re-participate total. No attrition effect has so far been detectable, and 13 adults, now aged 32–38 years, have been already interviewed. All these interviewees have been pleased to be re-contacted, consider the exercise of comparing past with present very entertaining and useful, and have demonstrated a relative eagerness to share how their life has turned out and a relative curiosity to know how the researcher's life has fared seven years on. Overall, ours is an intimate and informal conversation with a 'known' stranger. This has again allowed the researcher to be perceived as a 'particular kind of confidant, the kind that disappears after the interview' (at least for seven or more years), and to whom secrets can more easily be told, making him/her the 'receptor of words to which not even those the closest to us have access to' (Lahire, 2002/2004, p. 33).

The following table shows the range of life course instruments employed in the 2009 and 2016 sets of research (Table 1). Both used the combination of the life grid and the biographical interview to improve qualitative and subjective data collection and analysis, while simultaneously seeking to maintain the actual order of the narrated events and thereby escape Bourdieu's 'biographical illusion' (Bourdieu, 1994/1997; Nico, 2016a). In this regard, Bourdieu states that

> the narrative, whether biographical or autobiographical, for example, the discourse of the interviewee who 'opens up' to an interviewer, offers events which may not all or always unfold in their strict chronological succession (anybody who has ever collected life histories knows that informants constantly lose the thread of strict chronological order) but which nevertheless tend or pretend to get organised into sequences linked to each other on the basis of intelligible relationships. The subject and the object of the biography (the interviewer and the interviewee) have in a sense the same interest in accepting the postulate of the meaning of narrated existence (and, implicitly, of all existence). (Bourdieu, 1994/1997, p. 54)

The interference of the life calendar in the interview, as an instrument that is capable of challenging previous and pre-determined views of the past, and stimulating new reflexivity on the causal and emotional links between events of life – links that might be 'discovered' during and because of the interview – is a positive one. It allows the

Table 1. Life course research methods used: a summary.

	Participant recruitment	Collection and co-production of data			
		Biographical interview (transversal to all data collection)[a]	Life course calendar[b]	Past reality check	Locus control exercise
Round 1 – 2009	Intermediated by shared friends, co-workers or acquaintances	Conversation about time and timing of events, relationship between the events, understanding and explanation of the course of life. Aspects related with locus control exercise (only in 2016) and with the chronology of the	Used as the structural script for the interview – from birth to date of the interview. Analysed conjointly and separately in vertical content analysis and holistic form analysis.	Selected quotations from 2009 became part of the 2016 script as conversation-teasers, icebreakers and caricature quotes from the past.	Not used
Round 2 – 2016	Re-contacted directly	events respond to a more rigid script, contrary to the rest of the co-produced interview. Interview is recorded, transcribed to word files, and subjected to content analysis.	Used as the structural script for one part of the interview – from 2009 to 2016. Analysed conjointly and separately in vertical content analysis and holistic form analysis.		Table completed during the interview, with the most relevant (positive and negative) moments from 2009 to 2016, and the effect on them of agency, significant others, working and living conditions, crisis and chance

[a]The 2009 interviews lasted an average of 2h30m, while the 2016 interviews have lasted 2h on average so far. Interview transcripts were not reviewed by participants, but they are able to access their life calendar and transcript if they ask to do so. None of the interviewees has made such a request in 2016, and only two did so in 2009.
[b]Data not analysed here due to the small number of second-time participants.

biographical – objective and subjective – information to be shared in a more detailed and accurate format. At least since 1999, more research and publications on the combination of the life grid with semi-directed interviews have been presented as leading to new forms of understanding and qualitative results (Parry, Thomson, & Fowkes, 1999). Despite this, and although the life grid is very often employed in life course research, its combination with qualitative and biographical interviews is still not that common. Previous uses do show, however, how this combination enables the relationship between the individual experience and the identification of historical or individual key moments to improve the transparency of the relationship between the interviewee and the interviewer/ researcher, and allows a holistic understanding of the phenomenon by promoting the interdependence of the rapports about the various events and facilitating the recapitulation of the life course narrative (Parry et al., 1999).

In an attempt to make the most of the new, updated and re-reflected material on the 2009–2016 window of observation, the 2016 research used two new data collection and co-production methods: the 'past reality check' and the 'locus control exercise'.

The instrument I have called 'past reality check' allows for an adjustment between the 2009 and 2016 narratives (about values and practices). It consists of a selection of polemic, representative and/or paradigmatic quotes from the 2009 interview, which in some way demonstrate the most representative issues, opinions and/or plans at the time. The goal of using these old quotes is to act as an icebreaker and to set the past as the reference for the discourse, making it harder to completely re-write the (recent) past. As developed below, the quotations selected so far mostly had to do with: work and consumption ethics, homeownership and renting, and emotional rupture cycles.

The instrument I have called 'locus of control exercise' is partly inspired in psychology. It allows the individual to situate her/his most relevant life events on a scale from agency to structure (Table 2). An effort was made to make this scale correspond to the life course principles, such as agency, linked lives, and cultural and historical location, and these principles were adapted to the research design.

The scale is conceived as starting with a category of *agency*, where individuals are seen as completely responsible for their own actions and options,[1] followed by the *linked lives* category, which assumes that each individual's actions have intra- and inter-generational consequences.[2] However, in other cases this correspondence between the operative scale and the life course principle is not that linear. This is because one of the principles of life course research is broad enough to merge social, economic, geographical and historical backgrounds – that is, to sum up a substantial part of the sociological-analytical framework of social differentiation. As Elder and Giele put it, 'this principle underscores the multiple layers of human experience, the social hierarchies, cultural and spatial variations, and the social/biological attributes' (2009, p. 12). In the same text, by giving an example of this life course principle, these important life course authors distinguish between the level of 'the Great depression', shared by all (which would correspond to the Portuguese *Crisis*' in the present article), and other – more socially grounded – variables, which differentiate the effect of the historical context of the Great Depression. Similarly, in the present article the latter variables would correspond to the interviewees' 'socio-economic situation'.

Under this life course principle of the 'historical time and place', the remaining correspondence used in the data collection instrument included a *social location* category that considered close social context,[3] followed by a *historical location* category in which the *crisis* was the only element.

Lastly, and outside the scope of the life course research, one category considered that the 'unobserved heterogeneity' in statistical analysis simply corresponded to 'chance'.[4] The challenge put to the participants was to quantify in percentage terms the effect of each of these categories on their relevant life events (Table 3). Immediately before their interviews, interviewees were asked to provide a list of 'relevant' life events.

Emergent concerns and changes: lives and mindset

This set of results is mainly based on the 'past reality check' instrument, with three emergent trends found. The first has to do with the levels and values associated with

Table 2. Correspondence between life course principles and categories in the locus control exercise.

Agency	Linked lives	Social location	Historical and geographical location	'Unobserved heterogeneity'
Your own choices	Family and close friends – events and circumstances	Socio-economic situation	The *'crisis'*	'Chance'

Table 3. Example of the table shown in the interview.

Event	Your own choices	Family and close friends – events and circumstances	Social and economic situation	The 'crisis'	Chance	Total
Marriage	45	45	10	0	0	100%
Unemployment	0	0	20	70	10	100%
...						

consumption, use of credit and loans and savings practices or ambitions. Many of the 2009 interviewees demonstrated a very strong aversion to debt and would not have or use credit cards, even if it might have helped them overcome some difficulties towards the end of each month. Using credit cards or taking out loans was not considered an option, even when bank accounts were dangerously close to zero. In 2016, however, although these interviewees' discourse was very similar and true to the core values transmitted in 2009, practices had been slightly adjusted.

This adjustment is socially stratified. On the one hand, for those with less qualified[5] and badly paid[6] occupations, credit card use had become more flexible. Although not on a daily basis, credit cards were now used to schedule holidays or travel, the expectation being to pay off the debt immediately on receipt of the extra holiday or Christmas 'month' (by law, salaried Portuguese workers receive 14 months of pay, with the extra 2 paid before annual holidays and before Christmas), and with the reassurance of being in a common economic partnership (civil union or marriage). In these cases, this was done to maintain a certain 'young' lifestyle that is more common in couples (as yet) without children. On the other hand, among individuals with conservative financial values who had managed to achieve an ascendant social mobility trajectory in the past seven years and enter a consensual union, the adjustment to the crisis was surprisingly higher. Although possessing the means to maintain or improve a certain lifestyle, these individuals tended to be hyper-conscious of the crisis, reducing their consumption habits to a minimum and developing saving strategies involving low-rate, low-risk investments or early payment of mortgages.

Summing up, for those with the same 2009 values regarding consumption, savings strategies and resort to credit, (i) the individuals with more precarious and/or worst paid occupations adjusted their values to practices oriented towards their daily lives, aiming at improving them and from time to time having a holiday or other 'luxury' that was normally out of their financial league; (ii) while the ones with more stable and/or well-paid occupations tended to reorient their consumption values and practices towards the future by saving money and/or anticipating mortgage payments.

A second emergent trend is linked to a dividing issue in 2009: opinions on homeownership and renting. In 2009, some interviewees were strongly against homeownership; all those who have already been re-interviewed in 2016 had changed both their views and their practices in this respect. From a significant original aversion to buying a home, which was said to create a life-long debt, which they would always live to pay off and would be an inhibiting factor for a putative geographical mobility or migration project, these individuals were now more tempted to become homeowners (some already had). The three motivations for buying a home are well documented in the literature and apply, autonomously or conjointly, to these cases (Winstanley, Thorns, & Perkings, 2002, p. 815). One set of motivations has to do with the lifecycle model in which a change of residence serves the need for more space to accommodate the changing age and sexual composition of the family structure. The second set of motivations has to do with economic rationality, in which these residential changes are treated as the result of economically rational decision-making. Finally, a third set of motivations to change or buy a home is the environmental aspect, meaning that people choose to buy or change their residence according to where and near whom they want to live. All this means that the lifecycle effect has maintained a certain predominance, even in contexts of *crisis*, leading these individuals to buy apartments near their families of origin and with the aim of accommodating their own families in the future.

These sets of motivations are not mutually excluded by the participants, but instead appear conjointly in their discourses, in a process of accumulating reasons that together increase their propensity to see homeownership as positive and act accordingly. The profile of this set of re-interviewees may also help explain this tendency towards homeownership. They included people who had already left home in 2009, in order to live with a partner or spouse, live alone or live with friends or flatmates, so they had already taken the plunge of leaving the parental home and committing to a monthly obligation to pay rent. What they rejected was the long-term commitment of a mortgage, which they refused because of the uncertainty they perceived in their lives at the time, the relative flexibility they wanted to have in their lives, and also in some cases, because of left-wing anti-property political views (this was the least important reason). So while this set of reasons explains why these interviewees opted for rented apartments when they decided to leave their parental home in or prior to 2009, the combination of the lifecycle model, the economic rationale and the environmental aspect explains why they had experienced an increased tendency to choose homeownership seven years later.

The third emergent trend entailed voluntary and involuntary ruptures – mainly involving professional well-being or romantic relationships. In 2009, some participants displayed a low tolerance for precarious situations, be they emotional of professional. They considered rupture to be a positive action, a necessary harm, a long-term investment in happiness. In 2016, these and other participants displayed this same approach to life, but with some distinctions with regard to the particular sphere of life in question. While in 2009 rupture cycles were more directed at emotional and romantic trajectories (Nico, 2016b), in 2016 they mainly concerned the professional sphere. In fact, especially for those who began working very young, before or during their university studies, long-term precariousness had become intolerable. They had proven to themselves and others that they are working-class individuals, with early achieved independence and residential autonomy, but they had also gathered information about their rights as workers, their entitlement to well-being, and the processes that can lead to burnout. They now had 'chosen' to say 'enough is enough' to this long-term precariousness, and as a consequence had experienced transitional unemployment episodes. A couple of quotes will illustrate these intolerable experiences of precariousness and moments of rupture and non-conformity.

> Yesterday I heard a guy on the news saying 'it's better to have a precarious job than to be unemployed'. Hmmm, really? Not in my opinion. If you think you can be precarious for 9 years, like me. When I started working there I would cry because of the physical tiredness, I was not used to being on my feet the whole day, I only had one day off a week ... But then the mental tiredness came. The work environment is bad, people are unhappy

working there and I would sometimes get home in a really bad mood (for my daughter). And I thought; I don't want this for me, I need to get out, need to leave this environment. And you know? It is a relief, to have the possibility to start something new. (Julia, bachelor's degree, unemployed from fashion shop, rented apartment, civil union, one child)

There are many forms of non-dignifying work, and people have to know about that. I and everyone else from Architecture knew that. It was fantastic: we had to have our own car, computer, two languages, Autocad, of course. 'Come here, I'll let you work here!'. I found that statement about being "better to have a precarious job than to be unemployed. I thought 'yes, it's also better to have hepatitis B than aids, but the best is to have none of that, right?!'. (Jorge, almost graduate, bank manager, single, homeowner)

Serendipity: contractions and red flags

Some counter-intuitive results emerge from the analysis of the locus of control exercise, especially bearing in mind that it came at the very end of each interview, in an attempt to summarise information shared in the previous couple of hours. The information analysed here, although regarding the same 13 re-interviewees, refers to 66 relevant life events listed by them. After each interview, these were coded as to their impact (positive/negative/ambivalent), their dimension of life (family, work, school, health, home, other) and their occurrence (relevant events/relevant omissions of events[7]).

The list of relevant life events in the past seven years is the first source of surprise. Transition to adulthood is indeed a demographically dense period of life (Rindfuss, 1991), but some spheres of life are denser (more events per period of time) than others. There is a delay in entering conjugality in Portugal, a high age at the first child, and a very low birth rate, while precariousness and informal work are important characteristics of the Portuguese labour market. Additionally, these aspects were emphasised during the *crisis* period. As such, and particularly given the latter aspect of the situation, one might have expected most relevant life events to be work-related. However, the data reveal a big gap between the number of work-related events in the interviewees' lives and the number they considered relevant. Almost half the life events deemed relevant were family-related: romantic relationships (beginnings or breakups), parenthood, marriage, divorce and so on, whereas only about a quarter were work-related. To an extent, the 'persistence of the family life cycle' (Elchardus & Smits, 2006) is thus resistant to the economic *crisis*. In a way, it is the events that have the least to do with the *crisis* that are considered relevant, are part of the biography of identity that these individuals choose to embrace and share. In their discourses, there is a denial of the *crisis* as central to their identity. The *crisis* does not define them.

When it comes to the effect of the crisis, you can write down 'zero' for everything. The crisis did not have any influence on my decisions and career. I even think I grew in those periods of alleged crisis. (Ricardo, graduate, car salesman, homeowner, married, one child)

The financial crisis does not have any effect in my career. If it did, it would have ruined it. (Jorge, almost graduate, bank manager, single, homeowner)

Family events were mentioned more than any other as having been important in our seven-year window of observation. This may be linked to two interrelated aspects. One is that overall, the participants tended to list positive aspects and events more than negative ones. When summarising their seven-year life period, they tended to attach a positive view to their biography, mentioning the aspects that, 'at the end of the day', mattered most to them and best defined their progress in life. This is an act of implicit resilience which, when it comes down to it, supports their discourse and their interpretation of life. The second aspect is related to the first: the most frequently mentioned family events were in fact turning points and/or irreversible events in people's lives. By this, we are (and the participants were) referring to events such as marriage, and having a first or second child.[8]

A second source of counter-intuitive results has to do with the fact that between school/studies, family and work, the latter is actually the one that returned the lowest proportion of negative impacts. Unemployment was the event with the greatest responsibility for this result, in two ways: by not even being mentioned as relevant (compared to other life events); and by being mentioned as a 'positive' event (in the long term). The shared stories demonstrate how these unemployment events can be seen as positive. The reason is again related to long-term precarious situations in the labour market, which after several years reach the point at which they are unbearable and 'force' the individual to take a pause on the road to burnout or depression. This ability to 'pause' enabled interviewees to subsequently see this as a positive action, which was necessary in order to break dangerous cycles of long-term precariousness, decreases in emotional well-being, conformism and identity marasmus.

A third set of unexpected results can be seen from Table 4, which shows the distribution of the mean percentage attributed to the effect of the different categories of the agency-structure scale on relevant life events. We can see that with regard to general issues, the impact tends to decrease on the agency-structure scale. This means that generally speaking, the individuals believed it was their own agency (48.6%), followed by their families and friends (26.7%), their social context (11.2%) and only then the *crisis* (7.1%) that determined their life events. 'Chance' is the only predictor that scored below the *crisis*. This might mean that predictors for meaningful life events which fell well outside the individuals' control may have been left out of the narrative accounts about their trajectories, regardless of the actual impact they actually did or did not have in terms of shaping their life course.

Two other aspects of note are concentrated in the 'the *crisis*' column. In fact, according to the individuals' views, of all the influences their professional trajectories may have been subjected to, the *crisis* was the least important (3.7%). In their discourses, interviewees tended to individualise the explanation of their trajectories: their actions, their bosses'

Table 4. Importance attributed to different life events (agency-structure scale) (mean percentage).

	Your own choices	Family and close friends – events and circumstances	Social and economic situation	The 'crisis'	Chance
Family	53.83	29.17	7.33	5	5
Work	53.33	12	16.33	3.67	8.33
School	60	0	40	0	0
Health	40	60	0	0	0
Home	36.67	40	20	0	3.33
Other events	35.71	29.29	12.5	18.93	2.14
Total	48.56	26.74	11.21	7.12	4.77

decisions, their co-workers' attitudes. Even the negative work-related events can in a sense be read asocially, as if the *crisis* provided not a context, but an interpretative vacuum. On the other hand, the effect of the *crisis* on 'other' events is significantly high (18.9%). The *crisis* belongs to 'others'. Unemployment of parents, bankruptcy of a relative, migration of a best friend[9] – the examples are numerous. Interviewees displayed a somewhat bipolar approach to the *crisis*: they were bystanders with regard to the effects of the *crisis* on the 'other' people in their lives, and they were (or became) immune to the *crisis* themselves. It is nonetheless important to highlight that in this case the effect of linked lives is considered negative; the *crises* of others, in which family members occupy an important quantitative and qualitative place, are indeed those that illustrate the effect of the *crisis* in more detail.

Conclusions

This follow-up study means that the trajectories, plans and expectations of young Portuguese adults have not only been updated, but past and present were literally confronted with one another in a co-production interview. At a certain point, the individuals were asked to specifically reflect on and quantify the effects of the *crisis* on the several dimensions of their lives in the previous seven years. Results go to the heart of the discussion on a distinction between 'biographies of choice' and 'discourses of choice' (Nico & Caetano, 2017). This is because in 2009 the *crisis* was slightly present in discourses, but absent from actual trajectories, but in 2016 the contrary was verified. The presence of the *crisis* and its many effects at the micro-individual level was clear in the 2016 interviews, in which the events and conditions in the labour market were identified, described and sequenced; but it is also evident that this protagonism disappeared when the interviewees were challenged to interpret their life events as satellites of the *crisis*. This apparently asocial reading of their life trajectories, which is not the same thing as a lack of political literacy or political participation, reinforces the concern about the 'epistemological fallacy of the late modernity' as Furlong and Cartmel eloquently put it when they said that 'blind to the existence of powerful chains of interdependency, young people frequently attempt to resolve collective problems through individual action and hold themselves responsible for their inevitable failure' (Furlong and Cartmel (1997/2007, p. 144).

There is also evidence that this fallacy may possess a politically significant meaning, in the sense that it could be a result of neo-liberal discourses which uphold the idea that 'we are what we choose to be'[10] – an idea that helps produce a generational discourse which denies the context in an individual's own biography, thus neglecting its historical location and interpretation. Although probably involuntarily on the part of some influential sociologists, individualisation theories fit the neo-liberal discourse like a glove. After all, (young) people would like to acknowledge themselves as authors of their own lives, and the canvases on which they visualise and project their life goals, ambitions and plans are equally white for everyone, be they middle or upper class, rural or urban, poorly or highly educated, etc. What this research shows is that the appropriation of individualisation discourses by political agents may not be a one-way street, but part of a circular movement in which the dissemination of this individualised neo-liberal discourse is able to re-contaminate the individual's discourses and ways of thinking.

These conclusions would not have been possible without a wide window of observation and a combination of quantitative and qualitative approaches to life stories. 'Time matters' (Abbott, 2001). Phenomena such as long-term precariousness in the labour market are invisible in the statistics collected about young people; and phenomena like this are responsible for the apparent contradictions in young people's discourses and biographies and an apparent lack of agency and action. People are indeed capable of providing an explanation for their actions, and in that should lay our concerns as social scientists and citizens. 'If men define a situation as real, it is real in its consequences' (Thomas theorem).

Notes

1. Explained in the script as 'your own responsibility, choices, merit or fault' in a category called 'your own choices'.
2. Explained in the script as 'events or circumstances of those closest to you' in a category called 'family and friends'.
3. Explained in the script as 'your social and financial situation: expenses, difficulties, work stability, etc'. In a category called 'social and economic situation'.
4. Explained in the script as something out of their control, attributed to change, to luck, good or bad.
5. No higher education, or less than that.
6. Equal to or less than the Minimum Wage plus 200 euros.
7. For example, not reporting a pregnancy, a promotion, etc.
8. Given that this a follow-up study, it is also possible that the interviewees were affected by the social desirability that tends to contaminate qualitative interviews. In this specific case, this may even have been exacerbated by an unconscious need on the part of interviewees to show how life had improved, or at least that the positive elements were more significant that the negative ones.
9. The measures taken at the urging of the Troika proved difficult to measure the 'deepening of the current brain drain, especially among young people, with its vicious-circle-type amplifying effects on declining competitiveness' (Graça et al., 2011).
10. Translated title of the former Portuguese Prime-Minister's autobiography.

Disclosure statement

No potential conflict of interest was reported by the author.

Funding

This research was supported by Fundação para a Ciência e Tecnologia, under grants SFRH/BD/27314/2006 and SFRH/BPD/76580/2011.

Notes on contributors

Magda is a sociologist specialising in Youth, Social Trajectories and Life Course Research and Methods. She is a researcher at CIES-IUL and an active member of the Pool of European Youth Researchers of the EU-CoE Youth Partnership. She is currently developing a follow-up study with young people interviewed before the Portuguese *crisis*. Some of her most relevant chapters on these topics are 'Young people of the "Austere Period": Mechanisms and effects of inequality over time in Portugal' (with Nuno de Almeida Alves, by Palgrave Macmillan) and 'Beyond "Biographical" and "Cultural Illusions": European Youth Studies: Temporality and Critical Youth Studies', by Brill.

References

Abbott, A. (2001). The historicality of individuals. *Social Science History, 29*(1), 1–3.

Amaral, J. F. D., & Lopes, J. C. (2016). *Self-Defeating austerity? assessing the impact of fiscal consolidations on unemployment* (WP13/2016/DE/UECE, working paper).

Beck, U. (1992). *Risk society. Towards a new modernity.* London: Sage.

Bertaux, D., & Delcroix, C. (2000). Case histories of families and social processes: Enriching sociology. In Prue Chamberlayne, Joanna Bornat, & Tom Wengraft (Eds.), *The turn to biographical methods in social science. Comparative issues and examples* (pp. 71–89). London: Routledge.

Bourdieu, P. (1994/1997). *Razões práticas: Sobre a teoria da acção* [The logic of practice]. Oeiras: Celta.

Brückner, H., & Mayer, K. U. (2005). De-Standardization of the life course: What it might mean? And if it means anything, whether it actually took place? *Advances in Life Course Research, 9,* 27–53.

Carmo, R. d., & Matias, A. R. (2016). *O desemprego Jovem em Portugal e na Europa.* Retrieved from https://observatorio-das-desigualdades.com/2016/12/20/dossie-tematico-o-desemprego-jovem-em-portugal-e-na-europa/

Elchardus, M., & Smits, W. (2006). The persistence of the standardized life cycle. *Time and Society, 15* (2–3), 303–326.

Elder, G.Jr. (1974). *Children of the great depression.* Chicago, IL: Chicago Press.

Elder, G. (1994). Time, human agency, and social change: Perspectives on the life course. *Social Psychology Quarterly, 57*(1), 4–15.

Elder, G. H., Jr.. (1985). Perspectives on the life course. In Glen H. ElderJr. (Ed.), *Life course dynamics. Trajectories and transitions, 1968-1980* (pp. 23–49). Ithaca, NY: Cornell University Press.

Elder, G. H., & Giele, J. Z. (2009). Life course studies: An evolving field. In Glen H. em ElderJr., & Janet Z. Giele (Eds.), *The craft of the life course research* (pp. 430–445). New York, NY: Campus Verlag.

ElderJr, G. H., Johnson, M. K., & Crosnoe, R. (2002). The emergence and development of life course theory. In Jeylan T. Mortimer, & Michael J. Shanahan (Eds.), *Handbook of the life course* (pp. 3–19). New York, NY: Kluwer.

Furlong, A., & Cartmel, F. (1997/2007). *Young people and social change.* New York, NY: Open University Press.

Giele, J. Z., & Elder, G. H., Jr.. (1998). Life course research: Development of a field. In Janet Z. em Giele, & Glen H. ElderJr. (Eds.), *Methods of life course research. Qualitative and quantitative approaches* (pp. 5–27). Thousand Oaks, CA: Sage.

Goodwin, J., & O'Connor, H. (2015). A critical reassessment of the 'complexity' orthodoxy. Lessons from existing data and 'youth' legacy studies. In Peter Kelly, & Annellies Kamp (Eds.), *Critical youth studies for the 21st century* (pp. 28–52). Leiden: Brill.

Graça, J. C., Lopes, J. C., & Marques, R. (2011). The European sovereign debt crisis: The Portuguese case, economic sociology. *The European Electronic Newsletter, 12*(3), 38–47.

Henderson, S., Holland, J., McGrellis, S., Harper, S., & Thomson, R. (2007/2009). *Inventing adulthood. A biographical approach to youth transitions.* London: Sage.

Lahire, B. (2002/2004). *Retratos Sociológicos. Disposições e Variações Individuais.* Porto Alegre: Artmed.

Miller, R. (2000). *Researching life stories and family histories.* London: Sage.

Nico, M. (2011). *Transição Biográfica Inacabada. Transições para a Vida Adulta em Portugal e na Europa na Perspectiva do Curso de Vida* (PhD thesis). Departamento de Sociologia, Instituto Universitário de Lisboa, Lisbon.

Nico, M. (2013). Generational changes, gaps and conflicts: A view from the south. In *Perspectives on youth, European youth partnership series: 2020- what do we see?* (pp. 29–37). Luxembourg: Council of Europe and the European Commission Publication.

Nico, M. (2014). Variability of the transitions to adulthood in Europe: A critical approach to de-standardization of the life course. *Journal of Youth Studies, 17*(12), 166–182.

Nico, M. (2015). Beyond 'biographical' and 'cultural illusions': European youth studies: Temporality and critical youth studies. In Peter Kelly, & Annellies Kamp (Eds.), *Critical youth studies for the 21st century* (pp. 53–69). Leiden: Brill.

Nico, M. (2016a). Bringing life "back into life course research": Using the life grid as a research instrument for qualitative data collection and analysis. *Quantity and Quality, 50*(5), 2107–2120.

Nico, M. (2016b). Romantic turning-points and patterns of leaving home. Contributions from a qualitative research in a southern European country. *European Societies, 18*(4), 389–409.

Nico, M. (forthcoming). *Youth inequalities: Generation and social class intersection in theory and in practice, perspectives on youth, European youth partnership series: Youth inequalities.* Luxembourg: Council of Europe and the European Commission Publication.

Nico, M., & Caetano, A. (2017). Untying conceptual knots: The analytical limits of the concepts of destandardisation and reflexivity. *Sociology, 51*(3), 666–684.

Nico, M., & de Almeida Alves, N. (2017). Young people of the 'austere period': Mechanisms and effects of inequality over time in Portugal. In Peter Kelly, & Joanne Pike (Eds.), *Neoliberalism, austerity, and the moral economies of young people's health and well-being* (pp. 125–149). London: Palgrave Macmillan.

Parry, O., Thomson, C., & Fowkes, G. (1999). Life course data collection: Qualitative interviewing using the life grid. *Sociological Research Online, 4.* doi:10.5153/sro.233

Rindfuss, R. R. (1991). The young adult years: Diversity, structural change and fertility. *Demography, 28*(4), 493–512.

Roberts, S. (2011). Beyond 'NEET' and 'tidy' pathways: Considering the missing middle of youth transitions studies. *Journal of Youth Studies, 1*(14), 21–49.

Roberts, S. (2012). One step forward, one step beck: A contribution to the ongoing conceptual debate in youth studies. *Journal of Youth Studies, 15*(3), 389–401.

Thomas, W. I., & Znaniecki, F. (1918). *The polish peasant in Europe and America.* Chicago: University of Illinois Press.

Thompson, P. (2004). Researching family and social mobility with two eyes: Some experiences of the interaction between qualitative and quantitative data. *International Journal of Social Research Methodology, 7*(3), 237–257.

Thomson, R. (2009). *Unfolding lives: Youth, gender and change.* Bristol: Polity Press.

Thomson, R., Bell, R., Holland, J., Henderson, S., McGrellis, S., & Sharpe, S. (2002). Critical moments: Choice, chance and opportunity in young people's narratives of transition. *Sociology, 36*(2), 335–354.

Williamson, H. (2004). *The Milltown Boys revisited.* Berg: Oxford.

Winstanley, A., Thorns, D. C., & Perkings, H. C. (2002). Moving house, creating home: Exploring residential mobility. *Housing Studies, 17*(6), 813–832.

Investigating the roots of political disengagement of young Greek Cypriots

Ioanna Christodoulou, Charis Pashias, Sotiris Theocharides and Bettina Davou

ABSTRACT

This study attempted to disentangle the issues underlying the marked drop recorded in political engagement of young Greek Cypriots. To reveal the dynamic processes through which people debate, disagree or convince each other towards the formation of political attitudes, eight focus-groups were carried out with a total of forty participants, equally distributed according to age and gender. The analysis showed that young Greek Cypriots appear uncertain for their future, pessimistic, cynical, and highly disillusioned with traditional politics. Contrary to what is observed in other European countries, young Greek Cypriots do not experiment with alternative forms of political action, remain inactive, and although the country's politicised culture of the past is still reflected in their theoretical discussions about social issues, they express embarrassment and confusion when asked to elaborate on how theory could be transformed into practice. They associate politics with corruption and economic interests, they are scornfully disillusioned with the European Union, and they emotionally distance themselves from important changes to come with the possible reunification of Cyprus. Young Greek Cypriots appear insecure, pessimistic, disoriented, uninspired, and in an urgent need to rediscover passion for ideas which they cannot any more find in traditional politics and forms of political action.

Introduction

Apparent political indifference of young people has been attributed to various sources: frustration that the political system does not provide answers to their needs and actual concerns (Spannring, 2008), neo-liberal policies of political socialisation that focus on individual responsibilities and solutions to what were once considered to be collective problems (Riley, Griffin, & Morey, 2013), changes in the meaning of political categories (Wörsching, 2008) and of what is politically meaningful for young people (Kiisel, Leppik, & Seppel, 2015) or a shift of young people towards alternative forms of political participation such as non-governmental organisations, local and community movements or cause-oriented activism (Ampe, 2013). Whatever the combination of causes may be, the current economic insecurity has further affected negatively young people's political attitudes, satisfaction with the economy and subjective well-being – although human values appear resistant to economic hardship and may thus contribute to resilience, (Reeskens & Vandecasteele, 2016). These effects appear to be stronger in countries with higher unemployment rates (Ampe, 2013).

Young people's turnout to elections has declined all over Europe (with the exception of the Check Republic and Lithuania) in recent years. In Cyprus, the percentage shows a dramatic drop (from approximately 80% in 2011 to less than 50% in 2014), together with a significant drop in political party membership and a significant decline of participation in alternative forms of political action in comparison to other European countries (Eurobarometer #375, 2013). Furthermore, regardless of the hundreds of civil society organisations registered with the Associations Commissioner (Charalambus, 2014), Greek Cypriot youth are the least likely from all Europeans to be involved in youth organisations or local organisations aimed at improving the local community, and are generally absent from organised youth activities such as sport, cultural or environmental organisations (Eurobarometer #375, 2013). Thus, although studies carried out more than 10 years ago with adolescent participants – now in young adulthood – had indicated regional differences, with southern European youth anticipating the most intense political participation (Amnå, Munck, & Zetterberg, 2004), the reverse appears to have happened at least for Greek Cypriot youth, even though Cyprus has a traditionally overpoliticised culture (Charalambus, 2014).

Cyprus has generally been a quiet country in terms of contentious acts and politics, due to a belief that protest is largely unnecessary and less effective than the institutional avenues of the political process or the cultivation of contacts and networks. In the last decade, however, an increased mistrust in political parties, institutions and the media has been observed, and Cyprus finds itself in a state of political as well as economic crisis (Charalambus, 2014). There is a growing dissatisfaction with politics and delegitimisation of the political system that began before the onset of the economic crisis, but continued and in some respects accelerated during the crisis years. The financial, social and energy crisis that the country has undergone seems to have resulted in a changing political climate, affecting Greek Cypriots' interest in politics and dropping the confidence in institutions such as political parties, politicians, United Nations, Cypriot and European Parliaments, Police and Justice (Orinos, 2013).

In conjunction with the above, the current financial crisis has significantly affected electoral behaviour. Both the democratic deficit, as defined by Chomsky (2001) and the delegalisation of the party system have found their way to periphery countries such as Cyprus. Referring to the case of Cyprus, Chomsky (2013) notes that the elimination of disparities and the convergence between the Left and the Right allows for the implementation of macroeconomic programmes, imposed by the European Union (EU) Commission, which result in austerity regardless of the political colours under which they masquerade. Besides, with the dire economics of recent years and the country counting close to 66,000 unemployed, recording the severest lack of job opportunities for young people, and with 45,000 citizens on the Guaranteed Minimum Income Benefit, Greek Cypriots are increasingly losing faith in their state and its institutions. The increase in protest votes (also known as blank or white votes), the emergence of new types of political parties, the decrease in party loyalty and the elevation of contemporary media into highly influential institutions, are some of the developments which have contributed to the distancing from the political arena. Hence why a lack of interest and a nihilistic approach to politics has exalted absenteeism in Cyprus into a dynamic phenomenon.

Added onto the above is a characteristic feature of the Greek Cypriot society which, in view of the fact that the country is an island, sees itself as cut off from global reality. Hence, there is a tendency for citizens to operate in an individualistic and opportunistic manner, distancing themselves from the public sphere and showing no interest in what is happening both in Cyprus and abroad (INEP, 2013). This is also indicated in an interpretation of the results of the European Social Survey attempted by Orinos (2013); the average Greek Cypriot is only partially interested in politics, tends to abstain from all forms of political participation and engages in politics mostly when there are personal contacts/relations with politicians or government officials, a fact which suggests that the phenomenon of clientelism is still going strong.

A look at the electoral behaviour of Greek Cypriots up until 2011 reveals that in a period of 30 years, and with the country's electorate growing by 70%, absenteeism, void ballot papers and blanks recorded an increase of 600%. Relevant data show a gradual and steady increase in abstinence, particularly during the period 2001–2011 which saw a total of three elections. It is worth noting that Cyprus holds the seventh-fastest rate of decline in voter turnout during this period (PMR, 2011). Abstinence tends to be particularly high in the European Parliament elections as well as in local municipal elections, and relatively lower in national parliamentary and presidential elections. In the 2014 EU parliament elections, absenteeism reached 56%, in the Cypriot parliament elections of May 2016 reached 33.26%, and in the Municipality elections of December 2016, absenteeism reached 45.20%. Apart from the low turnout at the ballot box, one must also consider the thousands of young people who come to voting age but fail to register in the electoral lists. Although there is no official data on the age of voters who choose to abstain from electoral procedures, opinion and exit polls suggest that the numbers are particularly high. The low levels of participation in elections match the low index of politicisation and involvement in politics and the public sphere of a society which was once traditionally politicised.

The media are also linked to this depreciation of politics. In Greece, data show that low levels of interest in politics are highly associated with the perceived unreliability of the media, and that young people consistently and unambiguously categorise 'politics' in a very negative manner, bestowing politicians with selfishness and malice (Demertzis & Armenakis, 2000). And it is not just politics which is seen in a derogatory way; it is also the left-right axis, while at the same time there is a convergence in the middle of the left-right political spectrum, with almost half of young voters placing themselves at its centre (Demertzis et al., 2008). In Cyprus, young people aged 18–24 are greatly influenced in their political views by relatives and friends, and much less so from political news broadcasted on television. In fact, figures show that they watch the news and political shows on TV much less frequently than all other age-groups, while remaining strongly distrustful of the accuracy, quality and truthfulness of the political information, and updates received from both state-run and public TV channels (Maniou, 2013).

The declining trends in young Greek Cypriots political interest are mostly derived from descriptive quantitative studies that certainly reflect tendencies of large samples of people but cannot provide information on the dynamic processes that generate these tendencies. Qualitative data are scarce, though necessary if we wish to understand the processes that underlie the observed measures, especially in a culture where young people still rely mostly on discussions with friends and relatives to obtain political information and where political opinions are mostly formed through face-to-face interactions (Maniou, 2013).

The present study had the purpose to investigate how political opinions and attitudes are formed as young Greek Cypriots interact through focus-group discussions. Collective activities are more suitable for discussing public issues or societal concerns than one-to-one interviews, and focus-groups promote self-disclosure in the sense that participants may feel more comfortable to disclose information in a discussion with people like themselves. Focus-groups may reveal the dynamic processes through which people debate, disagree or convince each other towards the formation of political attitudes. Our purpose in this qualitative study was to attempt to understand the crucial themes that underlie the dramatic drop in political interest of young of Greek Cypriots, which is recorded in quantitative studies.

The central research questions were 'what are the social and political issues that concern young Greek Cypriots today?', 'what sort of meanings they attribute to politics, political behaviour and ideology?', 'how they perceive their personal and communal future', and 'how would they try to influence politics with regards to their issues of concern?'

Method

Participants

Forty individuals, equally distributed according to age (18–24 and 25–35) and gender (20 males and 20 females), participated in a total of eight focus-groups (four per age-group), with five participants per group. Participants were homogenous in terms of education, i.e. they were either university students or university graduates, but diverse in terms political views and political interest according to their answers in a recruitment questionnaire. The two different age-groups had the purpose of bringing together individuals in similar life cycles which often determine which social issues are most important, i.e. very young adults generally still in education and/or in search for a career (18–24) and young adults managing a job and/or a family (25–35).

Materials

(1) Recruitment questionnaire (see Appendix (i)): It was created with Google Forms and was sent to interested individuals with the request to return it within a week. The questionnaire consisted items on personal information (name, gender, education, job, contact details), a question about political interest which participants had to rate from 0 (not at all) to 10 (extremely high), a question about political stance which participants had to rate from 0 (extreme left) to 10 (extreme right), and a question about whether they voted in the last parliamentary elections of May 2016.

(2) Focus-group interview guide (see Appendix (ii)): A semi-structured interview guide was developed to investigate the following basic themes: (a) involvement with / reflection on current social conditions (social problems and causes, possible solutions), (b) political concern and participation (investigation of meanings attributed to concepts such as politics, politicisation vs. party membership, ideology), (c) ideological questions (e.g. attitudes towards transsexuals, immigrants, the difference

between voluntarism and charity), (d) attitudes towards media (use of media as sources of political information, trust on media), (e) orientation towards the future in terms of personal development and the socio-political development of the country.

(3) Probing materials (see Appendix (iii)): Probing materials associated with specific questions of the interview guide were used to facilitate the discussion. These consisted of (a) 13 cards representing institutions that could contribute to handling social problems (e.g. EU, Church, Parliament, etc.), to probe discussion about trust in institutions, and (b) six pictures representing forms of political action (e.g. demonstrations, strikes, election, etc.), to probe tendencies towards political participation. Participants were asked to individually select institutions and forms of action, respectively, comment on their choice, and then discuss between them and reach consensus on the selection of the three most significant institutions and forms of political action. Reaching a 'consensus' was expected to reveal aspects of the dynamic process through which citizens influence each other in political discussions.

Procedure

Participants were recruited via posters placed in universities around Nicosia, which were inviting young people to participate in a study on social and political issues. Individuals who are interested to participate contacted the researchers by mail or phone, and were asked to fill in the recruitment questionnaire that was sent to them via email. Final selection of participants was made with the purpose to achieve within-group diversity in terms of political interest, political stance and participation in recent elections. Participants signed a consent form and were assured that anonymity would be maintained in reporting of the findings.

The focus-groups were carried out in the facilities of the Institute of Communication and Social Research at Frederick University, by two researchers who interchangeably in each group acted as moderator and assistant. The moderator followed a non-directive approach, assuring participants that there was no right or wrong answer, and that the purpose of the discussion was to express freely and exchange views on the topics discussed. After welcoming and a short introduction, the moderators followed the interview schedule presented above with a semi-structured moderating style, using the probing material at specified points during the discussion.

Duration of the sessions varied from 110 minutes to 130 minutes, including 10 minutes to welcome participants at the beginning of the session, as well as a 10-minute break. The whole sessions were video-recorded and were then transcribed for purposes of thematic analysis.

Results and discussion

Social and political issues concerning young Greek Cypriots

Public agenda questions were originally posed to participants with regard to the challenges they themselves face in everyday life, as well as the problems that they believe society is generally dealing with. The overall trend showed that unemployment is the most important area of concern, causing a sense of fear to both the unemployed and working individuals. This seems to stem from the current financial crisis, which adds a whole series of other fears (Hardt & Negri, 2012), particularly the fear of being out of work and thus not being able to survive. The older age-groups, comprising mostly of individuals currently in employment, gave more emphasis on work relations: 'Nowadays, employees feel fear because they know they are expendable. They are aware, that is, of the ease with which their employers can replace them' (female, 32).

Employment thus, which has traditionally been an aspiration for young people, associated with fulfilment of personal goals as well as with independence from family and a guarantee for personal security, has now become a very fragile goal. Not only because it has become increasingly rear for one to find a job related to one's studies, but also due to new forms of 'flexible' but not reliable working relations, which keep employees in a constant state of insecurity. This insecurity appears to undermine any sense of personal control and leads young people to a state of helplessness, where no action appears to promise any change – even in situations where action could be proved effective (Seligman, 1992). In an intense discussion on 'the wrongs of this world', younger participants concluded that they had no alternatives to propose, that 'the system' was to blame for everything, that they felt extremely uncertain for their future and were in no way optimistic about finding employment in their field of study. The general feeling that prevailed, especially among younger participants, was one of uncertainty, and this was reflected in statements such as: 'I feel that nothing is for granted. I cannot count on something, anything, like the previous generations did. I live in a permanent state of anxiety' (male, 32) and 'Such lack of constants. I wake up anxious every morning and I feel that in order to survive I have to compromise on a daily basis' (female, 23).

Another issue that came up concerned the state of education and culture in the country: 'In Cyprus, most people have master's degrees and doctorates, yet what does this mean? Our schools do not cultivate critical thinking … Our education system is in need of an upgrade … ', was a representative comment made by a female participant (24), a view which tended to prevail in both groups. Older participants in particular, who delved more into the subject, commented on how superficial education in Cyprus is, and that, no matter how well educated one is, one can be socially manipulated. This feeling reflects an issue put forth by Chomsky (1988) when noting that education is a form of indoctrination and that educated societies are constantly bombarded with propaganda, which they often espouse, since the educated classes are generally more likely to take it without questioning. We should note, however, that the issue of 'education' has been high in the media agenda during the past months, brought forward mainly in the context of discussions about the possible reunification of Cyprus, as a necessary reform that will enable the two communities to coexist.

Notably, the younger age-groups made no spontaneous mention of this very crucial issue in Cyprus' political agenda – namely the 'Cyprus problem' – whereas older participants discussed it thoroughly, airing all different views and perspectives. 'The Cyprus problem is part of our daily lives and it is linked to the economy. In the past, there were people who did not want just any solution, but today, they want it solved for financial reasons' (male, 34). This view reflects a general tendency within the society in recent years, both among the refugees of 1974 who are tired of waiting for a solution to the problem, as well as among the post-war generation that has been crushed by the financial crisis Cyprus has been suffering over the past four years. This generation, as a general tendency, is looking to benefit financially from the reunification of Cyprus, which they believe will expand the labour market and increase trade, a view enhanced by the overall rhetoric in the media.

Trust in institutions

Discussing trust relations and ontological security, Giddens (1990) elaborates on the necessity of the feeling of trust, as a permanent human need. The lack of trust experienced today, fills people with existential anxiety, which leads to feelings of anguish, confusion, betrayal, suspicion and animosity. This lack of trust seems to immobilise young people, preventing them from opposing or reacting against those things which they define as 'challenges/problems' in their lives, because they feel they cannot rely on anything or anybody. Another prevailing view was summed up in the following statement by a 35-year-old man who attempted to explain in his own way the depoliticised person forged by the corruption of democracy (Hardt & Negri, 2012): 'We remain apathetic. We have grown up surrounded by corruption and political scandals and yet, we do nothing. Perhaps the only way we can send a message is through our political absenteeism'.

Beyond the corruption noted by both age-groups, another issue raised was the lack of powerful politicians, which links to Castoriadis' (2006) notion of hyper-liberal politics. Young Greek Cypriots witness politicians who have no real programme, whose main agenda is canvassing for votes and staying in power. Hence why they look for young politicians, hoping they will not turn out to be the same. On the other hand, as Badiou (2010, p. 8) notes, 'In politics, it is thoughts, organisations and deeds that count.' Participants of both age-groups shared a common belief that the source of problems lies in the political and financial interests of people in power, and in the mishandling of political issues by those in government. 'It is a corrupt world. Especially politicians, they think only of their personal gain and are afraid of nothing and no-one. It is all a game of money and glory', according to a 32-year-old man. The dominant belief was that political corruption is at the root of social problems.

Younger age-groups made frequent references to the role that both traditional and new media could play in solving society's problems, provided – and this was something that was strongly 'demanded' – that they become more democratic. Younger participants, who reported to make frequent use of new media, tended to believe that these can actually contribute to the alleviation of social problems, though they were not in a position to clarify how this could be achieved, apart from complaining in the media to awaken others on social problems: 'Perhaps internet is the only means we have to be heard, to cry, to change the world' (man, 25). On the opposite end, the older age-group agreed that the role of media is crucial, yet they cannot replace formal education nor solve people's problems.

All participants considered education as the most significant institution that could ideally contribute to the alleviation of social problems, though especially the younger ones expressed a strong belief that the Cypriot educational system is in desperate need of a reform, mainly towards the cultivation of 'critical thinking' – which, however, echoes what is systematically repeated in the media, as we noted earlier. On the contrary, older participants, though they do acknowledge the need for an educational reform, maintain high expectations from political parties and the parliament, even though they apply harsh criticism to the country's political scene.

The stimulus card referring to the EU brought about scornful laughter to both age-groups, while participants looked at one another as if they wanted their feelings to be acknowledged and confirmed by everyone. In a half comic half serious tone, a 21-year-old woman noted. 'It shouldn't exist!'. The discussion came to more serious terms when some participants raised the incompetent way through which the 'Brussels Bureaucrats' (man, 23) managed the migration problem, and only one participant from a younger age-group acknowledged that some developments have, nevertheless, taken place, as for example, the establishment of the legal partnership agreement. Older participants engaged in a more exhaustive criticism about the discrepancy between the initial vision and the eventual progress of the EU, as well as about the experience of the integration of Cyprus's in the EU: 'Ten years ago we used to say "Hey, we are Europeans, perfect!"' (woman, 32), 'But it is a grievous structure […] incomplete, unfortunately, […] there is not really any unity' (man, 35). Though the whole discussion was very skeptical and critical, older participants generally tended to accept in the end that Cyprus has political reasons to belong to the EU, particularly due to the 'Cyprus Issue'.

The disillusionment with the EU is reflected in the increasing absenteeism of the general Greek Cypriot population from the European Elections, from 27.50% in 2004 to 56.03% in 2014.[1] It seems that Greek Cypriots were initially enthusiastic that Cyprus succeeded to enter the EU in 2004 without having resolved the Cyprus Issue, but never really experienced themselves as actual members of a larger European community. Keeping in mind that participants in the younger age-groups were too young to have own memories from 12 years ago, their scornful attitude may be reflecting older citizens' current narratives that Cyprus was better off before entering the EU, because the state decided for its own affairs. Older participants, on the other hand, who themselves had experienced some positive changes from Cyprus's integration in the EU, mainly the ability to study in the UK with lower tuition fees and less bureaucracy, and the ability to travel freely, were disillusioned from the recent financial policies and the 2013 Memorandum.

The meaning of politics and political attitudes

The first words reported when participants' were asked to make associations with the word 'politics' were 'corruption', 'scandal', 'economic interests', with no distinction made between politics itself and its representatives, the politicians.[2] 'Political clientelism, ensconced politicians and scandals. Isn't this, what politics is all about today?' wondered a 23-year-old female, with the remaining group agreeing and emphasizing even further, while a 31-year-old male participant stated in disappointment: 'I do vote, but these days I do it with a heavy heart'. Participants, especially from the younger age-groups, equated politicisation with involvement in party politics, and older participants where quite scornful when talking about party followers, who were often described as 'sheep' and 'brain-washed'.

The concept of 'ideology' appeared very confusing, especially for the younger age-groups. They could not easily define the word, and it was only after extensive discussion that they arrived in a rough conclusion that it has to do with the way a person thinks. Older participants could more freely provide some more concrete explanations, i.e.: 'Ideology is the set of values by which I set my compass. I use it to find the party I converge with the most' (female, 30). Yet, the general tendency was a distance from politics expressed in aphorisms such as, 'Ideologies are dead', 'Politics is an outdated concept', 'They (politicians) are all the same', which suggest unclear boundaries between right and left-leaning ideologies and an inclination towards being apolitical, amongst the younger generation.

Nevertheless, when the discussion turned to more practical issues which however do express ideological stance, participants came to more lively debates, as if it was the party-affiliation connotations of the word 'ideology' per se which brought about repulsion, and not the act of holding a systematic set of ideas about human life and society. For example, towards the current topic of public discourse in Cyprus on whether LGBTI citizens should have the legal right to adopt children, which recently had extensive publicity, younger participants were spontaneously positive. On the contrary, members of the older age-groups expressed reservations centreing on the argument that the Cypriot society is not ready yet for this. These reservations are well illustrated in the words of a 35-year-old female, with whom the rest of the group firmly agreed: 'Everyone has the right to do what they want ... but adopt children? How will these children deal with the racism? Wouldn't it be better for them to be adopted into healthy families?'.

With regard to immigrants, both groups shared the same view on payroll matters and hiring opportunities, with almost all participants declaring a strong support of equal rights and standing against racism, and supporting equal pay for local and foreign workers. It should be noted, however, that this progressive attitude towards immigrants stems mostly from principle rather than from experience, since Cyprus has not been in any way inconvenienced by massive immigrant waves, as for example, Greece. On the contrary, individual immigrants from Russia, Balkan countries or Philippines that have been moving in Cyprus during the past decades, have been integrated softly in local life, often taking jobs that Greek Cypriots would not deign or making significant business investments in the country.

Personal and communal future

Earlier in this paper, it was noted with surprise that the on-going, critical issue about the possible reunification of Cyprus was not spontaneously raised by participants when asked about what they considered as main social issues. When the moderators raised the topic, participants appeared unprepared and uneasy, as if despite the dimensions that the issue has taken in formal public discourse, they had not yet pondered on how such a change would affect their everyday lives. The whole issue appeared to be encountered 'in theory' with comments such as 'Well, we have been making this effort for years', expressed by a 20-year-old – too young, in fact, to have any personal experience of this 'effort' – but denied or distanced emotionally (Fridja, 2004) in terms of the interpersonal and social adaptions it would require.

To probe some discussion on the issue, the moderators posed the question in a more straightforward, personalised manner: Would you marry a Turkish Cypriot? After an awkward pause, the most common reaction in both age-groups was 'I don't know'. But this 'I don't know' seemed to have a different meaning in each age-group. Younger participants appeared not to have ever been concerned about the actual consequences of living together with the Turkish Cypriot community: 'I don't know, I have never thought about it' (man, 23). 'With all that we've been hearing all these years from our families, the school ... I don't know ... ' (woman, 25). 'I've never met a Turkish Cypriot, I have never been to the occupied areas, I don't know where all this leads to' (man, 20). While for older participants 'I don't know' mostly reflected skepticism: 'It is always difficult to coexist. Are we going to attend the same schools? On what basis? Talk about which history? About which religion? Which language, Greek or Turkish? Everything is difficult' (woman, 35). Many references, especially by female participants, were made to resistances that their families would have before the possibility of a mixed marriage, in a society which until the 1980s would consider 'foreigner' even a person from a different village. For some, 'A Turkish Cypriot is a Turk. Which means, he is a foreigner' (woman, 35).

Most participants in the younger age-groups reported that they had no relationships with Turkish Cypriots and/or didn't know any Turkish Cypriots, and/or have never visited the occupied areas. Older participants were split into two equally strong viewpoints, summed up in the following statements, respectively: 'If you fall in love, where the other person is from becomes irrelevant' (female, 30), and 'I am a racist. I will not betray my country and I do not forget what has come to pass' (male, 35). This second comment was made so emphatically and bitterly, especially the announcement 'I am a racist' (banging the hand on the table), that one would expect the remaining group to react in a more politically correct way. On the contrary, it was received in awkward silence as if it voiced the whole group's unmentionable thoughts.

Leaving the Cyprus Issue behind, when participants were asked to share how they imagined both their personal future and that of the country as a whole, the topic caused grave concern, as well as distress and embarrassment. Very few appeared optimistic that things would improve both in their own lives and in the overall situation in the country. The prevailing feeling was pessimistic: 'I do think about the future, but I'd rather think of the present' (male, 24). 'I get depressed when I think of the future' (female, 22). 'Ideally, I want a future where I am able to live in dignity' (male, 21). Interestingly, although asked about the future, most participants grabbed insistently to the present, as if it was their only defence to uncertainty: 'I get disappointed when I try to think about the future, so I turn back to present. Living day by day, because if you fall into depression you may give up on everything' (female, 22). 'I try to concentrate in the present [because] I get very anxious when I think of my personal future' (male, 35).

This combination of hopelessness, insecurity and clinging to the present, which reminds Giddens's (1990) cynical pessimism as a reaction to ontological insecurity, is illustrated in the words of a 26-year-old man: 'It is extremely difficult for me to think [about the future]. Probably I will be working until I die ... I hope not to get old still feeling the same apathy I feel today'.

Political participation and forms of action

When participants went through the process of selecting photographs depicting various forms of action, the two most chosen pictures were those depicting elections and a demonstration. This was rather surprising, considering all that was said before by both groups. In spite of the disillusionment with the political system and the declared absenteeism from electoral procedures which were distinctly expressed by both groups, it appears that young Greek Cypriots still consider elections to be a significant form of action, which can have a positive change on the political situation in the country. Demonstrations were also deemed by both groups as a significant means of action for political change, mainly via bringing people together. 'Voting is of outmost importance, even when we think it will not change anything. It is a form of action' (female, 32). This was a strange finding, given the fact that Cyprus has generally been a quiet country in terms of contentious acts and politics, and that Greek Cypriots tend to rely more on political processes or the cultivation of contacts and networks. When the moderators insisted on whether participants had themselves participated in any demonstrations, the discussion shifted to abstract complains about the necessary organisation of contentious acts that is lacking in Cyprus, and which turns people off from participating, because 'you end up looking like another quaint weirdo shouting in the streets' (male, 19).

Other forms of action mentioned, differed between age-groups. Younger participants tended to rely on the internet as a strong source for political action, which they thought provides a space for freedom of expression. Older participants, most of whom were employed or had been in employment before, believed that strikes are an important means of lobbying for better working conditions. Though they recognised that the general public is often inconvenienced during strikes, this did not change their unanimous decision to include striking as a legitimate and powerful form of action.

The internet appears to be the main media channel for the younger generation, though it is not seen as a 100% reliable source. Skepticism on reliability extends to traditional media as well. Discussions on media in all groups invariably ended with the conclusion that the media are driven by specific interests and their purpose is to manipulate the masses. Thus, the need for the democratisation of the media was also expressed: 'You can never be sure if what you are reading is actually true, but you have to stay updated' (female, 23).

These results bring forward a paradox. Young Greek Cypriots declare elections as the main mode for political influence but quantitative data show that they abstain from voting, and report demonstrations and strikes as a powerful means for political action, but these forms of political action are rarely observed in Cyprus. As if some inertia from Cyprus's strongly politicised culture until the very recent past still influences young people's values and ideas, at least in theory and in principle, but the rapid socio-political transformations of the recent years and the increasing feelings of uncertainty and distrust keep them from putting ideas to action. Fridja (2004) provides an explanation for this discrepancy between words and acts. No matter how motivated one is to act, the path from motivation to action is influenced by four determinants: (i) that an appropriate action repertoire be available, (ii) that it is acceptable in terms of costs and benefits, (iii) that the issue at hand is urgent and important and (iv) on the degree of social disapproval or support for the act. Considering not only the local but also the global fragile socio-political conditions, it is very difficult for citizens of all ages to estimate costs and benefits of any form action. This can also explain the younger age-groups' strong reliance on political complaining through the internet. Rather than being left in fear and without any hope for transformation, they rely on the illusion that media urge them to participate, to choose what they like, to air their views and to pay attention (Hardt & Negri, 2012).

Conclusion

As a social category which is constantly renewed, youth is always changing form, shaping society with it (Demertzis et al., 2008). It appears that the absence of an organised social structure leads to the absence of a stable reference point in the present, thus causing uncertainty for the future. Though interest in politics has always fluctuated, it seems that today there is a revival of hopelessness and apathy of the electorate, with a significant percentage of young voters failing to see a reason for participating in a process that involves promises with no guarantees and programmes without vision (Bauman, 1994). Thus, what we observe is the amplification of the phenomenon of political obsolescence and, consequently, of non-participation in politics. With the global economic system experiencing what is perhaps the greatest crisis in its entire period of growth, the political system seems to be undergoing the same.

Assuming that the crisis in Cyprus began with the haircut of 2013 – a very intense politico-financial event which caused quite a panic within society at the time – we cannot but note that, strangely, young people made no reference to this incident in any way, as if it never affected themselves or their families, as if its consequences have been collectively repressed. In addition, the Cyprus Issue, which is of top priority in Cyprus's current political agenda, was not raised spontaneously as a current social issue; when introduced by the moderators, it was treated as a matter of secondary importance which young people simply want it to be closed in whatever way, without having wondered about the changes it will bring about, as if they are psychologically denying to confront it. Notably, crossing back and forth into the occupied areas over the last 12 years does not seem to have brought them any closer to the Turkish Cypriots, with which they will have to co-exist if there is ever a Cyprus solution.

We could not help but observe that although our participants appeared concerned and talked freely and lively about issues concerning 'other people', e.g. the LGBTI community or the immigrants, they seemed astonished and puzzled when confronted with issues that would affect their personal lives. They tended to tangle these issues mostly through general theoretical discussions, as if they psychologically resisted them. Our young participants tended mostly to concentrate on the present, trapped in negative criticism and without being able to offer a counter-proposal, and felt uncomfortable discussing the future. Statements like 'I cannot rely on anyone' seem to imply that although they need to believe in someone or something, they are too disappointed and disillusioned to do so.

Young Greek Cypriots as most young people in Europe, appear extremely uncertain for their future, quite pessimistic and cynical, and highly disillusioned with traditional politics. They feel they have no constants around which to build their lives, and contrary to young people in other European countries (Ampe, 2013; Davou, in press; Davou, Demertzis, & Thanos, 2015), they are not experimenting with alternative forms of political action (e.g. non-governmental organisations, community movements). Although the country's politicised culture of the past is still reflected in their discourse when they discuss things 'in principle' – in a rationalised and intellectualised manner, they become embarrassed and confused when asked to elaborate on how these ideas could be transformed into action. Instead, they appear numb and immobilised, grabbing from the here and now in their everyday lives. Politics is associated with corruption and economic interests and ideology is an incomprehensible concept because of its petty-party politics connotations. They are scornfully disillusioned with the EU and distance themselves from important changes to come, such as the possible reunification of Cyprus.

The fact that participants of this study responded to an open call in a way constitutes them a self-selected 'sample', and this could be considered a limitation. However, apart from the fact that the purpose of qualitative research is to investigate deep processes and not to provide representative and generalisable results, if we assume that this self-selected 'sample' decided to participate in such a study exactly out of some interest in social and political issues, we could anticipate that those who did not chose to participate would exhibit similar tendencies in a much more dramatic degree. This, of course, remains to be investigated by future research. Apart from testing the generalisability of the trends found in this study, future research should be orientated towards the goals and pro-cedures that would bring young people back to active political participation. Young Greek Cypriots appear insecure, pessimistic, disoriented and uninspired. Their responses indicated that they are in an urgent need to rediscover the passion for ideas, which they cannot anymore find in traditional politics and traditional forms of political action.

Notes

1. Official results. Republic of Cyprus-Ministry of the Interior-Electoral Service-Department of Information Technology Services. http://results.elections.moi.gov.cy/English/EUROPEAN_ELECTIONS_2014/Islandwide.
2. Note that in Greek both words sound the same –politiki, although spelled differently –πολιτική vs. πολιτικοί.

Disclosure statement

No potential conflict of interest was reported by the authors.

Notes on contributors

Ioanna Christodoulou is Research Fellow at the Institute of Communication & Social Research, and Honorary Lecturer at the Department of Journalism, Communication & Media Studies, School of Humanities and Social Sciences, Frederick University, Cyprus. She also works as a journalist for Dias Publishing House, and she is the editor-in-chief of the documentary TV series «Kyprion Erga» for Megaone TV and a radio producer at URADIO 99.6.

Charis Pashias is Research Fellow at the Institute of Communication & Social Research, Frederick University, Cyprus. He also works at the Progressive Party of Working People (AKEL) in Cyprus as Coor-dinator of the party's Social Issues Bureau. In the past he has served as Head of the International Relations Bureau of United Democratic Youth Organization (EDON), and as Head of Press & Com-munication Bureau, and of the organization's newspaper 'Neolaia' (Youth).

Sotiris Theocharides is Associate Professor of Philosophy and Social Sciences at the Department of Journalism, Communication & Media Studies, School of Humanities & Social Sciences, Frederick

University, and Director of the Institute of Communication & Social Research at Frederick University, Cyprus. His research interests focus on the interaction of social science, philosophy (and ethics) and social critique in the Postmodern Era, as well as on the national–cultural and political interaction in Cyprus.

Bettina Davou is Professor of Cognitive Psychology, and Director of the Laboratory for Psychological Applications & Communication Planning, at the Department of Communication & Media Studies, School of Economics & Political Science, National and Kapodistrian University of Athens, Greece. She is Chartered Psychologist and Associate Fellow of the British Psychological Society. Her research interests focus on the cognitive and emotional parameters of mediated and interpersonal communication, as well as on the impact of collective emotions to social and political behaviour.

References

Amnå, E., Munck, I., & Zetterberg, P. (2004). *Meaningful participation? Political efficacy of adolescents in 24 countries*. Paper presented at emerging repertoires of political action: Toward a systematic study of post-conventional forms of participation at ECPR joint sessions of workshops, Uppsala. Retrieved December 28, 2016, from https://ecpr.eu/Filestore/PaperProposal/e8a5f984-6738-4c7b-bebf-f2e385562b0f.pdf

Ampe, E. (2013). *Youth and democracy: The changing face of youth political engagement*. Council of Europe Report. Congress of Local and Regional Authorities. CG (23) 9 Final. Retrieved December 30, 2016, from https://wcd.coe.int/ViewDoc.jsp?p=&id=1980145&direct=true#P48_2286

Badiou, A. (2010). *The communist hypothesis*. London: Verso.

Bauman, Z. (1994). *Alone again: Ethics after certainty*. London: Demos.

Castoriadis, C. (2006). *Είμαστε υπεύθυνοι για την ιστορία μας* [We are responsible for our history]. Athens: Polis. [in Greek].

Charalambus, G. (2014). *Political culture and behaviour in the republic of Cyprus during the crisis*. PRIO Cyprus Centre Report, 2. Nicosia: PRIO Cyprus Centre.

Chomsky, N. (1988). *Language and politics*. Montreal: Black Rose.

Chomsky, N. (2001). *Δύο ώρες διαύγειας* [Two hours of lucidity]. Athens: *Livanis*. [in Greek]

Chomsky, N. (2013). Global media forum, June 2013. Retrieved from ww.youtube.com/watch?v=btlgQs0UDxY

Davou, B. (in press). Vicissitudes of emotions and political action: An example from the Greek crisis. In *Oxford research encyclopedia of politics*. London: Oxford University Press.

Davou, B., Demertzis, N., & Thanos, V. (2015). Συναισθήματα, κίνητρα και πολιτική συμπεριφορά στην Ελλάδα της κρίσης [Emotions, motivation and political behavior in Greece during the crisis]. In N. G. Georgarakis & N. Demertzis (Eds.), *Το πολιτικό πορτραίτο της Ελλάδας: Κρίση και αποδόμηση του πολιτικού* [The political portrait of Greece. Crisis and deconstruction of the political] (pp. 29–50). Athens: Gutenberg and National Centre for Social Research. [in Greek].

Demertzis, N., & Armenakis, A. (2000). Η πολιτική κουλτούρα και τα μέσα επικοινωνίας. Η περίπτωση των φοιτητών της Αθήνας [Political culture and the media. The case of Athenian students]. *Greek Political Science Review*, 23(16), 34–71. [in Greek].

Demertzis, N., Stavrakakis, G., Davou, B., Armenakis, A., Christakis, N. Georgarakis, N. Boubaris, N. (2008). *Νεολαία: Ο αστάθμητος παράγοντας* [Juvenescence: The non-standardized factor?]. Athens: Polytropon. [in Greek].

Eurobarometer # 375. (2013). Retrieved December 30, 2016, from http://ec.europa.eu/assets/eac/youth/library/reports/flash375_en.pdf

Fridja, N. (2004). Emotion and action. In A. Manstead, N. Fridja, & A. Fischer (Eds.), *Feelings and emotions: The Amsterdam symposium* (pp. 158–173). Cambridge: Cambridge University Press.

Giddens, A. (1990). *The consequences of modernity*. Cornwall: Polity Press.

Hardt, M., & Negri, A. (2012). *Take up the Baton*. Argo Navis author services. Retrieved from http://faculty.washington.edu/mpurcell/declaration.pdf

INEP. (2013). Ινστιτούτο Ερευνών Προμηθέας [Prometheus research institute]. *Political participation*. Unpublished manuscript. [in Greek].

Kiisel, M., Leppik, M., & Seppel, K. (2015). Engaged and critical? The young generation's political participation in EU countries. *Studies of Transition States and Societies, 7*(3), 52–66.

Maniou, T. (2013). *Τηλεόραση, κοινωνία και πολιτικές ειδήσεις* [Television, society and political news]. Athens: Epikentro. [in Greek].

Orinos, N. (2013). A glance at the political interest in Cyprus - evidence of the European social survey. *International Journal of Business and Social Science, 4*(8) [Special Issue -July 2013], 6–17.

PMR. (2011). Pulse market research. *Polling Data, Last 30 Years.* Retrieved from Pulse Market Research: www.pulse.com.cy

Reeskens, T., & Vandecasteele, L. (2016). Hard times and European youth. The effect of economic insecurity on human values, social attitudes and well-being. *International Journal of Psychology,* doi:10.1002/ijop.12387

Riley, S., Griffin, C., & Morey, Y. (2013). The rise of the 'pleasure citizen': How leisure can be a site for alternative forms of political participation. In K. N. Demetriou (Ed.), *Democrasy in transition: Political participation in the European Union* (pp. 61–76). New York, NY: Springer-Verlag.

Seligman, M. (1992). *Helplessness: On development, depression and death.* London: D.H. Freeman.

Spannring, R. (2008). We vote and then we suffer. Survey results in the light of young people's views on participation. In J. Benedicto, and A. López Blasco (Coordinators), Young people and political participation: European research. *Young People's Studies Magazine, 81*(June), 45–66.

Wörsching, M. (2008). Making a difference? Political participation of young people in the UK. In J. Benedicto, and A. López Blasco (Coordinators), Young people and political participation: European Research. *Young People's Studies Magazine, 81*(June), 91–104.

Appendices

Appendix (i) Recruitment questionnaire

1. Name (not to be disclosed in reporting of the findings)
2. Contact details
3. Age (tick): 18–24   25–35
4. Educational level (tick): Lyceum Undergraduate degree Postgraduate degree
5. Where would you politically place yourself in the Left – Right axis (choose a number)
   Extreme Left   Extreme Right
   0   1   2   3   4   5   6   7   8   9   10
6. How would you describe yourself in terms of political interest (choose a number)
   Not at all   Highly interested
   0   1   2   3   4   5   6   7   8   9   10
7. Did you vote in the last elections? Yes   No

Appendix (ii) Interview guide

(a) *Political thinking*
   - What are the main problems of your everyday life?
   - What are the major social problems?
   - What are the causes of these problems?
   - How are we supposed to solve these problems?
(b) *Political participation*
   - What comes to your mind when you hear with the word 'politics' (leaving vague the singular and plural meaning in Greek which means either 'politics' or 'politicians').
   - What means to be a 'politicised' person (how is politicalisation distinguished from political party membership)
   - What comes to your mind when you hear the word 'ideology'? Can you think of some ideologies?

- Examples of ideological stance (LGBTQ: Should they adopt children? Turkish Cypriots: Would you marry a Turkish Cypriot? Immigrants: e.g. payroll and cover for professional positions).
(c) *Media and the internet*
- Do you read and/or listen to the daily news? From which source?
- How valid and reliable are the media?
(d) *Attitudes towards Future*
- How do you imagine Cyprus to be in the future?
- How do you imagine yourself, as an elder, in this country in the future?

Appendix (iii) Probing materials

(a) Cards
Which institutions can contribute in the solution of your problems and the society's problems? (Choose three)

- European Union
- Church
- Parliament
- Government
- Businesses
- Banks
- Youth organisations/political parties
- Municipalities
- Education
- Syndicates/Unions
- Army/Police
- Mass Media
- Courts
*Reach a consensus
(b) *Pictures*
What kind of action would you choose?
Strike

Demonstration

Elections

Charity

Internet activity (collecting signatures and chatting)

Praying (religious activities)

* Consensus (3 pictures)

Index

Note: Page locators with **bold** indicate tables